The OLE MISS EXPERIENCE

First-Year Experience Text

THE OLE MISS EXPERIENCE

Editor: Leslie Banahan
Program Coordinator: Dewey Knight

Contributors: Lindsey Abernathy, Ty Allushuski, Seph Anderson, Toni Avant, Bradley Baker, Leslie Banahan, Ian Banner, Camp Best, Brad Campbell, Casey Cockrell-Stuart, Donald Cole, Kevin Cozart, Erin Cromeans, Robert Cummings, Melissa Dennis, Wesley Dickens, Joseph Dikun, Laura Diven-Brown, JoAnn Edwards, Kyle Ellis, Karen Forgette, Tom Franklin, Kathy Gates, Susan Glisson, Wendy Goldberg, Alex Hicks, Travis Hitchcock, Kate Hooper, Mariana Jurss, Dewey Knight, Guy Krueger, Brandi Hephner LaBanc, Ge-Yao Lin, David Magee, Kendall McDonald, Blair McElroy, Stephen Monroe, Lindsey Bartlett Mosvick, Alice Myatt, Natasa Novicevic, Cecilia Parks, Patrick Perry, Jennifer Phillips, Greet Provoost, Mariana Rangel, Thomas Reardon, Ollie Rencher, Stacey Reycraft, Holly Reynolds, Rebekah Reysen, Shannon Richardson, Nishanth Rodrigues, Valeria Ross, Marc Showalter, Whitman Smith, Jennifer Stollman, Katie Tompkins, Charles Tucker, Beth Whittington, Ryan Whittington, and Noel Wilkin.

A special thanks to University of Mississippi Communications — especially to the extraordinarily talented photographers Robert Jordan, Kevin Bain, and Nathan Latil.

ISBN #: 978-1-936946-48-8
Eighth Edition

PRINTED IN CANADA
through a partnership with Friesens Printing

Note From the Editor
Leslie Banahan

Congratulations and welcome to the Ole Miss Experience!

You are a new student at the University of Mississippi, and you hold in your hands one of the most valuable tools for college success. Each section of this text has been written by an expert who wants to help you excel in the classroom and earn your degree from the University.

Students begin college with different strengths. For some of you, college life will be easier than for others. Some of you come well-prepared and with natural gifts for literature, science, math, language, time management, study skills, and test-taking strategies. Others have had to work long hours to earn the grades to gain a seat at the University. Some of you have photographic memories, but others struggle to memorize each new term, date, and concept. Some of you are at ease in the classroom, eager to ask questions and engage in discussion. Others may be introverted, filled with anxiety at the thought of being called upon, and determined to sit in the back of the class and avoid eye contact with the instructor.

You hold in your hands one of the most valuable tools for college success.

Some of you will make friends easily and manage your new freedoms and responsibilities with seemingly little effort. Most of you will have the occasional bad day, when roommates are irritating, professors unreasonable, the bank account overdrawn, dirty clothes piled to the ceiling, and four tests to study for before the weekend arrives. On the down-and-out days, take a deep breath; go for a walk in the Grove (better yet, study in the Grove); call home for an encouraging word; play a pick-up game of basketball in the Turner Center; do something for someone else; consider what life would be like if you weren't a college student; read this text; and repeat to yourself: **I can do this.**

Consider this textbook your map to success at Ole Miss. Call or e-mail the authors; seek help when you're confused, uncertain, or just plain homesick. We are here to serve you. Enjoy the Ole Miss Experience!

Sincerely,

Leslie Banahan

Leslie Banahan, *Editor*

THE UNIVERSITY of MISSISSIPPI

CENTER FOR STUDENT SUCCESS AND FIRST-YEAR EXPERIENCE

Dear Students,

Welcome to Ole Miss and the First-Year Experience!

We have designed this course to help you, as first-year students, make a positive transition to the university, develop a better understanding of the learning process, enhance your academic skills, acquire essential life skills to insure your success and to begin your exploration of the career and major that are best for you. During the semester, you will be introduced to the mission, values, and constituencies of the University of Mississippi and the ethical and social concerns that you may face as a member of our community.

One of our former EDHE students describes the First-Year Experience as "a wonderful way to become familiar with Ole Miss, acquire effective study skills, learn how to manage your time, and to discover just who you are. It gave me a lot of connections and I learned about so many helpful services I was actually able to use!"

This text actually focuses on the University of Mississippi with information about its history, traditions, and values, as well as the academic and other support services available to you. The faculty and administrators of the University have assembled here a virtual cookbook of the ingredients (resources) that are essential for your success. As a member of our Ole Miss family, you are strongly encouraged to learn about the breadth and depth of the help that is available to you and make good use of all of it. We care about you and your success!

Hotty Toddy,

R. Dewey Knight
Associate Director for First-Year Experience

350 Martindale | Post Office Box 1848 | University, MS 38677 | (662) 915-5970 | Fax: (662) 915-1268 | www.olemiss.edu | cssfye@olemiss.edu

Dean of Students

Welcome to the University of Mississippi! You have made a wonderful decision to attend a great public university, and I hope your time at Ole Miss is full of opportunities for you to learn, grow, and participate in amazing experiences.

Although you will be faced with a number of choices in the coming weeks and months regarding your educational path, you have already made a wise decision to enroll in EDHE 105 or 305 as these courses can provide a strong foundation for your Ole Miss experience. Not only will you become familiar with resources that are available to enrich and support your academic pursuits, but you will also explore all the awesome opportunities that Ole Miss provides outside the classroom. I hope you take advantage of both academic and co-curricular offerings that interest you.

This course – and really, your entire experience in college – allows you to learn more about yourself. You will be challenged, inspired, frustrated, excited, and amazed (among other emotions) throughout your time here. This is part of what being in college is all about, and if you are not experiencing some of these feelings from time to time, then you are not capitalizing on all Ole Miss has to offer. Growing and learning – both in-and-outside the classroom – are integral parts of being a college student.

So, once again, welcome to this special place we call Ole Miss! We are so glad to have you join us, and I hope your experience here is all you are hoping for and more. This course will certainly equip you with the tools to create fantastic opportunities for yourself. The next steps will be yours to take!

Hotty Toddy!

Melinda Sutton Noss

Melinda Sutton Noss, Ph.D.
*Assistant Vice Chancellor for Student Affairs
and Dean of Students*

Table of Contents

FYE Textbook, 2018 Edition

The University of Mississippi: 13
    The Value of a Liberal Arts Education 15
    Living the Creed at the University of Mississippi 20
    University History. 23
    Race and the University of Mississippi 51
    Diversity and Inclusion: Exploring Similarities and Embracing
    Differences 71
    Bonus: History of Disability and Disability Rights 92
    Hotty Toddy and Other Traditions 97

Section I: College Survival 101. 117
Chapter 1: Ole Miss Doesn't Have Homeroom 119
    Bonus: Ole Miss Support Tools 122
    Bonus: Learning the Language of Ole Miss 130
    Common Reading: Building Community through Books 138
    Bonus: Tom Franklin on Creativity 140
Chapter 2: Not-So-Soft Skills: Emotional Intelligence and Grit 141
Chapter 3: Civility is So Much More than Southern Hospitality. 151
Chapter 4: Time Management—the Key to Success. 169
Chapter 5: Active Listening and Effective Note Making. 179
Chapter 6: Learning Styles. 188
Chapter 7: Our Library 203
Chapter 8: Reading College Texts. 211
Chapter 9: The Department of Writing and Rhetoric. 219
    Bonus: The Gertrude Castellow Ford Center
            for the Performing Arts 234
Chapter 10: Academic Dishonesty and Plagiarism 237
Chapter 11: Communication and Technology. 247
    Bonus: The Good, the Bad, and the Awful of Social Media. 254
Chapter 12: Test-Taking Strategies 261

Chapter 13: Academic Advising and Registration 267

    Bonus: Rebels Abroad. 280

    Bonus: Health Professions Advising Office 284

Section II: Wellness 285

Chapter 14: Make a Difference—Get Involved! (social dimension) 289

    Bonus: Robert's Rules of Order 298

Chapter 15: Red, Blue, and Green (environmental dimension) 301

Chapter 16: The LGBTQ Alphabet Soup: Sexual Orientation and
Gender Identity (emotional and physical dimensions) 313

Chapter 17: Relationships (social, emotional, and sexual dimensions) 323

    Bonus: Suicide: A Preventable Condition. 331

Chapter 18: Mindfulness for Stress Management (physical, emotional, and
spiritual dimensions). 333

Chapter 19: Financial Literacy (financial dimension) 347

Chapter 20: Finding Your Way: Career Exploration (financial, intellectual,
emotional, and social dimensions) 369

Chapter 21: Sex and Sexual Health (emotional and sexual dimensions) 383

Chapter 22: Substance Use and Misuse: Alcohol and Other Drugs
(physical and social dimensions). 393

Chapter 23: Physical Fitness (physical, emotional, and social dimensions) 409

    Bonus: Spirituality: Taking Care of the Soul (spiritual dimension) . . . 420

Chapter 24: Eating Healthy at Ole Miss (physical, emotional, and
social dimensions). 423

Chapter 25: Violence Prevention and Campus Safety (emotional, social, and
environmental dimensions). 437

Campus Resources 445

1848

The University of Mississippi

Introduction
The Value of a Liberal Arts Education
By Holly Reynolds

The University of Mississippi is the flagship liberal arts university in the State of Mississippi. What does this mean? And, what is the value of a liberal arts education?

From the origins of Western civilization in the ancient world comes the concept of a liberal arts education. The term comes from the Greek word *eleutheros* and the Latin word *liber*, both meaning "free." For free (male) citizens to fully participate in Athenian democracy, they needed certain skills in critical thinking and communication developed through a broad education in seven disciplines: the trivium, or verbal arts, consisting of grammar, logic, and rhetoric; and the quadrivium, or numerical arts, consisting of arithmetic, astronomy, music, and geometry. Such an education celebrated and nurtured human freedom and early democracy. The term liberal arts education does not mean an education that indoctrinates students in the political ideology of liberalism or the thoughts of those labeled as political liberals.

In modern times, we can look to the American Association of Colleges and Universities (AAC&U) for a contemporary understanding of this concept.

> "Of all the civil rights for which the world has struggled and fought for 5,000 years, the right to learn is undoubtedly the most fundamental."
> **W.E.B. DuBois, 1949**

Liberal Education is an approach to learning that empowers individuals and prepares them to deal with complexity, diversity, and change. It provides students with broad knowledge of the wider world (e.g. science, culture, and society) as well as in-depth study in a specific area of interest. A liberal education helps students develop a sense of social responsibility, as well as strong and transferable intellectual and practical skills such as communication, analytical and problem-solving skills, and a demonstrated ability to apply knowledge and skills in real-world settings. The broad goals of liberal education have been enduring even as the courses and requirements that comprise a liberal education have changed over the years. Today, a liberal education usually includes a general education curriculum that provides broad learning in multiple disciplines and ways of knowing, along with more in-depth study in a major (aacu.org/leap).

You regularly will hear proponents of a liberal arts education cite some combination of the skills listed above as the mark of a well-educated citizen who is able to fully participate in our society, economy, and democracy. Those trained in the liberal arts are ready for the widest array of career options. Liberal arts education is still about nurturing human freedom by helping people discover and develop their talents. Many of you have at least an implicit understanding that you enrolled at the University of Mississippi to acquire or deepen these areas of knowledge and skills mentioned above. Understandably, many students and parents are focused on preparing for the workforce in an ever-changing American economy. A liberal arts education is the best preparation for such uncertainty. Better yet, it prepares you for a meaningful life.

Faculty members developed a vision for the liberal arts education that is the basis for every undergraduate degree on campus. Look at the core curriculum and the learning outcomes listed in the Degree Requirements section of the Undergraduate Academic Regulations link in the online catalog. There is a common core curriculum of 30 hours of course work that is the framework for your freshman year courses. This core curriculum sets the liberal arts foundation for your degree. And, when combined with the courses in your major and your co-curricular learning experiences, the core curriculum should enable you to:

"When we ask about the relationship of a liberal education to citizenship, we are asking a question with a long history in the Western philosophical tradition. We are drawing on Socrates' concept of 'the examined life,' on Aristotle's notions of reflective citizenship, and above all on Greek and Roman Stoic notions of an education that is 'liberal' in that it liberates the mind from bondage of habit and custom, producing people who can function with sensitivity and alertness as citizens of the whole world."

Martha Nussbaum, 1998

"At UM, all students must complete a general education curriculum that is strongly rooted in the liberal arts, which encourages creativity, critical thinking, empathy, and being a strong communicator. These skills are highly transferrable in industry and essential to our society – which becomes more and more complex each year."

—Lee Cohen, Dean of the College of Liberal Arts

1. study the principal domains of knowledge and their methods of inquiry;
2. integrate knowledge from diverse disciplines;
3. analyze, synthesize, and evaluate complex and challenging material that stimulates intellectual curiosity, reflection, and capacity for lifelong learning;
4. communicate qualitative, quantitative, and technological concepts by effective written, oral, numerical, and graphical means;
5. work individually and collaboratively on projects that require the application of knowledge and skill;
6. understand a variety of world cultures as well as the richness and complexity of American society; and
7. realize that knowledge and ability carry with them a responsibility for their constructive and ethical use in society.

Connect the courses you are taking this semester with the learning outcomes listed above. Sometimes it is very easy to make the connection due to the title of the course. In other cases you may need to look at the course objectives or description on the syllabus and think about our larger goals for your education. Now, imagine a web of 100-level through 400- or 500-level courses that connect together to form your undergraduate degree. The connections between these courses are real and come from the above list. You are not simply "checking off courses" on a degree sheet. You are building an interactive set of skills and content knowledge for a liberal arts education, whether it is for a degree in history, forensic chemistry, social work, or accountancy.

But you don't have to take my word for the value of a liberal arts education. Employers regularly espouse the positive qualities of a liberal arts education. Let's see how the skills and knowledge listed from the UM catalog show up on a few national employer surveys.

Each year, the National Association of Colleges and Employers (NACE) surveys its employer members. From the *Job Outlook 2015* report, the top five skills or qualities desired in job candidates were the ability to:

1. **work in a team structure**
2. **make decisions and solve problems**
3. **communicate**
4. **plan, organize, and prioritize work**
5. **obtain and process information**

Hart Research Associates surveyed 318 employers in 2013 for a report to the Association of American Colleges and Universities titled "It Takes More Than a Major: Employer Priorities for College Learning and Student Success." The respondents highlighted the importance of innovative, creative thinking as well as ethical judgment, integrity, and intercultural skills. They underscored the value of the liberal arts education and increasingly pointed to application of knowledge during your years at the University.

• More than three in four employers say they want colleges to place more emphasis on helping students develop five key learning outcomes, including **critical thinking, complex problem solving, written and oral communication, and applied knowledge in real-world settings**. Employers endorse several educational practices as potentially helpful in preparing college students for workplace success. These include practices that require students to conduct research and use evidence-based analysis; gain in-depth knowledge in the major, analytic problem-solving, and communication skills; and apply their learning in real-world settings.

• **Employers recognize the importance of liberal education and the liberal arts.** The majority of employers agree that having both field-specific knowledge and skills and a broad range of skills and knowledge is most important for recent college graduates to achieve long-term career success. Few think that having field-specific knowledge and skills alone is what is most needed for individuals' career success. Eighty percent of employers agree that, regardless of their major, college students should acquire broad knowledge in the liberal arts and sciences. When read a description of a 21st century liberal education, a large majority of employers recognize its importance. Seventy-four percent would recommend this kind of education to a young person they know as the best way to prepare for success in today's global economy.

• **Employers endorse a blended model of liberal and applied learning.** Across many areas tested, employers strongly endorse educational practices that involve students in active, effortful work—practices including collaborative problem solving, internships, research, senior projects, and community engagements. Employers consistently rank outcomes and practices that involve application of skills over acquisition of discrete bodies of knowledge. They also strongly endorse practices that require students to demonstrate both acquisition of knowledge and its application.

The University of Mississippi campus is full of these opportunities. Faculty members across our campus intentionally foster these skills and opportunities. Student services staff members work diligently to help you connect with enrichment opportunities beyond the classroom. Seek out these opportunities while you are here.

Take these messages to heart. Be conscious of how each course and co-curricular activity will add these skills, values, knowledge, and experiences to your resume. Build a digital portfolio to showcase your liberal arts education for future employers or graduate/professional school admissions committees. You will get a valuable education and prepare yourself for a rich, meaningful life.

Glossary

Flagship liberal arts university – the finest, most important university in a state that has the liberal arts education at its core.

Liberal arts education – an approach to learning that empowers individuals and prepares them to deal with complexity, diversity, and change. It is an education needed to maintain a free society and enable the full development of individual talent.

Critical thinking skills – skills that allow one to reason well, including the abilities to clarify goals, values, and assumptions; evaluate evidence; and determine outcomes based on that evidence.

Work ethic - belief in the moral benefit and importance of work and its inherent ability to strengthen character.

Analytical skills – ability to separate an object or an idea into constituent parts to classify and understand it, draw conclusions, or solve problems.

(Academic) discipline – a field of study or branch of knowledge, such as history, business management, or chemistry.

REFERENCES

Association of American Colleges and Universities. (2013). It Takes More than a Major: Employer Priorities for College Learning and Student Success. Washington, D.C.: Hart Research Associates.

Association of American Colleges and Universities. Retrieved from aacu.org/leap/index.cfm

National Association of Colleges and Employers. (2015). Job Outlook 2015. Retrieved from naceweb.org/Research/Job_Outlook/Job_Outlook.aspx

About the Author

Holly Reynolds, *Associate Dean in the College of Liberal Arts*
Assistant Professor of Political Science

Holly Reynolds earned her Bachelor of Arts in political science from Louisiana State University and Ph.D. in political science from Rice University. She joined the UM faculty in 1997 and became an administrator with the College of Liberal Arts in 2002. Dr. Reynolds' areas of specialization are comparative politics, Latin American politics, and transitions to democracy. She has received the Cora Lee Graham Award for Outstanding Teaching of Freshmen in the College of Liberal Arts.

Living The Creed
at The University of Mississippi

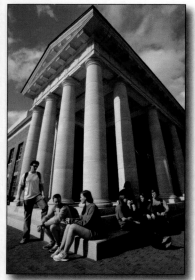

By confirming your admission and enrolling in courses at the University of Mississippi, you have accepted the responsibility of being a member of our campus community. This campus community may be unlike any other community you have been a part of in your past. In fact, I hope it is different. I say that because placing yourself in a new environment is one of the most educational and transformational experiences you will ever have in life. It opens your eyes and your mind to those who are different from you, to alternative approaches to getting things accomplished, and it will force you to decide who you really are as a citizen of our world.

So, exactly what does being a member of this community mean? The Creed of the University of Mississippi can be your compass in answering that question:

The University of Mississippi is a community of learning dedicated to nurturing excellence in intellectual inquiry and personal character in an open and diverse environment. As a voluntary member of this community:

I believe in **respect for the dignity of each person**

I believe in **fairness and civility**

I believe in **personal and professional integrity**

I believe in **academic honesty**

I believe in **academic freedom**

I believe in **good stewardship of our resources**

I pledge to **uphold these values** and **encourage others to follow** my example.

You have moved into your residence hall or apartment and are living—at least initially—with complete strangers. You are going to class and are joining organizations with students from diverse backgrounds. You are likely to walk across campus and hardly recognize anyone. You are meeting students who look different from you and talk differently than you. You will find students who share your spiritual background and those who reject the existence of deities.

These experiences may scare you or force you to think twice about your decision to come to Ole Miss; I assure you, this is the **best decision you have ever made**. Keep an open mind; get to know others who, seemingly, are unlike you. Treat others as you would like to be treated, and you will find that you have more in common with them than you initially thought. You also will find that it is fun to learn about others' backgrounds, traditions, and heritage. These are the things that make each of us special and proud of our history. Everyone has a story. Listen and learn.

Social challenges are one thing, but a **large** number of first-year students indicate that they are overwhelmed academically. If you don't fall into this category, good for you! I hope you will extend your talents to your fellow students and help them with an algebra problem or another assignment – that would be living The Creed! If you do find your academics challenging, you are not alone. I recommend you talk to your professors, seek out support from the many academic resources we have on campus, or ask a friend to study with you and tackle assignments together. At the end of the day what matters most is that you allow yourself the freedom to explore new subjects so you can confidently select a future career. Apply yourself, *don't cheat yourself*. If the topic is difficult (and we hope it is), your faculty expect you to ask more questions. Be curious and courageous with your academic career—you will never regret the choice to honestly expand your mind.

Being a member of this community requires you to possess an ethic of care. We expect you to:

care enough to respect yourself,

care enough to respect others,

and care enough to respect our campus.

So, go to class and get what you are paying for – an education and an expanded world view that will make you a competitive applicant for your dream job. Take time to recognize the students, faculty and staff who walk by you on campus. Smile at others and say *"hello;"* as we say at the University of Mississippi—*"Everyone Speaks!"* Lastly, respect the buildings, the grounds, your residence hall, and your classrooms. There are thousands of staff members on campus who work hard to make our campus the most beautiful in the country—help them keep it that way. Whether it is a football Saturday in The Grove or a quiet Tuesday night early in the Spring, please be a positive role model and live our Creed. You can never go wrong if you use the Creed as a compass to guide your behavior, attitudes, and decisions.

I look forward to watching you live The Creed. I have high expectations for all of our students; I know you will meet, and likely exceed, them! I look forward to watching you grow and learn as a member of this amazing, diverse, exciting, and caring community.

Welcome to the Ole Miss family – I am thrilled you are here!

About the Author

Brandi Hephner LaBanc

Vice Chancellor for Student Affairs and Associate Professor of Higher Education

Vice Chancellor Hephner LaBanc received her undergraduate degree in accounting from the University of Akron, her Master's degree in higher education administration from Kent State University, and her doctorate from Northern Illinois University. She takes great pride in her role as a student advocate and thoroughly loves working at Ole Miss. Be sure to introduce yourself if you see her at a student event or walking on campus.

University History

By Thomas Reardon and Leslie Banahan

The University of Mississippi is the oldest and best known of Mississippi's public institutions of higher learning. The University has a rich history of producing scholars and leaders who have had influence on every segment of society. Today the University has buildings that house modern technology. Residence halls serve as homes to students, and intercollegiate sports can be enjoyed in some of the finest facilities in the country. The faculty is made up of men and women who come from all over the world and the total enrollment is more than 24,000.

The campus scene today is far different than it was in the founding, early years of the University of Mississippi. Ole Miss has survived the intrusion of power hungry politicians, wars, storms, riots, and the wear of the years. Today, she stands strong as a great university among her peers.

This is a brief look at the University of Mississippi since its founding in 1848. It is far from complete or thorough. For those interested in reading in-depth about the University and its history, David Sansing's *The University of Mississippi: A Sesquicentennial History* is a great account of the University's history. William Doyle's *An American Insurrection: The Battle of Oxford, Mississippi, 1962* is a riveting account of the integration of the University. For extensive coverage of the struggle of African-American students at the University, Nadine Cahodas' *Let the Band Play Dixie* is an excellent read.

The founding and early years

In February 1840, James Alexander Ventress brought a bill before the Mississippi State Legislature that would provide for the location of a university for the state of Mississippi. The bill was passed by both houses of the legislature and signed by Governor Alexander McNutt on February 20, 1840. In an address to the legislature in 1839, McNutt sent a message to the lawmakers in which he noted, "Patriotism, no less than economy, urges upon us the duty of educating our children at home. Those opposed to us in principle cannot safely be entrusted with

OXFORD

MISSISSIPPI CITY

the education of our sons and daughters." The birth of the University of Mississippi arose from the need to spend monies for "seminary lands" that had been sold by the state. There also was a sense of urgency to provide local higher education for students without the influence of those who did not embrace the "ways" of the state of Mississippi. Seeking to preserve a way of life, the founders believed that education is the process by which a culture ensures its existence and transmits itself across time. These founders' resistance to change, which they viewed as their right, if not their obligation, thus created the University of Mississippi as a bastion in defense of "the Southern way of life."

February 21, 1840, one day following the passage of the bill to establish a state university, the legislature appointed a special committee to locate a site for the new university. After almost a year, the committee came back to the legislature and presented a list of sites. After much deliberation, on January 27, 1841, Oxford was selected over Mississippi City (on the Gulf Coast) by a vote of 58 to 57. The University was chartered by an act of the Mississippi State Legislature on February 24, 1844, and placed under the supervision of a board of 13 trustees, of which Ventress was the first appointed. James Alexander Ventress is known as the "father of the University" and Ventress Hall is named after him. The land for the new university was purchased from local land owners whose names were Stockard and Martin.

PRESIDENT
George Frederick Holmes (1848-49)

Elected to serve as president when he was only 28, George Frederick Holmes is distinguished as the University's youngest president, its first president—and its most transitory president. He served only five months, due to illness in his family and difficulties in maintaining discipline on campus. Born in 1820 in Georgetown, British Guyana, Holmes was reared in England but journeyed to Canada and the United States in his late teens to teach and practice law. President Holmes was a prolific writer; many of his essays were published in the *Southern Quarterly Review* before he was 25. He taught briefly at Richmond College and the College of William and Mary before coming to The University of Mississippi in 1848. Holmes helped inspire and organize the University's Hermaean Literary Society, which existed until 1946.

George Frederick Holmes was elected by the trustees as the first president of the University and on November 6, 1848, he welcomed the first students to the University of Mississippi. In an effort to avoid any appearance of indulging in aristocracy, the University had an open admissions policy, even to the extent of extending an offer of free admission to "any young man desirous of entering the University, but unable to pay for tuition." Eighty students, some no older than sixteen, became the first class of students. All were from Mississippi with the exception of

Did you know?

The Lyceum building, with a portico reminiscent of the Grecian Ionic Temple near Athens, originally included recitation and lecture rooms, a laboratory, a library and museum, and several society rooms.

one young man who was from Memphis, Tennessee. The open admissions policy proved a failure. Only 47 remained through the full term with five being expelled, eight suspended, 12 allowed to withdraw, and eight whose records show "absented themselves, whereabouts unknown."

Holmes's tenure as president of Mississippi's first state university was short lived. He left the University to return to Virginia in early March of 1849, and his absence was officially attributed to his ill health and that of his child. Perhaps more pertinent to Holmes's departure was the failure of an honor system that he had attempted to institute and the unruly nature of the students who first came to the University of Mississippi.

Augustus B. Longstreet replaced Holmes as president in 1849. Longstreet was a southerner by birth and had distinguished himself as a lawyer, judge, writer, and minister. Longstreet's tenure witnessed the first significant growth of the University from the original 80 students in 1848 to 232 students in 1856. Referred to by students as "Old Bullet" or "The Judge," Longstreet was a strict disciplinarian. After becoming involved in a dispute with political parties and criticized for being absent from the campus in his role as a businessman and clergyman, Longstreet resigned his position as president in 1856, and one year later became the president of the University of South Carolina.

F. A. P. Barnard and the Civil War

The next president of the University of Mississippi would leave an indelible mark on the institution. A young professor of Mathematics and Natural Philosophy, Frederick Augustus Porter Barnard, a native of Massachusetts and a graduate of Yale, worked from 1831 to 1838 at the American Asylum for the Deaf and Dumb and at the New York Institution for the Deaf and Dumb. In 1838, he accepted the chair of Mathematics at the University of Alabama in Tuscaloosa and from 1848 to 1854 served as professor of Chem-

PRESIDENT

Augustus Baldwin Longstreet (1849-56)

Born in 1790, Augustus Baldwin Longstreet was the first of four Yale graduates to serve as president of the University, and he was the first of three presidents to be an ordained minister. A man of many trades, Longstreet worked as a lawyer, legislator,

judge, and journalist in Georgia, where he started his own publication, *The Sentinel*, in Augusta. He also was a prominent author. His *Georgia Scenes*, a collection of humorous stories, was published by Harper in 1840.

Longstreet served as president of Emory College in Oxford, Georgia, and of Centenary College in Shreveport, Louisiana, before being elected to the post at the University of Mississippi. During his tenure, several social fraternities were organized, the School of Law was started and a professorship of governmental science and law was added to the faculty.

Did you know?

Barnard Observatory was modeled after the Russian Imperial Observatory and the observatory at Harvard University. It was to have nothing but the best, including a 19-inch telescope (the largest in the world at the time). Although the building itself was completed in 1859, the delivery of some of its equipment was delayed by the Civil War.

istry and Natural Philosophy.

Barnard was elected to the faculty of the University of Mississippi in 1854 as professor of Mathematics and Natural Philosophy. Barnard set about with all of his energy to make the University of Mississippi a great institution of higher learning. He disagreed with the existing system of student discipline as designed by Longstreet, especially the daily visitation to students' rooms by faculty members. With a free and flexible manner that won him the devotion of the students, Barnard saw the need for the students to have a life outside of the classroom and promoted the building of a student gymnasium and the establishment of literary societies. The gymnasium was one of the first in the nation for an antebellum college. For his focus on students, Barnard was praised by the student magazine "for endeavoring to infuse into the minds of students a love for…profound critical scholarship and high toned unblemished moral character."

Barnard wrote to the Board of Trustees of the University in 1858 and promoted an idea called "universitas scientiarum," which was a comprehensive plan to make the University of Mississippi "a true university that included all branches of science, medicine, agriculture, law, classical studies, civil and political history, and oriental learning." Although the faculty was dubious, the Board approved the "universitas scientiarum" plan with the exception of a training program for elementary and secondary education, a school of agriculture, and a school of engineering. With the adoption of this program, the title of "President of the University" was changed to "Chancellor of the University."

CHANCELLOR

Frederick Augustus Porter Barnard
(1856-61)

Frederick A.P. Barnard was the University's first "chancellor" (the title was changed from "president" in 1858), and he was perhaps its most ardent and idealistic proponent. He aspired to make the University the greatest scientific institution in the world, establishing an ideal that has challenged and inspired his successors. Born in 1809, he graduated from Yale in 1828 and began teaching. In 1838, he accepted a position teaching mathematics and natural philosophy at the University of Alabama, and, in 1854, he accepted a similar position at the University of Mississippi. Shortly after assuming the presidency in 1856, Barnard convinced the Legislature to appropriate funds to order the largest telescope in the world for the University and to construct an observatory for it on campus. The observatory (now called Barnard Observatory), which today houses the Center for the Study of Southern Culture, was completed, but because of the Civil War the telescope was diverted to Chicago, where it remains today at Northwestern University. Barnard, a minister and musician, left Oxford during the Civil War and became president of Columbia University, where he remained for 25 years. He is the only University of Mississippi chancellor to be elected as an undergraduate to Phi Beta Kappa.

Did you know?

The Lyceum bell, built by the Buckeye Bell Foundry of Cincinnati, was probably cast in early 1847 and installed when the building was constructed. It is the oldest bell at a university or college in America.

Throughout Barnard's tenure, the University was attacked by newspapers and lawmakers for being located in Oxford and for "pandering to the wealthy aristocracy." The attacks and constant criticism contributed to Barnard's weariness and frustration and led him to conclude that the University of Mississippi "was a thing too far above the ruling stupidity of the day to be a success." Barnard's status as Chancellor was most severely damaged by the "Branham Affair."

Branham was a physician in Oxford and the son-in-law of former president Longstreet and the brother-in-law of faculty member L. Q. C. Lamar. Branham had held Barnard responsible for undermining the authority of Longstreet in his last days as president and had waited for the opportunity to seek revenge against Barnard.

May 12, 1859, while Barnard was out of town, two students entered Barnard's faculty house. One of the students, Samuel B. Humphreys, allegedly raped and brutally beat a slave of the chancellor. Humphreys was called to a hearing before the faculty on May 23. He was found not guilty on counts of entering the Chancellor's residence and assaulting the slave because at the time the word of a slave against a white man was not admissible in court. In a second vote of the court, Humphrey was "morally convicted." Barnard was not satisfied with the ruling of the faculty and took it upon himself to write Humphreys' parents and request that they withdraw their son from the University, which they did. The young man applied for re-admission in the fall, but Barnard denied his admission, which not only prompted a small rebellion by students but also provided Branham an opportunity to bring into question

CHANCELLOR

John Newton Waddel (1865-74)

One of the University's original trustees and faculty members, Waddel was 36 when he came to the University of Mississippi in 1848, where he remained until the Civil War. An ordained Presbyterian minister, Waddel had served as commissioner of army missions for the Confederate Army in 1863 and had preached many sermons to troops. After the war, he was a highly influential and stabilizing force for the University and the community, encouraging the revival of the Alumni Association and student organizations. With the idea of revising the curriculum here, he visited leading universities in the North and East, ultimately achieving a new curriculum similar to that of the University of Michigan. Waddel was a graduate of the University of Georgia, where his father had served as president. He worked as a cotton farmer in Alabama, taught at the Willington Academy in South Carolina and established the Montrose Academy in Jasper County, Mississippi, before he was elected chair of the Ancient Languages Department at the University of Mississippi. He resigned the chancellorship to become secretary of education for the Presbyterian Church of the United States.

Did you know?

Architect William Nichols designed the original campus, laying it out on a circle which was emblematic of the Greek concept of perfection. Nichols also is well known for having designed the layout of Central Park in New York City.

Barnard's stand on slavery and state's rights. Again, rumors were circulated that Barnard had denied Humphreys' testimony on the basis of "negro testimony."

Upset and frustrated, Barnard requested of Governor John R. Pettus that the charges against him, especially his stance on slavery, be subjected to the "fullest and most searching investigation." Pettus convened the Board of Trustees, who heard testimony in March 1860. Even though Barnard owned slaves himself, he had misgivings about the institution of slavery and would later denounce it. But on that day in 1860, the chancellor of the the University of Mississippi stood before the Board of Trustees and declared, "I am as sound on the slavery question as any member of this board."

The Board of Trustees absolved Barnard of the charges, yet he remained subject to criticism by the evangelical clergy and the press. When Mississippi seceded from the Union on January 9, 1861, Barnard found the beginnings of his way out of the University of Mississippi. Upon returning from Washington February 2, 1861, Barnard discovered a campus stirred by the fire of secession and the rumors of war. Flags of the Confederacy flew from windows, and students stole and burned books favoring the abolition of slavery on the campus grounds. May 1, 1861, the University Greys, later Company A of the 11th Mississippi Infantry, boarded trains for Corinth and left the University to defend "their way of life." Other students had enlisted elsewhere, and the campus was ghostly, prompting Barnard to write, "We are indeed inhabitants of solitude...Our University has ceased to have visible existence." During the Civil War, the University served as a hospital for both Confederate and Union troops.

In the fall of 1861, when only four students arrived to enroll, the Board held an emergency meeting in Jackson and voted to close the University of Mississippi. At that time,

CHANCELLOR
Alexander Peter Stewart (1874-87)

The only Civil War general to serve as chancellor of the University of Mississippi, Alexander Peter Stewart walked away from a $6,000-a-year job with the St. Louis Mutual Life Insurance Company to take the job here—which paid about $2,500 a year. Stewart's tenure was marked by firsts. Baseball was introduced to the University in 1876. The University's first Ph.D. was granted in 1877. The University became coeducational in 1882. And the first woman faculty member was appointed in  1885. Born in 1821, Stewart was a graduate of West Point Military Academy, and he taught mathematics at Cumberland University in Tennessee before the start of the Civil War. Stewart entered the Confederate Army as a major, was promoted rapidly and was appointed lieutenant general on June 23, 1864. Stewart was a commander in the Army of Tennessee and was distinguished in the battles of Shiloh, Perryville, Murfreesboro, Chickamauga, and Missionary Ridge.

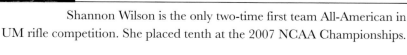

Barnard was relieved of his duties as the third president and the first chancellor of the University. In May 1864, Barnard was elected president of Columbia College and distinguished himself as a great educator. Barnard College was named in his honor.

F. A. P. Barnard fought numerous battles as chancellor of the the University of Mississippi. His dream of "universitas scientiarum" was never realized, but it was the initial dream of the University becoming a great institution of higher education. In a way, his connections saved the University during the Civil War. While most of Oxford was burned by Union troops led by General A. J. "Whiskey" Smith in 1864, much of the campus was spared. General William Tecumseh Sherman, a friend of Barnard's with whom he had taught at Louisiana Seminary, had issued an order that the campus be spared. In a letter he had written to Barnard, Sherman noted —

"When I rode through the grounds of the college, I thought of you... and... thought I saw traces of your life, of which I remember you spoke."

One of the buildings that was spared was the new observatory which was to house, at the time, the world's largest telescope. Today it is Barnard Observatory and houses the Center for the Study of Southern Culture.

Post-war years

The University of Mississippi reopened its doors to students in the fall of 1865 under the leadership of Chancellor John Waddel. The faculty members expected no more than 50 students, but were surprised when 86 showed up. The number of students grew over the academic year and swelled to 107 before the term ended. This new group of students was much like the entering class in 1848. Five were juniors, 41 were sophomores, 50 were freshmen. In addition, there were 40 "partial course" students and 57 preparatory students. The preparatory students were those who could not meet admission requirements to the University. Tuition and "fuel" ex-

CHANCELLOR
Edward Mayes (1887-91)

Edward Mayes was the first native Mississippian and the first University of Mississippi alumnus to become chancellor of the University. Born in Hinds County in 1846, Mayes served as a private in the Fourth Regiment of Mississippi Cavalry during the Civil War.

When the University reopened after the war, Mayes was the first non-Oxford student to arrive—in October 1865. He was one of only 193 students enrolled at the University that year. After graduating in 1868, Mayes practiced law in Coffeeville and Oxford. He was selected to teach law at the University in 1877. During his tenure, Ventress Hall was constructed as the University's first library building. Mayes returned to his law practice at the end of his term, and he later served as dean of the Millsaps School of Law. Among his most notable writings is a history of education in Mississippi.

Did you know?

Robert Khayat (B.A. Education '61, J.D. '66) Chancellor Emeritus of UM, has quite a list of accomplishments. He was an Academic All-American football player and was chosen as an All-SEC catcher for the 1959 and 1960 SEC Champion baseball teams. He was an All-Pro kicker for the Washington Redskins. Most recently, he received a silver medal from the 2014 Independent Publisher Book Awards for his memoir, *The Education of a Lifetime*.

penses were $75 dollars a year, and students were charged $15 dollars a month for boarding fees.

National events brought about by the end of the Civil War and the emancipation of slaves began to change the landscape of higher education in Mississippi. The Morril Land Grant Act of 1862 created Alcorn A&M College for the education of freed slaves. In addition, Mississippi Agricultural and Mechanical College, now Mississippi State University, opened its doors to students in 1880 and attracted the sons of Mississippi's blue collar workers, in contrast to the University in Oxford, which was seen as the school of the "aristocracy." Mississippi A&M came to be known as the "People's College."

In 1874, Alexander "Old Straight" Stewart succeeded Waddel as Chancellor. His immediate challenge was to stop the alarming enrollment decline that was beginning to occur. The enrollment of 302 in 1873 fell to 208 in 1874, to 131 in 1875, to 125 in 1876. As a result of their concern for the University, the Board published a pamphlet entitled "Where Shall I Send My Son?" It included a history and description of the University and made reference to the high morals and strong religious element "in the student body." Within the pamphlet, the public was assured by the faculty and citizens of Oxford that since the war "drinking, gambling, extravagance, and dissipation of every kind have been diminishing." The Board stated categorically, "There are no sons of rich men there." The pamphlet proved an effective recruiting tool. Enrollment jumped from 125 in 1876 to 471 in 1877.

CHANCELLOR
Robert Burwell Fulton (1892-1906)

Another University of Mississippi alumnus, Robert Burwell Fulton served as chancellor longer than any of his predecessors and deserves credit for establishing the School of Engineering (1900), the School of Education (1903), and the School of Medicine (1903).

Born in 1849 in Sumter County, Ala., Fulton graduated with honors from the University of Mississippi in 1869. After teaching stints in Alabama and New Orleans, Fulton returned to Oxford in 1871 as assistant professor of physics and astronomy. He achieved full professor status in 1875 and was the first director of the Mississippi Weather Service. His leadership was largely responsible for the organization of the National Association of State Universities; he served as its president for five consecutive years. During Fulton's tenure, football was introduced to the University (1893), and the University's first printed annual was published (1897). Its name, *The Ole Miss*, soon became synonymous with the University of Mississippi.

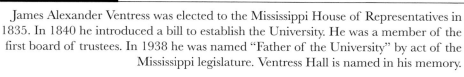

Did you know?

James Alexander Ventress was elected to the Mississippi House of Representatives in 1835. In 1840 he introduced a bill to establish the University. He was a member of the first board of trustees. In 1938 he was named "Father of the University" by act of the Mississippi legislature. Ventress Hall is named in his memory.

The changing campus

The University would make a major change in 1882 when women were first admitted as students. They were not allowed to dine with men and were required to live off campus or in the homes of faculty members, and were provided separate study rooms. The first women students quickly established themselves as a presence at the University. In the first class to graduate with women students, Sally Vick Hill received the highest honors. In 1885, Sarah Isom McGehee was appointed the first woman faculty member at the University. She was a tutor of elocution. The Sarah Isom Center for Women and Gender Studies was established in her honor and memory in 1981 to address the changing roles and expectations of women students, faculty, and staff. The University has been a leader in providing educational opportunities for women. Eleven women entered the University when its doors were opened to women. Today, women make up more than half of the student body, and a woman has served as Provost. Five women have served as vice chancellors.

As early as 1850, Greek letter societies became a part of the University during Longstreet's term as president. He had been a member of the Mystic Seven at Emory University and helped establish the chapter at the University of Mississippi. Records show that Delta Kappa Epsilon was the first fraternity on campus and was established in 1850. By the time the Civil War started, there were nine fraternities on the Ole Miss campus. All closed with the onset of the conflict and the first to reopen after the war was Sigma Alpha Epsilon in 1866. In 1881, the Greek societies came under strong attack by

CHANCELLOR
Andrew Armstrong Kincannon (1907-14)

Born in Noxubee County in 1859, Andrew Armstrong Kincannon was the second Mississippi native to serve as the University's chief administrator. Striving to make the University of Mississippi a progressive school, he pointed to other top state schools around the country, such as the University of Michigan and the University of Wisconsin, to inspire an attitude of enthusiasm and growth. After graduating from the National Normal University of Ohio in 1884, Kincannon taught at Mississippi A&M College (now Mississippi State University), was superintendent of the new public school system in Meridian, and was president of the Industrial Institute and College (now Mississippi University for Women) before being elected chancellor of Ole Miss. During his tenure, the University grew in size and reputation: some of its younger graduates were among the first of a growing list of Rhodes Scholars; the School of Pharmacy opened in 1908; and, in 1911, *The Mississippian*, the University's student newspaper, was started under the auspices of the YMCA and two literary societies. But there was increasing animosity in the legislature toward the University: fraternities and sororities were banished by law in 1912.

Our football stadium, Vaught-Hemingway Stadium, is named for Coach John Howard Vaught, our most winning football coach of all time, and Judge William Hemingway, long-time chair of the Athletics Committee.

the Board for appearing to exist only for the sons of wealthy men. These groups narrowly escaped banishment by the Board of Trustees.

CHANCELLOR
Joseph Neely Powers (1914-24; 1930-32)

Joseph Neely Powers is perhaps best known as an educator for his role in establishing the agricultural high schools that would become the basis for the community college system in Mississippi. A native of Havana, Ala., Powers was born in 1869. He taught in several rural schools and later served as a principal and superintendent. Governor James K. Vardaman appointed Powers as state superintendent of education, a post to which he was subsequently elected. Powers enjoyed enormous popularity as chancellor of the University of

Mississippi, although he was subjected to scandal and political favoritism during the political administrations of Governor Theodore Bilbo and Governor Lee Russell. He was voted out of office by the University's trustees in 1924 but was reappointed for a brief, turbulent period in the early 1930s. Powers is credited with the establishment of the School of Commerce. In another notable action, he permitted William Faulkner, the future Nobel Prize winner, to enroll at Ole Miss without a high school diploma—as a special student.

The public began to lose faith in Chancellor Stewart because of his inability to control student discipline problems. Numerous complaints about student discipline were recorded. Throwing rocks at passing trains, annoying passengers at the depot, gambling, hazing of students, kangaroo courts, drinking, cheating, and disrespectful behavior toward faculty all became fodder for the state press, for sermons from pulpits and for general conversation. In 1876, it was reported that "tying balls of fire to the tails of calves on dark nights to see them run across campus" had become a favorite pastime. This led to the prohibition of faculty keeping livestock on campus.

Stewart also found himself dealing with the problem of student housing. The dormitory system that constituted the mixing of boys from the "preparatory school," some as young as the age of 13, with older students, some of whom were now veterans of the Civil War, had long been a source of problems for the administration and faculty. Weekly room inspections were instituted, and the enforcement of this was uneven at best with some faculty members taking the duties seriously and others arguing that it was inconsistent with the atmosphere that should be promoted on a college campus. The inconsistent enforcement of this practice contributed to the student misconduct. Stewart decided to resign his position in July, 1886. In a bold move, the trustees abolished the *chancellor* title and allowed the faculty to elect a person from the faculty to serve as a chairman of the faculty. The faculty unanimously elected Edward Mayes, the first native-born Mississippian and alumnus of the University to so serve.

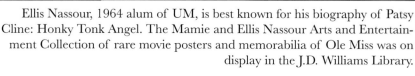

Did you know?

Ellis Nassour, 1964 alum of UM, is best known for his biography of Patsy Cline: Honky Tonk Angel. The Mamie and Ellis Nassour Arts and Entertainment Collection of rare movie posters and memorabilia of Ole Miss was on display in the J.D. Williams Library.

In 1889 another major reorganization of the academic framework of the University took place. Degree requirements were changed, making nineteen departments (or schools) inside the Department of Science, Literature, and the Arts. There also was a Department of Professional Studies, but it consisted only of the School of Law. The title *chancellor* was reinstated, and Mayes continued serving in that position, with the full support of the board and faculty colleagues.

Mayes was unusually energetic and spoke to audiences throughout the state about the University. He earlier had written at length about the debt the state owed the University as a result seminary funds having been misused. Though he and Senator James Z. George, a supporter of Mississippi A & M, had earlier disagreed on this matter, Senator George later assisted the University "in securing...an additional grant of land from the United States Congress." Under the leadership of Mayes and with the assistance of funding from the state, buildings were renovated, streets were laid, a new library was constructed, the first fraternity house (for Delta Psi) was built, the Mississippi Historical Society was founded (in 1890), and graduate student fellowships were created.

Mayes then made the tough decision to terminate Professors Hutson, Johnson, Quinche, Sears, and Latham because of continual complaints about their competence as teachers. It was a move that rankled some who thought the professors' years of service warranted a nobler end than firing. But Mayes followed through.

Although he had many enthusiastic followers, some of whom suggested him for various political offices, others never forgave Mayes for his decision. Perhaps because of this ill will (no doubt spurred by the fact that Quinche committed suicide shortly after his fir-

CHANCELLOR

Alfred Hume (1924-30; 1932-35)

Alfred Hume was the first University of Mississippi chancellor to possess an earned doctorate, and he was perhaps one of the most dedicated to the University, devoting nearly 60 years of his life to the school. A Tennessee native born in 1866, Dr. Hume began teaching mathematics and astronomy at the University of Mississippi immediately after he received his doctorate from Vanderbilt University. Besides serving two terms as chancellor, he was called upon three additional times to serve as acting chancellor.

Dr. Hume made many enduring contributions to the University. In 1927, he organized the graduate program into an administrative entity of its own. He started a significant building program, which included plans for the construction of Fulton Chapel, Bondurant Hall, the gymnasium, the high-school building, Lewis Hall, the School of Law, the cafeteria, six dormitories for men, one women's dormitory, Hemingway Stadium, and the Field House. Fraternities were allowed to reorganize. Most significantly, however, Hume is credited with preventing Governor Theodore G. Bilbo from moving the University to Jackson.

Did you know?

Albert Taylor Bledsoe was the first professor hired at the University of Mississippi, where he taught mathematics and astronomy. He became the interim president of the University when President Holmes left the campus in the spring of 1849. In 1854 Bledsoe left the University to teach mathematics at the University of Virginia.

ing), Mayes elected to return to the law profession; he submitted his resignation in 1891 and joined a law firm in December of that year.

Chancellor Robert Fulton succeeded Mayes and took it upon himself to enhance the beauty of the campus. One of his most lasting and endearing contributions to the geography and spirit of the campus was a wooded area set aside in the center of the campus that would become known to generations of University of Mississippi students and alumni as "the Grove." With Fulton at the helm, the nature of life outside of the classroom changed dramatically. Ricks Hall, a women's dormitory was built, and the Parthenic Society, a women's literary society, was founded. Fulton also built a male dormitory for 200 students that included a large dining hall.

Student activities also became so popular in the 1890s that the YMCA began publishing a handbook for new students. Clubs and organizations included the Glee Club, the YMCA, the Mandolin and Guitar Club, the University Orchestra, and the Minstrels, a traveling music troupe. Academic clubs listed were the Science Club, the University Teachers Club, the Press Club, the Sketch Club, and the Dramatic Club. The Kodak Club, the F.O.X. Social Club, and the Cotillion Club were listed as social organizations. There were two "shooting clubs" included in the YMCA handbook. One was a gun club and the other was "unrestricted and open to all crap shooters." Women's clubs included were the Talkatani Club, the SSS Club, the YWCA, the Women's Athletic Association, the Tennis Club, and the Gymnasium Club.

The first student newspaper, *The University Record*, appeared in 1898 and was published once a week on Wednesdays. *The Record* folded in 1902 and was replaced by the *Varsity Voice*. In 1911, *The Mississippian* replaced the *Varsity Voice*, and it remains today as the student newspaper of the University of Mississippi and the oldest student newspaper in the state.

CHANCELLOR
Alfred Benjamin Butts (1935-46)

A recognized scholar and law professor, Alfred Benjamin Butts was born in 1890. He received a B.S. degree from Mississippi A&M College in 1911 and a Ph.D. from Columbia University in 1920. While head of the Department of Education and Sociology at A&M, he spent summers teaching at numerous universities around the country, including at Yale, where he earned a law degree in 1930. Dr. Butts' most daunting task upon assuming the chancellorship in 1935 was to restore the University's accreditation, which had been lost during the Bilbo administration. This was achieved in 1941. Dr. Butts is credited with pulling the University through the Great Depression. To his credit, a substantial amount of construction was achieved despite economic difficulties: the Student Union (Weir Hall), the Physics and Astronomy Building (Lewis Hall), 21 new faculty houses, and 17 sorority and fraternity houses. Also during Dr. Butts' term, the name "Rebels" was selected for the football team.

The University becomes Ole Miss

There would be no single event that would have a more lasting effect on the University of Mississippi than the naming of the initial yearbook published in 1897. In a contest to name the yearbook, which was dedicated to the University Greys, Elma Meek suggested the name OLE MISS. Within two years students and alumni were using the name of the yearbook as a name for the University.

Four years prior to the naming of the yearbook, the University played its first football game in 1893. Fulton is remembered for bringing many outstanding and memorable faculty members to the University of Mississippi, but none would rival Alexander Bondurant for his role in the formation of the identity of the University. A Harvard-trained Latin professor, Bondurant introduced intercollegiate football to the University, coached the first team, and guided the program through its early years. The University of Mississippi played its first football game November 11, 1893, at University Park on campus against the Southwestern Baptist University of Jackson, Tennessee, before a large crowd. The "Oxford" team won 56-0.

Fulton had served honorably as chancellor but found himself embroiled in controversy over growing dissention between the Greeks and non-Greeks. The recommendation for abolishing the system went before the Board of Trustees, but Fulton intervened and

CHANCELLOR
John Davis Williams (1946-68)

John Davis Williams was chancellor for 22 years, and his influence on the University was profound. During the years of growth after World War II, he reorganized the administrative structure of the rapidly expanding University. He kept the University open and stabilized during the difficult period of integration in 1962. He saw the University experience a revival of athletics (the football teams were consistently successful during his term as chancellor). He helped the University celebrate its Centennial (an event highlighted

by the publication of Dr. J. Allen Cabaniss' *A History of The University of Mississippi*). A Kentucky native born in 1902, Williams was the first and only chancellor to hold the Ed.D. (Doctor of Education) degree. In 1955, he oversaw the establishment of the Medical Center campus in Jackson and the transition from a two-year medical program to a four-year school that was fully accredited. Three years later (1958), the School of Nursing was added on the Jackson campus. Doctoral programs were authorized in biology, physics, political science, and psychology, and Carrier Scholarships were established to attract the best students. Also during his long tenure, the University built an alumni headquarters and celebrated its unique relationship with William Faulkner.

became the target of public ridicule. Eventually, the Board voted to relieve Chancellor Fulton of his duties. Fulton was followed by Andrew Kincannon who pledged in his early

The Mississippi community colleges that send the most students to UM are Northwest CC, Itawamba CC, Northeast CC, and Holmes CC.

CHANCELLOR
Porter Lee Fortune Jr. (1968-84)

Porter Lee Fortune Jr. was chancellor during a period of remarkable growth and development. Born in 1920, Fortune served as a naval officer during World War II and saw action in the South Pacific, where he was awarded the Bronze Star. After receiving his Ph.D. from the University of North Carolina at Chapel Hill, he joined the faculty at Mississippi Southern College (now the University of Southern Mississippi), where he later served as dean of the university and graduate school. During his first 10 years as chancellor of the University of Mississippi, Dr. Fortune saw enrollment increase by 40 percent and black enrollment increase from 17 students to 733 students. Dr. Fortune is remembered for helping to smooth the way for both black and white students during the civil rights move-

ment. During his administration, funds were finalized for the construction of the Ole Miss Union; the Turner Health, Physical Education, and Recreation Center; the athletic dormitory; the chemistry building (Coulter Hall); Dorothy Crosby Hall; the Kate Skipwith Teaching Museum; Anderson Hall; the Lamar Law Center; and the J.D. Williams Library addition. The schools of Health Related Professions and Dentistry were added to the Medical Center during his chancellorship, as was the School of Accountancy on the Oxford campus. New programs under his administration included women's studies, African-American studies, communicative disorders, social work, and court reporting. Other legacies of the Fortune administration include the University of Mississippi Foundation, the Chancellor's Trust, and the Alumni Hall of Fame. But Chancellor Fortune may be best-remembered for promoting the development of the eastern part of the campus as a culture center—including the acquisition of Rowan Oak, the William Faulkner property, and the Skipwith property—which attracts visitors and scholars from around the world.

remarks to transform the University from an "aristocracy" to a "democracy." Kincannon established an Honor Council vested with authority over a wide range of discipline problems. This organization would be the predecessor to the Associated Student Body which still operates today. He also used the largest state appropriation to date to enlarge the infirmary, provide an updated water and sewage system for the campus, construct a laundry building, and build a new men's dormitory. Kincannon also dealt with accusations of misappropriation of University monies, a scandal involving paying football players. Perhaps the greatest controversy with which Kincannon had to deal was the decision of the state legislature to prohibit "secret societies" (fraternities). Charged before the state legislature for "encouraging dissipation, wasting money, discouraging study and scholarship, interfering with the literary societies, and destroying the college spirit by promoting cliques," the fraternities had little chance. The law would remain in effect until 1926 when the legislature passed a law allowing secret societies on campus. Kincannon dealt with the same issues that plagued many of his predecessors, and he resigned in 1914 stating that "he was unwilling for the school to become a political chattel."

Joseph Neely Powers succeeded Kincannon in 1914, and by 1916 was enjoying an unusually high enrollment of 641 students. Unfortunately, the physical

Did you know?

The top undergraduate programs in number of majors in fall 2014 at the Oxford and regional campuses were: Accountancy (962), Biology (868), Elementary Education (697), Psychology (642), Integrated Marketing Communications (596), Marketing (586), Exercise Science (585), and Criminal Justice (557).

structure of the campus was inadequate to accommodate the large number of students, and the financial situation left by Kincannon made it difficult to provide new facilities. During World War I, many of the students left for service. Those who remained were busy preparing for military service, and the campus took on the appearance of a military base. After the war, campus enrollment swelled, and the legislature was forced to appropriate money to build and refurbish facilities. With this money, a new science hall was built, as well as three new men's dormitories and one women's dormitory. In 1923, enrollment on the Ole Miss campus reached more than 800 students.

Alfred Hume replaced Powers in 1924. His tenure as Chancellor would coincide with the 1927 election of Governor Theodore Bilbo, who wreaked havoc in higher education in Mississippi. Shortly after his election, Bilbo initiated an effort to relocate the University to Jackson. Chancellor Hume fought him on this and in an address before the Board of Trustees, he eloquently pleaded, "Gentlemen, you may move the University of Mississippi. You may move it to Jackson or anywhere else. You may uproot it from the hallowed ground on which it has stood for 80 years. You may take it

CHANCELLOR
Robert Gerald Turner (1984-95)

The second youngest of the University's chancellors, Gerald Turner is credited with boosting the University's enrollment and with significantly increasing endowment funds. Spearheading the University's first capital campaign solely for academic enrichment and following that with a campaign to raise funds to bring athletics facilities to SEC standards, Dr. Turner oversaw a private fundraising effort that resulted in gifts to Ole Miss of more than $100 million. During his chancellorship, the University's endowment increased from $8 million to $64 million. A Texan, Dr. Turner received his Ph.D. in psychology in 1975 from the University of Texas at Austin. He advanced rapidly through a succession of teaching and administrative positions at Pepperdine University and later served as vice president for executive affairs at the University of Oklahoma before being named chancellor of the Uni-

versity of Mississippi. During his administration, seven new academic programs were introduced and six federally funded national centers were established: the Jamie L. Whitten National Center for Physical Acoustics, the National Center for the Development of Natural Products, the Marine Mineral Research Institute, the Center for Computational Hydroscience and Engineering, the National Food Service Management Institute, and the Center for Water and Wetlands Resources. The Mississippi Supercomputing Center was established on campus, and externally funded research programs increased more than 300 percent. Twelve Barnard Distinguished Professorships were created from private funds, and the University's 23rd Rhodes Scholar, Mississippi's first African-American honoree, was named. Minority enrollment increased 85 percent, and the University received two Peterson Awards for Excellence in Graduate Admissions for Minority Students. More than $200 million in new construction was completed, initiated, or approved on the Oxford and Jackson campuses prior to his departure to become president of Southern Methodist University in Dallas, Texas, in May 1995.

Did you know?

Ansu Sesay was 1998 consensus All-American and SEC Player of the Year. The two-time All-SEC led Ole Miss to consecutive SEC West titles and NCAA tournament berths. He played in the NBA with the Seattle Sonics and Golden State Warriors.

CHANCELLOR
Robert Conrad Khayat (1995-2009)

A respected academician and administrator, Robert Khayat was a professor of law and served as associate dean of the School of Law, vice chancellor for university affairs, and director of the Sesquicentennial before being named Chancellor of the University of Mississippi in 1995.

He received his bachelor's degree in education from Ole Miss in 1961 and graduated with honors with his Ole Miss law school class in 1966.

As a student-athlete, Chancellor Khayat demonstrated that athletes can succeed academically and be active in student life. During his undergraduate years he was tapped for membership in ODK, was active in the YMCA and served on ASB committees. Named an Academic All-American football player in 1959, he led the nation in kick-scoring in 1958 and 1959 and was selected to play in the 1960 College All-Star game. He played for the Washington Redskins from 1960-64 and was a member of the 1961 NFL Pro Bowl team.

Chancellor Khayat joined the Ole Miss faculty in 1969 as a law professor. While on leave from Ole Miss during 1980-81, he earned a master's degree in law from Yale University on a Sterling Fellowship. He returned as a law professor in 1981, advancing to the position of associate dean. He served as Ole Miss vice chancellor for university affairs from 1984-89. On leave from the University, he became the first president of the NCAA Foundation with a mission of promoting academic and personal development opportunities for college athletes.

He returned as law professor in 1992 and later began chairing the University's 150th anniversary celebration. The School of Law student body chose Professor Khayat as their 1993-94 Outstanding Law Professor of the Year, and the school's *Mississippi Law Journal* staff established a scholarship in his name in 1995.

He has served as Oxford-Lafayette County Chamber of Commerce president and was named Oxford's Citizen of the Year. The National Football Foundation presented him with the Distinguished American Award in 1987 and 1989. He also was featured in the 1987-88 and 1988-89 NFL yearbooks for achieving success after football, where he was cited as "one of the NFL's best examples of a successful scholar-athlete."

During his 14 years at the helm, Chancellor Khayat made an indelible impact on the University through enhancing the learning environment, increasing enrollment, and heading two capital campaigns generating almost $775 million in private support. The University created the Sally McDonnell Barksdale Honors College, Croft Institute for International Studies, Lott Leadership Institute, and Winter Institute for Racial Reconciliation while he was chancellor.

Chancellor Khayat spearheaded the effort that resulted in UM's becoming the first public institution of higher learning in Mississippi chosen for a Phi Beta Kappa chapter, thus establishing a climate of excellence for all endeavors at the University of Mississippi. Also during his tenure, Ole Miss hosted a presidential debate, announced its 25th Rhodes Scholar, and inaugurated the first black president of the alumni association.

from the surroundings that have become dear to the thousands who have gone from its door. But, gentlemen, don't call it Ole Miss." The Board voted to keep the University in Oxford, which angered Bilbo, who removed Hume as chancellor and appointed former

Did you know?

Tony Dees was a 1992 Olympic silver medalist (110-meter hurdles) and two-time All-American. Dees was a five-time SEC champion (60-yard hurdles, 110-meter hurdles, 200 meters).

Chancellor Powers. In addition to Hume, 179 employees at the four major institutions of higher learning in Mississippi were fired. This became known as "Bilbo's Purge." Because of Bilbo's interference in higher education, all institutions in the state lost their accreditation granted by the Southern Association of Colleges and Schools.

After Martin Conner was elected governor in 1931, a new Board of Trustees was appointed, Powers was dismissed, and former Chancellor Alfred Hume once again was appointed Chancellor. He only served until 1935 when he retired to become chairman and professor of mathematics, positions which he held until he was 80 years of age. Hume Hall, home of the mathematics department, is named in his honor and memory.

Campus growth and the Rebels

Alfred Benjamin Butts became Chancellor in 1935 and is recognized as the most visionary Chancellor since Barnard. He was the first to assume the role of fundraiser for the University, which prospered under his leadership. In 1939, 55 building projects were underway on campus. Among the additions to the campus were Guyton Hall, the cafeteria (Johnson Commons), a gymnasium, an athletic field house, a women's dormitory, six men's dormitories, a new law school, University High School, and an 18,000 seat football stadium, Hemingway Stadium. In addition, Weir Hall was built as the first student union building and housed the bookstore, the post office, the Grill, a game room, a barber shop, a clothing store, and meeting rooms.

Chancellor Butts steered the University through World War II. The enrollment on campus dwindled from more than 1400 in 1941-1942 to a mere 800 students in 1944.

CHANCELLOR
Daniel W. Jones (2009-2015)

July 1, 2009, Dr. Daniel W. Jones became the Sixteenth Chancellor of the University of Mississippi. Prior to his appointment, Dr. Jones was Vice Chancellor for Health Affairs, Dean of the School of Medicine, and Herbert G. Langford Professor of Medicine at the University of Mississippi Medical Center (UMMC) in Jackson. He served as the UMMC's chief executive officer for six years overseeing the five schools and the medical center.

Dr. Jones is a native Mississippian who graduated from Mississippi College in 1971 and earned his M.D. in 1975 at the University of Mississippi Medical Center and completed his residency in internal medicine there in 1978. He had a private practice in Laurel, and in 1985, he went to Korea as a medical missionary.

During his six year term, he focused on servant leadership for the betterment of all Mississippians.

Did you know?

Savante' Stringfellow was a 2000 Olympian, 2001 World Championships silver medalist (long jump), and three-time NCAA champion (long jump). He was a six-time All-American and four-time SEC champion (long jump).

Many professors had been called away in the service of their country. During the war, University students served in medical units for both the Army and the Navy, the Specialized Training and Regiment Unit, and a unit of the Army Specialized Training Program. Campus life went on as normally as it could during the war years. With most of the male student body enlisted in military service, new roles fell to women on campus. For the first time in the history of the University, a woman, Maralyn Howell Bullion, was elected president of the Associated Student Body. Subsequently, women also were elected for the first time to the positions of editor of the yearbook and the student newspaper. One hundred and thirty-seven Ole Miss men lost their lives in World War II.

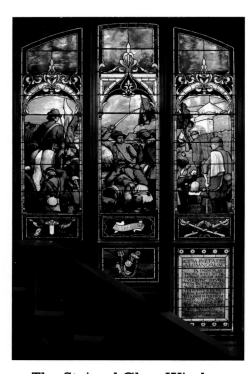

The Stained Glass Window at Ventress Hall.

While Dean Malcolm Guess had promoted a campaign to create a friendly campus by having placards placed around campus stating, "Ole Miss, everybody speaks!", the campus might have seemed anything but friendly in the aftermath of the war. During the 1945-46 academic year, enrollment surged to 2,005, the largest enrollment in the history of the University, and two and a half times that of the preceding year. Tensions were high with long lines, inadequate housing, and a shortage of teachers.

In addition to dealing with the challenges of the burgeoning student body numbers, Butts also faced growing criticism for his retention of Harry Mehre as football coach. After the 1945 season and Mehre's third consecutive losing football campaign, alumni became disgruntled and put pressure on Butts to fire Mehre. Also, Butts had received reports that Mehre had been inebriated at the Florida game earlier that year. The Chancellor had made the decision to fire Mehre but under pressure the coach submitted his resignation on December 5, 1945. Students had become so frustrated with the Chancellor and the football coach that they burned both in effigy after the firing. The Board of Trustees dismissed Butts in January, 1945.

Chancellor J. D. Williams, football and integration

John Davis Williams became the twelfth Chancellor of the University of Mississippi in

June, 1946. He faced the same challenges that had brought about Chancellor Butts' firing. Before he left the office of Chancellor, Butts appointed Harold "Red" Drew head football coach. When Drew left to take the same position at the University of Alabama in 1947, Chancellor Williams promoted Ole Miss Assistant Coach John Howard Vaught to the position of head coach. Williams' decision to promote Vaught would have long-lasting, positive effects on the University of Mississippi. As head coach from 1947 through 1970, Vaught compiled an amazing record. His teams were 190-61-12 with three national titles. In addition, he won six Southeastern Conference titles, 18 bowl games, and coached 27 All Americans. The 1959 Ole Miss team was voted by the Southeastern Conference as the Team of the Decade.

Football in the 1950s and 1960s was a facet of Ole Miss that shaped the image of the University. Another was that in 1959 and 1960, Ole Miss had back-to-back Miss America winners in Mary Ann Mobley and Lynda Lee Mead. The combination of winning football teams and beauty queens led *Sports Illustrated* to feature the University in a 1960 article entitled, "Babes, Brutes, and Ole Miss: Successful football and dazzling Miss Americas are the products of Mississippi's hell-for-leather tradition."

Ole Miss beauty queens and gridiron victories were only a part of the administration of Chancellor Williams. Williams faced burgeoning student numbers as war veterans returned to college. From the late 1940s through the 1960s, the campus expanded at an amazing rate. Dormitories for women and men were built. An engineering building, a school of education, an alumni center, and a continuing education center were built. The building of the University library, which now bears Williams' name, was the most significant construction project of his administration.

Throughout its history, the University had dealt with major challenges, but no two were more difficult or had a more lasting effect than the issues of political interference and race. Civil rights became a major issue on the national landscape in the late 1940s and throughout the sixties. It was during the University's centennial in 1948 that the Confederate flag became a part of Ole Miss athletics. In the 1950s, students celebrated Dixie Week with a reenactment of secession, Robert E. Lee beard-growing contests, mule races, and ceremonial consumption of mint juleps.

In 1950, the student editor of *The Mississippian*, Alvin Krebs, wrote an article supporting the integration of the University. Krebs became a target of scorn and derision and a cross was burned on the lawn of his dormitory. Throughout the decade of the 1950s, the issue of race would resurface again and again. One of the most glaring examples of paranoia involving race at Ole Miss occurred in 1958 when both a current and a former state legislator charged members of the Ole Miss community with subverting the "Mississippi way of life." The two filed a 36-page document to the Board of Trustees, charg-

Did you know?

Dave Peege earned first team All-American honors in back-to-back years (1984-85). As a sophomore in 1983, Peege was selected to the All-SEC first team and took medalist honors at the SEC Championships. In 1984 Peege helped lead the Rebels to the SEC Championship and the team's first ever NCAA Championship appearance.

ing Director of Religious Life, Will Campbell, for playing ping pong with a black man; the Dean of the Law School for publicly stating that Mississippi must obey the Supreme Court; a School of Education professor for bragging about being born in the North and for making fun of a female student with a southern drawl; and the chair of the history department for challenging the military strategy of Robert E. Lee. They also suggested that Ole Miss might be a "Communist cell." Chancellor Williams met with the Board of Trustees in 1959. The board cleared the University of all charges.

1962

When a young African-American Air Force veteran from Kosciusko decided to enter the University of Mississippi, a significant chapter in Ole Miss' history would be written. James Meredith saw Ole Miss as a symbol of white prestige and power, a "finishing school for the sons of the elite." After 18 months of Meredith's persistence, the University's delay tactics, and innumerable legal battles, Judge John Minor Wisdom ordered James Meredith admitted to the University of Mississippi on June 26, 1962. The University did all within its power to block Meredith's admission.

After lengthy legal wrangling, Meredith prepared to enter the University in September 1962. September 29, 1962, Governor Ross Barnett, a staunch segregationist, addressed a crowd of 40,000 fans in Jackson Memorial Stadium at half time of the Ole Miss – Kentucky football game. Stirring the crowd into frenzy, Barnett avowed, "I love Mississippi. I love her people, our customs. I love and respect her customs." In secret, Barnett had been communicating earlier in the day with President John F. Kennedy and his brother, Attorney General Robert Kennedy, about how to get Meredith safely on to campus.

Meredith arrived on campus Sunday, September 30, accompanied by a phalanx of U. S. Marshalls. He was placed in Baxter Dormitory where he would live during the school year. In the meantime, as students began arriving back on campus after the weekend and the football game in Jackson, a crowd started to grow in front of the Lyceum. Many of those who gathered in the Circle were not Ole Miss students. As the night wore on, violence ensued. Gunshots were fired sporadically at the U.S. Marshalls. Bricks were thrown. Both rioters and Marshalls were injured. Cars were overturned and burned. In the end, two people were killed, the inner campus was scarred, and on Monday, October 1, 1962, James Meredith enrolled in the University of Mississippi.

There have been numerous articles, books, and documentaries produced about the integration of Ole Miss. It was a dark time for the University. *An American Insurrection: The Battle of Oxford, Mississippi, 1962*, by William Doyle, is an excellent account of the events of that time.

Did you know?

Peggie Gillom-Granderson was a four-year starting forward (1976-80) and a career leader in points (2,486) and 1,271 rebounds. As a senior she was named to the SEC All-Tournament team and was a finalist for the Wade Trophy.

Enrollment dropped on campus from 5,042 in 1962 to 4,707 in the fall of 1963. In the fall of 1964, the University enrollment rebounded, and 5,159, the largest number of students to that date, entered Ole Miss.

The sixties

Chancellor Williams continued to lead the University through its recovery. He faced problems that were familiar to most university presidents. Students misbehaved, participated in panty raids, and tested the limits of the administration's patience. In October 1967, 800 students marched on the town square in support of legalizing beer in Oxford. Another "beer riot" occurred in December when students became rowdier, smashing parking meters, turning over trash containers, and hurling bottles. In the end, 58 students were arrested.

The assassination of Dr. Martin Luther King, Jr. on April 4, 1968, had a profound effect on the African-American students at Ole Miss. From the time that James Meredith entered the University in 1962 until 1968, there was little public notice of the black students on campus. Black student life was non-existent compared to the numerous opportunities offered to white students. Tensions ran high on the weekend following the death of Dr. King, and black students protested when the American flag was not lowered to half mast. Soon after, the black students sent a memorandum

The Meredith Monument on the Ole Miss Campus.

to the new Chancellor, Dr. Porter Fortune. In the memorandum, the students cited an atmosphere of bigotry, bias, and prejudice, and accused administrators, officials, teachers, and workers of the University of perpetuating that atmosphere. In the memorandum there were 16 demands, including hiring black faculty and staff, granting a charter for the Black Student Union, and recruiting black athletes.

After a tense two-year period, the situation came to a climax when on the night of February 25, 1970, 61 black students marched onto the stage at Fulton Chapel where a traveling group, *Up With People*, was performing. All were arrested, and later that night

Did you know?

Armintie Price Herrington is one of only two players in NCAA history to amass 2,000 points, 1,000 rebounds, 400 assists, and 400 steals. Her senior year, she was named to the ESPN.com All-America first team as well as the Kodak/WBCA All-America team.

another 28 were arrested for continuing the protest at various locations. When the Lafayette County jail was filled with students, the remaining students were bused to the State Penitentiary at Parchman. In the fall of 1970, Ole Miss hired its first black faculty member, signed its first black athlete, and established a Black Studies Program. Within the next few years, the University met almost all of the demands of the students' memorandum.

During the 1960s there was minimal Vietnam war protest. What was billed as the "biggest anti-war demonstration in Mississippi," attracted 200 students because it was competing against the pep rally prior to the Ole Miss – Alabama football game. Only 200 students showed up in Fulton Chapel to hear faculty members, alumni, and students speak out against the war.

In 1974, the University abolished curfew for women students. This had been preceded by the abolition of a dress code for women that disallowed wearing shorts. Women who were walking across campus to a physical education class were forced to wear a raincoat over their shorts. Also abolished was the practice of "signing out" dates. Women who left residence halls with dates had been required to list where they were going and with whom.

Chancellor R. Gerald Turner

After 16 years as Chancellor, Porter Fortune retired in 1984. The Board of Trustees of Institutions of Higher Learning elected R. Gerald Turner to serve as the fourteenth Chancellor of the University of Mississippi. When Chancellor Turner took office, he had three primary goals for the University: increase the University's endowment, reverse the enrollment decline, and repair the University's public image. Perhaps Turner's greatest gift to Ole Miss was his ability to make alumni believe in the responsibility of giving back to the institution. He launched the Campaign for Ole Miss and worked arduously to raise funds for the University. He spoke to alumni groups, visited civic clubs, called on corporation CEOs, spoke at schools and churches, and spent endless hours away from the University selling its merits. After two and a half years, the Campaign for Ole Miss was completed and exceeded original expectations. A total of $61.7 million was raised for the University. Two years later, Turner initiated the Drive for Athletics and appointed Archie Manning chair of the drive. This fundraising effort resulted in $11.6 million raised for athletics and the subsequent construction of Oxford-University Baseball Stadium, the Starnes Athletics Training Center, and the Palmer Salloum Tennis facility.

Turner went beyond private giving and sought federal funding for campus projects. He relied on the support of Mississippi's powerful congressional delegation. During the 1980s and 1990s, the Center for Computational Hydroscience and Engineering and the Center for Wetlands Research were expanded. In addition, the Jamie Whitten National

Did you know?

Danielle Johnson is Ole Miss's only four-time All-SEC honoree in soccer. She was a Scholar All-America selection as a senior and was a Freshman All-America selection in 2006.

Center for Physical Acoustics, the National Center for the Development of Natural Products, and the National Food Management Institute were established on campus. The National Center for the Development of Natural products is a part of the Pharmacy School and is now named for Senator Thad Cochran.

Chancellor Turner sought to meet the second of his goals by initiating a broad and expensive recruiting effort. This new program proved highly successful and enrollment rose from 8,715 in 1984 to 11,033 in 1992. During this time, there was a significant increase in the number of out-of-state students who chose to attend Ole Miss. Dr. Turner also made a commitment to recruit African-American students and doubled the number from 536 in 1984 to approximately 1,000 in 1992. From 1984 to 1990 the number of African-American graduate students rose from 22 to 305.

Turner's toughest challenge was improving the public image of the University. He led unsuccessful efforts to eliminate the Confederate flag from athletic events. He also had an ongoing battle with the fraternity system when, in the 1980s, there were reports of fights between football players and fraternities, hazing, an alcohol-related death, and other incidents. Even though the decision to cease the annual Shrimp and Beer Celebration had been made before Turner took over as Chancellor, he was blamed by students and alumni for its demise.

Embroiled in controversy over the association of the administration to the University Foundation and for firing the football coach for NCAA rules infractions, Gerald Turner accepted the presidency of Southern Methodist University in the spring of 1995. Turner made courageous and bold decisions on behalf of Ole Miss, and though not popular with many alumni and students, his contributions to the University of Mississippi are significant.

Chancellor Robert C. Khayat

The benefits that Ole Miss students enjoy today are the results of more than 160 years of hard work, sacrifice, leadership, and vision. Chancellors, faculty and staff, students, and alumni over the years have dedicated themselves to making the University of Mississippi a great university.

No person has done more to enhance Ole Miss than Robert C. Khayat, the fifteenth chancellor of the University. As an undergraduate, Khayat was a popular student who excelled in football and baseball. He was a member of the 1959 team of the decade and made All-SEC in baseball. Prior to becoming Chancellor in 1995, Khayat had been a professor in the law school, Associate Dean of the law school, and Vice Chancellor for University Affairs. Khayat wasted little time in achieving his goal of making the University of Mississippi one of the nation's premier universities. During his term as Chancellor, Khayat raised $778 million for academics and athletics. Due to his success in

Did you know?

Jennifer Soileau was a three-time All-SEC selection and a three-time NSCAA All-Regional selection. She is the Rebels' career leader in points (99) and points in a game (15) which also ties the SEC record.

fundraising, the University prospered with the opening of the Sally McDonnell Barksdale Honors College, the expansion of Vaught-Hemingway stadium to 60,000 seats, the expansion of Oxford-University baseball stadium, the establishment of the Croft Institute for International Studies and the Trent Lott Leadership Institute, the renovation and expansion of the J. D. Williams Library, the creation of the School of Applied Sciences, and the establishment of the Overby Center for the Study of Southern Politics and Journalism. In addition, during Khayat's tenure the University was the first public university in Mississippi to be granted a chapter of Phi Beta Kappa. The Gertrude Ford Center was built and quickly recognized as one of the premier performing arts centers in the South.

One of Khayat's lasting legacies is his leadership to rid Ole Miss of its association with the Confederate flag. He brought alumni, students, faculty and staff members, and coaches together in this effort. It was not an easy task, and many in Mississippi blamed Khayat for doing away with a part of Southern heritage. Khayat's life was threatened for taking the courageous stand.

While Khayat worked tirelessly to enhance academics and athletics, he also put emphasis on enhancing the beauty of the Ole Miss campus. In 2008, the Ole Miss Landscape Services Department was awarded the Scenic Communities of Mississippi award by the Mississippi Urban Forest Council. The campus has been recognized by national publications as one of the most beautiful campuses in the United States, and was listed as The Most Beautiful Campus by *Newsweek* in 2011.

In May 2008, the University of Mississippi opened its doors on all campuses to a record enrollment of 17,601 students, and *Forbes* magazine ranked it as one of the Top 25 universities in the United States. September 26, 2008, the eyes of the world were on the University of Mississippi when the first Presidential Debate was held in the Gertrude Ford Center. Every major national network and media outlets from around the world came to Oxford. Tom Brokaw, Katie Couric, Shepard Smith, Bob Shieffer, and other news giants covered the event. Classes were canceled the afternoon of the debate, and more than 6,000 came to the Grove to participate in the Rock the Debate festival that featured music, speakers, southern food, and a live telecast of the debate on two giant screens.

Khayat embodied the characteristics of many of his predecessors. He shared Barnard's dream of making the University a great institution. Like Chancellor Fulton he valued and maintained the beauty of the campus. He capitalized on Butts's and Turner's commitments to fundraising. Many of Khayat's predecessors led the University through turmoil and tough times. As Chancellor, Khayat did the same with resolve and vision.

Chancellor Daniel W. Jones

As with numerous other Chancellors, Dr. Dan Jones's first year was eventful — if not

Did you know?

Genevieve "V" Shy is the only player in school history to have earned All-SEC honors in volleyball three times (1993, 95, 96) and still ranks among the league leaders in blocks. Her 196 solo blocks for her career is third all-time in Southeastern Conference history. She put down 502 blocks in her career, ranking first all-time at Ole Miss.

tumultuous. Early in his first year, Chancellor Jones was approached by students who complained about the chanting of "The South Will Rise Again" at the end of the traditional pre- and post-game anthem "From Dixie with Love" which had been played at football games for 20 years. The song "From Dixie with Love" is a combination of "Dixie" and "The Battle Hymn of the Republic," the anthems of the Confederacy and the Union during the Civil War. Disgruntled because the foam-headed cartoon character, Colonel Rebel, had been dropped as the on-field mascot in 2003, a small group of students started the chant at the end of "From Dixie with Love." Students who entered the University after 2003 picked up the cheer, and it became more audible. For some, it was seen as a harmless expression of southern pride. For others, it evoked memories of segregationists in the 1950s and 1960s singing "Glory, glory segregation. Glory, glory segregation. The South shall rise again" to the tune of "The Battle Hymn of the Republic."

Prior to the Northern Arizona game in November 2009, Chancellor Jones issued a statement warning students that "From Dixie With Love" would no longer be played if the chant continued. Students ignored the warning and chanted it loudly after the song was played. On Monday after the game, Chancellor Jones asked the band to quit playing the song.

"Here at the University of Mississippi, there must be no doubt that this is a warm and welcoming place for all," Dr. Jones wrote in a letter to the University community. "We cannot ever appear to support those outside our community who advocate a revival of racial segregation. We cannot fail to respond."

Although supported by many, Jones's decision was met with outrage from some within and outside of the University community. The issue came to a head November 21, 2009, when 11 members of the Ku Klux Klan protested on the steps of Fulton Chapel on the day of the Ole Miss–LSU football game with tens of thousands of people on campus. The KKK was shouted down by a crowd of more than 300 onlookers and were taunted with shouts of "Go to hell, KKK!" A group of counter protesters led by the Associated Student Body and One Mississippi, stood 50 yards away. They wore T-shirts that read, "Turn your back on hate," and read out loud, over and over again, the Ole Miss Creed. The counter protest crowd numbered approximately 200 and included students, faculty, staff, alumni, and football fans, including some from LSU.

In the fall of 2009, ASB president Artair Rogers and Cardinal Club president Peyton Beard approached Chancellor Jones about a new on-field mascot for athletic teams. Dr. Jones agreed to consider it if the students voted to have one and they did.

On April 15, 2011, the University dedicated the Robert C. Khayat Law Center. The featured speaker was best-selling author John Grisham, an Ole Miss law graduate and a former student of Khayat's. The new law center was built at a cost of $50 million and cov-

Did you know?

Brittney Reese was a 2008 Olympian, and the 2009 and 2010 World Championships gold medalist (long jump). A two-time NCAA champion (long jump), a five-time All-American and a five-time SEC champion (long jump, high jump), she also was selected as SEC Field Athlete of the Year three times.

ers 130,000 square feet. It is located at the southwest corner of the campus. The first law school classes were held in the Lyceum in 1854.

In keeping with Chancellor Jones' investiture theme of service, the Associated Student Body, under the leadership of President Virginia Burke, sponsored the University's initial Big Event. The Big Event is a day of service modeled after a program begun at Texas

A&M University. More than 1,200 students spent Saturday morning, March 26, 2011, volunteering in Oxford and Lafayette County. The next year, more than 3,000 students completed 300 community projects as part of The Big Event. Today, the Ole Miss Big Event is the largest single day of community service in the state.

Despite success in the metrics typically used to evaluate leaders in higher education, Chancellor Jones had a strained relationship with the Board of Trustees of the Institutions of Higher Learning. He was notified in the spring of 2015 that his contract would not be renewed. There was a public outcry against the Board's decision, including a large on-campus rally organized by students and attended by students, faculty, staff, and alumni. A few months later, Dr. Jones accepted the position of Professor of Medicine, Director of Clinical and Population Science, and the inaugural Mr. and Mrs. Joe F. Sanderson, Jr. Endowed Chair in Obesity, Metabolic Diseases, and Nutrition for the Mississippi Center for Obesity Research at the University of Mississippi Medical Center.

Provost and Vice Chancellor for Academic Affairs, Morris H. Stocks, was named interim chancellor, and a national search for the next chancellor was launched by the IHL Board. In October 2015, Dr. Jeffrey S. Vitter was named the seventeenth chancellor of the University of Mississippi and Distinguished Professor of Computer and Information Science. He assumed office January 1, 2016, and quickly appointed a transition team and launched a comprehensive listening and learning tour known as the Flagship Forum. Between late January and early May 2016, Dr. Vitter met with more than 200 faculty, student, staff, alumni, and community groups across UM campuses, the state, and the nation. Four pillar themes emerged from these meetings, forming the foundation of strategic planning efforts and forging a path to advance the University's flagship status as a great public international research university.

A native of New Orleans and renowned computer scientist, Vitter graduated in mathematics with highest honors from the University of Notre Dame in 1977 and earned a Ph.D. under Don Knuth in computer science at Stanford University in 1980. He also holds an M.B.A. from Duke University. He previously served for five and a half years as provost, executive vice chancellor, and Roy A. Roberts Distinguished Professor at the University of Kansas. Prior to joining KU, he served in leadership and academic roles at Texas A&M, Purdue, Duke, and Brown.

Committed to academic excellence, Chancellor Vitter has overseen the University during a time when enrollment numbers and metrics of success have climbed, including incoming student ACT scores and grade point averages. During February of his first year as chancellor, the University received Carnegie R1 "highest research activity" designation — a status afforded to only the top 2.5% of the nation's colleges and universities. Also during his first year, Chancellor Vitter hosted multiple powerful events, including the U.S. Department of Education's Back-to-School Bus Tour, the first ever University-wide Town Hall, the CEO Technology Summit, and the Innovation and Entrepreneurship Panel.

Chancellor Vitter's leadership has been characterized by full engagement with the University and local community. A frequent social media user, he communicates about what is happening on campus and engages thousands of University stakeholders through his messages. He is a strong proponent of the UM Creed and has launched several initiatives to foster respect and diversity at the University, including the establishment of the Chancellor's Advisory Committee on History and Context.

During his first year, Chancellor Vitter strengthened strategic relationships with key decision makers and stakeholders, including the State Institutions of Higher Learning Board of Trustees, to ensure the University's role in advancing higher education opportunities in Mississippi. He also strengthened ties among all UM campuses to enhance the University's standing and impact.

He has focused on the University's role in serving the state of Mississippi, recognizing and promoting the University's ability to address pressing issues and promote economic and community development. Chancellor Vitter has been a strong advocate for the role of the medical center campus in improving the health of Mississippians and serving as the preeminent complement to local hospitals and sustainable community healthcare.

In 2017, through his "Flagship Constellations Initiative," he has encouraged University parties to form innovative, multidisciplinary research and creative achievement clusters to accelerate and inspire solutions to some of the world's great challenges where no one discipline has all the answers and collaboration across the disciplines is key.

Chancellor Vitter is a champion for the transformative power of education. In his November 2016 investiture address, he described education as "the great enabler that helps people lift themselves above their circumstances and disadvantages" and stated that there is "nothing more important to the future of our society than higher education."

Glossary

James Alexander Ventress – Brought the bill before the Mississippi State legislature to establish a state university in 1840. Appointed first member of the original board of 13 trustees to oversee the newly chartered University in 1844. Because of this, Ventress is known as the "Father of the University" and Ventress Hall, which houses the College of Liberal Arts, was named in his honor.

Universitas Scientiarum – Chancellor F. A. P. Barnard's far-reaching, comprehensive plan in 1858 to make The University of Mississippi "a true university that included all branches of science, medicine, agriculture, law, classical studies, civil and political history, and oriental learning."

Sarah Isom McGehee – Appointed the first female faculty member at The University of Mississippi in 1885. The Sarah Isom Center for Women and Gender Studies at the University was established in her honor in 1981.

Chancellor Robert Fulton – His most lasting and endearing contribution to the geography, spirit, and aesthetics of the University was preserving the wooded area in the center of the campus that would later become known to generations of University students and alumni as "The Grove."

Elma Meek and OLE MISS – She suggested the name OLE MISS be used for the first yearbook for the University in 1897. Within a couple of years, students and alumni were using the name of the yearbook as an affectionate name for the University.

John Howard Vaught – Head coach of the Ole Miss Rebel football team from 1947 to 1970. During his tenure, Vaught compiled an amazing record of 190 wins and only 61 losses. His teams won three national titles, six Southeastern Conference titles, and 18 bowl games. He coached 27 All-Americans and the 1959 Ole Miss team was voted the SEC Team of the Decade.

James Meredith and 1962 – The young Air Force veteran from Koscuisko was the first African-American student to enter and integrate The University of Mississippi. Meredith enrolled October 1, 1962. Between September 30th and October 1st, a rebellious mob clashed with U. S. Marshalls and Federal troops in front of the Lyceum over the court-ordered admission of Meredith. Two people were killed, and the event marked a decisive turning point in the Civil Rights Movement and the history of public school desegregation in the South.

About the Authors

Thomas Reardon, *Dean of Students Emeritus*

Thomas Reardon worked in higher education for more than 30 years. Known to everyone at Ole Miss as 'Sparky,' Dean Reardon is retired.

Leslie Banahan, *Assistant Vice Chancellor for Student Affairs*

Leslie Banahan provides oversight for the University's Career Center, Counseling Center, Health Services, Campus Recreation, Disability Services, and the Center for Student Success and First-Year Experience. She has written and spoken extensively on orientation programs, first-year students, crisis intervention and managment, and parents of today's college students. Ms. Banahan is the co-author of *Navigating the First College Year: A Guide for Parents and Families.* She attended Louisiana State University and the University of Mississippi, earning degrees in Journalism, Sociology, and Higher Education and Counseling. She tries to follow her dad's advice: Work hard and be nice to people.

Race and the University of Mississippi

By Susan M. Glisson and Charles H. Tucker

History, despite its wrenching pain, cannot be unlived,
however, if faced with courage, need not be lived again. Maya Angelou

Fair warning: some things in this chapter are going to be uncomfortable. Not because it is a radical concept – science has been proving it in bits and pieces for years – but because it addresses something most of us learned from our friends, family, and the media while we were growing up and now accept as bedrock fact.

So, about this whole race thing...

Let's hit the big one first: There is no such thing as race. In 2003 an international team of scientists completed The Human Genome Project, a 13 year undertaking to map the human genetic blueprint. They discovered a lot of things, and are continually discovering more as they analyze their results. But one of the biggest things they discovered is this – there is no genetic difference between the so-called "races." None. Nor could they find any biological distinctions. According to scientists the differences in appearance, hair color and texture, skin tone, etc., are all superficial and are adaptations to climate and other environmental conditions. In short, humans come in one style – human. Many different scientific teams in many countries have verified these results and expanded upon them since then.

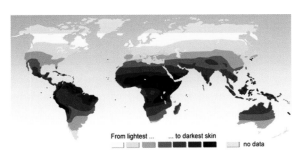

From lightest ... ... to darkest skin | no data

As it turns out, skin color is almost completely a function of how much UV sunlight an ethnic group receives in the fall. More sunlight means darker skin.

(Anthropologist George Chaplin)

How it all started

If there is no such thing as race, where did the idea come from, then? Why, we invented it. Not us in this classroom, of course, but our ancestors. In other words, it is a social construction invented as a way to organize and eventually control people.

Although some of the first recorded accounts of the concept arose around 500 years ago during the Middle Ages, anthropologists and psychologists believe it goes back to the earliest days of mankind, back to when mankind lived in small nomadic groups, hunting and gathering, constantly on the move. Theirs was a cruel, scary world, filled with predators and harsh weather. Food was hard to come by and in short supply, as was water, in some cases.

It was during this time when various tribes first encountered people who were new to them. Sometimes these encounters were pleasant. But most often they were not. The strange people would take their food by force, or not allow them access to the water.

Out of protection, and in constant competition for meager resources, these ancestors of ours developed a sense of "outlanderism," the automatic belief that anyone who was not a part of your tribe was an outlander and might be coming to harm your people and take your resources.

Here's an interesting bit of psychology: no species ever forgets a danger. Through one mechanism or another, it passes the memory down from generation to generation. Unfortunately, that memory remains in place in the subconscious, even when circumstances change and the once useful defense mechanism is no longer necessary. It is through this particular mechanism, outlanderism, that some scientists believe the once protective notion that people who do not look like you must mean you harm became a dangerous context for intergroup relations as time evolved. Mankind viewed the world as having two basic categories of people in it – "us" and "them," with "them," the outlanders, being anyone a particular group did not know, live in the same place as, recognize, or, in some cases, physically resemble. Because an outlander could sometimes look like one of them, it essentially focused on people from other groups, that is, people they did not know. This system worked for a while.

The transition between "outlanderism" to racism as a social order evolved through the development of anti-semitism, religious intolerance by Christians for Jews. The early church, which eventually grew into the Catholic Church, initially believed that Jews could convert to Christianity and thus become acceptable. Over time, a much more insidious conviction developed, that Jewish souls and bodies were unconvertible and that evil was in their blood. That being the case, then they must be a different type of creature, and a bad one at that, they reasoned.

It was in the late nineteenth century with the creation of the classification of "race" that things began to get nasty. While outlanderism was essentially a protective reaction, race was used in a far more sinister way. Governments used the created classification of race to falsely define some populations as inferior and to justify discriminating against them and withholding resources for their support and development.

It is important to note that before this time race wasn't always attached to skin color. The British, for example, considered the Irish, Scots, and Welsh as separate and distinctly inferior races. They were outlanders or others, people not of their group, and therefore morally inferior and more like animals than humans. That belief still lingers on among some in the British Isles today.

The Big S (And, no, we don't mean Superman.)

Another development that influenced the concept of race was the enforced and unpaid labor system of race-based slavery. Slavery existed prior to racism. The Greeks and Romans and Egyptians had slaves. Some African and Native American tribes enslaved conquered enemies. In the British Isles, the British conquered the Scots and the Irish and made slaves of them all. In fact,

virtually every culture that has ever existed has used slavery to increase its labor pool. But it wasn't until the fifteenth century that race and slavery were linked.

Imagine if your community relied on slave labor to bring in additional crops that you needed to feed your people. And imagine that, over time, you had difficulty preventing these slaves from escaping. You see, you had stolen them from neighboring tribes or conquered people who, by and large, looked a lot like you. If they managed to escape and make their way back home, it was easy for them to blend in and hide among the other villagers. Or worse, hide for a while, scrub off in a stream someplace, find some clothes and pretend to be a free man in another village. Who would know? In Europe, that was a real issue. What to do...?

The solution, or so it seemed to the conquerors in Western Europe, was to force others into unpaid labor who did not look like them. But where to find them?

Somewhere... across the sea, somewhere....

During the late fifteenth century, Europe began exploring the globe. Columbus, Magellan, and other explorers sought out new lands and reported back, describing lands ripe for the taking. Sponsored by governments and private corporations (yes, they were around way back then), Europeans sailed into North and South America and the Caribbean and after encountering and, in some cases, completely annihilating native populations by virtue of their superior firepower and disease, discovered mineral and culinary treasures that they'd never seen before – silver, gold, jewels, spices, CHOCOLATE!

But, unlike the travel brochure-like descriptions of the explorers, that wealth was not simply lying on the ground waiting to be carried off. It had to be mined, harvested, packed, and loaded. That required hard, sometimes dangerous work.

It wasn't long before the Portugese and Spaniards, followed by the British, French, and Dutch hit upon an answer – let's use these conquered people as free labor! They don't look like us, so they can't blend in with us. And if they do run off, we can find them easily. And if we happen to be over there, we can conquer some more.

This launched an economic boom in Europe.

Europeans justified this unsettling proposition by evolving concepts of color-based race. In other words, the merchants who were making money off slave labor defended their actions by saying that what they were doing was a form of labor that only targeted inferior populations who, therefore, deserved such treatment. After all, if they were equal, they would look like us.

The Portuguese, followed by the Spanish and the British Empires, began to barter for and steal Africans for a growing slave trade.

This slave trade grew in force as these same merchants, explorers, and conquerors reached shores that were new to them. Largely enslaving or killing the native populations living in these new lands, these slave traders began a vicious triangle. They captured or bought Africans, largely from West Africa, and brought them across the "Middle Passage" of the Atlantic Ocean to what they called the "New World," the islands of the Caribbean, and the eastern shores of North America.

The enslaved persons who were not able to survive being constantly shackled, fed poorly, and beaten were simply cast overboard to their watery graves. Scholars estimate that slave traders forced as many as 25 million Africans from their homelands to make this terrible journey. Only 11 to 13 million made it to the New World. Of that great number, traders brought only about 400,000 enslaved people to the new British colonies in America; the rest worked on sugar plantations in the Caribbean in conditions so horrific that most died soon after arriving.

ON BOARD A SLAVE-SHIP.

Ironically, it was in the so-called Age of Enlightenment during the late seventeenth and early eighteenth centuries that race and slavery became inextricably intertwined. While slavery as a labor system of unpaid, forced labor, had existed for centuries, it was Western Europeans who refined it by using presumed racial inferiority to justify the enslavement of African people.

In general, this combination meant that "blackness" was inferior and what was not black was superior.

Life in the New World

So, as Britain founded thirteen colonies in the New World during the seventeenth century, each colony used slavery as a labor system and protected that system legally.

In addition, the British also allowed indentured servanthood as a form of labor in the colonies. Indenture meant that you could sign on to work for a set period of unpaid labor, but after serving your time, you could become free. Only Europeans could be indentured servants.

The difference between slavery and indenture was that black people were deemed slaves, because of their presumed inferiority, and only white people could work their way into freedom. So, the United States grew based on a continuum of unpaid and paid labor: at one end were those deemed black and unfree and at the other end were those deemed white and free.

In the New World, the plantation economy developed slavery because of a lack of available laborers. Gradually understanding the dangers and abuses of the indenture system, individual business operations sought out a steady and plentiful supply of labor.

Despite claims that "all men" were created equal and deserving of liberty, our founding fathers did not believe blacks should be included in those claims. And so, they founded our country on a profound contradiction: they simultaneously declared that "all men are created equal" while legally protecting the rights of whites to own other human beings, who were black. To remove any doubt about the existence of this contradiction, they codified it in the new nation's Constitution, which declared that enslaved persons were not even fully human, while boasting that the document would "secure the blessings of liberty to ourselves and our posterity."

This journey to create the idea of race, having now moved from otherness to declaring that other human beings are inferior to justify mistreating them, continued to evolve.

In the eighteenth and nineteenth centuries, Southern defenders of slavery, including Thomas Jefferson, described the institution as a "necessary evil." After the invention of the cotton gin in 1793, which made harvesting and processing cotton much easier, Southern slaveholders claimed a need for increased enslaved labor to meet the growing demands of Europe for its cotton. Remember this point: it's important.

Just as slavery grew, so too did its dissenters. Along with rebellions by enslaved persons, there was a growing and intensely successful global movement to abolish slavery. This prodded defenders of slavery to reject the "necessary evil" doctrine and to declare instead that slavery was a positive good, that it brought Christianity and civilization to a "savage" people.

Scholars have noted the paradox that racism exists more easily in a society, such as the United States, that aspires to equality. It was because of this principled claim that our society had to find a justification of why some could not be considered equal. Thus, these two competing ideas fought for supremacy in the American mind.

As the two philosophies grew— slavery versus freedom, inferiority versus superiority – the opinions, strategies, and tactics of both sides became entrenched. Pro-slavery theologians used Christianity, particularly verses from the Old Testament, to justify slavery. Control over slaves increased; slaveholders prevented slaves from learning to read, and slave patrols monitored open roads to help return escaped slaves to their plantations. In addition, pseudo-scientists published annals attempting to link phrenology, or the size of one's head, to intellectual capacity and declared enslaved blacks to be inferior due to presumed smaller brains. Pro-slavery economists suggested that enslaved persons must be happier than paid Northern laborers because their owners provided their food and shelter. (The numbers of slaves who attempted to resist or escape belied this assertion, however.)

Go West, young man!

As the nation expanded into new territory across the continent, the issue of slavery grew more divisive. Armed conflicts over whether a new state would be "free or slave" foreshadowed the Civil War. With the acquisition of the Louisiana Purchase, free states became concerned that slave states would have an unfair advantage. Thus emerged the Compromise of 1820.

The compromise had two parts: the northern part of Massachusetts became Maine and was admitted to the Union as a free state at the same time that Missouri was admitted as a slave state, maintaining a balance of 12 slave and 12 free states.

The second part of the compromise consisted of an imaginary line that was drawn at 36 degrees 30 minutes north latitude. This line came to be known as the Mason-Dixon

Line. According to the compromise, all parts of the Louisiana Territory lying north of the Mason-Dixon Line would be free. There was a loophole, however. The act provided that fugitive slaves "escaping into any... state or territory of the United States...may be lawfully reclaimed and conveyed to the person claiming his or her labour or service" — and in the free territories, "slavery and involuntary servitude ... in the punishment of crimes" was not prohibited.

Meanwhile, in Mississippi

This is where that important bit about slave labor and cotton we told you about earlier comes into play. In Mississippi, cotton had become THE cash crop. Large plantations produced bales and bales of cotton, harvested by crews of slave labor, which were sold at a very tidy profit to the textile mills in New England and Europe.

The plantation owners who reaped the profits of those crops built palatial estates, complete with antebellum mansions and fruit orchards. They married and had children. These children grew up and were for the most part educated at local schools (except for some of the girls, who were sent back East to finishing schools). The young men were sent off to a university. Their parents could afford to send them to the best schools, so they went away to Harvard, Yale, and, in some cases, Oxford and Cambridge in England. There, they studied, partied, attended some classes, and eventually returned home.

But many were not the same when they returned. Some of the young men it seems, actually read their assignments on philosophy, religion, and political science. Upon their return, they looked at the social system of Mississippi and the "southern way of life" based on slavery, and found it wanting. They made these misgivings known to their parents, who were less than pleased. After all, their parents were at the top of the social order that their heirs wanted to topple. The parents then did what many parents do when their children question their decisions – they blamed the teachers.

Their solution was simple: create their own schools that taught a philosophy more in keeping with theirs.

Professor Charles Eagles wrote in *The Price of Defiance*: "There was also a sense of urgency to provide local higher education for students without the influence of those who did not embrace the 'ways' of the state of Mississippi. Seeking to preserve a way of life, the founders believed that education is the process by which a culture ensures its existence and transmits itself across time. These founders' resistance to change, which they viewed as their right, if not their obligation, thus created the University of Mississippi as a bastion in defense of 'The Southern Way of Life.' "

On February 20, 1840, the Mississippi State legislature passed a bill to establish a state university to do just that. In short, The University of Mississippi was created explicitly to perpetuate the philosophy of race-based slavery and white supremacy.

Up on Capitol Hill…

The abolitionist versus pro-slavery debate continued to rage. First there was the Compromise of 1850 and the infamous Fugitive Slave Act. According to the compromise, Texas would relinquish the disputed land it had gained after the U. S. War with Mexico (remember the Alamo?) but, in compensation, be given 10 million dollars — money it would use to pay off its debt to Mexico. Also, the territories of New Mexico, Nevada, Arizona, and Utah would be organized without mention of slavery. (The territories would make that decision for themselves when they applied for statehood.) The slave trade would be abolished in the District of Columbia, although slavery would still be permitted. Finally, California would be admitted as a free state.

In exchange for the pro-slavery faction accepting this imbalance, the Fugitive Slave Act was passed. This controversial piece of legislation required citizens to assist in the recovery of fugitive slaves, no matter how long they had been living in a free state. Furthermore, it denied a fugitive's right to a jury trial. If former slaves (or free persons of color accused of being escaped slaves) protested or sought to prove their freedom, special commisioners heard the cases. These commissioners were paid $5 if an alleged fugitive was released and $10 if he or she was sent away with the claimant. The Act called for changes in the process for filing a claim, making the process easier for slaveowners. Also, according to the Act, there would be more federal officials responsible for enforcing the law.

The federal government continued to go to great lengths to protect the property rights of white Southerners to own black people. In 1857, the U.S. Supreme Court heard the case of an enslaved man who sued for his freedom after having been brought to a free state by his owner. In the ruling, known today as The Dred Scott Decision, the majority of the Court ruled that since blacks were "beings of an inferior order, and altogether unfit to associate with the white race, either in social or political relations, and so far inferior that they had no rights which the white man was bound to respect."

Just two years later, Charles Darwin published *On the Origin of Species*, which advanced the concept of evolution. Defenders of slavery appropriated Darwin's work to argue that whites had evolved to be superior while blacks had not.

In response, many Abolitionists moved from attempts to persuade others to join their cause through public meetings and newspaper articles to legal challenges. Some, like abolitionist John Brown, even suggested and engaged in armed conflict.

By the time of Abraham Lincoln's inauguration as President in 1861, eleven Southern states, including Mississippi, had seceded from the Union; each one of them noted prominently in their articles of secession that slavery was the main cause of their leaving the Union.

The University of Mississippi, which had been founded in 1848 to teach young men to uphold the ideology of slavery, shut down during the war and its entire student body joined the Confederacy as the "University Greys."

Post-war

While the end of the Civil War may have settled the question of the supremacy of the Union, it only complicated the nature of race. Where before one could safely, though not completely, assume that a slave was a black person, now everyone was "free," to the extent that no one was supposed to be forced to work for another without pay. Since slavery

> When a tradition gathers enough strength to go on for centuries, you don't just turn it off one day.
>
> Chinua Achebe

also had produced multiracial children, often through the rape of enslaved women by their owners, there were many new citizens who could pass as white.

And so began a new development in the evolution of the social construct of race: the idea of whiteness.

"White" is another sociological construct. But unlike most group descriptors, which focus on who does belong, "whiteness" focuses on who doesn't. It wasn't based on a fixed definition. Place of origin, skin and eye color, and hair texture could or could not be factors. In fact, some groups considered "white" today – the Irish, Greeks, and Italians, for example – were not initially included, but were assimilated over time.

Southern states and municipalities began to enact laws to define who was white and who was black. In places with populations of multi-racial persons who could pass for western European (Louisiana, for example) the notorious "one-drop" rule meant that any person who had even one ancestor who had been held a slave, or who had African ancestry (free or not) was considered black. And those who were deemed black could not vote or claim many other rights of citizenship, and so could not legally challenge the laws that oppressed them.

In 1890, the state of Mississippi became the first Southern state after the Civil War to pass a new state constitution. It was the first Southern document to codify segregation, which meant the legal disenfranchisement of all blacks as well as an enforced legal separation in all aspects of daily life—from hospitals and schools, to whom one could marry and where one might be buried. Every other Southern state followed Mississippi's example and passed similar constitutions. Not to be outdone, federal authorities weighed in as well.

In 1896, the Supreme Court ruled in *Plessy v. Ferguson*, that "separate but equal" was the law of the land. The case had arisen from a man in Louisiana, Homer Plessy, who could pass for white and who hoped, through his case, to stop the flow of new laws that infringed on new rights of black citizens. The *Plessy* decision was a turning point in the developing concept of whiteness. It was clear that going forward all the advantages of citizenship would remain only for whites and would be denied to those defined as black. There was a caveat to this awarding of advantages; only certain privileges would be awarded to all whites. In the end, those rewards included just enough benefits to keep poor whites from joining with blacks to challenge the political, social, and economic power of elite whites.

In the wake of the 1890 constitution, white Mississippians used economic and physical intimidation, as well as legal restrictions, to discriminate against blacks. The Mississippi Delta, for example, which had been largely settled, cleared, and prepared for cultivation by freed slaves, and which could boast of predominantly black land ownership in the 1880s and 90s, became a political center of power in the state by the 1920s, dominated by white plantation owners whose sharecropping and tenant system of labor ensured that blacks and many poor whites would never earn enough to get out of poverty. These plantation owners obtained their land largely through illegal thefts or violent intimidation of previous black owners. It was during this same period of time that the University of Mississippi also became known as "Ole Miss," a name suggested by Elma Meek in a contest to name the yearbook. It quickly became the school's nickname, and eventually a controversial one, as its origin was a term of affection used to describe the wife of a plantation owner.

Jim Crow era

The 1890s to the 1940s can be described as a racist regime in the American South. The earlier attempts to use science to justify such treatment lived now in a eugenics movement, which was a global effort to create a "master race" of whites and manifested itself in the United States in immigration restrictions, the prohibition of interracial marriage, and forced sterilizations of black women. Indeed, during this same period, Nazi Germany in the 1930s modeled many of its laws, including those against intermarriage, or "miscegenation," on those of the American South. The newly forming apartheid regime in South Africa also modeled its laws on those of the American South. Segregation laws went far beyond controlling who could vote or who one

could marry, to determining where one could eat or live or go to the hospital—even what Bible you could touch when pledging an oath in court. Those who violated these ordinances met with economic intimidation such as losing their homes or job or with lynching. In fact, the state of Mississippi had more lynchings per capita than any other state in this period.

Despite the dark period of "Jim Crow" segregation in Mississippi, there were always many blacks and some white allies who challenged the segregated system. National efforts to challenge the system supported state work and in the wake of World War II, significant changes began to occur. In Mississippi, led largely by black war veterans such as Medgar Evers and Amzie Moore, who had fought for democracy abroad but returned home to second-class status, local organizers challenged segregation. Many suffered economic intimidation and sometimes violence or death, but they refused to give up the struggle.

While the predominant ethnic groups in the state were blacks and whites, there always have been other ethnic groups present. Within the racially stratified system of both Mississippi and the country at large, immigrant populations moved into the state and worked hard to be defined culturally as whites to gain the privileges of white skin. Italian parents in the Mississippi Delta had to sue the state in the 1950s for their children to be considered white and therefore allowed to attend white schools. Jewish and Chinese settlers straddled between the two predominant cultures, working in arenas that served both populations but were never truly accepted by either. And much later, on the Gulf Coast, Vietnamese immigrants created homogeneous enclaves of fisherfolk in an attempt to protect themselves from the larger, divided culture. This pattern repeated itself around the country, framed by different waves of immigration at different historical periods. But each new population was judged and defined through the lens of the black and white division.

The aftermath of World War II initiated changes nationally and within the state. Because of the combined efforts of both state and local black leaders and their white allies, calls for civil rights reform increased. The National Association for the Advancement of Colored People (NAACP) launched a judicial initiative to dismantle segregation methodically in education, beginning with higher education in the 1940s. In the wake of the Holocaust, many who had previously engaged in or tolerated racism now saw its horrible ultimate conclusion and began to work to prevent similar developments. And increasingly, during the Cold War and the decolonization of Asia and Africa, the United States was under great pains to show that daily life under capitalism and democracy lived up to its stated ideals to resist the propaganda of the Soviet Union and its claims of the supremacy of communism.

In 1948, reformers within the Democratic Party successfully included, for the first time in a political party, civil rights in the Democratic Party platform. In response, half of the Alabama Democratic delegation and all of the Mississippi Democratic delegation walked out of the convention in protest. These white supremacist protestors created a new political party that year called the "Dixiecrats." To show their support of the Dixiecrats, the Ole Miss student body began to fly Confederate flags, and the band played the song "Dixie" at athletics events.

Increasingly, the symbols of The University of Mississippi sent a message that the campus was a haven for those who opposed civil rights for all. Simultaneously, for some courageous black citizens like James Meredith, who called the University "the temple of white supremacy," their intent to desegregate the public facility grew as well. In 1954, as the Supreme Court issued the *Brown v. Board of Education* decision, which declared that the doctrine of "separate but equal" in schools was inherently unequal, Medgar Evers applied for admission to the University's law school. Its segregation policy prevented his admission, but his courageous application brought him to the attention of the NAACP, which hired Evers to become its first full-time field secretary for admissions. Less than ten years later, Evers assisted James Meredith in his attempts to enroll in the University.

In 1955, at least two white men in Tallahatchie County murdered fourteen-year-old Emmett Till, a black child from Chicago visiting his uncle for the summer. The men had been told that Till had whistled at one of their wives and this transgression of racial customs was enough for them to sentence him to death. His mother insisted that Till's casket remain open at his funeral so that the world could see what racism, the prejudice plus the power of whites in Mississippi, had done to her child. A photo appeared in the black magazine *Jet*, and Mississippi's reputation as a bastion of white supremacy only increased.

Civil rights groups began to determine ways to target the state for reform, while defenders of what they called the "southern way of life," sought to resist such efforts. It was perhaps inevitable that a climactic confrontation would occur. In 1962, that showdown happened at Ole Miss. Kosciusko, Mississippi, native James Meredith applied for admission to the University that year. While the University began a process of denying Meredith admission on the basis of his race, supported by then Mississippi governor Ross Barnett, national civil rights groups sought the intervention of President John F. Kennedy. Kennedy and his representatives negotiated with Barnett for Meredith's safe admission, but the clash intensified as many Oxonians and students as well as citizens across the state rallied for Barnett to defy the President. They were joined by pro-testors who came from other states to defend white supremacy at Ole Miss.

On September 30, Meredith came to campus under the protection of U.S. Marshals. Returning crowds of students, many of whom had been encouraged to resist Meredith's admission in a speech by Governor Barnett at the football game in Jackson on the previous weekend, learned of Meredith's presence on campus and began to gather in protest in front of the Lyceum. Bricks that had been delivered for new construction on The Circle became weapons in the hands of students. Students also fashioned Molotov cocktails to throw at the U.S. Marshals surrounding the Lyceum. Injured marshals retreated into the Lyceum and were soon joined by students who had been detained.

As the night wore on, other protestors from around the state and region joined the riot; many brought guns. Students began to retreat from The Circle and the armed insurrection of the remaining protestors began. Calm came only when federalized National Guard members, many of them native Mississippians, ignored their own biased training against blacks and slowly took control over the campus. The violence was not contained on campus alone that night; many black Oxonians reported later that rioters invaded their communities and inflicted injuries. On campus, many were injured and two people were killed: a French reporter and a local repairman. No one has ever been found responsible for their deaths.

On the morning of October 1, 1962, Meredith officially enrolled in the University, becoming the first black student to be allowed to attend the school. His safety that year required armed soldiers, who guarded him on campus; other Army personnel patrolled the streets of Oxford to keep order. Students enrolled at the time harassed Meredith throughout the year. Those who lived above his room in Baxter Hall would bounce basketballs on the floor throughout the night. When Meredith entered the cafeteria to eat meals, students turned their backs on him. And if he sat at a table of students, they would all leave. The few who attempted to reach out to him received death threats in return. Despite this intense pressure, Meredith persevered. Since he had transferred from Jackson State Col-

"Neither revolution nor reformation can ultimately change a society, rather you must tell a new powerful tale, one so persuasive that it sweeps away the old myths and becomes the preferred story, one so inclusive that it gathers all the bits of our past and our present into a coherent whole, one that even shines some light into the future so that we can take the next step forward. If you want to change society, then you have to tell an alternative story."

Ivan Illich

lege, he graduated in the spring of 1963, wearing a button upside down that protestors had worn as a message to keep him out of Ole Miss. It said, "Never."

In the wake of the events of 1962, student enrollment dropped. Faculty who spoke out in support of Meredith, such as Professor James Silver, were forced to leave. Silver would write of the realities of segregation and the events on campus in his book *The Closed Society*. For many black leaders in the state, the book was an important first public acknowledgment by a white Southerner that segregation was wrong. There would be no single event that would have a more lasting effect on the University of Mississippi than the desegregation of the University in 1962.

The University has struggled to overcome that dark time. Many of the black students who attended the University after Meredith in the 1960s and 1970s also suffered harassment and intimidation. Some who protested such treatment were expelled. Black enrollment finally began to increase significantly in the 1990s, under the tenure of Chancellor Robert Khayat, who personally visited predominantly black high schools and churches to recruit students.

Sometimes the University has been too hesitant to move forward, forced to negotiate between alumni who have nostalgic views of the past and new students who bring differing perspectives on race. And sometimes, its efforts have gone unnoticed by a nation that would rather keep Mississippi as a scapegoat for negative race relations. Many of the battles over its racial past and present have come over the symbols of the University. Over the years, conflicts about the Confederate flag and the playing of the song "Dixie," have ignited the campus. So, too, has conflict raged over the official team name and mascot of the University, the "Rebels" and "Colonel Reb." Many view these symbols as connected to a robust and familial past, while others view them as relics of a time when blacks were not allowed on campus.

In 1997, then-President Bill Clinton inaugurated an unprecedented national conversation on race. "One America: The President's Initiative on Race" marked the first time a sitting president had called for such a dialogue without the catalyst of a major crisis. It suggested, on a federal level, the importance of dealing positively with race relations on a daily basis. Accepting the challenge to prod grassroots efforts, The University of Mississippi hosted the only deep-South public forum for One America. Preceded by dialogue, groups representing ten constituency topics ranging from the arts to education to religion, the event highlighted elected delegates from each group. Sharing the insight and hopes of the more than 160 participants, the representatives crafted a frank yet civil discussion on one of our nation's most difficult subjects.

The President's staff hailed The University of Mississippi's experience as the single most successful of the entire Initiative year. That recognition encouraged the University to formalize its dialogue process with the creation of an institute to promote racial reconciliation and civic renewal. Founded in 1999, the William Winter Institute for Racial Reconciliation works in communities and classrooms, in Mississippi and beyond, to support a movement of racial equity and wholeness as a pathway to ending and transcending all division and discrimination based on difference. An additional result of the One America success included the awarding of a Phi Beta Kappa chapter to the campus, whose original application had been turned down in 1962 because of the riot.

In 2002, the University undertook its own initiative on race. Called "Open Doors,"

the year-long series of events commemorated the desegregation of the University. An opening public event on October 1, 2002, focused on an apology by Chancellor Khayat for the exclusion of blacks from the University along with a moving ceremony led by Khayat and James Meredith to dedicate the space between the Lyceum and the J. D. Williams Library. More than 2,500 participants heard keynote speaker Myrlie Evers-Williams, whose husband Medgar had been assassinated in their Jackson driveway in 1963; Evers-Williams extolled the attendees to be bold in seeking racial justice and healing. During the weekend-long event, the University undertook an oral history initiative about its past and welcomed back unsung heroes of its integration, such as the U.S. Marshals and soldiers who had protected Meredith, as well as the few students and white allies who had encouraged integration, including *Daily Mississippian* editor Sidna Brower Mitchell and Episcopal priest Duncan Gray. Workshops and lectures continued throughout the year and an International Conference on Race concluded the 40th anniversary commemoration.

The University hosted the first presidential debate of the 2008 campaign. The historic event, which included the nation's first black presidential nominee of a major party, Barack Obama, reflected the strides made by the University in race relations. Because of the success of those efforts, the Presidential Commission determined that the unavoidable references to race that would occur during the event would be handled respectfully and honestly by the University. The event, coupled with the 40th anniversary commemoration success, began to turn public opinion in favor of the University, which had fully accepted its role and obligation to lead the nation in developing positive race relations.

On November 6, 2012, a growing crowd of students, largely white, gathered on campus to protest the re-election of President Barack Obama. Grainy cell phone footage quickly circulated evidence of their anger, through social media, and once again, in lightening quickness, the nation began to distance itself. Initial media reports on the morning of November 7 assumed that nothing had changed at the University. But this time, student leaders from One Mississippi, supported by faculty, staff, and administrators, made a call for peace and unity and were able to coalesce more than 700 participants that night at a candlelight vigil in front of the Lyceum. While it is clear that we have much work to do to continue to move forward in race relations, a new generation of students is learning from the past and refusing to repeat it.

Challenges will continue. While the vestiges of legal segregation are gone, the social and economic legacies of racism remain, both in Mississippi and the nation at large. Thirty-three percent of children in Mississippi, disproportionately black, live in poverty. In most quality of life indicators such as housing, education, health care, economics, and criminal justice, black Mississippians are much more likely to suffer the brunt of inequity. These structural inequities are undergirded now not necessarily by racist intentions, but through implicit bias or policies enacted in the past that discriminated based on difference.

Implicit biases are the unconscious attitudes formed as early as childhood, based on society's cues about racial prejudice. They are reinforced through social segregation, the tendency we have as human beings to stay in groups that are composed largely of people who look like us. Despite intentions to promote equality and inclusion, these attitudes can remain hidden catalysts for our behavior because our brains are wired for implicit bias. Filtering through the billions of pieces of information that bombard us by the minute, our brains learn to make short cuts, based on cultural messages. If the larger culture sends messages of inferiority, that difference is bad, that equality is only for some people, our brains pick up on those messages, whether we want them to or not.

Thus it is important to understand several ideas: none of us who are alive today invented "race" or racism. But since race as a social construct is a human creation, it can be replaced by something better, a more perfect human creation. And while we did not invent racism, we have inherited a responsibility to understand its effects and to undo them, especially the unearned privileges that those with white skin share.

Racism has been remarkably resilient in adapting to new contexts, so it requires us to be continually vigilant to undo it. If we know the difficulties, such as implicit bias, that make understanding and change challenging, we can begin to unlearn those behaviors and learn new ones that are inclusive and just. All it takes is intention, and a

> Find out about your implicit bias here
> HARVARD IMPLICIT BIAS TEST TO
> SEE YOUR HIDDEN BIASES:
> implicit.harvard.edu/implicit/

willingness by us to be a part of a safe space that allows for open and honest questioning to build relationships despite perceived differences. It also requires us as a society to work intentionally to undo generations of disadvantage and oppression so that there is an equal playing field for everyone. Supreme Court Justice Harry Blackmun argued in a 1978 decision that upheld affirmative action: "[I]n order to get beyond racism, we must first take into account race. There is no other way. And in order to treat some persons equally, we must treat them differently. We cannot—we dare not—let the Equal Protection clause perpetuate racial supremacy."

What if, in the end, we began to think of our identities as not based in our physical characteristics, as solely in the realm of our bodies, or even in some essentialized concept of culture, but based in our spirits, in the highest values to which we aspire? What might the world look like then?

Dr. Donald Cole: My University of Mississippi Experience

I entered the University of Mississippi in 1968 as a freshman with the blessings and concerns of my parents and many other community friends and leaders. I was a young, black man excited about attending the University of Mississippi, our state's flagship institution. The University had been integrated for about six years, but I did not realize that it was not yet fully integrated. At the time of my enrollment, there were still many staff members who had never served an individual like myself; faculty who had not taught a black person; and students who had not sat in a classroom with a black person. Naive to this, I entered with optimism and enthusiasm, but within weeks my optimism and enthusiasm were eroded by event after event of demonstrated racial displeasure for my presence on campus. I was not alone in experiencing this unchecked hostility, but complaints by my fellow black students and me didn't seem to matter. Our pleas for help to allow us to feel that we belonged and mattered fell on deaf ears.

These unmet requests by students of color led us to stand together. During a time when the entire country was experiencing protest (Vietnam War, women's issues, civil rights), black students enrolled at the University banded together to protest against the tacit acceptance of behaviors that demeaned black students on campus. We asked for increased recruitment of black students, integration of the faculty, and integration of athletics teams. The national culture at the time was "march and protest," and we did. One such march resulted in all the protestors being arrested and jailed. Some were taken to the state penitentiary at Parchman. Subsequent University judicial procedures suspended eight students, and (unfortunately) I was one of those suspended from the University. This forced me to enroll in another university to complete my undergraduate and master's degrees, but I applied for admission to a doctoral program at the University of Mississippi in 1977.

My eligibility to enroll after having been suspended was questioned, but I was granted admission. Upon my return to campus, I recognized that much about the University had changed. Black faculty had been hired, black athletes were part of the intercollegiate teams, and the University was working to disassociate itself from the confederate flag. I remained in the background during my graduate days; quite different from the outspoken student who entered in 1968. I graduated in 1985 with a doctorate in mathematics. Although I failed to obtain a bachelor's degree from the University of Mississippi, I succeeded in earning my doctorate. In 1993, I was invited to apply for, and was then hired, as Assistant Dean of the Graduate School and associate professor of mathematics. Today, I am a proud alum and member of the University's academic community. I have a unique personal timeline of our institution's struggle and success with racial dialogue from the 60s to today. With still much work ahead, I am proud of the progress that we have accomplished and that we have positioned ourselves to be a national leader in racial reconciliation.

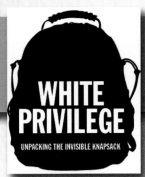

Excerpts from:
White Privilege:
Unpacking the Invisible Knapsack

I decided to try to work on myself at least by identifying some of the daily effects of white privilege in my life. I have chosen those conditions that I think in my case attach somewhat more to skin-color privilege than to class, religion, ethnic status, or geographic location, though of course all these other factors are intricately intertwined. As far as I can tell, my African American coworkers, friends, and acquaintances with whom I come into daily or frequent contact in this particular time, place, and time of work cannot count on most of these conditions.

1. I can, if I wish, arrange to be in the company of people of my race most of the time.

2. I can avoid spending time with people who I was trained to mistrust and who have learned to mistrust my kind or me.

3. If I should need to move, I can be pretty sure of renting or purchasing housing in an area that I can afford and in which I would want to live.

4. I can be pretty sure that my neighbors in such a location will be neutral or pleasant to me.

5. I can go shopping alone most of the time, pretty well assured that I will not be followed or harassed.

6. I can turn on the television or open to the front page of the paper and see people of my race widely represented.

7. When I am told about our national heritage or about "civilization," I am shown that people of my color made it what it is.

8. I can be sure that my children will be given curricular materials that testify to the existence of their race.

9. If I want to, I can be pretty sure of finding a publisher for this piece on white privilege.

10. I can be pretty sure of having my voice heard in a group in which I am the only member of my race.

11. I can be casual about whether or not to listen to another person's voice in a group in which s/he is the only member of his/her race.

12. I can go into a music shop and count on finding the music of my race represented, into a supermarket and find the staple foods which fit with my cultural traditions, into a hairdresser's shop and find someone who can cut my hair.

13. Whether I use checks, credit cards, or cash, I can count on my skin color not to work against the appearance of financial reliability.

14. I can arrange to protect my children most of the time from people who might not like them.

15. I do not have to educate my children to be aware of systemic racism for their own daily physical protection.

16. I can be pretty sure that my children's teachers and employers will tolerate them if they fit school and workplace norms; my chief worries about them do not concern others' attitudes toward their race.

17. I can talk with my mouth full and not have people put this down to my color.

18. I can swear, or dress in second hand clothes, or not answer letters, without having people attribute these choices to the bad morals, the poverty, or the illiteracy of my race.

19. I can speak in public to a powerful male group without putting my race on trial.

20. I can do well in a challenging situation without being called a credit to my race.

21. I am never asked to speak for all the people of my racial group.

22. I can remain oblivious of the language and customs of persons of color who constitute the world's majority without feeling in my culture any penalty for such oblivion.

23. I can criticize our government and talk about how much I fear its policies and behavior without being seen as a cultural outsider.

24. I can be pretty sure that if I ask to talk to the "person in charge," I will be facing a person of my race.

25. If a traffic cop pulls me over or if the IRS audits my tax return, I can be sure I haven't been singled out because of my race.

26. I can easily buy posters, post-cards, picture books, greeting cards, dolls, toys, and children's magazines featuring people of my race.

27. I can go home from most meetings of organizations I belong to feeling somewhat tied in, rather than isolated, out-of-place, outnumbered, unheard, held at a distance, or feared.

28. I can be pretty sure that an argument with a colleague of another race is more likely to jeopardize her/his chances for advancement than to jeopardize mine.

29. I can be pretty sure that if I argue for the promotion of a person of another race, or a program centering on race, this is not likely to cost me heavily within my present setting, even if my colleagues disagree with me.

30. If I declare there is a racial issue at hand, or there isn't a racial issue at hand, my race will lend me more credibility for either position than a person of color will have.

31. I can choose to ignore developments in minority writing and minority activist programs, or disparage them, or learn from them, but in any case, I can find ways to be more or less protected from negative consequences of any of these choices.

32. My culture gives me little fear about ignoring the perspectives and powers of people of other races.

33. I am not made acutely aware that my shape, bearing, or body odor will be taken as a reflection on my race.

34. I can worry about racism without being seen as self-interested or self-seeking.

35. I can take a job with an affirmative action employer without having my co-workers on the job suspect that I got it because of my race.

36. If my day, week, or year is going badly, I need not ask of each negative episode or situation whether it had racial overtones.

37. I can be pretty sure of finding people who would be willing to talk with me and advise me about my next steps, professionally.

38. I can think over many options, social, political, imaginative, or professional, without asking whether a person of my race would be accepted or allowed to do what I want to do.

39. I can be late to a meeting without having the lateness reflect on my race.

40. I can choose public accommodation without fearing that people of my race cannot get in or will be mistreated in the places I have chosen.

41. I can be sure that if I need legal or medical help, my race will not work against me.

42. I can arrange my activities so that I will never have to experience feelings of rejection owing to my race.

43. If I have low credibility as a leader I can be sure that my race is not the problem.

44. I can easily find academic courses and institutions which give attention only to people of my race.

45. I can expect figurative language and imagery in all of the arts to testify to experiences of my race.

46. I can choose blemish cover or bandages in "flesh" color and have them more or less match my skin.

47. I can travel alone or with my spouse without expecting embarrassment or hostility in those who deal with us.

48. I have no difficulty finding neighborhoods where people approve of our household.

49. My children are given texts and classes which implicitly support our kind of family unit and do not turn them against my choice of domestic partnership.

50. I will feel welcomed and "normal" in the usual walks of public life, institutional and social.

Glossary

Race— A social construct (with no biological validity) that divides people into distinct groups by categorizing them based on arbitrary elements of physical appearance, particularly skin color.

Racism— Racism exists when one ethnic group or historical collectivity dominates, excludes, or seeks to eliminate another on the basis of differences that it believes are hereditary and unalterable. From George M. Frederickson's *Racism: A Short History*

Prejudice— An attitude or opinion – usually negative – about a socially defined group (racial, religious, nationality, etc.) or any person perceived to be a member of that group, formed with insufficient knowledge, reason, or deliberation.

Power — Access to individuals, social groups, and institutions that own and/or control the majority of a community's resources, as well as the ability to define norms and standards of behavior.

Racial Stereotype— An image applied to an entire group of people (or a member of that group), assuming that those characteristics are rooted in significant and essential differences.

Institutional Racism— The ways in which institutions – social, political, educational, cultural, financial, religious, medical, housing, jobs, criminal justice – create and/or perpetuate systems that advantage white people at the expense of people of color.

White Privilege— Unearned advantages that benefit whites (whether they seek such benefits or not) by virtue of their skin color in a racist society.

White Supremacy— Once used only by racist groups such as the Ku Klux Klan, the term also is used in anti-racism work to describe the historically based, institutionally perpetuated system of domination and exploitation of people of color by white people, and which maintains white peoples' position of relative wealth, power, and privilege.

Reverse Racism— A term commonly used by white people to equate instances of hostile behavior toward them by people of color with the racism people of color face. This is a way of ignoring the issue of who has the power.

Internalized Racism— The misinformation and distortions that people may have about themselves and their cultures as a result of living in a racist society.

Non-racist— Term used by those who consider themselves "color-blind," a claim that in effect denies any role in perpetuating systemic racism, or any responsibility to act to dismantle it. Institutional racism is perpetuated not only by those who actively discriminate, but also by those who fail to challenge it (silence = consent).

Anti-racist— An anti-racist is someone who makes a conscious choice and persistent effort to challenge white supremacy, including her/his own white privilege, and to actively oppose forms of discrimination against people of color.

Social construct— A mechanism, phenomenon, or category created and developed by society; a perception of an individual, group, or idea that is created or "constructed" through cultural or social practice.

Separate but equal— A legal doctrine in United States constitutional law that justified systems of segregation. Under this doctrine, services, facilities, public accommodations, and public schools were allowed to be separated by race, on the condition that the quality of each group's public facilities was the same.

Affirmative action— Policies that take factors including race, color, religion, sex, or national origin into consideration in order to benefit an underrepresented group in areas of employment, education, and business.

Jim Crow era and laws— State and local laws enacted in the United States between 1876 and 1965 that mandated segregation in all public facilities in the Southern states of the former Confederacy. Separate but equal laws during this time led to conditions for blacks that were inferior to those provided for whites, systematizing a number of economic, educational, and social disadvantages.

Lynching— An execution conducted outside of legal authority by a mob, often by hanging, but also by burning at the stake, in order to punish an alleged transgressor and to intimidate, control, or manipulate a population of people.

These definitions were compiled over the last few years and are based on definitions originally created by the Challenging White Supremacy Workshops.

About the Authors

Susan M. Glisson,
Former Executive Director of the William Winter Institute for Racial Reconciliation

Susan M. Glisson is the former executive director of the William Winter Institute for Racial Reconciliation at UM. She holds a Ph.D. from the College of William and Mary and specializes in the history of race and religion in the United States, especially in the black struggle for freedom.

Charles H. Tucker,
Former Associate Director of the William Winter Institute for Racial Reconciliation

Charles H. Tucker is the former associate director of the William Winter Institute for Racial Reconciliation at UM. He holds a degree in mass communications and journalism from Jackson State University and previously worked as a newspaper reporter and photographer.

QUOTES FOR REFLECTIONS AND JOURNAL WRITING:

"Unless someone like you cares a whole awful lot, Nothing is going to get better. It's not."

Dr. Seuss
The Lorax

"If you simply try to 'do unto others as you would like them to do unto you' then you could wind up doing things to others they might not enjoy as much as you do. . . . An even more 'finely tuned' rule might be what some call 'The Platinum Rule,' namely, 'Do Unto Others as They Would Have You Do Unto Them.' In other words, take time to learn about your neighbor's tastes, their mood, their nature, and their temperment, before you start 'doing' things 'unto them.' Treat others the way they want to be treated."

Edward Babinski,
Leaving the Fold: Testimonies of Former Fundamentalists

"I tell my students, it's not difficult to identify with somebody like yourself, somebody next door who looks like you. What's more difficult is to identify with someone you don't see, who's very far away, who's a different color, who eats a different kind of food. When you begin to do that then literature is really performing its wonders."

Chinua Achebe

Diversity and Inclusion: Exploring Similarities and Embracing Differences

By Toni Avant, Ge-YaoLin, Shawnboda Mead,
Greet Provost, and Valeria Beasley Ross

Congratulations on your enrollment at the University of Mississippi. You are now an official member of the higher education community. Today's higher education communities (colleges and universities) include students from all over the world. These students and other members of the university community embody a range of different perspectives, beliefs, cultural practices, languages, socioeconomic experiences, and traditions. The university community also has people who differ from one another based on race, gender identity, sexual orientation, political beliefs, abilities, and religious practices.

Diversity in higher education is comparatively different to what colleges and universities included just a few generations ago. It is likely that our college community's diversity is dramatically different from that of your high school community. For starters, the University of Mississippi's student body includes people from more than 90 countries. This chapter provides you with an introduction to diversity. Additionally, it highlights the expectations and requirements for membership in your new and diverse community.

What is Diversity and What Does It Have to do With Me?

Diversity as an idea includes acceptance, respect, and recognition that individuals are unique and different. These differences can include religion, sexual orientation, ethnicity, race, gender, socio-economic status, age, physical abilities, religious beliefs and practices, political beliefs, and other ideologies.

Conceptually understanding the definition of diversity requires exploration of these differences. The University provides students opportunities to deeply explore differences through curricular and co-curricular activities. These activities provide a plethora of opportunities for engaging experiences on diversity and multicultural-related topics. Our college community promotes embracing and celebrating multiculturalism and diversity

rather than simple tolerance.

The University of Mississippi is a community that includes and promotes civility and respect in its mission and core values. As a new member of this community, you are expected to model the ideals expressed in the Creed, abide by the policies included in *The M-Book*, and embrace the pillars of *Respect the M*. So, explore the rich, diverse fabric that makes up our University community, and seek out those individuals and experiences that are different from those most comfortable and familiar to you.

The buzz words? Yeah, you've heard them all before!

You have probably heard all the buzz words – race, ethnicity, stereotyping, diversity, judgment, acceptance, tolerance, inclusion. Perhaps you have wondered how these words apply to you and why they are important. Perhaps you have contemplated that if we all just hung out with the people we like or those we are familiar with, wouldn't our organizations, our communities, our country, or the world be just fine, if not better off? Maybe, but think again. Is this really what the world is like beyond the comfort of your own front door?

Your opportunity

Is it not more likely that you will face situations where you will interact with others who are not like you? Others whose cultures, values, and behavior are peculiar, unusual, perhaps funny, or downright offensive to you? Have you ever considered that your values and behavior may be unusual or offensive to someone else as well? The point here is that you are now part of a wonderfully diverse environment at the University of Mississippi. Some of your fellow students, hall mates and roommates, your professors, and later on your co-workers and supervisors, neighbors, nurses, doctors, lawyers, or landscapers will be "those others." While you are a student at the University of Mississippi, you have the perfect opportunity to develop and practice those skills that will help you to be accepting and inclusive, to be an effective member of your workplace and community, and to learn to be a "good citizen." There is an old saying, "Knowledge, practice, attitude." It suggests that to effect positive change in your behavior, it is important to first understand yourself, to practice good habits, and to stand accordingly in the world.

Did you know?

Songwriter Jim Weatherly (Class of '64) has received more than 30 awards from the American Society of Composers, Authors, and Publishers. His songs have been recorded by The Indigo Girls, Kenny Rogers, and Charlie Pride.

Respect the M

The University of Mississippi's mission, vision, and statement of institutional core values proclaims: "In pursuing its mission, the University of Mississippi promotes inclusiveness in its student body, faculty, and staff and requires respect for all individuals and groups." With this in mind, the *Respect the M* campaign was launched in the Summer of 2013 during Orientation.

The foundational pillars of *Respect the M* include:

Respect Others' Opinions

Pay Attention	Listen
Acknowledge Others	Think the Best, Be Patient
Be Inclusive	Avoid Hateful Speech
Don't Speak Ill of Others	Check Your Biases

The logo for *Respect the M* uses the University's official colors. The inclusion of these colors in the logo was intentionally chosen to identify *Respect the M* as a University of Mississippi initiative. Additionally, the inclusion of the official University colors connects the idea to the larger institutional mission. "The University of Mississippi" encircling the logo further reflects the inclusive message intended by *Respect the M,* and the circular arrow demonstrates that *Respect the M* is a continuous lifestyle. The large M represents the University of Mississippi's full community and seeks to emphasize that we are a diverse community working toward a common goal. Most importantly, the breaks in the circle support sustainability of this initiative and allow for new tenets and pillars to be added over time as the fabric and reach of our institution continues to change and grow.

THE BUZZ WORDS AND WHY THEY ARE MEANINGFUL

Diversity

Diversity refers to the uniqueness of a population, be it local, national, global, or within specific organizations or communities, including, but not limited to, its overall make-up of race and ethnicity, gender and age, class, disability, religion, gender identity or expressions, or sexual orientation. Diversity is our different experiences, moral and religious beliefs, socio-economic backgrounds, languages and nationalities, tastes in music and art, all coming together in a way that contributes positively to our community.

Diversity at the University of Mississippi is a state of mind. The variety of backgrounds, experiences, and points of view contained in our community of students, scholars, faculty, and staff strengthens our campus as a whole and provides for an enriching environment in which all students can develop and practice skills that help them to un-

Did you know?

Ole Miss alum Harold Crump, Vice President of Hubbard Broadcasting, gave Oprah Winfrey her first television news anchor job.

derstand themselves and others, to be good citizens, and to contribute meaningfully to their communities, whether on a local or global scale.

However, diversity by itself is not enough. Diversity, in and of itself, is mostly about numbers and representation, and it is not enough to focus on numbers alone. In other words, diversity cannot be an end in itself. Diversity must also be about inclusion. Inclusion is the objective and focus of diversity.

Inclusion

Inclusion exists when we act in a manner that recognizes and respects individual similarities and differences in others so that they and their efforts are valued and viewed as a significant part of a particular organization or community whose contributions aid that organization's or community's objectives. Inclusion is about everyone; it is about respecting diversity, respecting each others' differences and similarities, and it is about building meaningful community together in which each member is valued. Inclusion means celebrating and embracing differences in a positive and constructive way. It is therefore important to recognize the diverse needs of different people, whether they are fellow students, co-workers, community groups, or population groups in general.

Race and ethnicity

So, what is race really? And what is ethnicity? While some use the words ethnicity and race interchangeably, they are not the same. Ethnicity refers to having cultural or national similarities. The word ethnic comes from the Greek word ethnos, meaning nation, people. The Oxford English Dictionary defines ethnic as "(of a social group) having a common national or cultural tradition, such as language."

The definition of race has transformed over time. Race has been used in the past to describe a "category of humankind that shares certain distinctive physical traits" (Merriam-Webster Dictionary). More recently, and per the U.S. census, the U.S. government defines race as a self-identified, self-reported social and cultural concept that places an individual into one of many global groups. Race is thus neither biological nor scientific, but a social construct utilized to categorize people based on phenotypical characteristics such as skin color, ancestry, or country of origin.

In the U.S., as elsewhere, data on race is generally collected through a census. A census is a numerical account of all citizens based on socioeconomic, biological, sociological, and psychological markers (ehow.com). In the U.S., a national census occurs every ten years. The first census was taken in the late 1700s, the most recent one in 2010. During

Did you know?

Virtually 100 percent of our accountancy master's graduates are placed in well-paying jobs, and many students have employment offers as early as 15 months before they graduate.

this time, the U.S. population has changed and has become increasingly diverse.

There are arguments for and against collecting data on race. Arguments in favor of collecting race data center on the importance of recording significant changes in the diversity of our population. This, according to proponents of collecting race data, helps monitor the civil rights of our whole population and guards against discriminatory practices in employment, voting rights, healthcare, financial lending, housing standards, and access to education and training.

Arguments against collecting data on race tend to center on the irreconcilability of the government's standardized race categories and the fluid, rapidly-changing racial and ethnic reality of the U.S., in part due to increasing intermarriages and expectant preference for multiracial designations. For example, is President Obama black or white? What about Mariah Carey, Alicia Keys, Dwayne "Rock" Johnson, or Drake? What race are their children? Collecting data per standardized race categories, opponents argue, provides an inaccurate picture at best.

Data on race also has been used to re-establish political districts and electoral boundaries, a practice referred to as gerrymandering: to attempt to manipulate geographic boundaries to achieve desired electoral results. This may establish political advantages for, or hinder, a particular group of constituents, be it a political party or a racial, linguistic, religious, or class group.

PAUSE FOR THOUGHT: What is your ethnicity? Where did your ancestors come from? Africa, Asia, Europe, the Middle East, South America (as we know those regions today)? Who were your ancestors' ancestors? Consider your own ethnicity. Would you say that everyone who shares your ethnicity is the same?

Bigotry, racism, and stereotyping

Even though our population has become diverse, discussions focusing on race and race relations are still sensitive ones. Conversations about race elicit emotions ranging from rational to irrational, from love to hate to indifference.

Bigotry is the "irrational suspicion or hatred of a particular group, race, or religion" (Rogets II, 1995). A bigot is a person who exhibits intolerance and animosity towards those of differing beliefs or opinions and is adamant about the accuracy of his or her own views. Bigotry generally refers to someone who is hostile to those of a race, ethnicity, nationality, sexual orientation, or religion other than his or her own. Racism, per the definition of the Anti-Defamation League, is "the belief that a particular race is superior or inferior to another, that a person's social and moral traits are predetermined by his or her inborn biological characteristics." Stereotyping is defined by the Oxford English Dictionary as "something continued or constantly repeated without change." It is easy to make assumptions about groups of people, basing those assumptions on stereotypical characteristics that we ascribe to particular identities. These stereotypes may be based on our own experiences, impressions gained by characters in movies or TV programs, or perhaps even discussions with family and friends.

Bigotry, racism, and stereotyping can lead to micro-aggressions and more explicit acts of bias. Micro-aggressions are "the everyday verbal, nonverbal, and environmental slights, snubs, or insults, whether intentional or unintentional, which communicate hostile, derogatory, or negative messages to target persons based solely upon their marginalized group membership" (Sue, 2010). In "35 Dumb Things Well-Intentioned People Say: Surprising things we say that widen the diversity gap," Dr. Maura Cullen discusses intent vs. impact. Even well-intentioned micro-aggressions can cause harm and have a lasting impact. Well-intentioned statements such as "I don't see color" and "What are you?" are problematic and minimize the cultural heritage of others. While micro-aggressions are generally discussed from the perspective of race and racism, any marginalized group in our society may become targets: people of color, women, LGBT persons, those with disabilities, religious minorities, and so on.

Micro-aggressions can be based upon any group that is marginalized in this society. Below are a few examples (Sue, 2010):
• A White man or woman clutches her purse or checks his or her wallet as a Black or Latino man approaches or passes by. (Hidden message: You and your group are criminals.)
• An Asian American, born and raised in the United States, is complimented for speaking "good English." (Hidden message: You are not a true American. You are a perpetual foreigner in your own country.)
• A female physician wearing a stethoscope is mistaken as a nurse. (Hidden message: Women should occupy nurturing and not decision-making roles. Women are less capable than men.)
• A young person uses the term "gay" to describe a movie that she didn't like. (Hidden message: Being gay is associated with negative and undesirable characteristics.)
• When bargaining over the price of an item, a store owner says to a customer, "Don't try to Jew me down." (Hidden message: Jews are stingy and money-grubbing.)
• A blind man reports that people often raise their voices when speaking to him. He responds by saying, "Please don't raise your voice; I can hear you perfectly well." (Hidden message: A person with a disability is defined as lesser in all aspects of physical and mental functioning).

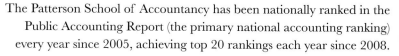

Did you know?

The Patterson School of Accountancy has been nationally ranked in the Public Accounting Report (the primary national accounting ranking) every year since 2005, achieving top 20 rankings each year since 2008.

DISCUSSION

What has been your personal experience with bigotry or racism? What are some of the stereotypes you have heard about your race or ethnicity, country, region, state, home town, religion, gender, interests, or the way you look? How do you react to stereotypes? Do you fit those stereotypes? If you don't – and we strongly suspect this is the case – how does it feel to have assumptions made about you based on stereotypes? What can you do to combat misguided beliefs about yourself, about others?

Writing and Reflection:

Consider the following questions and write your responses in five sentences or less. After answering all of the questions, take the most meaningful line from each of your responses. You have just created a poem.

- Do you treat people differently based on their race or ethnicity?
- When did you first realize your race?
- When did you first experience or witness an act of discrimination, and how did you respond?
- How would you define privilege?
- What is your attitude about same-sex relationships?
- What are your views on religious practices?
- If you could enact one rule about diversity and inclusion for you and your peers, what would that rule be?

Easier said than done? Your personal challenge!

In his most legendary speech, Dr. Martin Luther King, Jr. said: "I have a dream that my four little children will one day live in a nation where they will not be judged by the color of their skin but by the content of their character" (King, 1963). While we cannot be "color blind" or "difference blind," and while difference and diversity continue to cause conflicts, now is the time to get beyond judgment and stereotyping, beyond discrimination and exclusion. You have an opportunity to develop and practice acceptance and inclusion.

We encourage you to regard your fellow students as individuals. Get to know them. Get to know their names. Get to know them personally. The more you know about them, the more you will realize that you may have a lot more in common than meets the eye, and that each student brings his or her own individual attributes to our campus community. The more you get to know them, and they you, the more you will appreciate the inappropriateness of assumptions and judgments, and the value of appreciation and inclusion. In the words of Dr. King: "We have made of this world a neighborhood and yet we have not had the ethical commitment to make of it a brotherhood. But somehow, and in some way, we have got to do this. We must all learn to live together as brothers or we will all perish together as fools" (King, 1968).

ASSIGNMENT:

Breaking Down the Barriers in Small Steps.

Some students have claimed that the Union Food Court is the most segregated place on campus during the lunch hour. Visit the Food Court and ask to sit and dine with a group of students who are racially or ethnically different than you. Reflect on your experience by writing a one-page paper contemplating the following: What perceptions or stereotypes did you have about the group with whom you selected to dine? What were some of the perceptions that group had about you? How easy or difficult was this task, and why? Did you discover any common interests or similarities between yourself and the lunch group? Any differences? Would you repeat this experience if it were not an assignment?

Easier said than done? A challenge of leadership!

Inclusion at the systemic level, as an organization, campus, town, city, state, or nation can be more challenging to address than inclusion on a personal level. All systems, regulations, or policies, regardless of who or how many people are impacted, are, at least in part, informed by the personal knowledge, understanding, and convictions of those charged with making decisions. These decisions impact the community at large. In many diverse societies, there are groups of people whose voices are heard and whose needs are met, and there are others who are not heard and their needs are not met. To effect change towards inclusion as a member or a leader of a community, it is important to understand key concepts such as majority, privilege, and power.

Majority refers to abundance, to what is considered mainstream, normal, or popular. Privilege suggests advantage, opportunity, and rights, even freedom. Power implies authority, control, influence, or even supremacy. The intersection of majority, privilege, and power can create opportunities or barriers for communities, within organizations, workplaces, towns or cities, or institutions, especially when the connection between these concepts is not examined or addressed. Majority, privilege, and power can combine to create inequalities and inequities, but communities also can work together to ensure a balanced environment for all their members. Local governments or executive boards oftentimes create rules and policies to protect the interests of all groups to offset the "tyranny of the majority" that can otherwise evolve.

Our hypothetical community

Consider for a moment the religious practices in a hypothetical community where people subscribe to various denominations of faith. Imagine that the members of the Hindu faith are the largest in membership, have the most worship facilities, and the greatest financial resources. They represent the majority faith in our hypothetical town. Imagine that those of the Hindu faith control the worship opportunities for all religions in the community. What might that mean for them and for those who are not of the Hindu faith? What if this majority group always has the first opportunity to access or use the community's resources, or be allowed to schedule their events – booking facilities and listing events on community calendars – before any of the other groups? What would the implications be for those who practiced Christianity, Judaism, or Islam? When majority, privilege, and power rest predominantly in the hands of one group, a system of inequality is likely to develop. This is referred to as the "tyranny of the majority." The results can rapidly evolve into inequality, inequity, and injustice and can breed civil and political unrest. In the U.S., the historical division of race and wealth has facilitated a system of privilege and power (Hurtado, et al., 1998). The intersection of power and privilege has "produced unequal distribution of jobs, wealth, income, and access" (Dwyer, 2006; Iverson & Iverson, 2009).

"We have made of this world a neighborhood and yet we have not had the ethical commitment to make of it a brotherhood. But somehow, and in some way, we have got to do this. We must all learn to live together as brothers or we will all perish together as fools."

Dr. Martin Luther King, Jr.

Our real community

In the world of higher education in the U.S., distinct types of institutions have been established: private and public institutions, predominantly white institutions (PWI), and historically black colleges and universities (HBCU). How the concepts of privilege and power intersect at each of these types of institutions varies. At PWIs, such as the University of Mississippi, their impact is often analyzed in terms of recruitment, access, and retention. PWIs are aware that privilege and power, if not attended to, can have negative implications for their institutions. Therefore, academic programs, scholarship programs, and special offices often are established to ensure that students representing non-major-

Did you know?

Ole Miss alumni work for leading international accounting firms and Fortune 500 companies. They also own small (and not-so-small) businesses and head government and not-for-profit agencies. The diverse careers of our graduates reveal the extraordinary ways this degree proves valuable. Accounting truly is the language of business.

> "Voices that are silenced or ignored, for whatever reason, represent not only an injustice but also a valuable resource that has been wasted, a tragic waste of human capital."
>
> **James Padilla**
> **President,**
> **Ford Motor Company, 2005**

ity groups are provided with relevant services and access to counter the imbalance that minority groups might otherwise experience. These programs provide all students opportunities to interact and engage with students of races and ethnic origins different than their own, thereby embracing diversity and fostering inclusivity (Dwyer, 2006; Iverson & Iverson, 2009).

Recognizing when, where, and how majority, power, and privilege intersect can help you address systems and structures in organizations with the purpose of effecting change that fosters inclusion and unifies your community (Maher & Tetreault, 2009).

As you discuss the questions below, consider your familial influences, your past experiences and successes, and your knowledge of institutional cultural practices. It is important to consider these dynamics so that you have an awareness and appreciation for your opinions as well as those of others, and for how the intersection of majority, power, and privilege impact organizations and systems.

- How would you describe a typical undergraduate student, a professor, a roommate, or a classroom at the University of Mississippi?
- What is your perception of privilege on campus?
- What group (or groups) of students have the most access to resources, such as scholarships, study abroad opportunities, or tutors?
- In what ways do people like you become aware of the University of Mississippi?

The phrase *tyranny of the majority*, used in discussing systems of democracy and majority rule, is a criticism of the system in which decisions made by the majority place that majority's interests so far above those not belonging to that majority (i.e. minority), that the minority is actively oppressed – not unlike the oppression by a tyrant or despot.

Limits on decisions that can be made by such majorities have taken the form of constitutional limits on governmental powers, bills of rights, separation of powers, and checks-and-balances systems or procedures.

Adapted from John Stuart Mill

DIVERSITY AND INCLUSION IN THE WORLD, IN THE USA, IN YOUR HOMETOWN, and AT OLE MISS

Diversity in the world

On ethnic diversity

There are more than 7 billion people in the world today. More than 60 percent of them are Asians living on less than 30 percent of the land. Only about five percent of the world's people live in North America.

- 60 percent live in Asia
- 14 percent live in Africa
- 11 percent live in Europe and the nations that once made up the Soviet Union
- 8.7 percent live in Latin America and the Caribbean
- 5 percent live in North America (U.S. and Canada)
- 2.9 percent live in the Middle East
- 0.5 percent live in Oceania (Australia, New Zealand, and the Pacific Islands)

On language diversity

Linguists estimate that the world's peoples speak 5,000-6,000 languages. The most common "native" language is Mandarin Chinese. As compared to English as a native language, almost three times as many people in the world speak Mandarin Chinese, and almost twice as many speak Hindi or Bengali. The most common native languages spoken in the world are:

1) Mandarin Chinese
2) Hindi (India)
3) English
4) Spanish
5) Bengali (India and Bangladesh)
6) Arabic (its 15 major variants)

While English is not the "native language" of the majority of people in the world, it has the widest distribution, having become the second language of choice in many countries. Approximately 25 to 30 percent of humanity understands or speaks English to some degree.

Meanwhile, many languages of smaller ethnic groups are dying. Almost 50 percent of the languages in the world are no longer spoken by the children of these small ethnic groups. This is partly due to the increasing globalization of our economies and the global importance of the English language and Western (especially U.S.) culture. However, cultural diffusion has not been a one-way affair. For example, the English language contains words from more than 240 other languages. In less than one generation, the cultural influences of Asia and Latin America especially, have dramatically changed life in North America. (e.g. boogie, safari [African]; ketchup, wok [Asian]; coleslaw, frolic, furlough [Dutch]).

Did you know?

Two-time Grammy award winner, Nelly, and Grammy nominee, Dierks Bentley, have performed in the Grove.

On age diversity

There are currently 1.5 billion people in the world between the ages of 12 and 24; 87 percent of them live in the developing world. This includes India, China, and most of Latin America and the Middle East. The world population is forecast to grow from 7 billion in 2010 to 10.5 billion in 2050.

Globalization:

Globalization has made institutions of higher education rethink their overarching missions. Their focus has shifted to preparing students to become well rounded global citizens. In the 21st century, institutions of higher education inevitably must do more than ever to increase the global sophistication of their students, faculty, and staff, helping them to develop a global skill set that is much needed to succeed in the new world — a world in which the economy is borderless and is driven by technology.

Globalization Data:

■ "974,926 international students studied at U.S. colleges and universities in 2014-15" (2016 IIE OpenDoors Report).

■ "In 2015, the continued growth in international students coming to the U.S. for higher education had a significant positive economic impact on the United States. International students contributed more than $30.5 billion to the U.S. economy, according to the U.S. Department of Commerce" (2016 IIE Open Doors Report).

■ "304,467 U.S. students studied abroad for academic credit in 2013-2014" (2016 IIE Open Doors Report).

100 People: A World Portrait

A Global Education Toolbox

The world population has now reached **7 billion people**. This milestone inspired us to conduct research to update our statistics, and the changes over the past five years are remarkable. In 2006, only one person of 100 would have had a college education – today that number has jumped to seven thanks in part to advances in higher education in Asia.

If the World were 100 PEOPLE:

50 would be female
50 would be male

26 would be children
There would be 74 adults,
8 of whom would be 65 and older

There would be:

60 Asians

15 Africans

14 people from the Americas

11 Europeans

33 Christians

22 Muslims

14 Hindus

7 Buddhists

12 people who practice other religions

12 people who would not be aligned with a religion

12 would speak Chinese

5 would speak Spanish

5 would speak English

3 would speak Arabic

3 would speak Hindi

3 would speak Bengali

3 would speak Portuguese

2 would speak Russian

2 would speak Japanese

62 would speak other languages

83 would be able to read and write; 17 would not

7 would have a college degree

22 would own or share a computer

77 people would have a place to shelter them from the wind and the rain, but 23 would not

1 would be dying of starvation

15 would be undernourished

21 would be overweight

87 would have access to safe drinking water

13 people would have no clean, safe water to drink

Sources: 2012 - Fritz Erickson, Provost and Vice President for Academic Affairs, Ferris State University (Formerly Dean of Professional and Graduate Studies, University of Wisconsin - Green Bay) and John A. Vonk, University of Northern Colorado, 2006; Returning Peace Corps Volunteers of Madison Wisconsin, Unheard Voices: *Celebrating Cultures from the Developing World*, 1992; Donella H. Meadows, *Global Citizen*, May 31, 1990.

Diversity in the U.S.

When considering our diverse population, it doesn't simply boil down to race or ethnicity. There are many factors to consider to understand the big picture of what diversity actually means in our society. While race and ethnicity are two of the primary categories, gender, age, sexual orientation, and mental/physical abilities are also included in the primary dimensions of diversity. The secondary categories include geographic location, education, socioeconomic status, marital status, religious beliefs, and parental/family status. In the U.S., the total population is over 325 million, representing only 4.4 percent of the entire world's population. Let's take a closer look at the diversity in this country, based on 2016 data reported by the U.S. Census Bureau.

- 76.9 percent were Caucasian
- 13.3 percent were Black Americans
- 17.8 percent were Latino
- 5.7 percent were Asian
- 1.3 percent were American Indian or Alaska Native
- 0.2 percent were Native Hawaiian or other Pacific Islander
- 2.6 percent were two or more races
- 9.5 percent were 18-24 years old
- 61.9 percent were 18 to 64 years old
- 15.2 percent were 65 and older
- 37.9 was the median age in the U.S.
- 49.8 percent of males/50.2 percent females ranged in age from 18 to 64
- 13.2 percent of the U.S. population were born abroad

The median household income was $55,322.

The University of Mississippi's Oxford and Regional Campuses.

Take a brief look at the current and broad diversity of the student body at the University of Mississippi

- 76.7 percent are Caucasian
- 12.8 percent are Black; 4.4 percent are Asian; 3.5 percent are Latino
- 0.26 percent are American Indian
- 0.1 percent are Native Hawaiian/Pacific Islander
- 2.2 percent are multi-racial
- 55.1 percent are from the state of Mississippi
- 44.9 percent are from outside the state of Mississippi
- 4.2 percent are international, from countries other than the U.S.A. This group represents 82+ countries in the world
- 54.9 percent are women and 44.7 percent are men

The University of Mississippi did not always have the diversity it has today. In fact, the state of Mississippi and the University of Mississippi have dealt with their share of controversy regarding race. While the controversy created violent, malicious, and painful outbursts at times, it also served to raise the collective consciousness of intolerance and inclusion. This opened the door to engage in meaningful conversations about our differences and about how we relate to the notion of diversity and inclusion. Diversity and inclusion at the University of Mississippi are important, not only as a response to our institutional history but also as a way to provide a real world experience for all students.

Our student and faculty diversity serves to help make all students literate in understanding others, in getting along with others, and in learning how to successfully collaborate and compete with others, beyond their own personal and cultural comfort zones. This enables students to better understand the realities of the broader community and marketplace. A racially and ethnically diverse student body gives us a more realistic view of the world and helps students use their differences and similarities meaningfully to contribute to their communities, nations, and the world.

It is not uncommon for new students to experience a bit of "culture shock" when stepping foot on the University of Mississippi campus as new students. While you may think culture shock only happens when someone moves to another country, it can happen any time you are adjusting to a cultural environment that is markedly different than your previous living environment.

Student Testimonials

Summer Wigley—Recent Graduate from Jackson
"Attending college provides a multitude of opportunities to meet people similar and different from you. I challenged myself to embrace new experiences, have valuable conversations, and seek a better understanding of those around me. While I know that I will never be able to walk in someone else's shoes, I know that I can walk right beside them throughout our journeys."

Chase Moore—Senior from Horn Lake
"It is my desire to embrace similarities and differences in all aspects in life. To do so, I first consider my life, and everything that has shaped my beliefs, and then realize that each of the 7 billion people on this planet has their own narrative. Not one is the same. In order to be exposed to narratives, I have to at least attempt to befriend people of all walks of life."

The Division of Diversity and Community Engagement

Established in 2016, the Division of Diversity and Community Engagement coordinates the University of Mississippi's efforts to create and support a diverse, inclusive, and welcoming environment for all members of the community, including students, staff, faculty, and alumni. Under the leadership of Vice Chancellor Katrina Caldwell, the Division facilitates and encourages community engagement, develops partnerships to effectively facilitate transformation, and identifies and supports target areas to maximize the University's commitment to diversity, equity, and inclusion.

The Center for Inclusion and Cross-Cultural Engagement

The Center for Inclusion and Cross-Cultural Engagement opened in 2014. Located in Stewart Hall, the Center offers students a welcoming environment to interact, exchange ideas, and engage in programming and meaningful conversations that celebrate the cultures and heritages of our diverse community. The Center for Inclusion and Cross Cultural Engagement provides opportunities that prepare you for success in a multicultural society. From academic resources to peer mentoring and cultural programming, there is something for everyone! The desire is that, as a community, we interact with one another from a place of appreciation and acceptance, where all members are valued. The University of Mississippi is likely to be the most diverse community you will ever be part of in your life! The Center encourages you to embrace the difference and diversity around you!

The Office of International Programs

The Office of International Programs (OIP) is housed within the Division of Global Engagement. In addition to international recruitment and admission, OIP provides information and documents to support nonimmigrant student visa applications and assists international students and scholars with their cultural as well as educational adjustments, so they can complete their educational goals.

Multi-cultural or ethnicity organizations: The University of Mississippi has many organizations comprised of multi-ethnic memberships. These organizations host events and provide opportunities to dialogue about multicultural topics. Each of these organizations is registered through the Office of the Dean of Students. To view the website for these organizations and/or locate contact information, visit dos.orgsync.com/student_organizations.

African Caribbean Organization
Black Graduate Professional Student Association
Black Student Union (BSU)

Did you know?

Each spring, Ole Miss students contribute thousands of hours of volunteer work to the Oxford and Lafayette County communities thanks to the student-organized Big Event.

Cultural Connections Club
Cultural Connections Mentorship Program
Friendship Association of Chinese Students and Scholars
Gay/Straight Alliance
Indian Students Association
International Ladies Club
International Student Organization
Latin American Student Organization
Men of Excellence
Model United Nations
Muslim Students Assocation
PRIDE Network
Sistah Speak
Society of Black Sociologists
Taiwan Student Association
University of Mississippi German Club
University of Mississippi Gospel Choir
University of Mississippi Russian Club

Cultural events are held annually on the campus of the University of Mississippi.

Disability History Month
Hispanic Heritage Month
LGBTQ History Month
Native American Month
Black History Month
Celebration of Achievement
Fiesta Latina
Get Involved Now
Homecoming Step Show
India Night
International Fest
Multicultural Perspective
Homecoming Celebration Tent

Academic courses that address matters of diversity and inclusion:
African American Studies
Modern Languages and Culture Studies
Gender Studies
International Studies
Study Abroad
Southern Studies

Departments that engage in matters of diversity and inclusion:
Student Disability Services
The Center for Inclusion and Cross-Cultural Engagement
The William Winter Institute for Racial Reconciliation
The Sarah Isom Center for Women and Gender Studies
The Office of International Programs
The Croft Institute for International Studies
The Intensive English Program

Glossary

Acceptance: The Oxford English Dictionary defines acceptance as the agreement with or belief in an idea, opinion, or explanation. It also means recognizing and showing appreciation for our differences.

Bias: A prejudice or unreasonable judgment, view, or outlook drawn before gathering all the facts.

Bigotry: The Oxford English Dictionary defines bigotry as intolerance towards those who hold different opinions from oneself.

Census: The Oxford English Dictionary defines census as an official, periodic count or survey of a population, typically recording various details of individuals.

Discrimination: The Oxford English Dictionary defines discrimination as the unjust or prejudicial treatment of different categories of people or things, especially on the grounds of race, age, or sex.

Diversity: The Oxford English Dictionary defines diversity as the state of being diverse, variety. Diverse, as showing a great deal of variety, differences.

Ethnicity: The Oxford English Dictionary defines ethnicity as the fact or state of belonging to a social group that has a common national or cultural tradition.

Exclusion: The Oxford English Dictionary defines exclusion as the process or state of excluding or being excluded, and exclude as to deny access to someone from a place, group, or a privilege.

Micro-aggresion: The everyday verbal, nonverbal, and environment slights, snubs, or insults, whether intentional or unintentional, which communicate hostile, derogatory, or negative messages to target persons based solely upon their marginalized group membership.

Multicultural Competency: A process of learning about and becoming allies with people from other cultures, thereby broadening our own understanding and ability to participate in a multicultural process. The key element to becoming more culturally competent is respect for the ways that others live in and organize the world and an openness to learn from them.

Inclusion: The Oxford English Dictionary defines inclusion as the action or state of including or of being included within a group or structure.

Privilege: The Oxford English Dictionary defines privilege as a special right, advantage, or immunity granted or available only to a particular person or group of people.

Power: The Oxford English Dictionary defines power as the capacity or ability to direct or influence the behavior of others or the course of events; political or social authority or control; a person or organization that is strong or influential within a particular context.

Racism: An act by an individual or a group of individuals based on some bias or prejudice against another individual or group of individuals based on their race; a belief that based on racial categorizations, one group is superior to another group; attempts to deny a person or a group of persons' rights (including constitutionally granted rights) based on race.

Tolerance: The Oxford English Dictionary defines tolerance as the ability or willingness to tolerate something, in particular the existence of opinions or behavior that one does not necessarily agree with.

Stereotype: The Oxford English Dictionary describes stereotyping as something continued or constantly repeated without change.

REFERENCES

A Global Education Toolbox. *100 People: A World Portrait.* Retrieved from www.100people.org/statistics_100stats.php. Accessed 2/6/2012

American Religious Identification Survey (ARIS). Retrieved from www.americanreligionsurvey-aris.org/2010/02/

American Sociological Association. *Statement of the American Sociological Association on the Importance of Collecting Datat and Doing Social Scientific Research on Race.* Retrieved from www2.asanet.org/governance/racestmt.html. Accessed 2/13/2012.

Anti-Defamation League. www.adl.org/hate-patrol/racism.asp.

College Prowler. The University of Mississippi – Diversity. Retrieved from www.collegeprowler.coom/university-of-mississippi/diversity

Cappex. The University of Mississippi. Retrieved from www.cappex.com/colleges/University-of-Mississippi-Main-Campus-176017

Cullen, M. (2008). 35 Dumb Things Well-Intended People Say: Surprising Things We Say That Widen the Diversity Gap. Garden City, NY: Morgan James Publishing.

Dwyer, B. (2006). Framing the effect of multiculturalism on diversity outcomes among students at historically black colleges and universities. *Educational Foundations*, 37-59.

Erickson, B. L.; Peters, C. B.; & Strommer, D. W. (2009). Teaching First-Year College Students: Revised and Expanded Edition of Teaching College Freshmen. San Francisco, CA: Jossey Bass.

Gibson, C., & Jung,K. Historical Census Statistics on Population Totals by Race, 1790 to 1990, and by Hispanic Origin, 1970-1990, for the United States, Regions, Divisions, and States. U.S. Census Bureau. Retrieved from www.census.gov/population/www/documentation/twps0056/tabA-26.pdf

gladstone.uoregon.edu/~asuomca/diversityinit/definition.html

Grace, S., & Gravestock, P. (2009). *Inclusion and Diversity: Meeting the Needs of All Students.* Routledge, New York.

Hurtado, S., Milem, J.F., Clayton-Pederson, A.R., & Allen, W.R. (1998). Enhancing campus climates for racial/ethnic diversity: Educational policy and practice. The Review of Higher Education, *21*(3), 279-302.

Iverson, S.V. (2007). Camouflaging power and privilege: A critical race analysis of university diversity policies. *Educational Administration Quarterly*, *43*(5), 586-611.

Iverson, A. C. & Iverson, S. V. (2009). Addressing the structure of power and privilege: Implications for diversity efforts at PWIs. *The Voice.* Retrieved from www.myacpa.org/comm/social/Newsletter0309/newsletter_0309_power.cfm

Jones. R. A. (2005). Race and revisability. *Journal of Black Studies.* 35(5). 612-632.

King Jr., M. L. Remaining Awake Through a Great Revolution. Speech. March 31, 1968. The Martin Luther King, Jr. Research and Education Institute. Retrieved from mlk-kpp01.stanford.edu/index.php/kingpapers/article/remaining_awake_through_a_great_revolution/

Maher, F.A. & Tetreault, M.K. (2009). Diversity and privilege: We need to understand how privilege works before we can make diversity work. *Academe, 95*(1), pp. 17-20.

Martin, Megan. U.S. Census Definition of Race. Retrieved from www.ehow.com/facts_5589095_u_s_census-definition-race.html. Accessed 2/13/2012.

Nittle, Nadra Kareem. Race Relations. *What is Race?* Retrieved from racerelations.about.com/od/understandingrac1/a/WhatIsRac.htm. Acessed 2/13/2012.

Nittle, Nadra Kareem. Race Relations. *What is Race? Debunking the Ideas Behind this Construct.* Retrieved from racerelations.about.com/od/understandingrac1/a/WhatIsRace.htm. Accessed 2/13/2012.

Office of Institutional Research & Assessment. Retrieved from www.olemiss.edu/depts/university_planning/

Racial Equity Tools Glossary. Retrieved from racialequitytools.org/glossary

Roget's II. (1995). *The New Thesaurus*. 3rd Ed. Boston: Houghton-Mifflin.

Sansing, D. (1999). *The University of Mississippi: A Sesquicentennial History*. Jackson: University Press of Mississippi.

StrategyDriven. Diversity and Inclusion. Retrieved from www.strategydriven.com/2010/07/300/diversity-and-inclusion-what-is-diversity-and-inclusion/

Sue, Derald (2010). Micro-aggressions: More than just race. Psychology Today. Retrieved at psychologytoday.com/blog/microaggressions-in-everyday-life/201011/microaggressions-more-just-race.

The Oxford English Dictionary. Retrieved from www.oxforddictionaries.com

The White House. Office of Management and Budget. Standards for the Classification of Federal Data on Race and Ethnicity. Retrieved from www.whitehouse.gov/omb/fedreg_race-ethnicity

United States Census 1990. Your Guide for the 1990 US Census Form. Retrieved from www.census.gov/prod/1/90dec/cph4/appdxe.pdf

United States Census 2010. Explore the Form. Retrieved from 2010.census.gov/2010census/about/interactive-form.php

United States Census Bureau. 2009 American Community Survey. Retrieved from www.census.gov/acs/www/

U.S. Constitution Online. *I Have A Dream Speech*. Retrieved from www.usconstitution.net/dream.html

World Diversity Patterns. Retrieved from www.anthro.palomar.edu/ethnicity/ethnic_5.htm

About the Authors

Toni Avant has spent most of her career working with college students at public and private universities. She's an alumna of the University, and a first-generation college student, holding a B.A. in computer science and an M.A. in higher education. Ms. Avant is the proud parent of three sons, is actively involved in her community, and hopes one day to earn her black belt in Tae-Kwon-Do.

Ge-Yao-Liu, *Former Director of the Office of International Programs*

Ge-Yao Liu is currently the Director for the Center of International Programs at Humbolt State University. He received his B.A. in English from Guangxi Normal University in China and received his M.A. in Linguistics with an emphasis in TESOL from Brigham Young University in Provo, Utah. Ge-Yao has had 20 years of experience in international education in a higher education setting, both at two-year and four-year institutions, including international student/scholar services, international recruitment, admissions, credential evaluation, study abroad, ESL teaching and program supervising, and international outreach/partnerships. He also has worked, resided, and traveled internationally to many different countries.

Greet Provoost, *former Director of the Office of International Programs*

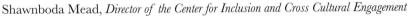

With a career in international education spanning more than 25 years, **Greet Provoost** earned undergraduate degrees in education and international politics from Belgium and the U.S., respectively, and a master's degree in international education from Australia. Ms. Provoost's travels, whether for work, education, or just plain fun, have taken her to some 43 countries on six continents to date. She is the Assistant Dean for Enrollment and Registration at Virginia Commonwealth University - Qatar.

Shawnboda Mead, *Director of the Center for Inclusion and Cross Cultural Engagement*

Shawnboda Mead joined the University of Mississippi in July 2014 as the inaugural Director of the Center for Inclusion & Cross Cultural Engagement. She works closely with student leaders in the Black Student Union, Inclusion Team, and MOST Mentoring Program and serves as co-chair to the Bias Incident Response Team. Ms. Mead earned a bachelor's degree in educational psychology from Mississippi State University and a master's degree in higher education administration from Western Kentucky University. She is passionate about helping underrepresented student populations succeed and providing cultural learning opportunities for all students.

Valeria Beasley Ross, *Director of Leadership and Advocacy*

Valeria Beasley Ross has a Bachelor of social science, a Bachelor of public administration and a Master of social science with a minor in African American Studies, all from the University of Mississippi. She is currently completing her doctoral degree in higher education.

History of Disability and Disability Rights

With approximately 52 million members, people with disabilities make up the largest minority group in the country. It is also the only minority group that anyone can join at any time. The U.S. has passed several laws designed to protect the rights of people with disabilities. The Rehabilitation Act of 1972 and the Americans with Disabilities Act (ADA) of 1990 are civil rights legislation enacted to remedy discrimination of those with disabilities.

Sometimes people are confused about why those with disabilities need a law to protect their civil rights. Before Congress would include those with disabilities as a "protected class" under civil rights legislation, it had to be proven that people with disabilities suffered prolonged discrimination and abuse based on the fact that they were disabled.

For instance, there was a time in history when people who had disabilities were kept prisoners in "asylums" with names such as the Connecticut "Asylum for the Education and Instruction of Deaf and Dumb Persons" and the "Hospital of Idiots, Lunatics, and Other People of Unsound Mind" in Virginia. Many states in America had "ugly laws" which stated that "any person who is diseased or deformed…so as to be a disgusting object…shall not expose himself to public view." People with disabilities were sterilized under state laws that legalized forced sterilization of those considered "feeble-minded, defectives, or idiots." In addition, it wasn't until 1975 that U.S. law required that children with disabilities be educated. Before that time, only 1 in 5 children with disabilities received an education.

Even higher education is not free from the history of disability discrimination. In August of 1962, during the same time that James Meredith sued to enter the University of Mississippi, a man named Ed Roberts, who became disabled at the age of 14 due to polio, sued the University of California Berkley for admission. Even though he met the admission criteria, Mr. Roberts' application was denied because of his disability. The University's reason for the denial? "We tried cripples once. It didn't work." Like James Meredith, Ed Roberts was only able to gain admission after much resistance and reluctance.

Twenty-seven years after the passage of the ADA, disability-related disparities continue to affect this population of Americans. In 2013, only 31.9% of adult Americans with disabilities were in the workforce compared to 63.5% of adult Americans without disabilities. Poverty rates for these two populations also are starkly different. In 2014, 28.5% of adults with disabilities were living under the poverty line. During that same year, only 12.3% of adults without disabilities were living under the poverty line.

Educational disparities also fall along the disabled/non-disabled line. In 2014, 20.9% of 24 year olds with a disability did not have a high school diploma. During that same year, only 7% of non-disabled 24 year olds did not have a high school diploma. College degree at-

Student Activity – Part 1

Imagine you are sitting in the Student Union and you see a student walking into the building. He walks unevenly and seems to have a lack of coordination and balance. You notice that he holds his hands in a rigid, uncomfortable way and that he has unusual facial movements. His phone rings and when he answers you hear that his voice and speech patterns are difficult to understand.

What is the first word you think of?

by Stacey Reycraft

tainment rates are equally discouraging with only 13.5% of people with a disability receiving a bachelor's degree or higher, compared to 34% for those without a disability.

According to a 2009 report from the United States Government Accountability Office, at least 10 percent of college students nationwide identify as having a disability. This number has increased with the passage of the ADA Amendments Act of 2009, which broadened the definition of disability. It is estimated that 11 − 15 percent of all college students may now identify as having a disability. Disability can include, but is not limited to "visible disabilities" such as mobility issues, blind/low vision, and deaf/hard of hearing and "invisible disabilities" such as chronic illnesses, learning disorders, ADHD, neurological disorders, and mental health issues.

Perceptions of Disability

The Merriam-Webster Dictionary defines perception as "the way you think about or understand someone or something." Our perception of someone or something impacts our behavior towards, expectations of, and understanding about that person or thing. Perceptions about disability can significantly impact how societies and individuals interact with those who have disabilities.

One way of identifying our perceptions of disability and how those perceptions impact our interactions with people who have disabilities is by using a Model of Disability as a guide or tool. These Models help define disability and the meaning of a person's disability as it relates to society as a whole. Models of Disability serve to provide a blueprint for how government policy makers, the medical establishment, social assistance organizations, and individuals should meet the needs of people with disabilities. The two most common Models of Disability are the Medical Model and the Social Model.

The Medical Model of Disability views disability-related limitations as caused solely by the disability itself. For instance, if someone in a wheelchair is not able to enter a building because of a stairway leading to the entrance, the Medical Model views this barrier as being a problem with the wheelchair instead a problem with the stairway. Through this model, focus is on finding a "cure" and providing treatment. Under the Medical Model, people with disabilities are expected to adjust to the limitations caused by the dis-

Student Activity – Part 2

Let's go back to our student activity. What was the word that you thought of when you imagined the student with cerebral palsy who walked into the Union talking on his phone? This word represents your perception of disability. Now which model of disability is represented by your perception?

Common words that people use when they see someone with a disability include helpless, broken, victim, sad, weak, abnormal, tragic, and incapable. These words characterize a Medical Model perception of disability. In contrast, disability-related perceptions that characterize the Social Model of disability use words such as normal, ambitious, intelligent, capable, funny, independent, healthy, and human. *Which Model of Disability does your perception fall under?*

ability and to change their behavior accordingly. The Medical Model sees disability as something that is broken and needs to be fixed. Within the Medical Model is a sub-model called the **Charity Model of Disability.** This model views those with disabilities as tragic victims who should be pitied and taken care of by others. Both the Medical Model and the Charity Model of Disability are paternalistic in nature and assume that others know what is best for the person with the disability.

The Social Model of Disability views disability-related limitations as caused by the relationship of the person to the environment. In the previous example, the Social Model of disability would view the barrier as resulting from the stairway and not the wheelchair. With this model, disability is a result of poorly constructed physical, social, and policy-related environments which limit or prevent the full participation of people with disabilities. The Social Model of disability is inclusive in nature and encourages pro-active, mindful planning and adjustments that allow the full participation of people with disabilities. This model was created by those with disabilities in a reaction to the lack of opportunities, choice, and self-determination provided under the Medical Model of disability. It views disability as a social justice issue because of preventable physical, policy, and attitudinal barriers that cause limited access to employment, education, housing, and other activities that are easily available to those without disabilities. While the Medical Model sees those with disabilities as dependent on society, the Social Model sees them as customers who have a right to access all that society has to offer.

Disability Etiquette

Many people hesitate to interact with those who have disabilities because they have no experience in doing so. They are unsure of how to approach someone with a disability or what to say. They feel self-conscious, uncomfortable or awkward, afraid of doing or saying the wrong thing. There also may be discomfort because seeing someone with a disability forces us to acknowledge our own fears of losing movement, independence, relationships, and the ability to do what we want. It forces us to face the delicate nature of life and how abruptly things can change. These feelings are normal, especially if someone has had limited or no interaction with someone who has a disability.

Below are some general tips that may help alleviate some of the discomfort that may occur when interacting with someone who has a disability. It is critical to remember that each person with a disability is an individual. Even those who have the same disability will be impacted differently and will have different life experiences, just like those without disabilities.

1. **Use Person-First Language.** While people with disabilities do have individual preferences regarding how they like to be addressed, until you know someone well enough to know their preference, always use person-first language. Refer to someone as "a person with a disability." Avoid the term "disabled person." If you know the person's diagnosis and it is important to the discussion, you can use that as well. For instance, someone diagnosed with autism should be referred to as "a person with autism" instead of an "autistic person."

2. **Be Careful with Terminology.** Terms such as crippled, crazy, lame, retarded, and deaf and dumb are outdated and are considered to be offensive when used to de-

scribe a person. Be cognizant of the terminology used when talking with or about a person with a disability. The word "handicapped" is used only for the physical environment, such as "handicapped parking" or "handicap door." Never use the word handicapped to describe a person. Also, many people with disabilities dislike euphemistic terms such as "differently abled" or "physically challenged." Never use "wheelchair bound" or "confined to a wheelchair." These terms suggest that the person is restrained or imprisoned in some way. In actuality, a wheelchair is a source of independence and freedom for a person who has difficulty with mobility. Instead, use "wheelchair user." Terminology has powerful implications so it is important to think carefully about what you are saying.

3. Don't Try and Help Unless Asked. People assume that someone with a disability automatically needs help of some kind. In reality, people with disabilities can usually get around and function perfectly fine. And more importantly, just like anyone else, a person with a disability will ask if help is needed. Adults with disabilities are adults, and they are fully capable of knowing when and if they need assistance.

4. Be Aware of Physical Contact. Some people with disabilities may need physical assistance in getting around, such as someone who is blind or has cerebral palsy. However, don't grab them even if you are just trying to help. Someone who is blind needs your arm as a guide and will measure his or her footsteps, speed, and direction by yours. Grabbing the arm of someone who is blind can disrupt coordination and balance. Allow the person take your arm. Grabbing someone with cerebral palsy also can cause difficulty with balance so again, allow the person to take your arm so he or she can control balance. Never touch a wheelchair, scooter or other mobility device because those who use them consider them to be part of their personal space. Also, never pet or feed a service animal without first asking the handler if it is okay. Service animals are working animals, and if you pet or feed them you can cause them to lose focus. A service animal must be able to concentrate on its job.

5. Be Respectful When Communicating. It shows respect for a person if you look directly at him or her when speaking. The same is true of people with disabilities. Always speak directly to the person with the disability. Never speak through the family member or friend who might be with the person with the disability. Never speak through the sign language interpreter. And never speak with the service animal (yes, sadly this happens!). Talk to the person as you would anyone else. Respect his or her privacy the same way you would anyone else. In other words, treat the person with a disability normally, as you would anyone else.

6. Never Assume Anything. People with disabilities know what they can or cannot do. Like people without disabilities, they have individual strengths, weaknesses, interests, talents, and needs. Don't assume that you know what they are capable or not capable of doing or how well they may or may not function in a particular situation. People with disabilities have the right to succeed or fail, just like everyone else. They deserve the opportunity to do so. Don't make decisions for someone with a disability without asking first.

7. Be Gracious Regarding Requests. If a person with a disability asks for assistance or for an accommodation it means that he or she feels comfortable doing so. This is a

positive thing, and your assistance will be appreciated. Conversely, do not be offended if you offer assistance and your offer is declined. This just means the person does not need assistance or prefers to handle the task independently.

Disability and the University of Mississippi

The University of Mississippi follows federal law and supports any qualified student with a disability who wants an opportunity to receive an education at our institution. Many offices collaborate on issues of access for students with disabilities. The Office of Student Disability Services provides direct classroom accommodations for qualified students; Facilities

Management and Facilities Planning manage accessibility of the built environment; the Center for Inclusion and Cross-Cultural Engagement ensures that disability is included in the University's diversity efforts; and Student Housing provides access to campus housing. In addition, faculty and staff work diligently on issues of access.

The University recognizes disability as a vital component of social justice, inclusion, and diversity and strives to ensure equitable and usable campus environments of all types, including physical, educational, and social. Most importantly, the University embraces the uniqueness and dignity of each individual person in accordance with the Creed.

REFERENCES

A Comprehensive time-line: isc.temple.edu/neighbor/ds/disabilityrightstimeline.htm

Institute of Education Sciences: ies.ed.gov/

Income and Poverty in the United States 2014, retrieved from census.gov

Lives Worth Living PBS Documentary pbs.org/independents/lives-worth-living/
    Nielson, K. E. (2012). *A Disability History of the United States (Revising American History)*. Boston, Massachusetts: Beacon Press.

Roberts, E. Independent Living USA, retrieved from ilusa.com/links/022301ed_roberts.htm

Schweik, S. M. (2009). *The Ugly Laws: Disability in Public*. New York and London: NYU Press.

United Spinal Association. "Disability Etiquette: tips on Interacting with People with Disabilities," retrieved from united-spinal.org

VonSchrader, S. L. and Lee, C. G. (2015). Disability Statistics from the Current Population Survey (CPS). Ithaca, NY: Cornell University Employment and Disability Institute (EDI). Retrieved from disabilitystatistics.org

About the Author

Stacey Reycraft, *Director of Student Disability Services*

Stacey Reycraft has been at the University of Mississippi since August of 1987, first as a student and then as a staff member. She is currently enrolled in the higher education Ed.D. program and works on issues of disability at the university level as well as state and federal levels.

Hotty Toddy and Other Traditions

By Seph Anderson and Thomas Reardon

The Alma Mater

The Alma Mater of the University of Mississippi is a beautiful song that has been sung and played at athletic events, commencement ceremonies, the inauguration of chancellors, funerals and memorial ceremonies, class reunions, and other special events. The song has great meaning and is held sentimental by alumni of the University. It was written in 1925 by Mrs. A. W. Kahle and her husband.

When the Alma Mater is played, there should be an attitude of respect. Those in attendance should stand, remove hats or caps, and sing the words.

The Alma Mater

Way down south in Mississippi, There's a spot that ever calls
Where among the hills enfolded, Stand old Alma Mater's halls.
Where the trees lift high their branches, To the whisp'ring southern breeze.
There Ole Miss is calling, calling, To our hearts' fond memories.
With united hearts we praise thee, All our loyalty is thine,
And we hail thee, Alma Mater, May thy light forever shine;
May it brighter grow and brighter, And with deep affection true,
Our thoughts shall ever cluster 'round thee, Dear Old Red and Blue.
May thy fame throughout the nation, Through thy sons and daughters grow,
May thy name forever waken, In our hearts a tender glow,
May thy counsel and thy spirit, Ever keep us one in this,
That our own shall be thine honor, Now and ever dear Ole Miss.

The Legend of Hotty Toddy

Nothing may be more shrouded in uncertainty than the origins of Ole Miss's Hotty Toddy cheer.

The first print appearance of the cheer surfaced in a 1926 *Mississippian*, but the true origin of the famous school cheer has no such definite beginnings.

In 1931, an Ole Miss music professor named Arleen Tye wrote a spirited song ap-

Hoddy Toddy is much more than a cheer to Ole Miss fans.

Heighty! Tighty!

Gosh A Mighty!

Who in the hell are we?

Rim! Ram! Flim! Flam!

Ole Miss, by Damn

propriately titled "Ole Miss." Important to note is that the song's chorus was, "Hi-ty Ti-ty Gosh a'mighty, Who the heck are we?"

While parts of the chorus are similar to today's version of Hotty Toddy, the remainder of Tye's "Ole Miss" doesn't make as much of a connection.

Ole Miss historian Gerald W. Walton poses a potential connection to World War II by suggesting, "Many associate the cheer with one used during World War II. Battle Cry and Band of Brothers contained versions of: Highty, Tighty, Christ almighty, Who the hell are we? Zim Zam, god damn, We're airborne infantry."

However, quite possibly the strongest and most logical connection actually stems from another university, Virginia Tech. Specifically, the Virginia Tech Regimental Band which began to be called the Highty-Tighties in 1919:

How did the cadet band come to be known as the "Highty-Tighties?" The cadet band website suggests:

> The origin of the name has been hotly debated for years — some claimed it was part of a cheer, others claimed it sprang from a trip to Richmond where the Corps and Band marched in honor of Field Marshal Foch, the supreme allied commander of WW-I. Supposedly the drum major had dropped and then recovered his baton while rendering a salute in front of the reviewing stand and someone in the crowd yelled hoity-toity. Southwest Virginia slang had supposedly turned this into Highty-Tighty. Like many legends there are bits and pieces of factual information from several events woven into a story — but the accepted story is, that just like "Hokie" began as part of a cadet cheer, so too, the name "Highty-Tighty" began as part of a cadet cheer.

As for that cadet band cheer, suggested to have come from a cheer when the band was housed in Division E of Lane Hall, cadet sources claim it originally went something like this:

Highty-Tighty! Christ Almighty!
Who the hell are we?
Rip, Ram, God Damn!
We're from Division E!

In all likelihood, the well-known Ole Miss cheer we know today developed over the years from several of these potential origins. In the end, it's the mythical nature of the cheer that adds to its legend.

Let's Call Them the Rebels

In a 1929 student-only contest by the *Mississippian* to name the team, Ole Miss student Dick McCool suggested the team be called the "Flood," in reference to the 1927 Mississippi River flood. After reviewing an estimated 800 student entries, the contest committee decided to go with the "Flood."

However, the new team name simply didn't catch on in the years that followed.

Having been referred to as the "Mighty Mississippians," "Flood," "Red and Blue" and "The Southerners" for periods of time prior to the program's first bowl appearance in the 1936 Orange Bowl, head coach Ed Walker was looking for a strong team name to further establish the program's presence on a national stage.

A major reason behind Walker's insistence was likely the name by which one sportswriter had casually referred to the Ole Miss team.

David Sansing notes in *The University of Mississippi: A Sesquicentennial History:*

> After an unimaginative sportswriter referred to the Ole Miss football team as the "Mudcats," the student newspaper decided it was time for another contest and a new name. In the 1936 contest, a committee of sportswriters selected the name Rebels, which was submitted by Ben Guider of Vicksburg. The name was a natural and quickly captured the imagination of Ole Miss students, fans, friends, alumni, and sportswriters.

The five finalist options put before the sportswriters through *Mississippian* sports editor Billy Gates' poll, were the Confederates, Ole Miss, Raiders, Rebels, and Stonewalls. In the end, Rebels received 18 votes, Raiders received two votes and Ole Miss received one vote.

Ever since that momentous final vote, University of Mississippi squads have been called the Rebels.

Did you know?

John Z. Kiss, former dean of the University of Mississippi Graduate School, is the recipient of NASA's Outstanding Public Leadership Medal. The prestigious honor recognizes nongovernment employees for notable leadership accomplishments that have significantly influenced the NASA mission.

James "Blind Jim" Ivy – "Perpetual Dean of Freshman Class"

The legend of James "Blind Jim" Ivy at Ole Miss began back in 1896, a mere three years after Bondurant coached the school's first football team. However, the peanut vendor's legend was actually born at an Ole Miss Baseball game. Losing to the University of Texas, Ivy began to loudly cheer for the Rebels. Come the end of the game, Ole Miss had prevailed, and Ivy was credited for helping to rally the red and blue.

From that day forward, Ivy would be an integral part of the campus fabric.

Called the "Perpetual Dean of the Freshman Class" for his close affiliation and care for the freshman class each year, he was known to give an opening address to the freshmen each fall and to lead the pajama parade, among other contributions.

Alongside a picture of Blind Jim with the freshman class, the 1924 *Ole Miss* states, "For over thirty years he has been one of the truest and most optimistic Ole Miss supporters. His courage is inspiring, and the spirit with which he has cheered the team has many times given heart to the weak and encouraged us to fight to the finish even though it were a losing one."

Blind Jim would remain a mainstay on the Ole Miss campus for nearly sixty years. Primarily a peanut vendor on campus for decades until a single food service company assumed all such duties in 1931, Ivy was considered one of the most loyal and truest Rebel supporters.

As much as Ivy cared for the University, its students and athletic teams, the feeling was mutual.

Dr. Gerald Walton writes in *The University of Mississippi: A Pictorial History*:

> In 1936, when he (Ivy) was about to lose his home to foreclosure, students and alumni raised about $425 to help him. In 1955, Ivy became too ill to attend Homecoming. A committee was formed to see to his needs; they raised more than $1,100, later used to pay for his medical and burial expenses.
>
> When Ivy died October 20 of that year, the *Daily Mississippian* ran a huge front-page banner headline and news story. Because he had gained celebrity status by then, several regional newspapers also reported the news of his passing, along with history. His memorial service at Second Baptist Church in Oxford, an all-black church, was a precedent-shattering integrated affair attended by more than five hundred people. The crowd was so large that many people could not even get in the door. The headline in the Oxford Eagle the next day read, "Blind Jim Mourned by Both Races."

Moreover, an entire page in the 1955 *The Ole Miss* is dedicated to the fervent Rebel.

Ivy is quoted as famously saying, "I've been following the Rebels for 50 years and I have never seen them lose a ball game yet." The dedication goes on to read, "Everyone who comes to Ole Miss knows Jim, and more than likely, if you have ever talked to him he will remember you also. He is known all over the United States for his undying loyalty for the Rebels. When things are not going so good for us out on the field, it is Jim who is the first to give a rousing Rebel yell and raise the Ole Miss spirit again."

Did you know?

Ole Miss grad Stephen Johnston was CEO of SmartSynch — a technology company that may change the way electric utility companies and consumers use energy. SmartSynch has raised more than $100 million in venture capital — the most ever by a single entity in Mississippi.

Frank Everett quote

During your time at the University, you probably are going to walk into an office and see on the wall Frank Everett's quote about Ole Miss. You might notice it on the wall of the main staircase in the Union. Some of your friends might have it posted on their Facebook page. And, most likely, you will hear it quoted in a speech before you graduate.

Everett, a lawyer from Vicksburg, gave these remarks as part of his introduction of Chancellor Porter Fortune at an alumni event in 1971. It was so well received that it was published in the Sunday paper two days later.

The opening paragraph is most frequently quoted:

Did you know?

When film director and Ole Miss alum Tate Taylor acquired the dramatic rights to the novel, *The Help*, he had no idea it would hit the bestseller list. The $100 million production (filmed in 2010 in Mississippi) places Taylor among Hollywood's elite film directors.

There is a valid distinction between "The University" and "Ole Miss" even though the separate threads are closely interwoven. The University is buildings, trees, and people. Ole Miss is mood, emotion and personality. One is physical and the other is spiritual. One is tangible, and the other intangible. The University is respected, but Ole Miss is loved. The University gives a diploma and regretfully terminates tenure, but one never graduates from Ole Miss.

Gamedays in The Grove

While Ole Miss students, faculty, and staff enjoy a tranquil, serene Grove most of the year, on six or seven Saturdays each fall the Grove becomes the scene of the finest tailgating experience to be found on the planet.

The Grove is known as the premier site in the country for football tailgating. In fact, *Sports Illustrated* ranked it as #8 on the list of all-time best sports experiences.

Having been applauded by *The Sporting News* as "The Holy Grail of Tailgating" and by *Business Insider* as one of the "Top 50 Trips to take in the United States," the Grove has truly become a national tailgating treasure.

It is yet another part of what makes being an Ole Miss student so special. Where some people come to experience the Grove once in their lives and others come for a few games each fall, you're afforded the opportunity to enjoy the majestic natural landscape throughout the school year.

The Grove's not only the place you'll experience your first home football weekend as part of the Ole Miss Family, but it is also where you will sit during commencement when you graduate.

The Founding Father of the Grove: Chancellor Robert Burwell Fulton

Former Chancellor Robert Burwell Fulton, an alumnus himself, is the person responsible for first preserving and growing the 10-acre campus landscape. It all began in 1889, when work began on a campus library. While the library was being built, now known as Ventress Hall, a nearby wooden fence enclosed the "inner circle" of campus.

Did you know?

Ole Miss alum Larry Speakes (former editor of *The Daily Mississippian* and *The Oxford Eagle*) served as press secretary for President Ronald Reagan.

Not too long after the library was finished, as new Chancellor, Fulton had the temporary fencing removed and made the decision to advance the campus east in the direction of what was at the time the railroad and train depot. Not only did he extend the campus beyond the "inner circle," but he also decided to enhance the newly-included campus grounds by adding a variety of trees and shrubs to the area.

In the 1902 *Ole Miss*, University of Mississippi student S. Lamar Field wrote a fitting poem, "Our Campus," about the natural beauty of the campus Fulton helped grow:

The chilling blasts have passed us by:
The gentle Spring greets us with cheer;
A panorama fills the eye
That looks upon the views now here.

The artist's hand, so deft and skilled,
And with imagination's aid,
Were weak to please the soul that's thrilled
By beauty such as here is laid.

Though fancy's ideal high may be,
If bound by earth's or nature's views,
No grander sight her eye can see.
Nor grander scenes her wishes choose.

The pink horizon in the East
Is brightened by the rising sun;
The shadow of the night has passed.
A cheerful song of birds begun.

The grass an emerald carpet rare,
And rich with diamond dew-drops bright,
Aglow with brilliance everywhere,
Creates a most imposing sight.

The weeping willow's graceful bow
To huge, gigantic, stately oak,
Salutes the squirrel seated low
As he, in glee, chats with his folk.

The sky, a canopy of blue.
With grace, is bent above the scene;
The sun beholds the brilliant view
And smiles upon this plot of green.

At last, but greatest of it all.
The Co-Ed comes, so rare and bland;
Upon this scene dark shadows fall
And leave it for the artist's hand.

It's telling that more than 100 years after Field wrote "Our Campus," his words and description remain ever so true.

The 1899 *Ole Miss* contains an entry entitled "The Devil Knows," in which a student writes about being visited by spirits in the original University chapel (now the Croft Institute for International Studies). Having been used as a hospital during the Civil War, many students believed parts of the campus were haunted by those lost during war.

Particularly interesting, though, are the references made about the land between the chapel and old train station. The writer suggested:

Did you know?

Former Rebel All-American Michael Oher's early life was the subject of the book and blockbuster film, *The Blind Side*. But Oher still had more to tell. In 2011, his own memoir, *I Beat the Odds*, hit bookstores.

"Everyone who visits the University of Mississippi is struck with the beauty of the place. Perhaps June and October never find a more splendid situation for their gorgeous displays in all our picturesque Southland than within that sacred Grove of the goddess of wisdom. But those mighty forest trees and vine-clad buildings often wear a gruesome aspect under the shade of night that banishes all memory of their beauty by day.

The University chapel was used as a Confederate hospital during the Civil War, and within that building and the surrounding groves, the deadly misfortunes of that fatal strife were in ample and ghastly evidence. Perhaps some cool-headed student residing upon that campus to-day has never noticed the weird and uncanny influence which those historic groves exert by night. If such is the case, I would ask that student, bearing in mind the mournful war record of the place, to choose some dark, starless night, best of all midnight in October, when a low east wind is mourning among the treetops and the sere autumn leaves float slowly to the earth, whispering vaguely the while, - choose such a night as this, and take a walk all alone around the chapel building and on down through those dark woods past the Dead House in the direction of the railroad depot."

The reference to "mighty forest trees and vine-clad buildings," along with the suggestion that students "walk all alone around the chapel building and on down through those dark woods past the Dead House in the direction of the railroad depot," almost assuredly refers to the area now known as the Grove.

The Glade Becomes The Grove

While the earliest of *Ole Miss* yearbooks reveal information that suggest the Grove has long been known as the "Grove," a photo in the 1928 *Ole Miss* shot behind the then-Law building and towards the train depot is entitled "The Ancient Law Building, From The Glade."

Whether referred to as the Grove or the Glade through the early 1930s, a photo in the 1935 *Ole Miss* shows a backdrop of the grassy plot labeled "The Grove." Moreover, the 1996 annual states, "In 1935, the Grove gets its name." Regardless of what faculty, staff, students, and locals called the 10-acre green spot, by 1935 the Grove or Glade would officially become the "Grove." It's remained the same ever since.

Did you know?

The new Center for Inclusion and Cross-Cultural Engagement was created to provide programs and services that encourage cross-cultural interactions and provide a physical space that is both nurturing and welcoming for students from diverse backgrounds.

Tribute to Chancellor Fulton's Vision

The 1907 *Ole Miss* yearbook was dedicated in Fulton's honor and proclaimed:

> And may these words sincerely show
> The love, the pride that men have failed
> At times to feel when power paled
> And greatness moved at ebb and flow
>
> You loved these trees, these walks, this life;
> You gave for them unswerving work
> And untold thought which in them lurk;
>
> That dares to scar this pulsing heart
> Of Mississippi. Broad and brave.
> You made it; drove in calm the wave
> That washed it safe in every part.
>
> It speaks in us, tho' some may chide;
> It speaks in us, tho' some may complain;
> It speaks in us one word not vain –
> It speaks the love no heart can hide.

It is remarkable that an alumnus, chancellor, and most importantly an individual who showed great affinity and love for the University of Mississippi is responsible for the Grove as it's known today. Well before tailgating in the Grove would even first take shape in the 1950s, Fulton's students knew their leader was doing something great.

The Beginnings of a Tailgating Tradition

Prior to the 1950s, tailgating and gameday camaraderie among students largely took place at fraternity and sorority houses on campus. However, legendary head coach John H. Vaught helped ignite a football frenzy at Ole Miss after his inaugural season at the helm in 1947.

In that season with the red and blue in 1947, Vaught's team won the school's first SEC Championship and claimed the school's first bowl game victory in the Delta Bowl, among other accomplishments. While there is not a specific year or game in which tailgating first took root in the Grove, there's no question the early successes of Vaught and Ole Miss

First-Team All-Americans tailback Charlie Conerly, end Barney Poole, fullback Kayo Dottley, and quarterback Jimmy Lear, amped up football excitement.

Come the 1950s, gameday crowds grew, and cars, trucks, and RVs began to park in the Grove for a true "tailgate" picnic alongside throngs of other fans on campus to watch the upstart Rebels. Patrons popped open their trunks, unfolded their card tables, opened their picnic baskets and coolers, and simply enjoyed the atmosphere of gameday in the Grove.

Tailgating in the Grove would continue over the next couple of decades until vehicles descended upon a rain-soaked Grove to tailgate before the October, 26 1991 homecoming game against Vanderbilt. With cars, trucks, and RVs having driven all over the grounds that afternoon, the Grove had been turned into nothing more than a muddy mess.

While vehicles first parked in the Grove to tailgate out of necessity to accommodate growing gameday crowds, it was clear to University officials that the Grove was beginning to suffer as a result of hosting so many vehicles.

Ahead of the very next home game in what had been another rainy week in Oxford, a decision was made by University administraters to no longer allow vehicles to be parked in the Grove.

More than twenty years later, that decision has turned out to be a wise one, as tens of thousands of college football fans now descend upon the Grove each time the Rebels play at home. From the rush of people setting up their tents and tailgating equipment beginning at 9:00 p.m. on Friday nights, to Ole Miss students donning their Sunday best for an afternoon in the Grove, gameday in the Grove has become a major affair.

Examining the Grove Grounds

In terms of specific types of grass in the Grove, the two predominant grasses are tall fescue and Bermuda 419. In noting the diverse climate and shade of various areas in the Grove, Landscape Services' website states:

"Generally, Landscape Services uses a tall fescue blend that can handle the deep shade of the Grove as well as the hot summer heat. Although tall fescue is a cool season grass and does great in the spring and fall, it does a fair job in deep shade if kept moist during the summer. Also, Bermuda 419 is used in full sun areas in the Grove."

As of early 2014, there were in excess of 150 trees in the Grove and some 75 in the neighboring Circle.

A variety of oak species are far and away the most prevalent in both areas. Specific to the Grove, the two most prevalent species of oak are the willow oak, followed by the water oak. It only takes a quick look above to notice the immense size of so many Grove trees. While willow oaks can near 130 feet at maturity, water oaks only grow to around 90 feet.

Many of the larger oaks likely were planted in the early part of the twentieth century,

Did you know?

Journalism alum Curtis Wilkie worked as a correspondent for the *Boston Globe* for 26 years. He is the author of several award-winning works of nonfiction, including *The Fall of the House of Zeus*. He now serves as the inaugural Overby Fellow at the Overby Center for Southern Journalism and Politics.

meaning there is only so much longer the stately trees have to live. The next time you walk through the Grove on your way to class, look to the sky to appreciate the towering beauty.

New trees continue to be planted that will grow larger in time, but unfortunately there's no way to replace aging trees that have helped give the Grove indistinguishable character. One day, they'll be gone.

Protecting and Preserving the Grove

In 1983, a student group called "Save the Grove" made efforts to preserve the Grove from damage being caused by revelers pulling their vehicles into the Grove to tailgate. Just one year earlier in 1982, tailgating in the Grove had been ruled off limits entirely while a lengthy landscaping project took place.

Ahead of tailgaters arriving for the Memphis State game in 1983, their first time tailgating since the Grove was ruled off limits during the previous season, members of "Save the Grove" went out and strategically laid blankets around trees in the Grove to try and keep vehicles away.

A few years later, the senior class of 1986 made its class project "Preserve the Grove." Among several different fundraising efforts, members of the class charged five dollars to everyone who wanted to park and tailgate in the Grove.

Finally, as previously mentioned, vehicles were forbidden in the Grove following the muddy mess that was created when tailgaters parked in an extremely wet Grove during the 1991 Vanderbilt game.

Today, the Green Grove Initiative through the University of Mississippi Office of Campus Sustainability is doing its part to keep the Grove green. Founded in 2009, during each home game student volunteers walk from tent to tent with Green Grove recycling trash bags and encourage tailgaters to do their part to keep the Grove green.

UM Landscape Services shares the following gameday facts and figures:

Landscape Services places 500 thirty-five gallon plastic waste cans and approximately 200 cardboard boxes in the 11-acre Grove and Circle areas on the day before each home game.

More than 200 additional fifty-five gallon barrels are placed around the campus perimeter to assist with refuse demand.

An additional 12 to 30 dumpsters (20 or 30 yards each) are placed on campus to remove all waste that is generated in the Grove and around campus.

In 2012, Landscape Services removed a total of 489 tons of waste from the Grove.

This is the equivalent of 16 M4 Sherman tanks (30 tons). The Central Arkansas game produced 42 tons of waste while the Texas game produced 87 tons. The 87 tons removed from the Texas game is greater than the weight of an empty space shuttle (82.5 tons).

The collective efforts of these groups are clearly helping keep the Grove clean and green, so that the treasured campus space may continue to be enjoyed for decades to come.

The Walk of Champions

In the heart of the Grove lies the affectionately-named "Walk of Champions," a brick-paved path beginning near the Ole Miss Student Union and crossing through the Grove.

Upon being hired as head coach in 1983, Billy Brewer began walking with his players from the old athletics dorm (Kinard Hall) across campus to the stadium before every home game. While the Rebels' Saturday strolls to the stadium were first comprised of different game day routes, the path Brewer took with his team beginning in 1985 would become a Saturday staple.

Looking for a way to try and include his coaches and players in the pre-game revelry of the Grove on game day, Brewer felt leading his coaches and players through the fan-frenzied Grove would add to the players' game day experience. The players, coaches, and fans alike enjoyed the atmosphere, and a new game-day tradition was born.

Approximately two hours before kickoff at every home game, Ole Miss team buses pull up alongside the Walk of Champions entrance to the cheers of thousands of fans. Those lucky enough to stand alongside the actual brick-path get to do more than just watch coaches and players make their way through the crowd. The path-side patrons get the opportunity to reach out and high-five their coaches and players.

Named in honor of the 1962 undefeated, national champion Ole Miss Rebels, experiencing the Walk of Champions on a Saturday has become a time-honored tradition in the Grove.

The Pride of The South

Just over an hour after fans have cheered Ole Miss coaches and players traveling down the Walk of Champions, there is another game day experience in the Grove.

Nestled just steps behind Ventress Hall inside the Grove, in an area surely to have been part of that which Fulton had fenced off when the library was being built in 1899, the University of Mississippi Band, *The Pride of the South*, performs its pregame medley in an area to the right of the Grove stage.

Children are perched on trees, toddlers sit atop their fathers' shoulders, and all within sight of the band squeeze together to take in the sights and sounds. It's the perfect culmination to pre-game in the Grove.

Initially formed as merely a small, student-led campus organization, the University of Mississippi Band became an official institutional organization in 1928. That year, Chancellor Alfred Hume selected Roy Coates to be the first Director of Bands to serve with faculty status.

Interestingly, the UM Band website suggests, "Coates's initial marching band used instruments, uniforms, and equipment donated by the National Guard. Not until 1934 did the Rebel Band own full dress uniforms, purchased by funds solicited by the general student body."

Crimson of Harvard and Navy Blue from Yale

So how did Ole Miss's colors become red and blue? When Ole Miss began playing football in 1893 and was training to play five games that year, the players discussed what colors to wear. According to Dr. A. L. Bondurant, the first coach of Ole Miss football, one of the managers spoke up and noted "that the union of the Crimson of Harvard and the Navy Blue of Yale would be very harmonious and that it was well to have the spirit of both of these good colleges." From that day forward, Ole Miss's colors have been red and blue.

The Ole Miss colors are a union of Harvard Crimson and Yale Navy Blue.

Eternally Undefeated, No. 38 Chucky Mullins

The legacy of Ole Miss Rebel Roy Lee "Chucky" Mullins is as rich and storied as any that preceded or may follow him at the University.

The legend of "Chucky" began in Russellville, Alabama.

Having lost his mother at a young age and without a father in his life, Mullins was raised by family friend and local recreational center worker Carver Phillips and his wife. Under the excellent care of the Phillipses, Chucky would make a name for himself growing up as an athlete in Russellville.

When Ole Miss Head Coach Billy Brewer offered Mullins a football scholarship, little did he or anyone else on the Ole Miss campus know what type of impact the exuberant young man and athlete would have on the place he loved so much.

Redshirted his freshman year, No. 38 Chucky made it his mission to show coaches just what he was capable of doing on the football field. The next season as a sophomore, Mullins began to make a name for himself and found playing time on both special teams and defense.

On October 28, 1989, the Rebels hosted Vanderbilt for Homecoming on a beautiful fall day in Oxford. However, spirits on the Ole Miss campus would quickly turn grim when Chucky failed to get up after what initially appeared to be a routine defensive collision.

A stunned crowd at Vaught-Hemingway Stadium sat in silence as Mullins didn't pop back up after the play. Something was wrong, very wrong. Mullins was taken off the field on a stretcher to the local hospital before being airlifted to a hospital in Memphis. It was there that it was revealed the Rebel had shattered four vertebrae in his cervical spine. It was a daunting discovery for a young man just hours earlier so full of life.

After undergoing operations and spending 114 days in the hospital, Mullins was transferred to the Spain Rehabilitation Center in Birmingham where he underwent extensive rehabilitation work. Never down or discouraged, the upbeat young man was determined to return to the Ole Miss campus to earn his degree and to be back around his teammates.

As is chronicled in Micah Ginn's film, *Undefeated: The Chucky Mullins Story*, one of the highlights of both Mullins's and his team's time following the devastating injury came at the 1989 Liberty Bowl in Memphis.

It was in the tunnel of the Liberty Bowl that Mullins was brought in and wheeled off the ambulance to wish his teammates well against Air Force, and memorably stated, "It's Time" before every Rebel in shouting distance erupted in cheer.

Mullins returned to Oxford in 1990 and began taking classes again in the spring of 1991. His undefeated spirit served as daily inspiration to both Ole Miss students he would visit with on campus and certainly his teammates. Things were as back to normal as he could have hoped, and Chucky was happy.

Sadly, on the morning of May 1, 1991, he stopped breathing and was immediately rushed to the hospital where he would pass away only days later from a blood clot.

While his time on earth and with his Ole Miss teammates and family had ended, the "never quit" attitude that defined the spirited competitor and human being would live on.

Today, Chucky's spirit remains alive and well at Ole Miss. Since 1990, a leader on the Rebel defense has been selected each year by coaches to receive the Chucky Mullins Courage Award. Additionally, the award winner receives the honor of wearing Mullins's No. 38 during the upcoming season.

While No. 38 was retired in 2006, and no player wore the jersey through the 2010 season, the retired number made its way back onto the jersey of the award winner beginning in 2011 and every year since.

Today, Ole Miss coaches and players are reminded of Mullins's legacy and can-do attitude during each home game as they touch the Chucky Mullins statue above the inscription "Never Quit" when entering and leaving the locker room.

The Ole Miss Creed

As the University approached the year 2000, there was discussion among Chancellor Robert Khayat and others about the development of a creed for the University. A committee of students, faculty, staff, alumni, and community members was appointed, and it undertook the task of writing a statement that succinctly explained what the University believed. After consulting the University of South Carolina about The Carolinian Creed, the task force held focus groups with campus, University, and local constituencies. More than 1,500 persons participated in lengthy, sometimes intense, discussions about what Ole Miss valued and believed.

After the committee reviewed the information provided by the first focus groups, another round of discussions was conducted. The initial draft was presented to the Chancellor and the Executive Management Council in late 2002, and in 2003, the University of Mississippi officially adopted *The Ole Miss Creed*.

The Ole Miss Creed is the standard by which members of the University community attempt to live. Since its adoption, it has been used as a basis for discussion in trying times and often is used by instructors in classroom situations. The senior class of 2005 left as its class memorial The Ole Miss Creed monument in front of the Lyceum.

The Ole Miss Creed

The University of Mississippi is a community of learning dedicated to nurturing excellence in intellectual inquiry and personal character in an open and diverse environment.
As a voluntary member of this community:
I believe in respect for the dignity of each person.
I believe in fairness and civility.
I believe in personal and professional integrity.
I believe in academic honesty.
I believe in academic freedom.
I believe in good stewardship of our resources.
I pledge to uphold these values and encourage others to follow my example.

The University Memorial Ceremony

In 2008, Chancellor Khayat issued a proclamation that designated "University Memorial Day" would be observed on the last Thursday of classes of the spring semester. As with any community, the University is saddened by the loss of one of its members. At the end of the work day on University Memorial Day, the University community gathers in Paris-Yates Chapel for a ceremony to remember those who have died in the past calendar year. Those remembered include students, faculty, staff, faculty/staff emeriti, and special friends of Ole Miss.

During the ceremony, names of the deceased are read and friends or family members place a gardenia in water in their memory. The Peddle Carillon tolls once for each of those being remembered.

Rebel Run

Rebel Run is the latest of many game day traditions at Ole Miss where fans welcome freshmen to the campus by inviting them to a free game and the opportunity to run across the football field before kickoff. Each year, thousands of students participate in this exciting event.

Red, Blue, and Green

Chancellor Dan Jones signed the American College and University Presidents' Climate Commitment in 2014. Chancellor Khayat had first signed the agreement in 2008. The University of Mississippi also has become a LEED (Leadership in Energy and Environmental Design) campus and vigorously promotes sustainability efforts through programs of energy conservation and recycling, as well as sponsoring Green Week each Spring.

Rebel Black Bear

In the fall of 2009, students approached newly appointed Chancellor Jones with the idea of selecting a new mascot for Ole Miss athletic teams. Ole Miss had been without an official on-field mascot since 2003, when University officials decided to remove Colonel Rebel from the sidelines at athletic events. Ole Miss was the only school in the SEC without an identifiable mascot to represent its athletic teams. ASB President Artair Rogers and Cardinal Club President Peyton Beard, with the assistance of the student group One Mississippi, conducted a survey to see if students were interested in voting on whether or not they wanted to consider a new on-field mascot. In the ensuing referendum, more than 3,000 students voted, and an overwhelming 74 percent voted a resounding YES in support of a student-led effort to develop and propose a new on-field mascot that represented the spirit and energy of today's Ole Miss Rebels.

The Rebel Black Bear made his debut at the Blair Batson Children's Hospital at the University Medical Center in Jackson on April 5, 2011, and appeared on campus for the first time at the Ole Miss/Kentucky baseball game on April 16, 2011.

The Landshark Becomes Our Official Mascot

In September 2017, the Associated Student Body (ASB) sponsored a campus-wide student vote to determine whether or not there was student support for changing the school's mascot from the Black Bear to the Landshark.

More than 4100 Ole Miss students took part in the ASB poll, with 81% of student voters indicating they were in support of changing the University's official mascot to the Landshark. As a result, on October 6, 2017, Chancellor Jeffrey S. Vitter officially announced that the University would move forward with the Landshark as the school's official mascot.

The Landshark Legacy

At Ole Miss, Landshark is a term that was first adopted by the Rebel football team's defensive unit. As part of that identity, defensive players celebrate big plays by putting a hand to their forehead in the shape of a shark fin. A battle cry of "Fins Up" also contributes to the players' persona. With the popularity of both the players and the hand gesture, Ole Miss fans and student-athletes from other sports embraced the spirit of the Landshark, and in October 2017, the University announced the Landshark as the official mascot of the Ole Miss Rebels. The Landshark mascot is expected to be unveiled in advance of the 2018 football season.

Roots of the Landshark at Ole Miss date back to 2008. After four straight losing seasons, the Rebel football team returned to national prominence with a 9-4 record and a victory over 7th-ranked Texas Tech in the Cotton Bowl. Leading the charge was a defensive squad that ranked fourth in the nation in rushing defense and included All-American Peria Jerry and eventual All-SEC standout Jerrell Powe.

The term Landshark originated that season from senior linebacker Tony Fein, an Army veteran who served a one-year tour in the Iraq War before arriving in Oxford. A two-year letterman after transferring from Scottsdale (Ariz.) Community College, Fein was the 2008 recipient of the Pat Tillman Award by the Military Order of the Purple Heart. Fein passed away in October 2009, but his legacy at Ole Miss continues through the Landshark. olemisssports.com/trads/landshark.html

The Ole Miss Big Event

Service has been a part of the Ole Miss Community since the school's beginning in 1848. UMSFusion, an annual service event developed in 2003, gave students of the University of Mississippi an excellent opportunity to volunteer in the Oxford/Lafayette community. As this event continued to grow year after year, it became evident that the students of Ole Miss were committed to providing assistance and service to the members of the surrounding communities.

After visiting Texas A&M University in College Station, Texas, in 2010, student leaders and staff from Ole Miss were excited by the idea of a large-scale, one-day community service project similar to Texas A&M's "Big Event." Soon thereafter, the decision to take

service to the next level in Oxford and Lafayette County was made by the leaders of the ASB and the Division of Student Affairs. In Spring 2011, more than 1,200 students participated in the first Ole Miss Big Event. Braving wind, rain, and hail, students gathered in the Union to kick off the BIGGEST community service project in Ole Miss history. On March 31, 2012, in only the second year of the event, more than 3,000 students volunteered to work in 300 community projects to say, "Thank you Oxford and Lafayette County." In just a few years, The Ole Miss Big Event has become an important and valued tradition of the University and the surrounding community.

The Columns Society

Begun in 2008, The Columns Society is a group of 14 men and 14 women selected from the sophomore and junior classes to serve as the official student hosts for the University. The Society is based upon the principles of humble service, leadership, and integrity. The Columns Society serves the University of Mississippi at all functions where it is desired to have students welcome guests and visitors to our campus.

The Columns Society, coordinated by the Division of Student Affairs, provides services to the offices of the Chancellor, the Provost, the Vice Chancellor for Student Affairs, Athletics, Alumni, and Development.

Named after one of the prominent symbols at the University of Mississippi, the columns that support the Lyceum, The Columns Society seeks to advance the University of Mississippi through humble service. No opportunity to serve the University is considered too small. Membership in the Columns Society is highly selective and requires a significant commitment to serve Ole Miss, always with humility and integrity.

About the Authors

Seph Anderson, *Early Entry Program Academic Advisor for the School of Pharmacy*

Seph Anderson received his B.B.A. (marketing) and M.A. (higher education and student personnel) from the University of Mississippi. He served students and families in the Office of Financial Aid at Ole Miss for nearly a decade, before moving to the School of Pharmacy. Since 2008, he has taught a section of the First-Year Experience course, in which he is able to follow his passion for helping freshmen successfully transition from high school to college. Seph has written about Ole Miss Football, Oxford, and Ole Miss history in *RebelNation*, *Invitation Oxford*, *Experience Oxford*, *Bleacher Report*, and hottytoddy.com. Seph is a passionate Rebel football fan and enjoys spending time with his wife and two young daughters.

Thomas Reardon, *Dean of Students Emeritus*

Thomas Reardon worked in higher education for more than 30 years. Known to everyone at Ole Miss as 'Sparky,' Dean Reardon is retired.

Section I:
College Survival 101

Chapter 1
Ole Miss Doesn't Have Homeroom
by Leslie Banahan, Whitman Smith, and Katie Tompkins

Welcome to Ole Miss, and congratulations on choosing to take EDHE 105 or 305. We don't have homeroom, *in the traditional sense, or like most of you had in high school*, but the EDHE classes are intended to provide you with a home base where you feel comfortable asking questions, seeking answers, and expressing your concerns, desires, and accomplishments during your first year. These courses are designed to help you in your transition to the University, and we'll start by helping you develop some good habits that will serve you through college and beyond.

Five simple habits that lead to success

1. Go to class. Every day, go to class, even when it's hot, cold, raining, or snowing. Sure, you know this is important, but we remind you because every year there are students who don't go to class, and the results aren't good. Did you know, for instance, that you can fail a course based solely on poor attendance? Many professors require attendance and will lower final grades if students miss more than two or three classes. Will going to class guarantee you an A? No, but skipping class almost certainly guarantees that you will NOT earn an A.

Studies show that students who sit closer to the front of class simply make better grades.

Alternative Course Options.

For most of you, your first year of college is the first time in your life that you have been in control of your schedule, managed your own time, and exclusively made your own decisions about what you do throughout the day. The idea of NOT having to be in specific places at specific times can be intoxicating, and for some students, long mid-afternoon naps begin to feel like a necessity rather than a luxury. For other students, more personal time is an opportunity to work, have an internship, or engage in more student organizations.

In this brave new world, options such as online courses and independent study may seem like a perfect fit. When handled responsibly, they certainly can be. However, too often students jump into these type of courses without understanding the requirements and expectations, and what they envision as a surefire way to make a good grade without a regularly scheduled time commitment can end in disaster. Online and independent study courses are not recommended for freshmen, but if you consider this option later in your academic career, the following information will be helpful.

Online Courses

For most online classes, the majority of course content is available through the web, but there might be a required live element. Many online courses require proctored tests. A few even have a required online meeting in a virtual classroom or in a live classroom setting. Online learning is flexible and convenient, but it also is more challenging.

■ **Persistence.** Students who are successful in online courses are those willing to work through technical problems. They seek help and assistance when needed, keep a daily course work schedule, and continue through challenges. To help with persistence and avoid technical problems, confirm technical requirements and test your computer to make sure it works with all the online tools, and know who to contact for assistance with any issue you may have.

■ **Time-management and preparation.** Avoid procrastination by developing a plan of action for assignment completion and having a daily "to do" list. Read your course syllabus to create these lists. Schedule time for yourself to log in to your course two to three times a week and schedule study times and time for assignments/discussions.

■ **Communicate and connect.** Use communication tools built into Blackboard to communicate with your instructor. In the course syllabus, the instructor also will provide other ways to contact him or her. In traditional classes, instructors have visual cues and body language to know when a student is struggling. The online environment does not allow for these cues, so reach out. If you do not reach out, your instructor will not know. The same goes for your fellow classmates. Get to know your classmates, and create connections with them. The social tools and applications available today make building a learning community relatively easy.

■ **Motivation and independence.** To be successful in an online course, a student must be independent, self-motivated, disciplined, responsible, and mature.

■ **Appropriate study environment.** No matter the format of the course, whether it is online, hybrid, flipped, or traditional, every student needs a suitable study environment. Create your perfect study environment by locating a quiet space, avoiding games (consider uninstalling games on your computer), turning off your phone, and avoiding surfing the net or social media.

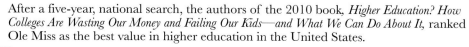

Did you know?

After a five-year, national search, the authors of the 2010 book, *Higher Education? How Colleges Are Wasting Our Money and Failing Our Kids—and What We Can Do About It,* ranked Ole Miss as the best value in higher education in the United States.

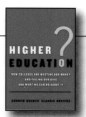

■ **Be active, be present.** Time-management plans of action and "to do" lists will help you be active and present in an online course. Professors teaching online courses expect students to log in to their online course two to three times a week. Check regularly for discussion posts, course announcements, course materials, and other important information. While checking for updates in your online course, get involved in a discussion and respond to your classmates' postings. This will enhance your learning experience and make you a more active member of that online community.

Independent Study

Most independent study (iStudy) courses are available online through Blackboard (Bb), but there are classes that are paper-based, with many courses available in both formats. Students enroll in iStudy courses by submitting a registration form, and lessons are submitted, graded, and returned to the student. The student must take a proctored midcourse test (some courses have two course exams) and then submit the remaining lessons. A final exam is given, and the student receives a grade for the course. Students typically have one year from the date of enrollment to complete the course but semester options are also available.

> **High School Versus College Classroom Hours Per Week**
>
> **High School 35 Hours**
>
> **College 12-15 hours**

When considering iStudy, remember:

- There are many restrictions and requirements placed on financial aid, and it is imperative that students using financial aid consult with the Financial Aid Office to determine eligibility, possible delayed aid disbursement, and completion deadline requirements. Do this before registering for an iStudy course.

- While the cost for each iStudy course is the same as in-state tuition for a three hour course, tuition is separate from standard tuition after 12 credit hours.

- iStudy courses require students to be self-motivated and good with time management. It is critical to keep moving ahead with readings and assignments. The course should be started as soon as you have your materials.

- Students must have approval from their academic dean's office to enroll in iStudy.

- Students are generally limited to two iStudy courses at one time. However, some academic areas further limit course enrollment, so you should always check with your academic advisor before planning to enroll in iStudy courses.

- If a student does not complete his or her course in one year, extensions may be given, but with additional costs.

Did you know?

Johnny Vaught is the only coach in Ole Miss history to win an SEC football championship. Three of his teams (1959, 1960, and 1962) won shares of the national championship, and Vaught's teams appeared in 14 straight post-season bowl games (a record at that time).

2. **Read your syllabus carefully and write down the important dates and deadlines in your planner.** It's a good idea to read each syllabus several times. There may be assignments in the syllabus that the instructor never mentions, which you are responsible for just the same. The syllabus is your road map to completing the course (your trip) successfully. After you have read it over a few times, highlight important assignments, deadlines, room changes, days you don't have class, etc. Next, get out your planner. Write the assignments from EVERY SYLLABUS in your planner. You might use different colors for different courses (red for math, blue for EDHE 105 or 305, green for history). When you are finished, you will be surprised how many assignments and tests hit at the same time. This is your clue to begin projects and papers well in advance of deadlines.

3. **Use a planner. Oh, you don't have a planner? GET ONE!** Many students use their phones or their laptops as planners. Certainly, this is better than nothing, but it is helpful to be able to see a week or even a month at a glance on something bigger than a phone screen. Writing it down, instead of typing it in, will help you remember and give you options for notes, questions, and diagrams that you may not have with an electronic device. (*Also, some instructors do not allow cell phones or laptops in class.*)

Ole Miss Support Tools

by Ty Allushuski and Mariana Rangel

Blackboard (Bb)

What exactly is Blackboard? It is a social media software tool used in many courses at the University of Mississippi. Blackboard allows instructors to post content for a course, including assignments, article links, attendance, grades, syllabus, videos, and announcements. Blackboard also accommodates blogs, discussion boards, and journals for teaching purposes.

Getting Started

You need an Internet browser to begin using Blackboard. Blackboard can be accessed via your University of Mississippi Web ID and password by visiting:

blackboard.olemiss.edu/

You also can find a link to Blackboard at the bottom of the Ole Miss Homepage. Your Web ID is the same as your University e-mail name (the part of your e-mail address before the "@" symbol). For example:

E-mail Address:	Web ID:
johndoe@go.olemiss.edu	johndoe

Once you have signed on to Blackboard, the my UM home page displays the following six default modules: My Announcements; My Courses; My Tasks; On Demand Help and Learning Catalog; Report Card; Tools. You can personalize which modules display by selecting Personalize Page on the upper right side of the home page.

My Courses

Click on an individual course in the My Courses module to display the course home page with six menu items on the left side of the webpage: Homepage; Content; Discussion; Groups; Tools; Help. Instructors for individual courses might choose to add additional menu options such as Assignments or Information, or give different names to the existing menu options.

Some features of the menu on the left include the ability to access and submit assignments, view the syllabus, view grades, and e-mail the instructor or other members of the class.

If you do not see your course listed, it may be because your instructor has not yet made the site available. If you have registered for the course, check back later. Contact your instructor if the course is not available when the semester begins.

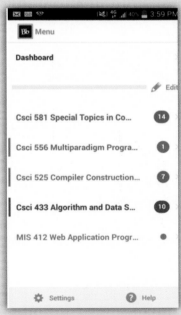

Blackboard App (Highly Recommended)

You can sync Blackboard to your smart phone by downloading the Blackboard app. One of the main advantages of having this application on your phone is that you will receive notifications regarding grades, course announcements, and content posting. For instance, if one of your instructors uploads a PowerPoint presentation that will be covered in class, you will receive an immediate notification, which will allow you enough time to read through and print the document to bring to class. Getting immediate notifications of course updates is a valuable tool, as it helps track your progress in your classes.

On Demand Help and Learning Catalog

This section of the Blackboard home page provides resources for using and understanding the many capabilities of Blackboard technology. Here you can find tutorials, short video clips, and other guides to help you navigate Blackboard.

Additional technical assistance is available through the University of Mississippi Information Technology Helpdesk. Contact the Helpdesk via e-mail (helpdesk@olemiss.edu) or telephone (662-915-5222).

Ole Miss E-mail

Your Ole Miss Gmail account is a critical component of your life as an Ole Miss student. Through this account, you receive official communication from the University, as well as important notices from your instructors. As a student, you are expected to check your e-mail at least twice a day, and faculty assume that you have received and read any communication sent via e-mail. "I didn't get the e-mail" is never an acceptable excuse, so make sure to check it frequently!

The IT Helpdesk website provides you with more information about your Gmail account at olemiss.edu/helpdesk/. Under the Frequently Asked Questions section, you can learn how to sync your Ole Miss e-mail to your smart phone, so that you get immediate notifications upon receiving an e-mail. It is strongly encouraged that you sync your e-mail to your smart phone. You also may choose to forward your Ole Miss e-mails to your personal e-mail account.

Lastly, it is wise to keep a separate e-mail account for your personal e-mails so as to reduce the amount of spam and other non-academic information you receive.

myOleMiss

One of the most important features of your myOleMiss portal is access to course registration (you can read more about this in the Academic Advising chapter of this text). In addition to allowing  you to register for classes, myOleMiss allows you to pay Bursar bills, apply for certain scholarships, accept financial aid awards, check your midterm and final grades, read and submit teacher evaluations, and check your registration holds. You are encouraged to take time at the beginning of the semester to become familiar with all of the tools offered through the myOleMiss portal.

Last words of advice:

Just like many other new experiences during your first year at Ole Miss, navigating these different online systems may be overwhelming. Remember that your instructors and advisors are here to help you, so do not hesitate to ask them questions about these systems. Your EDHE instructor is an excellent resource to help you become familiar with Blackboard, my-OleMiss, and your Ole Miss e-mail account.

4. Begin making contacts with three important groups of people: faculty, staff, and students.

Faculty: These are the professors, instructors, and graduate assistants teaching your classes. They make out tests and decide if there is going to be a pop quiz on Friday morning. They calculate and assign your grades. Introduce yourself, and show an interest in the class. Successful relationships with faculty are key to your college success.

Staff: These are the people who perform administrative tasks, take care of the buildings and grounds, manage the University's resources, plan for the future of the institution, and even teach a course or two along the way. Get to know them as they typically know the ins and outs of the University and can help you in a variety of ways.

Students: These are the people sitting next to you in class, living in your residence hall or apartment complex, walking along the campus sidewalks, and eating lunch at the next table. Introduce yourself, smile, and make an effort to get know people who are different than you. College is the perfect time to begin lifelong friendships; the process begins with you.

E-mail Etiquette

It seems that the more popular and expansive social media and smartphone technology become, the less capable we are in producing appropriate and effective e-mail communication. Many students equate e-mail with the forms of communication they use more frequently (such as texting, tweeting, and Facebook messages), and they assume that e-mail in college is just as casual. Big mistake, but easy to fix!

Consider *your audience*. When you send a text or tweet, it is most likely to a friend or family member. In college, e-mails are typically how you communicate with professors and instructors, potential employers, or administrators.

The e-mail you send influences people's opinions of you and can influence the type of treatment you receive as a student. If you send inappropriate, offensive, or poorly written messages, professors and administrators usually remember them and you, but not in a good way.

E-mail Etiquette
Do's and Don'ts

The Basics:

- Be concise and to the point.
- Answer all questions.
- Use proper spelling, grammar, and punctuation.
- Use complete sentences.
- Use proper structure.
- Use gender neutral language.
- Use correct name with appropriate title:
  - Use his or her name with the appropriate title: Dr., Professor, Ms./Mrs./Miss, or Mr.
  - Be sure to spell the name correctly.
  - Address the person receiving the message properly
- Identify who you are.
- Use signature.

> Dear Ms. Smith:
>
> I missed the History 105 class, (Section 1), on Friday. I will have my assignment on Monday.
>
> My Apologies,
> Maria Jones
> #001-23-456

The Don'ts

- Overuse the high priority option.
- Write in ALL CAPITALS.
- Leave out the message thread.
- Send an e-mail without reading it first.
- Overuse Reply to All.
- Use abbreviations and emoticons.
- Forward chain letters or virus hoaxes.
- Request delivery and read receipts.
- Ask to recall a message.
- Discuss confidential information.
- Send or forward messages containing libelous, defamatory, offensive, racist, or obscene remarks.

> mrs anne
> Iam not going to make it to class today cuase I feel terrible

Subject Lines

- The subject line should help the person receiving the message understand the reason for the message.
- Include a specific question or concern.
- Include a class assignment or title.
- Do not the leave the subject line empty.

Beginning Body

- The next sentence should explain who you are.
- Teachers or faculty members may be teaching hundreds students or several sections of the same course.
- Always sign your name at the bottom of the message; include your ID number.
- It is your job to explain who you are!

Incorrect Example:

Hey!!!

I didn't hear my alarm this morning and slept in. Oops! Did I miss anything important in class?

Correct Example:

Dear Ms. Morgenstern:

I overslept this morning and missed our EDHE class, section 106. I am really sorry and promise it will not happen again. I have gotten the class notes from Taylor and will be in class Wednesday morning, ready for the test. Again, I apologize for missing class.

Sincerely,
John Brown
#001-29-456

Professional E-mail Addresses and Signatures

Use your Ole Miss e-mail address when communicating with University faculty and staff. If you must use a different personal address, remember that readers can see it, and they won't be impressed with your maturity if your personal address is kutiegurl@yahoo.com.

Never assume that your reader will know who you are without a proper e-mail signature. Too often students treat e-mail like texting and forget that their e-mail address is NOT automatically connected to a name. I've heard many professors say that when they get a message from an e-mail address that doesn't immediately reference a student name, they simply ignore it and move on. Their time is valuable, and they won't waste it trying to track down your identity. Provide your full name (not a nickname) and your student ID number at the end of your e-mail message, and you will likely get a response.

Avoid personal statements about politics, religion, and other controversial topics in your e-mail signature when communicating with faculty, staff, or current or potential employers. It is easy to delete these before you press send, and you avoid the risk of offending your recipient.

Subject Lines

Always provide a brief explanation of the nature of your e-mail, such as "question about group project" in the subject line. An additional tip? Avoid subject lines that use phrases such as "urgent request." At best it annoys a professor when you've waited until the last minute, and at worst it makes them less likely to respond at all.

Greetings and Complimentary Close

"Hey!" is not an appropriate way to begin an e-mail to a professor or staff member. Use "Dear Professor (insert his or her last name). If the recipient is a staff member or instructor, use the name provided on the course syllabus, or use the University directory to get the correct name. If you cannot find a name or are not sure of correct spelling, open with Dear "Sir" or "Madam." To close, use a common complimentary close such as "Sincerely," or "Yours truly."

Content

Be concise. If your question or request is buried in the third paragraph, it is possible that your recipient will never read that far. If you must include a lot of information, break it into short paragraphs or bullet points.

DO NOT use slang, text message abbreviations, emoticons, all caps, profanity, or any offensive language in an e-mail. This is not a text message or your friend's Twitter account. Think of your e-mails as college papers. Write in complete sentences with correct grammar and punctuation, use spellcheck, and ALWAYS proofread for errors. Your recipient will be impressed, and you will increase your chances of getting the response you need.

Remember

Always check to make sure you have typed the correct e-mail address so your message gets to the intended recipient.

Check your syllabus to see if your professor has rules about e-mail, such as where to send it, what type of attachments are acceptable, etc. Do not assume your professor can open any attachment. If you are unsure, always ask well in advance of the assignment deadline and make other arrangements if necessary.

E-mail is forever. Always read your message before you send it. If you are upset, calm down before composing an e-mail you might later regret. Once the message is sent, you cannot take it back.

Always acknowledge an e-mail or reply from professors, staff members assisting you, potential employers, etc. When a professor goes out of his or her way to assist you and never receives an acknowledgment or thank you…it is remembered. A simple thank you now can equal a glowing recommendation letter in the future.

5. Take care of business. You might remember this advice from orientation, but it is worth repeating. As a college student, you have the absolute freedom to make your own choices, but with freedom comes personal responsibility. You can't enjoy the freedom of independent living without the responsibility that comes with making your own decisions. Choose wisely. Take care of academics first, and remember the values you have been taught by family, teachers, and friends. Rely on those values to guide your decisions.

Create a semester "To Do" list. It will help you organize your study time . . . and will help create a sense of accomplishment.

Learn the Language of Ole Miss

The University community has a language all its own. To help you better understand the terms, titles, and places you will encounter as a student, this guide to the language of Ole Miss is provided.

Academic Dean - Chief Academic Officer over a specific school or college; ex: Dean of the College of Liberal Arts, Dean of the School of Education, etc.

Academic Discipline - a field of study or branch of knowledge, such as history, business management, chemistry, etc.

Advisors and Counselors - there are multiple types of advisors and counselors available to assist you at the University. Academic Advisors help you plan your academic path towards a degree. Financial Aid Advisors help you identify and manage financial resources to fund your education and living expenses as a student. Career counselors help you develop a plan to reach your vocational goals.

Alma Mater - *Use 1*: Alma Mater is a beautiful song with great meaning and sentiment written specifcally for UM and played at special events; *Use 2*: an individual's college or university from which he or she graduates is called alma mater. Alma Mater is a Latin phrase meaning Nourishing Mother.

ASB - The Associated Student Body is the student government of the University which represents all students.

Blackboard - a web-based learning management system used by UM instructors to share important class information, assignments, and grades (blackboard.olemiss.edu).

Blue Book - a blank lined book, with a blue cover, used for written exams; can be purchased at bookstores both on and off campus.

Bursar's Office - manages student accounts, assesses tuition and fees, provides monthly billing statements, and processes payments and refunds. At many colleges and universities, this function is the responsibility of the business office; at Ole Miss we do not have a business office, rather we have a Bursar's Office.

Chancellor - the Chief Executive Officer of the University; at many universities the Chief Executive Officer is known as the president.

College and Schools - within the University, there are smaller academic units that are separated by subject or content area, for example: College of Liberal Arts, School of Engineering, School of Pharmacy, etc.; a student chooses a major that is housed within a specific college or school.

Commencement - the ceremony when degrees are conferred by the University; also known as graduation; it is held annually at the end of the spring semester.

Counseling Center - serves students, faculty, and staff. At the University Counseling Center you will find a team of dedicated professionals who strive to offer the best care possible in an atmosphere of caring respect. All services are offered in accordance with the legal limits of confidentiality.

Creed of the University of Mississippi - also known as the Ole Miss Creed, it is a statement of shared values of the University community.

Dean of Students - unlike an academic dean, this individual has responsibility for non-academic areas such as leadership, Greek affairs, campus organizations, etc.

Department - a smaller academic unit that is housed under a college or school, for example: under the School of Education at Ole Miss there is a Department of Teacher Education and a Department of Leadership and Counselor Education.

Department Chair - typically an academic department chair is a faculty member of the department who reports to the Academic Dean and is assigned to manage the department.

Faculty - academic professionals of the University; persons who are full, associate, and assistant professors as well as instructors.

Fall Convocation - a formal welcome to the University of Mississippi and presentation of all academic schools and colleges; at Convocation, students formally become student members of the University community.

Flagship University - the finest, most important university that has the liberal arts education at its core; the University of Mississippi is the flagship university in Mississippi.

Gertrude C. Ford Center - the premier entertainment venue in the University and Oxford community area; used for theatre productions, lecture series, film screenings, Broadway shows, concerts, ballets, and more.

Fulton Chapel - auditorium located on the Circle. Named for Chancellor Robert Fulton, this historic building hosts performing arts events, University meetings, Orientation sessions, and large lecture classes.

Galtney Center for Academic Computing - the 24/7 computer lab for students; this is especially helpful for students who have no laptops or whose laptops are broken.

Help Desk - located in Weir Hall; a phone and walk-in source of help for computer and IT problems; hours each day are 8:00 a.m. – 5:00 p.m., e-mail is helpdesk@olemiss.edu, and the phone number is 662-915-5222.

Hold - placed on a student's account or records and will not allow registration of courses, receipt of an academic transcript, graduation, etc. The student must contact the department from which the hold was placed to have it removed.

Hotty Toddy - a cheer, greeting, and/or salutation embraced by all Ole Miss students, faculty, alumni, and friends; legend claims the phrase to be in mocking of the attitude of Ole Miss students in the 1920s as hoity toity which evolved into Heighty Tighty and later Hotty Toddy.

IHL Board - The Board of Trustees of the Institutions of Higher Education of the State of Mississippi is the constitutional governing body of the State Institutions of Higher Learning which includes the University of Mississippi.

iStudy - iStudy@OleMiss classes are flexible and self-paced. This distance learning program allows students to learn anytime, anywhere. Most courses are available online through Blackboard. There also are classes that are paper based. Many are available in both formats.

Jackson Avenue Center (JAC) - multipurpose building located just northwest of the main campus on Jackson Avenue; Math Lab is located here.

Lyceum - Completed in 1848, the Lyceum was the first building constructed on campus. Over the years, it has served as both an academic and administrative center for the University. The Chancellor's Office, Provost's Office, and the Vice Chancellors' offices are located in the Lyceum.

M Book - a compilation of many different policies that affect students both in and out of the classroom; it is every Ole Miss student's responsibility to be familiar with the contents of *The M Book*.

Martindale Student Services Center - student support offices are located in this building which is next to the J.D. Williams Library and across the street from the Turner Center; the Center for Student Success and First-Year Experience as well as the offices of the Bursar, Registrar, Student Disability Services, Career Center, Study Abroad, Financial Aid, International Programs, Health Professions Advising, Admissions, and Orientation can be found in Martindale.

Meredith Statue - This monument honoring James Meredith, the first African-American to enroll at Ole Miss, was unveiled in October 2006. The statue depicts Meredith passing through the doorway of campus as he was formally admitted to the University.

myOleMiss - the online portal used to transact business with the University; it is accessed from the Ole Miss home page using your Web ID and password.

Office Hours - specific times when faculty members are available for student questions, concerns, or just to talk about a course or other college issue. All faculty must provide office hours to their students. Office hours for a particular course will be included in the course syllabus.

OUT - (Oxford University Transit) public transportation available to all students, faculty, and staff at no cost; routes connect various locations in Oxford and on the campus; a schedule for the various routes can be found online.

Paris-Yates Chapel - completed in 2001, the ecumenical chapel seats approximately 200 individuals and is embellished with an elaborate handmade pipe organ and carillon. Paris-Yates Chapel is located on the west side of the Quadrangle.

Provost - Chief Academic Officer for the University.

Quadrangle (Quad) - green space with large fountain in the center bordered by J.D. Williams Library on the east, Bondurant Hall on the south, Paris-Yates Chapel on the west, and Paul B. Johnson Commons on the north.

Rebel Market - an all you care to eat dining facility open Monday through Friday for breakfast, lunch, and dinner. One swipe of the Student ID Card allows students to choose from different dining stations in a comfortable and social atmosphere. Rebel Market accepts Meal Plans, Flex Dollars, Cash, Credit Cards, Debit Cards, and Ole Miss Express.

Registrar's Office - located on the first floor of the Martindale Student Services Center, this office is responsible for registration of students for classes, recording of grades on official university records, maintaining and supplying transcripts of students' academic work, processing withdrawals, and Commencement.

Rubric - grading tool (sometimes called a scoring sheet or guide) that identifies specific criteria used in grading student work; used especially in writing courses.

Scantron - paper form used to record answers for quizzes, tests, and examinations; scantrons are available in the ASB Office or at local bookstores; scantrons come in a variety of versions and formats so the instructor should be consulted regarding the version needed for the course.

Student Disability Services Office (SDS) - located on the second floor of Martindale Student Services Center, SDS provides classroom accommodations to all students on campus who disclose a disability, request accommodations, and meet eligibility criteria.

Study Abroad Office - located on the third floor of Martindale Student Services Center, makes available opportunities to study abroad all over the world.

Swayze Field - home field of Ole Miss baseball. The stadium at Swayze Field is known as Oxford/University Stadium (or OU Stadium).

Syllabus - an outline and summary of topics to be covered in a course; it will usually contain information about the instructor and his/her contact information, designated office hours, required textbooks, course requirements, due dates for assignments, test dates, and grading scale.

The Circle - the center of the University; the Lyceum stands at the apex of the Circle; original campus was laid out on the Circle to symbolize the Greek concepts of perfection and eternity which were the hopes held by founding trustees for the University.

The Daily Mississippian - (DM) founded in 1911, the campus newspaper is published Monday through Friday and is the only daily college newspaper in Mississippi; it is distributed free-of-charge throughout the campus and in Oxford.

The Grove - 10 acres located in the center of campus; site of Commencement, peace and solace, and the greatest tailgating in America on gamedays in the fall.

The Inn at Ole Miss - the Ole Miss alumni's luxury hotel located on the east side of campus; available to alumni, students, their families, and other visitors to the University.

The Manning Center - (Indoor Practice Facility or IPF) athletic complex named for alumni Olivia and Archie Manning, the patriarchs of the first-family of football in America; contains in-door practice field, locker rooms, training facilities, weight rooms, team meeting rooms, and the Grill at 1810.

The Pavilion - state-of-the art, $96.5 million facility opened in January 2016. Site for basketball games, concerts, and academic convocation, The Pavilion also has the largest hung video display in college sports and includes Steak 'n' Shake, Raising Cane, and Rebel Locker Room.

The Square - Courthouse Square of the city of Oxford; home of smart retail stores, stylish boutiques, gourmet restaurants, and bars; some describe it as the Center of the Universe.

The Turner Center - located on All-American Drive across the street from Martindale Student Services Center; on-campus recreation center open to all students.

TLO - (Transfer Leadership Organization) leadership organization for transfer students. tlo.ole-miss.edu

UPD - (University Police Department) University's police force with offices located in Kinard Hall.

Vaught-Hemingway Stadium - home of the Ole Miss football Rebels. Built in 1915, the stadium is named after Coach John Howard Vaught and Judge William Hemingway.

Vice Chancellor - title for leader of a division of the University, i.e., Vice Chancellor for Academic Affairs, Vice Chancellor for Student Affairs; at many colleges and universities these positions are held by vice presidents.

Web ID - an account name that gives you access to many UM systems such as e-mail, myOleMiss, Blackboard, and the campus wireless network.

Tough Times

What can get in the way of your success at Ole Miss? Even students who do "everything right" occasionally have tough times. Freshmen and new transfer students are particularly vulnerable to homesickness, roommate conflicts, fatigue, and the common cold.

Homesickness

Every new student experiences homesickness at some point during the first semester. Unfortunately, knowing it is going to happen doesn't prevent it. Most students get past it, though it may take some time. Here are some tips to help you get over the typical case of homesickness:

- **Do not** stay in your room. Being alone feeds homesickness.

- **Do not** avoid contact with people.

- **Do not** continually call home, call friends at home, or worse, go home. This feeds the feeling that you cannot make it in college. Fight through it, and stay on campus!

- **Do not** think you are in this alone– see above! There are many faculty, staff, and fellow students here to help.

- **Do not** think something is wrong with you. Homesickness is a normal part of being a new student.

- **Do** talk to people when you are on the bus! It's a great way to meet people.

- **Do** seek out new friends on your floor or at your apartment complex. Invite them in, or walk around and meet them.

- **Do** go to class! You need to keep a normal routine as much as possible.

- **Do** seek help – your community assistant, a professor you know, someone in Student Affairs (hint – your EDHE instructor), or the free and confidential University Counseling Center. We are here to help.

- **Do** continue to eat, exercise, and sleep (at night, not during the day).

- **Do** spend time outside!

- **Do** stay in Oxford for weekends! This is when you have time to really work on new relationships.

- **Do** volunteer to help others. This is a surefire way to quit thinking about yourself. (See the chapter on campus involvement for volunteer ideas.)

Roommate Issues – Whether you are living with your best friend or someone totally new, your chances for roommate conflicts are the same. This may be enhanced if you have never shared a room with another person. The key is to communicate your feelings and agree upon some basic rules. Talk with your roommate early about study habits, sleep habits, housecleaning, and personal space. Working out the details of sharing a small living space, sooner rather than later, will make life much more pleasant. And, don't be surprised that when you voice a complaint, your roommate has a complaint or two about you. (Read the chapter on relationships for more help with roommates.)

Fatigue and the Common Cold – If there was ever an expression that summed up new college students, it is, "Burning the candle at both ends." Of course, that means the candle burns out twice as quickly. It's understandable that you want to go to every event, meet tons of new people, go to football games, and in general not miss out on anything fun. And, there is no one to stop you from trying to do everything! After all, you are living with hundreds of fellow students and not your parents. Eventually, the college lifestyle will catch up with you, and you will be more tired than you have ever been and probably sick, too. Being sick and tired away from home is hard, and something you likely have not experienced.

Try to create a balance of social activities, exercise, personal hygiene, and healthy eat-

ing. Eat a variety of foods, because a steady diet of pizza, cheeseburgers, fries, and soft drinks leads to the "freshman 15" and a sluggish, sick feeling. Wash your hands often, keep your room or apartment reasonably clean, and try for at least seven hours of sleep most nights. Residence hall and apartment living at a minimum put you in close proximity with a lot of people, so the inevitable virus is bound to hit at some time or another. When you feel sick, go to the Student Health Center to see a physician or nurse practitioner. (*Check the resource guide at the end of the text for location and office hours.*)

It takes work to be a successful college student. EHDE 105 and 305 and this textbook will help you work smart and make the most of your Ole Miss experience. Dr. Ken Sufka, professor of psychology and pharmacology, advises, "Learning is not a spectator sport." Don't stay on the sidelines; get involved in your classes and campus life TODAY!

REFERENCES
Sufka, K. (2011). *The A Game.* , 1st ed., (p. 17). Taylor, MS: Nautilus Publishing Co.

Did you know?

With over 60,000 sound recordings in most audio formats; over 20,000 photographs; more than 1,000 videos; and over 6,000 books, periodicals, and newsletters, the Blues Archive at Ole Miss houses one of the largest collections of blues recordings, publications, and memorabilia in the world.

About the Authors

Leslie Banahan, *Assistant Vice Chancellor for Student Affairs*

Leslie Banahan provides oversight for the University's Career Center, Counseling Center, Health Services, Campus Recreation, Disability Services, and the Center for Student Success and First-Year Experience. She has written and spoken extensively on orientation programs, first-year students, crisis intervention and managment, and parents of today's college students. Ms. Banahan is the co-author of *Navigating the First College Year: A Guide for Parents and Families.* She attended Louisiana State University and the University of Mississippi, earning degrees in Journalism, Sociology, and Higher Education and Counseling. She tries to follow her dad's advice: Work hard and be nice to people.

Whitman Smith, *Director of Admissions*

Whitman Smith directs the activities of the Office of Admissions, the department within the Division of Student Affairs that is responsible for student recruitment, undergraduate applications, and orientation. Mr. Smith has a B.A.E. and M.A. from the University and has taught EDHE 105 for many years. He has worked for Ole Miss since 1990.

Katie Tompkins, *EDHE 105 Instructor,*
Prospect Research Analyst for University Development

Katie Tompkins is originally from Florence, Alabama, but now calls Oxford her home. She earned a B.A. in English from Ole Miss in 2002 and a J.D. from the University of Mississippi School of Law in 2006.

Common Reading: Building

Why A Common Reading Assignment?

We are a community of readers, and one of the first decisions a new student at the University of Mississippi faces is: "Will I read the UM Common Reading book — or will I blow off my first assignment?" It's an important decision and one that will set the course for academic success or failure. The common reading assignment is an early signal that college is about learning (despite the many distractions) and that UM students are expected to read and discuss a wide range of materials during their time at the University.

As part of the First-Year Experience, students and faculty have the opportunity to read and discuss one book. It's an assignment that strengthens the overall academic atmosphere of the University, connects students to peers and instructors, and provides opportunities for campus involvement.

Reading and discussion are integral parts of every student's college education, and the common reading experience provides students with the chance to read a compelling book, express opinions and questions about the book, and listen and react to others' differing opinions. Classes engage in small group discussions about characters, plot, dialogue, authors, and story content. Some of these discussions may challenge students' political, religious, or social beliefs; these challenges are a key component of the assignment. The ability to respectfully listen to diverse opinions and to articulate an opposing viewpoint are important skills necessary for success in higher education. The small and intimate environment of EDHE 105 and 305 classes facilitates and supports learning and practicing these skills.

> **Will I read the book — or will I blow off my first college assignment?**

In addition to talking about the book, students are expected to write about what they have read. The importance of learning to write in a clear, concise, and compelling manner cannot be overstated. The common reading assignment asks students to interpret, discuss, or react to a book or author; in return, faculty provide constructive feedback to help students improve their writing skills. The discussion and writing assignments developed from the common reading book model important facets of learning that students encounter again and again in their freshman, sophomore, junior, and senior years. It's the beginning of a different type of learning that is essential to college success.

Finally, the common reading assignment is developed to encourage students to relate personal experiences with what they read and to develop the ability to express viewpoints and draw parallels between characters in a book and the people they know in their families, communities, and the University. Often the common reading assignment has co-curricular events that encourage student involvement in lectures, plays, or concerts. It's another way to connect to the University and enrich the First Year Experience.

So, will you read the book? We hope so.

Community Through Books

by Leslie Banahan

2018 Common Reading Assignment

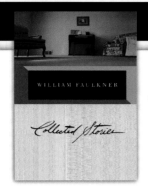

Collected Short Stories of William Faulkner

Ten short stories by one of the most acclaimed American authors of the 20th century have been selected for the University's 2018 Common Reading Experience. Nobel Prize-winning author William Faulkner's short stories are expected to be read by incoming Ole Miss freshmen and transfer students in advance of the first day of fall classes.

A committee of faculty, staff, and students chose 10 thought-provoking stories from the *Collected Short Stories of William Faulkner,* said Stephen Monroe, chair of the Department of Writing and Rhetoric and of the Common Reading Experience Steering Committee.

"In reading the stories together, our community will engage invigorating themes and Mississippi realities," Monroe said. "Before Faulkner became a Nobel laureate, he was a member of the University community, as both a special student and staff member.

"Everyone affiliated with UM should read at least a little Faulkner. I'm pleased that we'll have that opportunity this fall."

Faulkner studied at the University and wrote many literary classics at his home, Rowan Oak, which sits on 32 acres off Old Taylor Road. He lived and worked there from 1930 until his death in 1962.

When the Common Reading Experience was created in 2012, the founders anticipated focusing on a Faulkner work one year. This year, the committee worked with Jay Watson, Howry Professor of Faulkner Studies, to choose ten short stories from the 900 page *Collected Stories of William Faulkner.* *

Assigned stories are: *Barn Burning, Two Soldiers, Shall Not Perish, A Rose for Emil, Hair, Dry September, Uncle Willy, Mule in the Yard, That Evening Sun,* and *The Brooch*

*Michael Newsom, University Communications, contributed to this section of the text.

REFERENCE:

Laufgraben, J. L. (2006). Common Reading Programs: Going Beyond the Book (Monograph No. 44). Columbia, SC: University of South Carolina, National Resource Center for The First-Year Experience and Students in Transition.

Tom Franklin: on creativity

To be creative is to be messy, to allow yourself this. It's hard, especially if you're like me, if you don't like your hands dirty. My dad's a mechanic, and he wanted me to be one, too, but I turned wrenches the wrong way, left parts on the floor when I put transmissions back in. Washed my hands too much. So they put me in the office. Which I cleaned up. I'm a writer now, and in order to write a publishable novel and support your family, you have to sit down and crack your knuckles and write a first draft. You have to figure out what the story is, who the characters are. And in order to do this, you have to write a few bad sentences. You have to write some bad pages. Maybe even a lot of them. But doing that clears the pipes. I believe that writing (and other forms of creativity) comes from our subconscious minds, from the same place that dreams do; and in the way you're not really in control of your dreams, you're not entirely in control of your creative mind. It's down there, bubbling, even when you're not thinking about your novel, when your head's a dozen other places, your tarry subconscious swamp is blooping and burping, and if you're faithful to your art, if you write every day, even though it sucks, even though you're ashamed of how bad it is, you'll be there one morning writing, and suddenly the character you were half-heartedly pushing around on the page has said something brilliant, something hilarious, something you'd never say and hadn't thought of before. Where did it come from? From you. Your own subconscious mind, down there working for you. And it happened because you cleared those pipes and made a mess. So go make messes. Write bad sentences that you'll make better later. But also: Have fun. Oh, and by the way, I can't prove any of this. It's not scientific. In fact, I didn't even know I thought it until I sat down and wrote "To be creative is to be messy..."

Did you know?

The *Star Trek* character Leonard "Bones" McCoy attended Ole Miss in the mid-2240s, enrolled at The University of Mississippi Medical Center (Jackson) in the year 2249, and graduated as an M.D. with an expertise in space psychology in the year 2253.

Chapter 2
Not-So-Soft Skills:
Emotional Intelligence and Grit

by Patrick Perry and Rebekah Reysen

Think about a recent event that made you happy. Now think about an event that made you sad. Finally, think about an event that made you angry. If you are able, remember specific details of each of these events. Do you remember making any decisions after each of these events? If so, were you aware of your emotions during the decision-making process? Were the decisions you made small or perhaps more significant? Would the decisions be the same if your emotions were different or if you had been in more control of your emotions? The first part of this chapter explores the role emotions play in decision-making and your ability to be successful based on your ability to manage emotions. The second part of this chapter focuses on the importance of having grit to push through struggles.

Emotional Intelligence is defined as "a set of emotional and social skills that influence the way we perceive and express ourselves, develop and maintain social relationships, cope with challenges, and use emotional information in an effective and meaningful way" (Multi-Health Systems, 2011). Many times we associate successful people with their intellectual ability. Intellectual ability does contribute to success, but having a high IQ does not necessarily guarantee success. What about the ability to identify and control emotions, especially when making decisions? In the 1980s, the psychologist Dr. Reuven Bar-On struggled with the fact that there were individuals who possessed strong intellectual skills but were unsuccessful while others with average skills were successful (Stein & Book, 2011). Bar-On's research led him to create a measure called the Emotional Quotient or "EQ" (Stein & Book, 2011). The research of Bar-On resulted in the creation of the Emotional Quotient Inventory (EQ-I), an assessment that provides individuals information about emotional strengths and areas for potential improvement.

Why does developing my Emotional Intelligence matter?

Research indicates that a person's intellectual ability (IQ) develops until around seventeen years of age, but Emotional Intelligence, often referred to as "EI" may develop throughout the lifetime (Stein & Book, 2011). This is important because through practice and experience you may develop your emotional intelligence skills. Recent research findings indicate that having certain EI skills can positively impact your ability to be successful and graduate from college. In a study conducted by Sparkman, Maulding, and Roberts, the EI skills of social responsibility, impulse control, and empathy were predictors of enrollment and graduation (2012). National Career Services noted that although technical skills and knowledge can be taught, "soft skills" are what employers would like to have in employees' skill sets (2015). The soft skills identified by National Career Services as most commonly sought by employers include: communicating, making decisions, showing commitment, flexibility, time management, leadership, creativity and problem-solving, being a team player, accepting responsibility, and the ability to work under pressure (2015). Some research studies indicate that EI also may have a positive effect on your mental and physical health (Stein & Book, 2011). To summarize, research supports that developing your EI skills may increase your level of success in college as well as your success and well-being in life.

How do you develop your emotional intelligence? You will have many opportunities in college to develop your EI. Your choice to get up for an 8:00 a.m. class instead of sleeping late is exercising your impulse control. Making the decision to talk to your roommate about an issue in a meaningful and productive way instead of being angry or silent demonstrates your skill in assertiveness. Understanding that a poor grade may be due to your lack of effort versus the thought that the instructor is at fault for giving too difficult a test, is an indication that you are strong in your reality testing. When faced with multiple decisions under stress, being able to thrive and find solutions demonstrates your problem solving skills. The key is exercising emotional intelligence skills. To become better at managing your emotions you have to practice and learn what works and what does not work. This can be difficult because it means identifying your strengths as well as areas in which you may need to improve. Keep in mind that although managing your emotions effectively is not easy, it will lead to higher levels of success in college and life.

> "We all go through something in life.
>
> Sometimes you have to push past the pain."
>
> - Antoinette Tuff

Antoinette Tuff: Emotionally Intelligent Tough

The story of Antoinette Tuff and her actions to save students' lives at the Ronald McNair Learning Center near Atlanta, Georgia, in 2013 demonstrates how important effective management of emotions can be in a life and death situation. On the morning of August 20, 2013, Michael Hill entered the Ronald McNair Learning Center Elementary School with a weapon and hundreds of rounds of ammunition with the intent to harm those inside. Ms. Tuff, a bookkeeper at the school substituting for the receptionist on that particular day, was told by the gunman to call 911 and to state that he was going to start shooting (CNN, 2014). Ms. Tuff, instead of panicking, began a "calm" and "matter of fact" dialogue with the gunman that eventually led to his surrender (CNN, 2013).

During the time after Mr. Hill entered the elementary school until his surrender Ms. Tuff went through many emotions along with Mr. Hill. Her ability to listen and talk in an empathetic way with Mr. Hill saved many lives. Ms. Tuff calmly explained to Mr. Hill at several different times that he was not in this alone and that she cared for him and about his specific life circumstances. Ms. Tuff told Mr. Hill, "we all go through something in life" (CNN, 2014). Ms. Tuff's calmness and caring dialogue with Mr. Hill allowed her to be successful in convincing him to surrender without a single person being injured that day.

Using and Developing Your Emotional Intelligence

In fall 2014, as part of a pilot study at the University of Mississippi, students in some sections of EDHE 105 and 305 were given the EQ-I 2.0 instrument, designed to measure Emotional Intelligence. This study was conducted to provide students with information about their EI so they might better understand their emotional skills and areas in which they might improve. Hopefully by better understanding their EI, students would be better equipped to develop their skills through practice and be more successful in college and in life. One third of the students in the study indicated Impulse Control, Stress Tolerance, and Problem Solving as areas in which they could improve (Perry, 2015).

In general, college students are constantly facing challenges related to Impulse Control, Stress Tolerance, and Problem Solving so the results of this study are not surprising. The key is to formulate strategies to develop in these areas. For instance, let's say you are upset with a friend for not showing up to meet you at a movie. You begin typing a text message or e-mail explaining how upset you are and as you type you get angrier and angrier. Stop typing! Take a few breaths and think about multiple reasons why your friend might not have shown up. Perhaps your friend had an emergency and had to drive home to be

with family. Ask yourself if you think your friend would intentionally not show up to make you angry. Open your mind to multiple possibilities, and take the time to cool down before you allow your emotions to be hijacked. Give the situation a little time before you react, perhaps sleep on it as you consider the possibilities. Now, are you calm? Give your friend a phone call or go visit in person. What should you say first? In a calm but genuinely concerned voice, ask if everything is all right and tell your friend that you were concerned about her well-being because she did not show up last night when you had both agreed to meet. Give your friend the opportunity to explain without passing judgment. Your tone, demeanor, and general approach to this situation will make a huge difference! Do you think this approach is better than a text or e-mail? Why or why not? In this situation, if you do just one thing, take five minutes to settle down when you first feel angry or upset, this will allow you a little time to put everything in perspective before addressing the situation (Kannoy, 2013).

EI Exercises

The following exercises give you the opportunity to think about EI in a practical way with real life situations you may encounter. To get the most out of these exercises, be thoughtful in how you might handle each situation. Think of more than just one answer, and go through the results you might experience based on various possibilities.

Scenario #1

You are suddenly given an assignment in your Friday afternoon class that will be due on Monday afternoon. You had planned to leave campus following class for a weekend at home because your best friend is getting married, and you are in the wedding. You also planned to spend the entire day Sunday with your family and with friends from high school. The assignment you were given for your class is one that will take several hours to complete to earn a good grade. What emotions are you feeling as soon as you find out about the assignment? What do you do? Describe how your emotions will play a role in the decisions you make in this scenario.

Scenario #2

This week you have two tests and two papers due for your classes. This is also the week you have volunteered to work outside the Student Union every afternoon for an hour as part of your commitment to a student organization in which you are an officer. You have been notified by your supervisor at work that several employees are sick and that your request to be off from work to prepare for your class assignments this week is not approved; you need to work your shifts. Describe how you feel and how you might react. What are you going to do? What will be the results of the approach you take (positive and negative)?

Are you going to quit? No, because you have Grit!

Former Ole Miss Football Coach Billy Brewer told Roy Lee "Chucky" Mullins, "You're not big enough, you're not strong enough and you're not fast enough to play football at Ole Miss" (ESPN Storied, 2014). Chucky Mullins replied, "If you give me a chance, I'll never let you down" (ESPN Storied, 2014). Chucky was a role model for his determination, positive attitude, and grit. Recent research suggests that grit can play a significant role in your achievement of goals. Merriam Webster defines grit as firmness of mind or spirit; unyielding courage in the face of hardship or danger (2015).

Chucky was a role model for his determination and positive attitude. Today his jersey number 38 is a symbol of his Ole Miss grit.

Angela Lee Duckworth defines grit as passion and perseverance for long term goals; sticking with your future, day in and day out, not just for the week, not just for the month but for years, and living life like it is a marathon, not a sprint (AP Conference 2013).

Grit, like emotional intelligence, may be developed through practice and can have a positive influence on your current and future success. Chucky Mullins had countless opportunities in his life to give up when he faced adversity, but he chose to persevere and push forward instead, and with a smile. How do you face adversity and failure? Think about something that has posed a barrier to your being successful. As you progress in college and in your life you will face numerous obstacles, and your capacity to stick it out when faced with challenges and failure is a measure of your grit.

> **"If you're not failing every now and again, it's a sign you're not doing anything very innovative."**
>
> **– Woody Allen**

How Do I Develop Grit?

Educators and researchers are trying to better understand the extent to which grit plays a role in success.

Most agree that if you have characteristics of grit, generally you are more likely to be successful in achieving goals. Of course, this makes sense right? If you have a goal and you are persistent in working towards the goal you are more likely to achieve the goal. Do you think you are gritty? If so, great! Could you be grittier? Consider the following example of grit.

In an article by Tyler Tervooren, he describes how, as a child, he would take things apart that were broken to see how they worked and then try to repair them himself (2015). He started with the computer his parents purchased, but over time he developed the con-

fidence to attempt to fix pretty much anything. This process involved a lot of failure, but by breaking and repairing things, he was developing grit (2015). I am not encouraging you to break your computer so you can take it apart and try to fix it! However, it is important to develop your grit by attempting to do things that you may be uncomfortable doing if that is what is necessary to reach your goals. Think about the goals you have set for yourself. Some of the things you need to do to accomplish your goals will undoubtedly test your grit. Through practice and repetition you will be more successful and will become grittier and grittier.

Start Building Grit Today!

Successful individuals acquire grit in small ways every day. Duckworth said developing grit is "a marathon, not a sprint" (Xhelo, 2013). Taking this interpretation literally, for those of you who played sports in high school, you know that being a strong runner, soccer player, or football player takes practice, repetition, and persistence. Running an actual marathon begins Day 1 with something small, like walking for 20 minutes a day a few days a week. As the Greek Philosopher Aristotle said, "We are what we repeatedly do. Excellence, then, is not an act, but a habit."

This is good news! Because laying the foundation for success starts today. Or maybe

it has already started, and you are continually building upon your previous accomplishments. Motivate yourself each day to take one small step towards meeting your end goal. Getting back to the exercise analogy, let's say that you want to get in better shape. Do not try to drop 10 pounds in a week. Make it a realistic and sustainable goal that you can work on daily. You want it to be simple, like brushing your teeth. And you want to enjoy the process if at all possible. Here's an example:

Week 1: Get in Better Shape

Day 1: Make a list of reasons why you want to get in better shape. What is your definition of being in shape? Losing weight? Being able to run a seven-minute mile? What are the benefits? Are there any drawbacks? What do you need to do to reach your goal?

Day 2: Brainstorm exercises that you would find enjoyable, like taking your dog on a walk at Lake Patsy or at the South Campus Rail Trail.

Day 3: Take your dog for a 20-minute walk around the Square. Get some sunshine, some fresh air, and a cup of coffee. You will not only be in a better mood, but you will be fully caffeinated too. And your dog will want to take a nap, freeing you up for some afternoon study time.

Day 4: Go for a 20-minute walk with a friend around The Grove between classes.

Day 5: Repeat Day 3 or 4.

As you can see, change does not always have to be stressful, and you can always build up to more challenging goals. Start small so that you do not lose motivation.

If you want to set goals effectively, you can think about the SMART Goals acronym: *Specific, Measurable, Attainable, Realistic,* and *Time Bound* (Drucker, 1954; Doran, 1981). Here is how training to reach the goal of running a 5K can follow this method:

Specific - Run a 5K.

Measurable - Walk 20 minutes a day for one month.

Attainable - If your doctor says yes to exercise, then absolutely you can do it!

Realistic - Run a 5K in 3 months.

Time Bound - I am going to complete a 5K on a certain date and time.

Be kind to yourself while you are going through a change process. Remind yourself that everyone is different. What matters is how YOU are making changes, no one else.

Don't Forget about Passion

As you recall, grit is defined as perseverance AND passion for long-term goals. Do not forget the passion part. The great thing about being the unique person that you are (there is only one of you!) is that you can be enthusiastic about whatever you want. And, you can make a difference in society by translating what you are passionate about into a future career.

What are you passionate about? Start thinking about how all of the activities that you do on a daily basis translate into being a successful college student. The book *The A Game* by Dr. Ken Sufka (2013), which you should have in addition to this textbook, can point you in the right direction. Go to class. Take your own notes. Don't sit in the cheap seats. Make mind maps. Know what you don't know, etc. Practice these tips on a daily basis.

And beyond that, I want you to think about how passionate you are about being a college student. Are you willing to study for at least a couple of hours each day? Enjoying what you are studying and your major can make a huge difference in persisting to graduation.

Many students struggle with trying to find the right major (Scott, 2016). Knowing what you want to do for a living in a few years is not easy. If you already know what you want to do, that's great! More power to you! But if you don't know what to major in, or feel like your major is not a good fit, I want you to consider some important resources. These resources include the Career Center, where you can sit down with an advisor and brainstorm potential majors and careers. The Career Center also has the Strong Interest Inventory, an assessment that can connect your interests and abilities to majors and careers. There is a small fee to take the Strong Interest Inventory. Career Center staff are the experts on helping people find their passion.

You also can do additional research by perusing the Occupational Outlook Handbook website: bls.gov/ooh/ or completing a career assessment on your own, such as the Career Construction Interview (CCI; Savickas & Hartung, 2012). I also recommend job shadowing and getting an internship if you want to see what a career is like first-hand. For more information on careers, please refer to Chapter 13.

Another thing to consider is that there will be times when you simply feel burned out. When this happens, it never hurts to talk to someone about what is on your mind. If you have been feeling overwhelmed by something that has happened to you in your personal life, consider speaking with a counselor at the Counseling Center, even if it is just for one session. Counselors are grit masters and can help you build grit by managing stress.

The Center for Student Success and First-Year Experience's (CSSFYE) Academic Support Programs are another campus resource available to help you improve your study habits. You can attend one of their free DIY workshops on time management, test taking and analysis, or note making. To schedule a meeting or attend a workshop, go to their website: cssfye.olemiss.edu/student-support-programs/.

Success is built one day at a time in simple, SMART steps. Success is based not only on perseverance and habits, but on passion - who you are as a person and what you like to do. As Mahatma Ghandi once said, "Be the change that you wish to see in the world." We have great confidence in you!

REFERENCES

Doran, G. T. (1981). There's a S.M.A.R.T. way to write management's goals and objectives. *Management Review (AMA FORUM), 70(11)*, 35–36.Drucker, P. (1954). *The Practice of Management.* HarperCollins Publishers.*ESPN* (Producer). (2014). *It's Time* [TV Show].

Georgia school shooting: Antoinette Tuff hailed as hero - CNN.com. (2013, August 22). Retrieved February 26, 2015, from cnn.com/2013/08/22/us/georgia-school-shooting-hero

Kannoy, K. (2013). KISS Strategies for Improving Emotional Intelligence: 60 Strategies for Keeping It Simple, Specific. Unpublished Document

Merriam Webster Online. Retrieved April 6, 2015 from merriam-webster.com/

Multi-Health Systems. (2011). *Emotional quotient inventory 2.0 (EQ-i 2.0) user's handbook.* Toronto, Ontario: Multi-Health Systems.

Perry, P. (2015). Emotional Intelligence Pilot Study at the University of Mississippi in Fall 2014. Unpublished Data.

Research Shows Building This Trait Will Help You Outperform Natural Genius. Retrieved April 6, 2015, from riskology.co/outperform-genius/

Savickas, M. L. & Hartung, P. J. (2012). The Career Construction Interview. Retrieved February 7, 2016 from vocopher.com/CSI/CCI.pdf

Scott, E. (2016). Stress in College: Common Causes of Stress in College. Retrieved from stress.about.com/od/stdentstress/a/stress_college.htm

She survived a standoff with a gunman – could you? CNN.com. (2014, February 22). Retrieved February 26, 2015, from cnn.com/2014/02/22/us/tuff-survivor-gunman

Sparkman, L., Maulding, W., Roberts, J., (2012). Non-Cognitive Predictors of Student Success in College. *College Student Journal*, 46 (3), 642-652.

Stein, S., & Book, H. (2011). *The EQ edge: Emotional Intelligence and your success.* Ontario, ON: Wiley.

Sufka, K. J. (2011). *The A Game: Nine Steps to Better Grades.* Nautilus Publishing Company: Oxford, MS.

Tervooren, Tyler (2015). *Research Shows Building this Trait will Help You Outperform Natural Genius.* Retrieved April 6, 2015, from riskology.co/outperform-genius/

The University of Mississippi's Center for Student Success and First-Year Experience. (n.d.) Academic Support Programs. Retrieved from cssfye.olemiss.edu/student-support-programs/

True Grit – 2013 AP Annual Conference Keynote Dr. Angela Lee Duckworth. Retrieved April 4, 2015, from youtube.com/watch?v=BrkwrHSfsMY

United States Department of Labor. (2015, December 17). Occupational Outlook Handbook Homepage. Retrieved from bls.gov/ooh/

What are the 'soft skills' employers want? – National Careers Service. Retrieved February 26, 2015, from nationalcareersservice.direct.gov.uk/aboutus/newsarticles/Pages/Spotlight-SoftSkills.aspx

Xhelo, Gerta (Producer). (2013, April). Angela Lee Duckworth: The Key to Success? Grit. *Ted Talks Education.* Podcast retrieved from: ted.com/talks/angela_lee_duckworth_the_key_to_success_grit

About the Authors

Patrick Perry received his undergraduate degree in geography from the University of Memphis and his master's degree and Ed.D. in Leadership from the University of Memphis. Since 2008, he has been the Director of Luckyday Scholarship Programs at the University of Mississippi. He enjoys working with students to identify the best resources needed to reach their goals. In his spare time he enjoys playing tennis, running, watching sports, and spending time with his partner and two cats.

Rebekah Reysen received her undergraduate degrees in psychology and theatre from Purdue University, and her master's degree and Ph.D. in Counselor Education from the University of Mississippi. She is a National Certified Counselor (NCC), Licensed Professional Counselor (LPC), Distance Certified Counselor (DCC), and has published articles in a variety of counseling journals. Dr. Reysen coordinates programs for academically at-risk students and is passionate about helping students navigate their way through college.

Chapter 3
Civility Is So Much More than Southern Hospitality

by Jennifer A. Stollman

As a University of Mississippi student, you now are entering a different space. This is a space where thousands of people from across the nation and the globe are dedicated to learning and the support of learning—including faculty, staff, administrators, and students. As you have already determined, the University of Mississippi is a cosmopolitan space. People arrive and inhabit this campus carrying multiple life experiences, different political leanings, complex ideas about faith, and different attitudes about people. Our campus is enriched because we have so many people hailing from different ethnicities and races. They have come to the University of Mississippi for the same reasons that you have—to gain the knowledge and skills needed to achieve future professional and personal goals. As you soon will experience, such knowledge and skills happen in many spaces including classrooms, co-curricular events, athletic events, social activities, and through social media. Within these spaces, you will encounter people who possess different opinions, ideas, and ways of doing things. This is normal and to be expected. In fact this is one of the most attractive aspects of college campuses.

The University of Mississippi Creed:

One of the most important binding mechanisms on the University of Mississippi campus is the Creed. A creed is a series of philosophical statements that you voluntarily adhere to while you live, learn, work, and play on this campus. To best ensure the advancement of learning, research, civic, and personal growth, the University of Mississippi is a society reliant upon intellectual inquiry and upholding certain character ideals. These ideals serve as the framework by which all campus community members strive to live.

The College Campus as a Society With Many "Mini" Societies

College campuses are societies and in fact, exist as some of the most complex and difficult societies created and sustained by the United States. What makes the University of Mississippi a society is that different people from all walks of life, with different experiences and differing ideas engage each other for prolonged periods of times. The college campus is a shared space where, in addition to acquiring the necessary knowledge and skills to succeed in your chosen profession, people live their lives. You will make the transition from adolescence to adulthood and full-fledged citizenship. You will actualize. You will encounter and make new friendships. You will socialize, exercise, discover your political voice, and firm up your moral and intellectual compasses. Your groups of friends may change, political interests will form and change, intellectual pursuits will expand. You will move in and out of social and intellectual circles. You will join, drop out of, and join different campus social and political groups. Each of these formal and informal spaces and groups functions as a smaller society within the large campus society. You also will find that some of these societies may be permanent and others temporary. Classrooms, lecture halls, auditoriums, The Grove, Student Union, student organizations, and sorority and fraternity houses represent just a few of the smaller societies on campus. Unlike previous generations, you also have the benefit of virtual societies. Social media such as Twitter, Facebook, YikYak, and even independent SMS messaging serve as smaller societies. You may find that the larger society of the University and the smaller societies that you engage in have different standards of participation and expected behaviors. Be on the lookout for these expectations. Doing so will make your integration into those groups more enjoyable and successful.

The Creed of The University of Mississippi

The University of Mississippi is a community of learning dedicated to nurturing excellence in intellectual inquiry and personal character in an open and diverse environment. As a voluntary member of this community:

I believe in *respect for the dignity of each person.*

I believe in *fairness and civility.*

I believe in *personal and professional integrity.*

I believe in *academic honesty.*

I believe in *academic freedom.*

I believe in *good stewardship of our resources.*

I pledge to *uphold these values* and *encourage others to follow my example.*

Successful Conduct in University of Mississippi Societies

One of the most difficult and crucial things that you will do at the University of Mississippi is to successfully adjust to the campus society and its smaller societies. Because of your years of experience in your hometowns, your schools, your student learning and athletic groups, and your spaces of faith, you have become experts at participating in your home societies. Parents, relatives, spiritual advisors, and friends have taught you the rules and expectations for how to succeed in these societies. You have mastered so well the objectives and rules of each of the societies in which you claim membership that you probably do not even have to think about it. Well, now you have arrived in a totally different setting. Some of your knowledge and skills as a citizen in previous societies might work, but you  also may find that on campus, your previously used strategies are unsuccessful. You may find that you are unaccustomed to the expectations of a college campus society and its mini societies. This is normal and to be expected. Fear not, because with careful attention to these new societies' structures and behavioral expectations, you will integrate with little difficulty. Like your home societies, the college campus has its own rules. Because this is a space where debate and difference are encouraged, the University has developed a set of expectations to ensure that you develop your intellect and your professional skills in a safe and secure environment.

What you will find at the University of Mississippi and other college campuses is that the higher education society is different. Most societies strive for peaceful cohesion. Other American societies often rely on force or compromise for stability. For its productivity and success, the University demands and depends on difference and debate. Intellectuals—including faculty, staff, administrators, and students—accept that diverse people, opinions, ideas, experiences, methodologies, and perspectives are fundamental to ensuring continual discovery and advancing learning. Challenging ideas and observations are crucial to a university's success. It also is crucial to your own intellectual development. College campuses often are spaces of contention and not consensus. Critical reasoning depends on debate and argument to move thinking forward. In spaces beyond the college campus, arguing involves aggression—both verbal and physical. This is not the case on a college campus—in fact far from it. Constructing an argument requires logical thought, evidence, and calm exchanges of ideas. In doing so, individuals on college campuses assume the role of an intellectual. Reason and passion come together to create new thought and to develop professional skills. Ideally, at the University of Mississippi this activity is replicated daily and in multiple spaces. Every department and program relies on debate. What makes the University society effective, productive, and attractive is how people conduct themselves within their societies. To avoid doing harm to individuals on campus and to prevent chaos, the University adheres to normal standards of civility. Following standards of civility during your time on campus, both inside and outside of the classroom, maximizes your personal development while ensuring the personal development of others.

What is Civility—Definitions and Misconceptions

The term "civility" has been on the minds of Americans over the last several years. Perhaps because of the events of 9/11, economic crises, and continued uneven access to power, more and more American commentators from all ideological and identity positions have devoted countless hours and typed and uttered countless words on the topic of civility, or rather the existence of incivility in daily social interactions, entertainment, politics, and schools. Most have issued a call for civility and have persuasively argued that incivility has obstructed economic growth, political processes, and educational systems. Our own University, like every university across the nation, often has issues with civility—as campus individuals forget standards of civility when expressing their own opinions or fulfilling their own objectives and goals. Events related to racism, sexism, homophobia, and classism continue to happen on our campus. Anxieties provoke campus individuals and groups to marginalize or alienate members of minorities. This leads them to act out on the campus or through social media. Every time this happens the campus is thrown into chaos and is forced into a painstaking recovery process that takes time away from learning and development. Civility is thought to be difficult to define, and it is true that, depending on context, elements of the definition may be differently emphasized. In fact, there are several agreed upon definitions of civility.

Civility at the University of Mississippi IS:

- ■ Respecting the dignity and rights of everyone on campus.
- ■ Maintaining respect for and learning from people who have different experiences, ideas, and positions than you.
- ■ Remaining open to new ideas and actions.
- ■ Acting with integrity.
- ■ Demonstrating concern for others, their feelings, and their need for conditions that support their work and development.
- ■ Respecting the privacy of others.
- ■ Challenging discrimination, disrespect, and apathy.
- ■ Learning to live successfully with different people.
- ■ Seeking common ground for dialogues to begin and continue.
- ■ Maintaining a deep self-awareness.
- ■ An important act of humanity.
- ■ A continuous action, repeated in every campus encounter.

Misconceptions:

Civility at the University of Mississippi is NOT:

■ **About only being polite:** being polite is a solid place to start but civility (as demonstrated below) encompasses more than passive responses.

■ **About political correctness:** once an important phrase designed for American citizens to be more aware of their thought and speech with respect to racism, sexism, classism, ethno/religio-centrism, and homophobia, it has devolved into a meaningless phrase often used to mask anger at the groups it was designed to protect.

■ **About being restrained or silenced:** learning cannot effectively advance when people silence themselves. In fact, this encourages frustration and anger and actually inhibits learning.

■ **About being blind to existing racism, sexism, homophobia, and classism:** While we may wish that oppressive events or ideas were no longer present on this campus, this is not the case. Pretending so only encourages the maintenance and strengthening of these unproductive and harmful narratives.

How to be Civil on Campus

Now that we know what the components of civility are, we need to know how to behave in a civil manner. To ensure that disagreements in societies do not devolve into endless and unproductive arguments and potential violence, members define and subscribe to sets of rules and behaviors. It works similarly at the University of Mississippi. To protect and sustain our spaces of learning, experience, and exploration and to avoid chaos and harm, participants must accept and adhere to certain guidelines. The college campus, in addition to existing as its own society, prepares you for the many public, professional, and private societies that you are sure to engage in after you graduate. Learning and integrating civil behaviors now will absolutely assist you in advancing in your future careers, communities, and relationships. Here are some easy guidelines for civility. Johns Hopkins University professor, P.M. Forni has created a solid list of ways to ensure civility. Many of the ideas expressed and elaborated on in this section are drawn from or inspired by his thoughts.

Did you know?

Southern Living magazine selected Susan Glisson, director of the William Winter Institute for Racial Reconciliation, in 2013 as one who represents "the next generation of leaders forging a better future without forsaking a bitter past." Her mission is social justice – working to change the conditions that have created a legacy of inequities. She believes racism can be eliminated in her lifetime.

■ **Pay Attention**—Train your focus on the individual speaking. Try not to wander in your thoughts. Avoid answering phone calls and text messages when others are speaking. This can encourage misunderstanding and convey disrespect. If you encounter an emergency, politely excuse yourself and move far enough away to avoid disrupting the activity.

■ **Acknowledge Others**—Part of the Ole Miss culture is that we view the campus as a community. When you encounter someone in class and around campus, acknowledge his or her presence. Averting your eyes can unintentionally communicate that you view a person as unimportant.

■ **Think the Best**—Accept from the beginning that the individual you are engaging with has positive intentions.

■ **Listen**—Be sure to meaningfully listen to what another person is saying. Do not use this time to solely craft your next thought. Listening can avoid miscommunication.

■ **Be Inclusive** (language and action)—Strive to include people in your conversation. Avoid gestures or speech that signal secrecy or exclusion.

■ **Be Patient**—When encounters or ideas frustrate or anger you, remain calm in mind and body. Negative emotional responses inhibit rational thinking and lead to incorrect assumptions and conclusions.

■ **Speak Kindly**—Remember that you are speaking to someone who has feelings, who may be hurt by your words. Your words have the power to comfort, inspire, and move people.

■ **Don't Speak Ill of Others**—Doing so reveals that you are feeling unsure about yourself, trying to elevate yourself above others, competing in less valorous ways, and indicates that you are spending less time on improving your own intellectual and spiritual self. In your speech, do not encourage sexism, racism, homophobia, ethno- centrism, or classism. It is wrong and makes you appear ignorant. Speak up against and walk away from language that discriminates against others.

■ **Do Not Harass People**—Do not verbally or physically threaten faculty, staff, or other students by writing threatening letters, text messages, e-mails, or leaving disturbing voice-mail messages. Model the behavior you would like to see in others. Manage your emotions. Gather yourself before approaching people regarding difficult situations. Avoid persistently contacting faculty, staff, and students.

■ **Respect Others' Opinions**—This is perhaps one of the most difficult behaviors to achieve. Avoid belittling someone's opinions that are different from your own. Also avoid assuming that everyone must think like you. Criticism of your opinions should be listened to intently and rationally. You are not required to integrate others' ideas into your own. Preface your responses to ideas contrary to your own with wording that acknowledges that you heard what the individual said, that you understand how he or she might think that way, or that you had not thought about the topic in that particular way. This is known as "qualified disagreement."

■ **Expand Your Horizons**—Make time to learn more about a background or culture you are not familiar with to expand your own perspective, belief systems, and interpersonal skills.

■ **Work Collaboratively**—To maximize learning and skills development and effectiveness for course assignments, campus activities, and curricular events, make sure to work in a collaborative manner. Avoid tendencies to either inappropriately control or let someone else do your work.

■ **Be Agreeable**—Avoid adopting a negative attitude. There will be times when you may disagree, but recognize when disagreeability has become an impulse rather than a genuine response. To maintain your credibility, carefully choose when to disagree. In general and in public, adopt a friendly approach and positive tone. Avoid being disrespectful, offensive, or threatening. If you feel yourself going down a potentially dangerous road, remove yourself from the situation, and if necessary, seek assistance.

■ **Respect Other People's Time**—Avoid being late for classes, meetings, work, and campus events. Being tardy to class signals disrespect and is disruptive and distracting to professors and classmates.

■ **Accept and Give Constructive Criticism**—Be sure before you speak that your words are intentional, kind, and solely for the purpose of advancing someone's progress. Identify the problematic action or idea and don't criticize or attack the individual. Avoid resorting to obscenities and name-calling. Try to be empathic and deliver criticism in the way that you would want someone to deliver it to you. When criticism comes your way, receive it with an open mind and the notion that the individual delivering the comment has your best interests at heart. Remember to respect the work of others through positive comments.

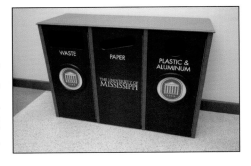

■ **Respect the Environment**—Strive to keep the campus environment clean; recycle if possible; do not use materials that harm the environment, yourself, or others; and adopt a conservationist attitude. Avoid wasting water and energy sources.

■ **Don't Shift Responsibility and Blame**—Accept responsibility for your actions and words. Understand where your responsibility begins and ends. Resist the tendency to avoid critically analyzing your own words and actions. This inhibits self-growth and respect for others.

■ **Protect Your Communities**—Uphold these standards of civility. Avoid doing and saying things that damage the reputation, productivity, integrity, and safety of your communities. In doing so, you protect and secure yourself and your well-being.

■ **Social Media and Civility**—(Some of this information is covered in Chapter 11 but bears repeating.) Many people do not recognize that the Internet is itself a giant society made up of an infinite number of mini-societies. As such, it is important to protect your reputation, your safety, and your privacy.

Adhering to the standards and behaviors listed above are an excellent place to begin your quest to observe a civility standard. Here are a few more (Many of the ideas expressed here may be found in or are inspired by Nancy Willard's work.)

■ **Avoid Hurtful Communication**—Once such communication is on the Internet it stays there. You and others may be impacted long after a hurtful message was sent.

■ **Avoid the Mistake of Assuming You are Anonymous**—Over the Internet, you are never completely anonymous. Every communication that you make and every site that you log on is recorded and can be accessed. While everyone is entitled to free speech under our country's constitution, you are not immune to the consequences of your actions.

■ **Consider How Internet Images and Statements Might Affect Your Professional and Personal Futures**—With increasing ease of access to the Internet, employers, colleagues, and friends can access information and images about you. Be careful how you construct your Internet persona. Privacy may be your right but it is also the right of others to make assumptions about you and your character based on what you have shared on the Internet.

■ **Avoid the "Everybody Does it" Mentality**—If you do something on the Internet that is considered either illegal or unethical you may be held accountable by law enforcement officials, University of Mississippi administration, and your fellow students.

■ **Avoid Manipulating and Being Manipulated**—Train yourself to recognize when you are using others for your own gain or are being used for someone else's gain. This can happen fast and often in intense situations or it could be a "slow burn." Watch for this and avoid it.

■ **Avoid Impulsive Behavior**—Always remember to carefully re-read your messages before sending them. To maintain your own civility and credibility, consider the impact of your words before you hit send, especially if you find yourself in a highly emotional state.

- **Assess the Credibility of Information Given to You**—Remember to check and rely on facts rather than assumptions. Make sure that before you act or react, you have as much credible information as possible to create the most reasonable and effective response.

- **Make Ethical Choices**—While active on the Internet—surfing and sending messages—make sure you maintain your ethical compass. Do not do things just because you can. Activities may be technically legal but can stray into the blurry area of not being ethical. Strive to be self-reflective about your activities on the Internet.

- **Avoid Using Electronic Devices When Inappropriate**—Difficult personal and educational conversations and productive labor are best accomplished in person. Using text messages, Twitter, Facebook, and e-mail to communicate can often lead to misunderstandings and miscommunications. Textual communication rarely communicates the intended tone.

- **Avoid Addictive Use**—Always consider the amount of time you spend on the Internet. Think about whether your time spent on the Internet is productive or if it is inhibiting your communication skills, your sociability, and your mental state. If you think you have a problem, consult a counselor.

Civility, Tradition and the University of Mississippi Campus

The University of Mississippi, like campuses across the nation, possesses many traditions that bind us as a society and a community. Looking across history and our landscape, we carry those traditions with us and pass them on to the incoming classes as part of their legacy. Sharing of traditions brings us closer as a society and creates common ground. Displays of tradition may be seen in our Alma Mater, our cheers, our mascot, The Grove, our clothing, in our residence hall rooms, apartments, houses, and cars. Traditions are only useful as long as they promote the best of what our University has to offer and strengthen ties among all members of the campus community. Because of this, traditions change. Traditions that previously seemed harmless are rediscovered as problematic. Sensitive to the feelings and ideas of  their members, colleges, including University of Mississippi, have ceased traditions that negatively impact its members and have replaced them with ones that inspire pride in the school. Traditions that exclude people or cause harm should be eliminated or adjusted. During our history, the campus has supported Colonel Reb, played *Dixie* during athletic events, displayed Confederate flags, and colloquially referred to the university as *Ole Miss*. We as a community should understand that these traditions emerged from our problematic legacy of racism. While many of us may cherish these traditions, we must understand the history of these campus traditions and how they cause injury and discontent for many of our campus community members. As responsible community members, we must consistently analyze those traditions that create an unwelcome environment or represent the University in a negative light. A society and a community cannot successfully and productively exist if its strength is drawn from harming, intentionally or unintentionally, others. Not to worry though, older and less useful traditions are regularly altered or eliminated to make space for even better ones.

The Benefits of Civility:

Acting civil is not a mere demonstration of being polite; provides many benefits to all members of a society or community. Civility guarantees:

■ **Respect for all regardless of who they are and what they believe**

■ **A safe environment that promotes learning and self-discovery**

■ **An ability to more effectively navigate through campus crises**

■ **Avoidance of unintentional gaffes**

Civility and the Active Bystander

One of the most effective ways to create productive and intelligent societies is to make sure that all of their participants are active bystanders. An active bystander is someone who observes a conflict or unacceptable behavior and then intervenes. The event might be something serious or minor, one-time or repeated, but the active bystander knows that the behavior is destructive to an individual or the society at large or likely to make a bad situation worse. (web.mit.edu/bystanders/definition/index.html). An active bystander takes steps that can make a difference. It is likely that while you are a student at the University of Mississippi, you will encounter uncivil or hostile language or action. You do not have to idly sit through the uncomfortable situation. This is your University and you should expect that this setting be safe, productive, and civil. If faced with an uncomfortable comment or situation, here are some questions to ask yourself and actions to consider:

■ **First**, you can assess a situation to determine what kind of help, if any, might be appropriate.

　　1. Notice out-of-the-ordinary actions and interactions.
　　2. Decide "in your gut" that something is amiss or unacceptable.

Did you know?

Clifford Ochs, professor of biology, conducts research on the Mississippi River. Students have been vital to his exploration. "Students in my lab are carrying out studies of many of the different types of organisms that occur in the river, from microbes to algae to benthos and fish. We are interested in how these organisms interact with each other."

3. Ask yourself, "Could I play a role here?"

4. If no one intervenes, what will likely happen?

5. Is someone else better placed to respond?

6. What would be my purpose in responding?

7. Assess your options for giving help.

8. Determine the potential risks of taking action:

    a. Are there risks to myself?

    b. Are there risks to others (e.g. potential retaliation against person being "helped")?

    c. Is there a low-risk option?

    d. How could I reduce risks?

    e. Is there more information I can get to better assess the situation?

    f. Decide whether to act at the time or later.

■ **Second**, an active bystander evaluates options and chooses a strategy for responding. For strategies while things are unfolding consider these actions:

1. Name or acknowledge an offense.

2. Point to the "elephant in the room."

3. Interrupt the behavior.

4. Publicly support an aggrieved person.

5. Use body language to show disapproval.

6. Use humor (with care).

7. Encourage dialogue.

8. Help calm strong feelings.

9. Call for help.

■ **Third,** for **strategies** after the fact, consider these actions:

1. Privately support an upset person.

2. Talk privately with the person acting inappropriately.

3. Report the incident, with or without names.

THE WILLIAM WINTER INSTITUTE
WELCOME TABLE GUIDEPOSTS

Be present and welcoming. Be 100% present. Set aside the usual distractions of things undone from yesterday, things to do tomorrow. Bring all of yourself to the work and participate fully. Practice hospitality. We all learn most effectively in spaces that welcome us. Welcome others to this place and this work, and presume that you are welcomed.

Listen deeply to learn. Listen intently to what is said; listen to the feelings beneath the words. Listen to yourself also. Strive to achieve a balance between listening and reflecting, speaking and acting. You will be invited to share in pairs, small groups, and in the large group. The invitation is exactly that. *You* will determine the extent to which you want to participate in our discussions and activities.

No fixing. Each of us is here to discover our own truths, to listen to our own inner teacher, to take our own inner journey. We are *not* here to set someone else straight, or to help right another's wrong, to "fix" or "correct" what we perceive as broken or incorrect in another member of the group. Be a community of learners; set aside perfectionism and fear of "messing up."

Suspend judgment and assumptions and seek understanding. Set aside your judgments. By creating a space between judgments and reactions, we can listen to the other, and to ourselves, more fully, and thus our perspectives, decisions, and actions are more informed. Our assumptions are usually invisible to us, yet they undergird our worldview and thus our decisions and our actions. By identifying our assumptions, we can then set them aside and open our viewpoints to greater possibilities.

Speak your truth and respect the truth of others. Say what is in your heart, trusting that your voice will be heard and your contribution respected. Your truth may be different from, even the opposite of, what another in the circle has said. Speaking your truth is not debating with, or correcting, or interpreting what another has said. *Own* your truth by speaking only for yourself, using "I" statements.

Did you know?

C. Edward "C. J." Rhodes (B.A. philosophy '04) delivered the keynote address at UM's Black History Month in 2012. "This is the 50th year of the University's integration…As we look back on the achievements and sacrifices of those from the past, this generation is challenged to do great things not just for themselves, but for others and the world as well."

Maintain confidentiality. Create a safe space by respecting the confidential nature and content of discussions held in the formation circle. What is said in this space, stays there; what is learned here, leaves here. Everyone gets to tell their own story for themselves.

Respect silence. Silence is a rare gift in our busy world. After you or someone else has spoken, take time to reflect, without immediately filling the space with words. Look inward and listen to yourself in the silence.

When things get difficult, turn to wonder. If you find yourself disagreeing with another, becoming judgmental, shutting down in defense, try turning to wonder: "I wonder what brought her to this place?" "I wonder what my reaction teaches me?" "I wonder what he's feeling right now?" You do not have to agree with another's story; but you do have to respect his or her right to tell his or her own story.

Trust the circle. In this setting, all voices are valued equally. All gifts are welcomed and respected. Within each circle is the genesis of renewal and the campus community well-being. The circle can be the instrument for creating a new campus community narrative for the sake of ourselves and future University of Mississippi campus individuals.

Conclusion:

This chapter has provided a lot of information to consider. While at the University of Mississippi, upholding the standards of civility and being aware of your own behavior and style of participation on campus will benefit yourself and others by creating and sustaining a space conducive to intellectual, professional, and personal growth. While you are a student at Ole Miss, consider regularly using this chapter as a resource. Refer to the chapter for appropriate conduct, advice on how to maintain good relations with other campus participants, how to ensure interpersonal communication success and how to effectively move through difficult interpersonal situations.

Did you know?

Patrick Woodyard (B.A. International Studies and Spanish '10), is co-founder and chief executive officer of Nisolo, a company that manufactures handmade leather shoes and accessories in Peru for sale in the U.S. His goal is to put producers first: "to pay fair wages and ethically produce goods that have a profound impact on the lives of people making the product, as well as their families."

EXERCISES

One of the best ways to preserve civility is to have a vested interest in the society and the members of that society.

I. Getting Started: Respect Activity (edchange.org/multicultural/activities/activity1.html)

- Ask everyone to find someone in the room they do not know.

- Instruct everyone to introduce themselves and spend five to ten minutes talking about respect. What does it mean for you to show respect, and what does it mean for you to be shown respect?

- After the allotted time, ask the participants to return to their seats, and open the discussion. What ideas did people discuss?

- Common responses include the "Golden Rule," looking somebody in the eyes, being honest, and appreciating somebody's ideas even when you do not agree with them.

- Each of these responses offers interesting points of reflection. They each are informed culturally and hegemonically.

- Once people have returned to the big group for processing the activity, be sure to inquire where people's notions of respect come from and who those notions serve and protect.

- Does everybody really want to be treated the way you want to be treated? Is it respectful in every culture to make eye contact with the person who is speaking?

- What if somebody's ideas are oppressive—should we still respect them? And to whose benefit?

- It is important to mention that respect is a crucial ingredient in any discussion but especially in a discussion of controversial issues such as racism, sexism, and economic injustice.

- The point is to learn from our differences—to understand each other's understanding. The point is *not* to agree. But the point, as well, is to reflect critically on our assumptions and socializations around the concept of respect.

- This activity touches many bases. First, it starts the crucial path toward building a community of respect. This is the first step in maintaining a constructive exchange regarding issues related to equity and social justice. At the most basic level, participants meet someone they did not know and exchange ideas with that person. Second, the community is built through an understanding of how the group perceives respect and how we negotiate its meaning. Third, the similarities and differences in participants' ideas about respect begin to show the first signs of similarities and differences within the group on a larger level, often in ways that reflect power and privilege.

Did you know?

The College Corps student leadership group in the College of Liberal Arts seeks to alleviate community poverty by placing student volunteers committed to long-term service with nonprofit organizations and schools in Lafayette County. Members serve 10 hours per week with a goal of 300 hours during the school year and receive a Segal Education Award at the year's end.

II. Who I Am Poems (edchange.org/multicultural/activities/poetry.html)

Preparing and Assigning:

This activity begins an active introspective process while continuing to provide opportunities for individuals to make connections with each other. Participants write short poems, starting each line with "I am," encouraging them to describe in their own words who they are and what's salient to their identities.

Objectives:

In any attempt to increase awareness and encourage self-development, it is crucial to engage participants in activities that call for introspection and self-reflection. It also is important to provide opportunities for participants to make connections across, and even within, identity borders. The "Who I Am" activity can provide a non-threatening starting point for encouraging self-reflective thought and introspection. It is a safe way for participants to think about and share the influences that have shaped their identities. Also, it continues the connection-making process as participants find unexpected similarities and differences between themselves and others in the group.

Instructions:

- Ask participants to take 10 to 15 minutes to write a poem called "Who I Am."

- Instruct them that the only rule is that each line begins with the words "I am..."

- Leave it open to their interpretation as much as possible, but suggest that they can, if they wish, include statements about where they're from regionally, ethnically, religiously, and so on; memories from different points in their lives; interests and hobbies; mottos or credos; favorite phrases; family traditions and customs; and whatever else defines who they are. Be sure to let them know that they will be sharing their poems.

III. Inclusion/Exclusion (edchange.org/multicultural/activities/inclusion.html)
This activity requires 30-45 minutes.

Purpose:

Participants share their experiences as students, exploring different ways people are made to feel "included" in and "excluded" from the learning process. Topics emerging from this activity include (1) the range of learning styles and needs in any group of people, (2) the importance of reflective practice and understanding one's own socialization, and (3) the power teachers have through both implicit and explicit actions.

Preparation:

Divide participants into small groups of four or five.

Did you know?

For the first time in the show's 28-year history, ESPN's "College GameDay" came to the campus of UM in October 2014. Broadcasting from the Grove stage, the nation watched as Rebel fans became fired up for GameDay. This was one of the biggest weekends in Ole Miss football history as the Rebels defeated the No. 1 ranked Alabama Crimson Tide.

Instructions:

◼ Ask participants to do a five-minute free write based on two prompts:

   ◼ Recall a time from your own schooling when you felt especially included, engaged, appreciated, and validated in the learning process.

   ◼ Recall a situation when you felt especially excluded, alienated, and invalidated in the learning process.

◼ Without being too directive, let students know that the reasons for their feelings of inclusion and exclusion could vary broadly, from the way a certain teacher taught to a lack of feelings of support to social reasons.

◼ In their small groups, ask participants to share the parts of their stories they feel comfortable sharing. Once everybody has shared both stories, ask them to reflect upon the similarities and differences in their stories.

◼ Return students to the big group and ask a few people to share their stories with the whole class.

◼ Request a volunteer to record brief notes about both categories of stories. (What makes students feel included? What makes them feel excluded?)

◼ Facilitate a discussion about the notes, examining consistencies and differences in individuals' stories and learning needs. Often I ask participants how many of them found it easy to recall both an inclusion and an exclusion story. Most participants respond that it was easy. This allows me to make the point that we, as teachers, have tremendous power—that even when we don't intend to do something wrong, we might do something that has a lifelong impact on one of our students. This is why developing reflective practice skills are critical to anybody committed to educational equity.

◼ Other sample questions to guide the conversation:

   ◼ What similarities do you observe among the situations in which people felt especially included in a learning process?

   ◼ What consistencies do you notice in the situations in which people felt excluded?

   ◼ Knowing that we have students with various needs and learning styles, what can we do to ensure we are including, engaging, and validating all learners?

Did you know?

UM assistant professor of chemistry and biochemistry, Amala Dass, has been awarded a $650,000 Faculty Early Career Development (CAREER) Program grant from the National Science Foundation. The grant will allow Dass and his students to continue research in the study of gold alloy nanomolecules, plus launch and sustain a summer chemistry research program for Mississippi high school students.

IV. Knowing the Community: Sharing Activity

Objectives:

■ Participants will learn the names of each person in the class, group, or community, as well as something about each person's background.

■ Participants will have a greater understanding and appreciation for the diversity within the group, while realizing that they have things in common with some of the people from whom they might have felt most distant.

Activity Description:

■ Participants should sit in a circle for this exercise if possible.

■ The facilitator should hand out a list of items for each participant to share with the group.

■ Items could include name/nicknames, ethnic background, where they are from and where their parents were born, which generation for their family they represent in the U.S., and one custom or tradition their family practices.

■ Give participants time to record some of their initial thoughts on these items.

■ Before you begin the exercise, instruct the participants to identify one or two people in the group who they do not know and to think about what answers they expect from those people. This part is not to be shared among group members, but can help people realize how they formulate ideas about people based on appearance.

■ Now you are ready to begin. It is important to tell the group that each person will be limited to about two minutes in order for everyone's voice to be heard. Once everyone has had an opportunity to share their information, ask the group to discuss what they have learned from the exercise.

Did you know?

A five-week fellowship in bioethics designed for juniors and seniors in the College of Liberal Arts offers a collaboration between the Medical Center and the Department of Philosophy and Religion. The program introduces students to real-world ethical issues that face medical professionals, while engaging with medical students in Jackson.

V. CORE VALUES (Group Exercises **Do Respect** by Madd-Steiny Productions | © Copyright 2011 Madd-Steiny Productions, LLC. madd-steiny.com)

■ Take a few minutes to identify your top three core values — the values that are most important to you right now.

■ As a small group, answer the following question: Is there any overlap between the core values each of you selected?

■ Break up into groups of about three or four. Each participant should share what he or she wrote with the others in the group.

    a. How can you live these values at the University?

    b. Does your campus align with these values?

■ **RESPECT IS...** Respect is an action, respect is a personal matter, and respect is powerful. **Write these down for all to see.**

■ As a large group, ask participants to think of more endings to the statement: Respect is...

■ Make the following quote available for all to see: *"I'm not concerned with your liking or disliking me... All I ask is that you respect me as a human being."* – *Jackie Robinson* Ask the participants to break up into small groups and have a brief discussion about the preceding quote.

■ **As a small group, answer the following questions:**

    a. Is it possible to respect and dislike someone at the same time?

    b. How can you show respect to someone if you dislike him or her?

    c. How can you respect someone if you disagree with him or her?

    d. Do you automatically respect someone if you like the person?

About the Author

Jennifer A. Stollman, former Academic Director for the William Winter Institute for Racial Reconciliation

Jennifer A. Stollman, Ph.D., focuses on creating and facilitating educational and professional development programs dealing with the issues of race and anti-racism. Her research and teaching interests include the study of race, class, and gender and the construction and deployment of individual and collective identities in American history.

Chapter 4
Time Management—the Key to Success

by Dewey Knight

As Coordinator of the First-Year Experience courses I often am asked by students and their parents, "What is the key to success at Ole Miss?" My answer is simply, "time management" — two words that most often determine the degree of success students achieve, both inside and outside the classroom, especially during their first year at the University.

Most students arrive at the University with little or no experience in managing their own time. From birth they have had their time managed for them by parents, teachers, coaches, and other adults. They have had their days and nights ordered for when to get up, where to go, when to go there, when to be home, when to study, and when to go to bed.

Then, suddenly, students are offered almost total freedom in how they use time—whether to go to class, whether to go out, whether to go to bed, etc. This new freedom is wonderful and most students will say it is one of the best things about college. But it can also be one of the worst! This new-found freedom can be destructive if not exercised carefully and responsibly. One of my former EDHE 105 students describes this transition from high school and home and no freedom to the University and Oxford and virtually unlimited freedom as like "moving from an Amish village to Las Vegas!" I think she expressed the change in lifestyle every new student experiences better than I have ever heard it.

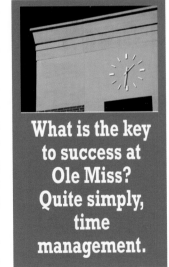

What is the key to success at Ole Miss? Quite simply, time management.

This chapter is about how to make the best use of the freedom you now enjoy. Managing time is a skill that takes practice to acquire. Time is limited, and it is your most valuable asset. Use it wisely and success and happiness will be yours. Misuse it and underachievement and unhappiness will result.

We will give you guidelines to help you better manage your time. On the assumption that people who want help managing their time probably don't *have* a lot of it, the guidelines are short and to-the-point. They aren't "magic pills" that will suddenly make you

Your new freedom brings with it many choices . . . and many challenges.

super-efficient and well-organized, but if you use them to improve the way you organize your time, you probably will find that your life is a little less stressful and, with any luck, you will have time to do more of the things that you enjoy outside of your college work.

If you are a full-time student, you have a full-time job. You may not think of college as a job, but consider this: You typically have 12-15 or more hours of class per week. In addition, you are expected to put in about two to three hours of preparation and production outside of class for each hour in class. This means that your work week is at least 36 to 60 hours long. College is a full-time occupation.

When lack of time is a problem, your first consideration should be the "big picture." Everyone should try to have a balanced life. If you don't think that your life is balanced, you may need to make some tough decisions. Should you take a smaller course load with fewer hours? Should you not be involved in so many student organizations? Should you give up a part-time job? Whatever your decision, you also should try to allow time for family and friends to keep that important balance. Now that you have considered the "big picture," it is time to improve your ability to manage your time, or in other words, manage yourself.

The Benefit of Being a Planner

Time management begins with the use of a calendar or planner with daily lists, taking the time to write down everything you must do so it gets done. If you sleep seven hours a night, you have 119 hours a week to do everything that you need to do. That, of course, includes everything from going to class, eating, sleeping, athletic events, getting ready to go out, going out, time-in-transit, studying, club meetings, social media, texting, surfing the "net," video games, shopping, laundry, telephone and television time, and everything in between. You must use all 119 hours a week to schedule everything you must do. Then you must stick to your schedule, which should give you an idea of your true priorities.

Instructors of EDHE 105 and 305 believe this information is critical to your success, so much so that we cover planners in more than one chapter of the text!

To begin, make a semester calendar. Use a wall or desk calendar for major exams, project and assignment due dates and meetings — basically the events that you must do and that do not change. Use your class syllabi to help you complete the calendar. You can use a pocket calendar, smart phone calendar, PDA, or paper planner as a reminder of classes, appointments, meetings, and errands. Study time should be scheduled at a ratio of two to three hours of study per hour of class.

Did you know?

"I've never been a quitter. It's not in my heart to give up. I don't think it should be in anybody's heart. I may give out, but I'll never give up."
Chucky Mullins

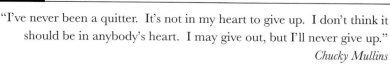

Moreover, a daily "to do" list should be made each day, either when you wake up in the morning or each night before you go to bed. The list should be kept short, no more than five or six items, both academic and personal. It's a good idea to prioritize the items and be specific, such as *read five pages in psychology*.

Get in the habit of using your calendar every day, and learn to say "no" so that you can meet your priorities.

Time Monitoring Exercise

Every successful change of habit begins with an assessment of where you are. For the next seven days, track what you do as you do it. First thing in the morning, jot down when you woke up. Then around noon, write down what you did with your hours between then and waking up. The more often you record your activities, the more useful this exercise will be to you. Mid-afternoon, pull this worksheet out again, and note what you've been doing in the intervening hours since noon. Do this again in the evening.

Time management begins with the use of a calendar or planner.

Use categories for filling in your time: class, study (name of class), social time, TV time, naps, meals, worship, meditation or other personal time, club meetings, exercise, shopping, social media, work, community service, etc. Don't be limited by this list, though. If you spend significant amounts of time doing other things (i.e. video games), then add those categories as well.

THIS IS IMPORTANT!!! You need to write down what you do as you do it, not at the end of the day, or even worse, at the end of the week. The information is *useless* if you attempt to retrace your steps for that long. You'll lose the richness of what this exercise has to offer. Don't take the lazy way out!

When you are done, tally up the number of hours spent in each category. Do you notice anything surprising, either good or bad? Even better—does this exercise give you any ideas on where you can recapture wasted time?

Here are two thoughts to consider: (1) Experts say you need to devote two to three hours of study time to every credit hour of class. If you are carrying 12 hours, that's 36 hours of study time. Even though it might seem like a burden, you need to PLAN for those hours. (2) What activities are both **UNNECESSARY** and **UNIMPORTANT**? Why the heck are you doing them? Is it because someone else wants or expects you to do so? Think about how you can eliminate timewasters—your degree is on the line, and it's worth it.

Did you know?

UM offers the state's only degree program in Mandarin Chinese, and the Department of Defense selected Ole Miss as one of four universities to train cadets and midshipmen as part of its ROTC Language and Culture Program.

Time Monitoring Exercise

HOUR	MONDAY	TUESDAY	WEDNESDAY	THURSDAY	FRIDAY	SATURDAY	SUNDAY
7-8 am							
8-9 am							
9-10 am							
10-11 am							
11-12 pm							
12-1 pm							
1-2 pm							
2-3 pm							
3-4 pm							
4-5 pm							
5-6 pm							
6-7 pm							
7-8 pm							
8-9 pm							
9-10 pm							
10-11 pm							
11-12 am							
12-1 am							
1-2 am							
2-3 am							
3-4 am							
4-5 am							
5-6 am							
6-7 am							

Track how you use your time. Note the times you spend for the following:

* Class
* Study
* Breaks
* Meals
* Spiritual activities
* Exercise
* Job
* Sleep
* Going out
* Time with friends
* Household chores/laundry
* Community service
* Social Media
* Getting ready to go out

Did you know?

The University partnered with the state of Mississippi and Toyota Motor Company to establish the Center for Manufacturing Excellence, which provides skilled workers for industries that locate in north Mississippi.

Procrastination

Procrastination is a basic human impulse. The term (derived from a Latin word meaning "to put off for tomorrow") entered the English language in the sixteenth century, and by the eighteenth century, Samuel Johnson was describing it as "one of the general weaknesses" that "prevail to a greater or lesser degree in every mind." The problem seems to be getting worse. According to Peirs Steel, a business professor at the University of Calgary, the percentage of people who admitted to difficulties with procrastination quadrupled between 1978 and 2002.

Philosophers are interested in procrastination for another reason. It's a powerful example of what the Greeks called *akrasia*—doing something against one's own better judgment. Professor Steel defined procrastination as willingly deferring something even though you expect the delay to make you worse off. The essence of procrastination lies in not doing what you think you should be doing, a mental contortion that surely accounts for the great psychic toll the habit takes on people. This is the perplexing thing about procrastination: although it seems to involve avoiding unpleasant tasks, indulging in it generally doesn't make people happy. In one study, 65 percent of students surveyed before they started working on a term paper said they would like to avoid procrastinating: they knew both that they wouldn't do the work on time and that the delay would make them unhappy.

Why Do Students Procrastinate?

Students, in general, procrastinate because of poor time management. Procrastination means not managing your time wisely. You may be uncertain of your priorities, goals, and objectives. You also may be overwhelmed with the task. As a result, you put off your academic assignments, or spend a great deal of time with your friends and on social activities, or worry about your upcoming examination, class project, and papers, rather than complete them.

Students also procrastinate because they have difficulty concentrating. When you sit at your desk, you may find yourself checking text messages or Instagram instead of studying. Your environment may be distracting and noisy (as are most residence halls and apartments). You may feel compelled to watch the latest YouTube video or try out the newest iPhone app. Perhaps your desk is cluttered and unorganized, and sometimes you sit/lie on your bed to study or do assignments. Have you noticed that all of these examples promote procrastination?

Some of us procrastinate because of fear and anxiety. You may be overwhelmed with the task and afraid of getting a failing grade, so you delay and delay getting started.

Students may procrastinate because of personal problems, lack of interest in the class or subject matter, fear of failure, or an unrealistic expectation of perfection.

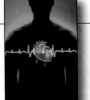

The Medical Center, with Tougaloo College and Jackson State University, is conducting the Jackson Heart Study, the world's largest study of heart disease risk factors in African-Americans.

Overcoming Procrastination

■ Set realistic goals. Don't try to do too much, and don't try to do everything perfectly.

■ Do school work when your energy is at its highest. If you are a morning person, do school work in the morning. If you are a night person, do school work at night.

■ Break large tasks into smaller ones. You don't want to be overwhelmed by the work you need to do so create smaller tasks from bigger ones. Then focus on completing the smaller tasks one at a time until you are finished.

■ Work for realistic periods of time. If you work best at one hour intervals, don't try to cram in two hours of study. Or if one-half hour at a time is best for you, then follow your own needs; do not study for long periods just because your friends do.

■ As much as you want to believe you do your best work under pressure, most often that's just not the case!

■ Avoid study marathons (like all-nighters).

■ Don't rely on energy drinks or drugs to "make up for lost time."

■ Mix activities. Switch subjects after a while, or try to alternate between doing things you enjoy with things that you find challenging or boring.

■ Create an effective place to do your school work. Make your work place comfortable but not **too** comfortable. Try to keep distractions to a minimum (such as phones, TV, and friends). Don't forget the importance of good lighting, and make sure you have access to the materials and supplies you need.

■ Allow extra time for unexpected things. The "unexpected" can be discovering that you really need at least five hours to write your English composition when you had only planned for three hours. And you don't want to wait until the last minute to do an important assignment only to get sick, or have your computer crash, or have the printer run out of ink.

■ Schedule time for yourself—for exercise, relaxation, and socializing.

■ Use your free time wisely. Make effective use of the time between classes or while you are waiting—for buses or friends, at the Student Health Center, etc.

■ Reward yourself when you finish a task on time. Make sure that the reward is suitable for the difficulty of the task and the time you spent on it.

■ Start NOW!

Successfully Managing Your Time at Ole Miss

The key to effective time management at Ole Miss is literally being your own boss. Instead of being accountable to teachers and parents, now you need to be accountable to you! As we have seen, one of the biggest stumbling blocks to time management is procrastination. However, the easiest way to avoid procrastination is to start by memorizing ten little two-letter words; "If it is to be, it is up to me." Here's how:

Did you know?

The first Olympic-size swimming pool in Mississippi was located on the campus on the west side of the then-Gymnasium which is now the Martindale Student Services Center.

1) Get—and use—a planner. No matter what kind it is, make sure you have one and you use it – EVERY DAY!

2) Set goals. Determine what you want to accomplish and set goals to accomplish it. Setting goals makes you more inclined to follow through with your plans and accomplish your tasks. Your life is a series of choices and decisions. You are actually managing these choices, not the flow of time.

3) Prioritize. Once you determine what you want to accomplish, you must prioritize your tasks. Figure out what must be done and what can be put on hold. Focus on the most important tasks before proceeding to the less important ones. Prioritizing makes you less inclined to procrastinate.

4) Learn to say no. You can determine how to spend your time or you can let others plan it for you by default. Knowing your priorities helps you stay focused. You are not being selfish if you choose to schedule your time according to your goals. Be careful with over-commitment, and don't attempt to do too much. Remember that every time you say yes to something, you are automatically saying no to everything else you could have done with that time.

5) Let yourself relax. Schedule certain days that are just for you. Don't study on those days, and don't make obligations to anyone else. Instead, use this time to do something that you really enjoy. It is important to have personal time—it can be renewing.

6) Plan ahead. Do you have a large research paper due the last week of the semester? Work backward in your calendar and figure out how much time you need to write it, how much time you'll need to research it, and how much time you'll need to pick your topic. If you think you'll need six weeks for the entire project, work backward from the due date and schedule the time into your calendar before it's too late.

7) Utilize spare time. If you have to wait in line or for class to start, use that extra time to review your notes or study for an exam. Have an hour between classes? Study in the coffee shop, the library or The Grove. Don't waste any time! You can accomplish a lot during this extra "found" time. This will allow extra time to complete larger tasks.

8) Know when you are most productive. Everyone has a time during the day when they are most productive. Whether this time is in the morning or at night, use it to tackle your most demanding tasks. Do less challenging activities when you have less energy.

Did you know?

Professor Alexander Bondurant organized our first football team in 1893. For the team's uniform colors, he chose the red of Harvard and the blue of Yale.

9) Plan for the unexpected. Sure, you just might be able to pull off two papers and a presentation during midterms week. But what happens if you catch the flu the night you're supposed to be pulling the all-nighter? Expect the unexpected so you don't have to spend more unplanned time trying to fix your mistakes.

10) Don't give up! Like any other skill, it takes time to learn how to manage your time. Even time management experts have days when their whole schedule falls apart. If yours does, don't give up on time management. Instead, pick up the pieces and start again the next day. Review your schedule at the end of each week to see what did and what didn't work for you. Build on your successes as you develop plans and time management strategies for the following weeks.

Good time management skills give you control of your life. Fortunately, all the time management skills can be learned. Learning them will allow you to maintain balance in your life and empower you to be successful. Your Ole Miss experience will be all that you, and we, want it to be!

Glossary

Procrastination: "To put off for tomorrow." A phenomenon manifested in 65 percent of college students that results in failed time management and less-than-desired success.

Time management: How one organizes and uses the 168 hours in each week to successfully meet academic, spiritual, social, emotional, and personal goals and expectations. The most critical skill needed for success in college and in life.

REFERENCES

Lynn, K. (2011). Eight steps for strong time management for college students. Retrieved from
collegelife.about.com/od/academiclife/a/timemanagement.htm?p=1

Martindale, G. (2010, November 5). Time management tips for college students. Retrieved from
stateuniversity.com/blog/permalink/Time-Management-Tips.html

Surowiecki, J. (2010, October 11). What we can learn from procrastination. *The New Yorker*.
newyorker.com/arts/critics/books/2010/10/11/101011crbo_books_surowiecki

Time management for college students. Retrieved from
timemangementhelp.com/college.htm

University Learning Center. Time management. Retrieved from
pennstatelearning.psu.edu/time-management

Did you know?

The speed limit on campus is 18 miles per hour. The jersey number 18 was worn by legendary Ole Miss quarterback Archie Manning, and it is in his honor that the speed limit is set.

SPEED LIMIT 18

About the Author

Dewey Knight, *Associate Director for the Center for Student Success and First-Year Experience*

Dewey Knight holds a Bachelor of Business Administration degree in advertising and a Master of Arts degree in higher education/student personnel. Both degrees are from the University of Mississippi. He is currently completing his Doctor of Philosophy degree in higher education at the University of Mississippi.

Chapter 5
Active Listening and Effective Note Making
by Dewey Knight

Knight's Law

Half of the final exam questions will come from the notes you missed in lectures.

Banahan's Corollary

The other half will come from the notes you can't decipher.

For centuries, the predominant method of instruction at universities and colleges has been lecture. The professor, an expert in his or her academic subject, imparts knowledge and understanding by oral presentations to students. This model of instruction has been referred to as the "sage on the stage." The all-knowing sage (your professor) presents from a podium or lectern to his or her students. The instructor is active while students assume a passive role.

> **The importance of class attendance can never be overstated. Students who go to class make better grades.**

Over time, visual aids (overhead projectors, PowerPoints, and handouts) have been utilized to supplement lectures. Attempts to move from this lecture model of instruction have been undertaken, but still the lecture dominates most collegiate classrooms. Most students do not have a learning style preference that favors learning in this environment. This is a challenge, and this chapter will help students address that challenge.

The fundamental challenge for many students is to be present for the lecture. The most basic strategy any successful student must employ is simply **go to class**. The importance of class attendance can never be overstated. Students who go to class make better grades. Test content, directions for assignments and papers, and discussion of subject matter are covered in class. Copying someone else's notes or listening to a tape recording are not the same as personally being in class to observe, listen, ask questions, and make notes. Your productivity once you get to class is dependent on your arriving rested, nourished, and with appropriate supplies (paper, pen/pencil, textbook, laptop, etc.).

Additionally, preparation before class is critical. Read the assignment. Unfortunately, many students, particularly freshmen, do not read the assigned materials. In fact, recent statistics indicate that only 22 percent of freshmen arrive at class having read the assignment. In addition to reading the assignment, it is important to review your notes from the previous class meeting. This will refresh your memory and provide context for what will be covered.

As we begin this section of the text, focus on the following key concepts. First, passive is the opposite of active. Second, hearing (passive) is not the same as listening (active). Third, note-taking (passive) is not the same as note-making (active).

Active listening vs. Passive hearing

Active is defined as being engaged and is characterized by energetic work and participation. Passive is defined as not participating readily or not being involved. Listening is an active process. Passively, one can hear simply by being conscious (awake) and perceiving sounds. Listening goes beyond just hearing as it involves thinking about the information. Listening requires energy, being alert, and being engaged.

Hearing and listening are not the same thing. Hearing is a physiological response, while listening involves proactively seeking to understand, think, and analyze. In short, when you listen you are actively involved!

Effective Listeners & Ineffective Listeners

- Actively look for something of interest
- Focus on content, not style
- Listen for main ideas and their organization
- Vary note-making tools according to content
- Work hard and maintain active body posture

- Tune out mentally
- Judge the delivery
- Listen for facts rather than main ideas/organization
- Do not vary tools based on content
- Are mentally passive and give up easily

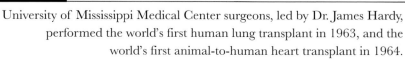

Did you know?

University of Mississippi Medical Center surgeons, led by Dr. James Hardy, performed the world's first human lung transplant in 1963, and the world's first animal-to-human heart transplant in 1964.

The most successful students learn to listen selectively. They focus on ideas, not just words. Throughout a lecture, they ask themselves, "What are the most important points the instructor is trying to get across?" Selective listening involves an awareness of what is and is not important enough to write down.

You will never be able to take down every word the professor utters and you should not even if you could. Instead, in discerning what is important (selectively listening), respond to the cues given by the instructor. These so-called listening cues are both verbal (what the instructor says) and non-verbal (what the instructor does).

Knowing what is important...

- **Ideas the professor repeats or spends a long time on**
- **Ideas written on the board or overhead or in the PowerPoint**
- **Ideas also covered in the text or course outline**
- **Change in pace, tone, emphasis, volume, or body language**
- **Clear cues: "This is important!" or "This will be on the exam!"**

Classroom seating

When you arrive at class is important. Be there on time (ten minutes early, if possible) and arrive prepared to learn.

Where you sit in class is important. Studies show that students who sit in the front and center of the classroom tend to achieve higher average exam scores (Rennels & Chaudhari, 1998). This is true even when students are assigned to these seats by their instructor. This indicates it is not simply that more motivated students tend to sit in the front and center of the room. Instead, the higher academic performance of students sitting front and center is most likely due to the learning advantages provided by these seating positions, such as the following:

When you arrive at class is important. Be there on time and arrive prepared to learn.

1) Better vision of the blackboard;
2) Better hearing of what is being said by the instructor;

For several years, ESPN has had at least one summer intern from the Meek School of Journalism and New Media, which also has had interns in New York at CBS News, NBC News, and Fox.

3) Better attention to what is being said because there are fewer (or no) people between them and the instructor to distract them;

4) Better eye contact with the instructor, which may increase the sense of personal responsibility to listen and take notes on what the instructor is saying.

So, when you step into the classroom, give serious thought to where you sit; make a conscious and strategic decision to head to the front and center of the class. This is particularly important in large lecture classes because as the class size gets larger, each individual tends to feel more anonymous, which may reduce your feelings of personal responsibility and your drive to stay focused and engaged. Thus, in large class settings, it is especially important to place yourself in a position that maximizes your ability to fight off distractions and stay involved.

Another advantage to sitting "up close and personal" with your instructor in large lecture classes is that it increases the likelihood your instructor will know you. This may work to your advantage at the end of the course if your total points fall between two grades. It is more likely that you will be given the benefit of the doubt because the instructor will remember you and that you sat up front—suggesting that you were an interested and motivated student. Furthermore, if you do well in the instructor's class and the instructor remembers you, you are well positioned to ask that instructor for a future letter of recommendation.

> **Another advantage of sitting up front? It increases the likelihood that the instructor will know you.**

Lastly, there is one other advantage to sitting in the front of the class. You are likely to feel less nervous about asking a question or making a class contribution because there will be no students sitting in front of you to turn around and stare when you do!

Note making vs. note taking

The most effective class notes are made (active), not just taken (passive). Learning to make notes effectively will help you to improve your study and work habits and remember important information. Often, students are deceived into thinking that because they understand everything that is said in class, they will remember it. This is so wrong! Write it down!

As you make notes, you will develop skills in selecting important material and in discarding unimportant material. The secret to developing this skill is practice. Check your results constantly. Strive to improve. Notes enable you to retain important facts and concepts and to develop an accurate means of arranging information.

There are many note making systems including: running text, informal outline, formal outline, word maps, and the Cornell note making system. The Cornell note making

Did you know?

Students who staff the S. Gale Denley Student Media Center are consistent recipients of the Grand Prize (Sweepstakes) at the Southeast Journalism Conference as well as individual prizes.

system is probably the most popular method of making notes and the one that is recommended to students who do not already have an effective system. The Cornell system was developed more than 40 years ago at Cornell University.

The Cornell Note Making System

Recall Column
2.5"

Reduce ideas and facts to concise jottings and summaries as cues for reciting, reflecting, and reviewing.

Record Column
6"

Record the lecture as fully and meaningfully as possible.

The format provides the perfect opportunity for following through with the 5 Rs of note making. Here they are:

1) RECORD. During the lecture, record in the main column as many meaningful facts and ideas as you can. Write legibly.

2) REDUCE. As soon as possible, summarize these ideas and facts concisely in the recall column. Summarizing clarifies meanings and relationships, reinforces continuity, and strengthens memory. Also, it is a way of preparing for exams.

3) RECITE. Now cover the column, using only your jottings in the recall column as cues or "flags" to help you recall and say facts and ideas of the lecture as fully as you can, not mechanically, but in your own words and with as much appreciation of meaning as you can. Then, uncovering your notes, verify what you have said. This procedure helps to transfer the facts and ideas into your long term memory.

4) REFLECT. Reflective students distill their opinions from their notes. They make such opinions the starting point for their own musings upon the subjects they are studying. Such musings aid them in making sense out of their courses and academic experiences by finding relationships among them. Reflective students continually label and index their experiences and ideas, put them into structures, outlines, summaries, and frames of reference. They rearrange and file them. Best of all, they have an eye for the vital—for the essential. Unless ideas are placed in categories, unless they are taken up from time to time for re-examination, they will become inert and soon be forgotten.

5) REVIEW. If you spend 10 minutes every week in a quick review of notes, you will retain most of what you have learned, and you will be able to use your knowledge currently to greater and greater effectiveness.

Abbreviations and symbols

Accustom yourself to using abbreviations and symbols when making notes. When it comes to note making, less is more. Develop a "shorthand" system that works for you. Try these tips: Write only the beginnings of words. Leave out small words such as "a" and "the" that won't affect meaning. (Don't leave out "in" or "on" which can affect meaning.)

Did you know?

The University of Mississippi has produced 25 Rhodes Scholars. Only six other public universities in the United States have produced more.

Leave out vowels inside words (you cn stll rd thm!). Just be sure you can understand your notes later!

Communicating with your professor

In the first chapter of this text, the importance of getting to know your professor was discussed. Building a relationship with your instructor can be a positive, rewarding, and beneficial endeavor. Instructor/student relationships are key to the success of both parties.

Even in large lecture classes, your professors can see you. Your posture and expressions send them messages as to your interest and level of engagement. Professors tend to engage with those students who seem to be most communicative.

Ask questions in class

■ Avoid irrelevant questions.

■ Maintain focus. Don't ask a question about what was just said if you weren't paying attention.

■ Give your instructor a place to start. Preface what you don't understand by saying what you *do* understand.

■ Think of a question and ask it!

A good note maker learns the instructor's style. Some lecturers start with a written outline, follow it, report key ideas, do not get off topic, and end on time. Other lecturers start with no outline, meander through various topics, write on the board, and sum up the lecture at the end of class. Pay close attention to the signals (verbal and non-verbal) that the lecturer sends.

Abbreviations and Symbols

&	and
<	less than
>	greater than
b/c	because
w/	with
w/o	without
@	at
#	number
=	equals (is, same)
☐	leads to (next, results in)
≈	approximately (similar)
Δ	change
/	or (per)
*	very important
etc	and so on
1st	first
ex	for example
cont'd	continued
reg	regular
form	formula
conc	conclusion
US	United States
WWI	World War I

Avoid distractions

Active listening is dependent on your being focused during the lecture. You must avoid distractions both external, and internal. External distractions include windows and doorways, classmates, cell phones (yours should never be active during class), seating choice, room temperature, and outside noises. A great many of these are beyond your control, but some are in your control. Make sure you avoid those in your control!

Internal distractions are all within your control. Make sure you exercise the control that is yours. Negative attitudes are barriers to your being an effective active listener and note maker. Try not to let personal worries and concerns enter your mind while in class. Avoid negative self-talk!

Lecturer's Signals...

- Writes on the board
- Repeats information
- Speaks more slowly
- Gives a definition
- Lists a number of points/steps
- Explains why or how things happen
- Describes a sequence
- Refers to information as a test item
- Changes tone of voice
- Uses body language
- Uses visual aids
- Refers to specific text pages

Negative self-talk

- So, who cares?!?
- I'm never going to remember all of this.
- I should never have taken this class.
- I wonder what I will do after this class…
- What a stupid question!
- I wish I weren't here…

Review your notes

Research confirms that students who review their notes within 24 hours of making them recall 70 to 80 percent of the information for a test. After class, be sure to re-read your notes as soon as possible. You should look for patterns and points that were repeatedly emphasized. Fill in the recall column (Cornell note making system) as you re-read your notes. Fill in portions of your notes that you had to speed through. Make sure you understand your abbreviations.

Did you know?

Ole Miss grad James Barksdale was the President and CEO of Netscape — one of the most successful early internet companies. He and his late wife Sally, funded the University's honors college — and a $100 million gift established the Barksdale Reading Institute.

Make the Most of Difficult Lecturers

Lecturer Characteristics	Suggestions for Students
Jumps from topic to topic; unorganized.	• Reorganize notes *after* each class. • Have three-ring binder with the aim of using a separate sheet of paper for each topic; reorganize the pages after class. • Record (with permission), and use the recording to help you reorganize the notes, by topic, after class.
Talks over students' heads; uses complex words and ideas.	• Review chapter to be covered. • Ask lots of questions. • Talk with the instructor outside of class to seek explanations.
Talks too fast.	• Review notes after every class — use text to fill in what you missed. • See the instructor during office hours to review what you missed or don't fully understand. • Ask the instructor to slow down and/or to repeat information.
Talks with a foreign accent.	• Sit in front of the room near the instructor. • Talk to the instructor one-on-one. This will help you get used to the instructor's manner of speech. • Ask the instructor to repeat the information.
***Boring* — presents information in a lifeless, boring manner.**	• Sit near the instructor. • Bring colorful supplies — at least create lively notes for yourself. • Ask questions and urge classmates to ask questions to enliven the presentation.
Condescending or impersonal towards students.	• See if you can talk to and form a relationship with the instructor. • Ignore it. • Seek help and personal affirmation out of class.
Is unprepared.	• Go to tutoring to fill in gaps. • Read and study the textbook before and after class. • Ask lots of questions and show interest. This might spur the instructor to prepare better for class.
Doesn't want to be bothered explaining material.	• Be persistent; keep asking questions. • Personally talk to the instructor after class — try to establish a working relationship. • Seek help from a tutor or another student.

It is important to review your notes at least once a week; don't wait until two or three days (or nights) before an exam for your review.

Conclusion

Active listening is the key to effective note making. Given the predominance of the lecture model of instruction, college students who make effective notes are in a position to be more academically successful. It takes lots of practice—both in actively listening in every lecture and in the making of notes. It's a skill set that once learned and mastered will serve you well throughout your academic career.

Glossary

Active is defined as being engaged and is characterized by energetic work and participation.

Hearing is a physiological response.

Lecture is the predominant method of instruction at universities and colleges wherein the professor who is an expert in his or her academic subject imparts knowledge and understanding by oral presentation to the student.

Listening is an active process that involves proactively seeking to understand, think, and analyze.

Listening cues are both verbal (what the instructor says) and non-verbal (what the instructor does) signals that indicate the material being covered or about to be covered is important.

Passive is defined as not participating readily or not being involved.

REFERENCES

Academic Skills Center at Dartmouth College. (2007). The Cornell note making system. dartmouth.edu/~acskills/docs/cornell_note_making.doc

Cuseo, J., Fecas, V.S., & Thompson, A. (2007). Thriving in college & beyond: Research-based strategies for academic success and personal development. Dubuque, IA: Kendall/Hunt.

Giles, R.M. et al. (1982). Recall of lecture information: A question of what, when, and where. *Medical Education, 16*(5), 264-268.

Lipsky, S.A. (2008). *College study: The essential ingredients.* Upper Saddle River, NJ: Pearson Education.

Rennels, M. R. & Chaudhari, R.P. (1988). Eye contact and grade distribution. *Perceptual and Motor Skills, 67*(October), 627-632.

About the Author

Dewey Knight, *Associate Director for the Center for Student Success and First-Year Experience*

Dewey Knight holds a Bachelor of Business Administration degree in advertising and a Master of Arts degree in higher education/student personnel. Both degrees are from the University of Mississippi. He is currently completing his Doctor of Philosophy degree in higher education at the University of Mississippi.

Chapter 6
Learning Styles
by Marc Showalter

The MBTI is the most widely used personality inventory in the world.

We come to college to learn. It often turns out that we end up learning most about ourselves. We don't all learn the same way. The Myers-Briggs Type Indicator (MBTI) is an instrument that helps you learn about yourself and your style of learning. This chapter is designed to help you apply the concepts of personality type to how you learn and how you can get the most out of your college experience.

Brief background on MBTI

The MBTI was developed by Isabel Briggs Myers and her mother Katherine Cook Briggs. It is based on Carl Jung's theory of type development. His theory suggests that seemingly random behavior is actually logical and orderly. The MBTI is the most widely used personality inventory in the world. It emphasizes that we each see the world through our own unique set of lenses. The constructive use of differences is emphasized, and each person is viewed as unique and valuable.

The MBTI offers us insight into how our personality type impacts our learning. Each type has a preferred way of learning, and understanding our preferences can help us be more effective learners.

Characteristics of Learners

E & I preferences — Where we focus our energy and attention

The preference for **Extraversion (E)** or for **Introversion (I)** tells us where we like to focus our energy and attention. Students who prefer Extraversion tend to focus on the outer world. They pay attention to those things going on outside themselves. They are energized by others and direct their energy outward. Students who prefer Introversion tend to focus on their own inner world. They are very aware of their feelings, thoughts and perceptions. They are energized by their inner experience and direct their energy there.

S & N preferences — How we take in and express information

The preference for **Sensing (S)** or for **Intuition (N)** tells us how we take in and express information. Students who prefer Sensing are aware of what is real, concrete—they can experience it with their senses (see, hear, taste, touch, smell). Their senses tell them what's happening here and now and they look for practical matters. They prefer specifics, facts, and figures to ideas and theories. Students who prefer Intuition are aware of relationships, patterns and meanings that go beyond what is actually presented. They like the big picture and trust their intuition about people and situations. The future, ideas, and possibilities are often more interesting than what is happening now.

T & F preferences — How we make decisions

The preference for **Thinking (T)** or for **Feeling (F)** tells us how we make decisions and judgments. Students who prefer Thinking make decisions objectively and don't let personal feelings sway their judgment. They do what is logical to their heads. They can make decisions in a detached way and pride themselves on their cool and logical analysis of the facts. Being fair and truthful is a guiding principle. Students who prefer Feeling make decisions based on what is logical to their hearts. They consider their values and the feelings of others when making choices. They are empathic, compassionate, and subjective in their decision making. Sometimes they take things too personally and have hurt feelings to show for it.

J & P preferences — How we organize our life

The preference for **Judging (J)** or for **Perceiving (P)** tells us how we like to organize and relate to the world. Students who prefer Judging like order, organization, planning, and structure. They prefer to get things done and don't like to play around until they have finished their work. Marking things off the list and moving on is important. They don't trust things that aren't well organized, and they take time very personally. Students who prefer Perceiving like flexibility, options, and freedom. They like to be available to new opportunities and don't want to do anything unless it is fun. They like to just "see what happens" and often wait until the last minute to complete projects. Time is more of a concept for them and they aren't hung up on that completion thing.

(Myers, 1998)

How the preferences affect learning

How the E (Extraversion) & I (Introversion) preferences affect learning

Es (Extraversion) act first and reflect later. They learn through interaction.

EXTRAVERSION

Cognitive style

The extraversion preference is expressed as a cognitive style that favors:

- Learning by talking and physically engaging the environment
- Letting attention flow outward toward objective events
- Talking to help thoughts form and become clear
- Learning through interactions, verbal and non-verbal

Study style

Extraverted study styles favor:

- Acting first, reflecting later
- Plunging into new material
- Starting interactions needed to stimulate reflections and concentration
- Having a strong external reason for studying, beyond learning for its own sake
- Avoiding distractions that will cut into their concentration
- Studying with a friend
- Studying to prepare to teach someone

Instruction that fits Es

The extraverting types do their best work with:

- Opportunities to think out loud; e.g., one-to-one with the teacher, classroom discussion, working with another student, action projects involving people
- Learning activities that have an effect outside the learner, such as visible results from a project
- Teachers who manage classroom dialogue so that extraverts have ways to clarify their ideas aloud before they add them to class discussion
- Assignments that let them see what other people are doing and what they regard as important

How the preferences affect learning

How the E (Extraversion) & I (Introversion) preferences affect learning

Is (Introversion) prefer quiet reflection. They learn in private, individual ways.

INTROVERSION

Cognitive style

The introversion preference is expressed as a cognitive style that favors:

- Quiet reflection
- Keeping one's thoughts inside until they are polished
- Letting attention flow inward
- Being engrossed in "inner events:" ideas, impressions, concepts
- Learning in private, individual ways

Study style

Introverted study styles favor:

- Reflecting first, acting after (if necessary),
- Looking for new data to fit into the internal dialogue that is always going on
- Working privately — perhaps checking one's work with someone who is trusted
- Reading as the main way of studying
- Listening to others talk about the topic being studied and privately processing what they take in
- Extraverting just when they choose to do so

Instruction that fits Is

The introverted types like learning situations that let them:

- Work internally with their own thoughts: listening, observing, lab work, reading, writing
- Process experience at their own pace
- Present the results of their work in forms that let them keep their privacy
- Have ample time to polish their work inside before needing to present it
- Have time to reflect before answering the teacher's questions
- Tie their studies to their own personal interests, their internal agenda

How the preferences affect learning

How the S (Sensing) & N (Intuition) preferences affect learning

Ss (Sensing) are careful to get the facts right. They desire concrete details in order to understand the facts.

SENSING

Cognitive style
The sensing preference is expressed in a cognitive style that favors:

- Being careful to get the facts right
- Memory of facts
- Observing specifics, absorbing data
- Starting with concrete experience, then moving to the abstract
- Aiming toward soundness of understanding
- Staying connected to practical realities around oneself
- Attending to what is in the present moment

Study style
The sensing preference is associated with a study style that favors:

- a practical approach to new material, looking for immediate usefulness
- beginning with the familiar, solid facts of their own personal experience, and distilling abstractions and principles from them

Instruction that fits Ss
Sensing types do their best work with:

- Instruction that allows them to hear and touch (as well as see) what they are learning
- Hands-on labs, materials that can be handled
- Relevant films and other audio-visuals
- Computer-assisted instruction
- First-hand experience that gives practice in the skills and concepts to be learned
- Teachers who provide concrete experiences first in any learning sequence, before using the textbook
- Teachers who show them exactly what facts and skills the adult world expects of them
- Teachers who do not move "too quickly" through material, touching just the high spots or jumping from thought to thought
- Assignments that allow them to start with known facts before having to imagine possibilities
- Skills and facts they can use in their present lives

How the preferences affect learning

How the S (Sensing) & N (Intuition) preferences affect learning

Ns (Intuition) get caught up by inspiration. They rely on insight more than observation.

INTUITION

Cognitive style

The intuition preference is expressed in a cognitive style that prefers:

- Being caught up in inspiration
- Moving quickly in seeing meaning and association
- Reading between the lines
- Relying on insight more than careful observation
- Relying on easy use of words more than on memory of facts
- Focusing on general concepts more than details and practical facts

Study style

Intuitives typically adopt a study style that includes:

- Following inspirations
- Jumping into new material
- Finding their own way through new material
- Wanting the big picture first before details
- Exploring new skills rather than polishing present ones

Instruction that fits Ns

The intuitive types do their best work with:

- Assignments that put them on their own initiative
- Real choices in the ways they work out their assignments
- Opportunities to be inventive and original
- Opportunities for self-instruction, individually or with a group
- A system of individual contracts between teacher and students
- Fascinating new possibilities
- Experience rich with complexities
- Work that stays fresh by calling for new skills, not just repetition of existing skills
- Teachers with a brisk pace, who don't go "too slowly"

How the preferences affect learning

How the T (Thinking) and F (Feeling) Preferences Affect Learning

Ts (Thinking) seek out objective truths. They analyze in order to discover logical principles.

THINKING

Cognitive style
A preference for thinking is expressed in a cognitive style that favors:

- Making impersonal judgments
- Aiming toward objective truth
- Analyzing experience to find logical principles
- Keeping mental life in order through logical principles
- Staying cool and free of emotional concerns while making decisions
- Naturally critiquing things, finding flaws to fix, aiming toward clarity and precision

Study style
The thinking preference is reflected in a study style that favors:

- Logically constructed subject matter
- Classrooms organized in logical systems
- Classrooms free from emotional distractions
- Interesting problems to analyze
- Wanting to bring logical order out of confused situations
- Wanting to get mastery over material

Instruction that fits Ts
The thinking types do their best work with:

- Teachers who are logically organized
- Subjects that show cause and effect relationships
- Subjects that respond to logic
- Feedback that shows them specific objective achievement

How the preferences affect learning

How the T (Thinking) and F (Feeling) Preferences Affect Learning

Fs (Feeling) seek out harmony and make caring judgments. They learn through personal relationships.

FEELING

Cognitive style

A preference for feeling is expressed in a cognitive style that favors:

- Making caring judgments
- Taking into account people's motives and personal values
- Attending to the relationships between people; seeking harmony
- Personalizing issues and causes that have high priority
- Staying tuned to emotional aspects of life
- Naturally appreciating people and things

Study style

Students who prefer feeling usually favor:

- Having topics to study that they care deeply about, with a human angle to them
- Learning through personal relationships rather than impersonal, individualized activities
- Warm and friendly classrooms
- Learning by helping, responding to others' needs

Instruction that fits Fs

The feeling types do their best work with:

- Teachers who value personal rapport with students
- Assignments that have a goal of contributing to others
- Receiving appreciation for them as persons
- Harmonious small-group work

How the preferences affect learning

How the J (Judgment) and P (Perception) Preferences Affect Learning

Js (Judging) seek predictability and consistency. They aim toward getting closure.

JUDGING

Cognitive style

Running one's outer life with a judging process is expressed as a cognitive style that favors:

■ From the beginning having a clear structure in a learning situation

■ Aiming toward completions and getting closure

■ Having life organized into an orderly plan

■ Looking for consistency, wanting to be able to predict how things will come out

Study style

J types typically adopt a study style that includes:

■ Planned and scheduled work, drawing energy from the steady, orderly process of doing their work

■ Wanting to know exactly what they are accountable for and by what standard they will be judged

■ Seeing assignments as serious business and persisting in doing them

Instruction that fits Js

The J types do their best work with:

■ Preplanned structure and a teacher who carefully provides it

■ Predictability and consistency

■ Formalized instruction that moves in orderly sequences

■ Prescribed tasks

■ Milestones, completion points, ceremonies to honor successful completions

How the preferences affect learning

How the J (Judgment) and P (Perception) Preferences Affect Learning

Ps (Perceiving) are open to new experiences. They are stimulated by something new and different.

PERCEIVING

Cognitive style

Running one's outer life with a perceiving process is expressed as a cognitive style that favors:

- ■ Open exploration without a preplanned structure
- ■ Staying open to new experiences
- ■ Managing emerging problems with plans that emerge with the problems
- ■ Having the stimulation of something new and different

Study style

P types typically adopt a study style that includes:

- ■ Spontaneously following their curiosity
- ■ Studying when the surges of impulsive energy come to them
- ■ Studying to discover something new to them
- ■ Finding novel ways to do routine assignments so as to spark enough interest to do the assignments

Instruction that fits Ps

The P types do their best work when:

- ■ They can pursue problems in their own way
- ■ They have genuine choices in assignments as with a system of individual contracts in which the students can negotiate some of the activities
- ■ Assignments hold their interest
- ■ Their work feels like play

(Lawrence, 1996)

What do all these letters mean to you?

Once you have an idea of your preference in each area, combining your four preferences gives you an overall pattern called type. There are 16 possible types and each one provides a way to help you understand yourself more fully.

The brief descriptions of each type included here give you some idea about how the four preferences work together. These general characteristics that are typically associated with each type give you additional information to help you understand how you learn best.

ISTJ

Quiet, serious, earn success by thoroughness and dependability. Practical, matter-of-fact, realistic, and responsible. Decide logically what should be done and work toward it steadily, regardless of distractions. Take pleasure in making everything orderly and organized – their work, their home, their life. Value traditions and loyalty.

ISFJ

Quiet, friendly, responsible, and conscientious. Committed and steady in meeting their obligations. Thorough, painstaking, and accurate. Loyal, considerate, notice and remember specifics about people who are important to them, concerned with how others feel. Strive to create an orderly and harmonious environment at work and at home.

INFJ

Seek meaning and connection in ideas, relationships, and material possessions. Want to understand what motivates people and are insightful about others. Conscientious and committed to their firm values. Develop a clear vision about how best to serve the common good. Organized and decisive in implementing their vision.

INTJ

Have original minds and great drive for implementing their ideas and achieving their goals. Quickly see patterns in external events and develop long-range explanatory perspectives. When committed, organize a job and carry it through. Skeptical and independent, have high standards of competence and performance – for themselves and others.

ISTP

Tolerant and flexible, quiet observers until a problem appears, then act quickly to find workable solutions. Analyze what makes things work and readily get through large amounts of data to isolate the core of practical problems. Interested in cause and effect, organize facts using logical principles, value efficiency.

ISFP

Quiet, friendly, sensitive, and kind. Enjoy the present moment, what's going on around them. Like to have their own space and to work within their own time frame. Loyal and committed to their values and to people who are important to them. Dislike disagreements and conflicts, do not force their opinions or values on others.

INFP

Idealistic, loyal to their values and to people who are important to them. Want an external life that is congruent with their values. Curious, quick to see possibilities, can be catalysts for implementing ideas. Seek to understand people and to help them fulfill their potential. Adaptable, flexible, and accepting unless a value is threatened.

INTP

Seek to develop logical explanations for everything that interests them. Theoretical and abstract, interested more in ideas than in social interaction. Quiet, contained, flexible, and adaptable. Have unusual ability to focus in depth to solve problems in their area of interest. Skeptical, sometimes critical, always analytical.

ESTP

Flexible and tolerant, they take a pragmatic approach focused on immediate results. Theories and conceptual explanations bore them – they want to act energetically to solve the problem. Focus on the here-and-now, spontaneous, enjoy each moment that they can be active with others. Enjoy material comforts and style. Learn best through doing.

ESFP

Outgoing, friendly, and accepting. Exuberant lovers of life, people, and material comforts. Enjoy working with others to make things happen. Bring common sense and a realistic approach to their work, and make work fun. Flexible and spontaneous, adapt readily to new people and environments. Learn best by trying a new skill with other people.

ENFP

Warmly enthusiastic and imaginative. See life as full of possibilities. Make connections between events and information very quickly, and confidently proceed based on the patterns they see. Want a lot of affirmation from others, and readily give appreciation and support. Spontaneous and flexible, often rely on their ability to improvise and their verbal fluency.

ENTP

Quick, ingenious, stimulating, alert, and outspoken. Resourceful in solving new and challenging problems. Adept at generating conceptual possibilities and then analyzing them strategically. Good at reading other people. Bored by routine, will seldom do the same thing the same way, apt to turn to one new interest after another.

ESTJ

Practical, realistic, matter-of-fact. Decisive, quickly move to implement decisions. Organize projects and people to get things done, focus on getting results in the most efficient way possible. Take care of routine details. Have a clear set of logical standards, systematically follow them and want others to also. Forceful in implementing their plans.

ESFJ

Warmhearted, conscientious, and cooperative. Want harmony in their environment, work with determination to establish it. Like to work with others to complete tasks accurately and on time. Loyal, follow through even in small matters. Notice what others need in their day-by-day lives and try to provide it. Want to be appreciated for who they are and for what they contribute.

ENFJ

Warm, empathetic, responsive, and responsible. Highly attuned to the emotions, needs, and motivations of others. Find potential in everyone, want to help others fulfill their potential. May act as catalysts for individual and group growth. Loyal, responsive to praise and criticism. Sociable, facilitate others in a group, and provide inspiring leadership.

ENTJ

Frank, decisive, assume leadership readily. Quickly see illogical and inefficient procedures and policies, develop and implement comprehensive systems to solve organizational problems. Enjoy long-term planning and goal setting. Usually well-informed, well-read, enjoy expanding their knowledge and passing it on to others. Forceful in presenting their ideas.

(Myers, 1998)

It's ok to not be sure about your type. Type isn't a complete explanation of everything you do, nor is it a perfect process. You are the expert on you so you get to decide what description fits you best. Once you have an idea of your type, you can look at how your type learns best.

Glossary

Myers-Briggs (MBTI) — an instrument designed to help determine personality type preferences. It is the most widely used psychological type instrument in the world.

Extraversion — Students who prefer to focus on the outer world. They are energized by others and direct their energy outward.

Introversion — Students who prefer to focus on their own inner world, personal feelings, thoughts, and perceptions and are energized by their inner experience and direct their energy there.

Sensing type — Students who tend to be aware of what is real, concrete and practical. Ss like details and dealing with the here and now.

Intuitive type — Students who tend to be aware of relationships, patterns, and meanings that go beyond what is actually presented. They like the big picture and trust their intuition about people and situations.

Thinking type — Students who prefer to make decisions objectively and don't let personal feelings sway their judgment. They do what is logical to their heads.

Feeling type — Students who prefer to make decisions based on what is logical to their hearts. They consider their values and the feelings of others when making choices.

Judging type — Students who prefer order, organization, getting things decided, planning, and structure.

Perceiving type — Students who prefer flexibility, staying open to options, new information, and freedom.

REFERENCES

Lawrence, Gordon, (1996). *People Types and Tiger Stripes* (3rd ed.) Gainesville, FL: Center for the Application of Psychological Type, Inc.

Myers, Isabel B., (1998). *Introductions to Type* (6th ed.) Palo Alto, CA: Consulting Psychologists Press, Inc.

About the Author

Marc Showalter, *Clinical Assistant Professor in Leadership and Counselor Education*

Marc Showalter has been working with college students and teaching freshmen for more than twenty years. A former director of the University Counseling Center, he now teaches full time in the School of Education.

Chapter 7
Our Library
by Melissa Dennis and Cecilia Parks

"A university is just a group of buildings gathered around a library."

— Shelby Foote, *Civil War Historian and American Novelist*

Getting to Know Our Libraries

The University Libraries include the John Davis Williams Library and the Science Library (located in the Thad Cochran National Center for Natural Products Research building). The J.D. Williams Library is the main library for the University community and houses books, journals, study space, and a Starbucks cafe. The Science Library primarily serves the School of Pharmacy and the Department of Chemistry and Biochemistry. Print and electronic library collections as well as online and onsite services are detailed on the library's website: libraries.olemiss.edu. Online services include access to electronic databases, subject guides, mobile website, chat box, and library news. You can access the library online through your phone, tablet, or laptop anytime.

Our library's mission is to support research, teaching, and learning at the University of Mississippi. **This means you should use the library to find sources for your academic work.** Library instruction in your classes will help you throughout the research process. Librarians teach basic research skills that allow you to find and evaluate sources and learn how to properly cite your work to avoid plagiarism. Your professors expect you to combine your own ideas with those of professionals, but only in a way that distinguishes your thoughts from theirs. When you properly cite your sources, you demonstrate an understanding of how academic writing works. (Read Chapter Ten for more information about plagiarism.)

We're Not Your High School Library

If you walk into the campus library and feel overwhelmed, you are not alone. Sometimes students feel like they already know how to find books from their experiences in high school or public libraries. However, academic libraries are different than public and high school libraries. Academic libraries have many more resources available for you to use, and you access many of these resources differently. For example, the University of Mississippi Libraries use the Library of Congress Classification System (LCC) to organize nearly two million volumes.

The LCC organizes books by call number. An item's call number is the address you use to find the book on the shelf. The LCC sorts items by subject (not title or author), so items on the same topic are arranged next to each other on the shelf. This means that, for example, books by William Faulkner and books about William Faulkner are together on the shelf. Every item (journals, DVDs, sheet music, books, etc.) is shelved according to the LCC, with the exception of microforms and government documents.

Every call number starts with a letter to indicate the basic subject heading. The call number breaks down into sub-headings after that, leading to a unique code of letters and numbers for each individual book. No two books have the same call number. This is why it is important to write down an entire call number and not just the first few letters and numbers. Sections such as PS 3500 or E 185 can easily have hundreds of titles.

QUESTION?

How does our library organize books?

Our library uses the Library of Congress Classification System (LCC) – An alphanumeric classification system that was first developed in the late nineteenth and early twentieth centuries to organize and arrange book collections of the Library of Congress. Because the system adequately organizes large collections, it has been adopted by several institutions, including ours. The LCC uses call numbers to organize materials.

For example, this year's Common Reading Experience selection is *The Collected Short Stories of William Faulkner*, by William Faulkner. This book has a call number of P93511.A86A1 1958. The first part of the call number, PS3511, shows that the book is shelved with the subject of American literature from the first half of the twentieth century. The second part of the number, A86 A1, is a code for the author's last name and the work's subject and title. Finally, the last part of the call number, 1958, is the year the book was published.

Did you know?

Cool Fact:

The J.D. Williams Library was the first building on campus with air conditioning. It was installed in 1951.

Listed below are the letters and titles of the main classes of the LCC:

A – General Works
B – Philosophy
C – Auxiliary Sciences of History
D – World History and History of Europe, Asia, Africa, Australia, New Zealand, etc.
E – History of the Americas
F – History of the Americas
G – Geography, Anthropology, Recreation
H – Social Sciences
J – Political Science
K – Law
L – Education
M – Music and Books on Music
N – Fine Arts
P – Language and Literature
Q – Science
R – Medicine
S – Agriculture
T – Technology
U – Military Science
V – Naval Science
Z – Bibliography, Library Science, Information Resources (General)

QUESTION?

What is a call number?

Use LCC call numbers to locate items in the library. An item's call number is the address you use to find the book on the shelf. The LCC sorts items by subject (not title or author), so items on the same topic are arranged next to each other on the shelf. Every call number starts with a letter to indicate the basic subject heading. The call number breaks down into sub-headings after that, leading to a unique code of letters and numbers for each book.

The J.D. Williams Library has three main floors for student use. Books are shelved according to their LCC call number on all three floors of the library, except for books about chemistry and pharmacy, which are housed in the science library. Each floor contains various tools for research assistance to accommodate a wide variety of users. The entire building has wireless access, with printing services available for laptop users (no software required but you must use Ole Miss Express to print).

Here is a brief breakdown of the library's floor plan:

First Floor

■ The first floor is considered a "talking floor" with several areas for group study and some individual study.

Did you know?

William Faulkner in his late teens and twenties spent a good deal of time at the University. For a number of years he lived with his parents on the University campus (his father was business manager, his relatives were members of the Board of Trustees, a great aunt was a librarian).

■ West Circulation Desk – check out books, pay fines (we e-mail you when a book is approaching its due date), check out materials reserved for a class, and pick up books from interlibrary loan (books we borrow for you from anywhere in the world). You can check out an iPad mini, Makey Makey Kit, or Raspberry Pi to create new projects. If you need white board markers, flash drives, headphones, portable power bricks, or other gadgets, come to the circulation desk. You need your Ole Miss ID to check out materials.

■ The IDEA Lab – contains our 3-D printer, large format plotter printer, collaboration spaces, and other tools and materials to turn your ideas into reality.

■ The Commons houses the Reference Desk, computers, print station, DVDs, scanners, and group study rooms. You need Ole Miss Express on your ID to print.

■ STUDIOone video creation and editing suite is located in the Commons with two computer classrooms at the end of the hall.

QUESTION?

What can you find in the Department of Archives and Special Collections?

1. Original documents or primary sources

2. Blues archive

3. Mississippi collection

4. Materials related to the University of Mississippi

5. Diaries, letters, scrapbooks, and financial records

6. Publications, photographs, recordings, and manuscript collections

■ Government documents – We have more than 2.5 million government documents in print, microform, map, and electronic formats. The library is the Regional Federal Depository for Mississippi and is also a Mississippi state documents depository.

■ LCC call numbers R – Z, as well as the Music Collection (call numbers M) and the Juvenile Collection (books for children and young adults).

Second Floor

■ The second floor is considered a "quiet talking" floor. There are several areas for individual study as well as three reservable group study rooms.

■ East Circulation Desk – check out books. You need your Ole Miss ID to check out materials.

■ Pilkington Study Area next to main stairwell is a good area to work in groups.

■ Baxter Room next to Starbucks Coffee Shop has Apple computers, group study areas, a SCANTRON machine, magazines, and newspapers.

■ LCC call numbers J – K and N–Q (Call numbers starting with "L" are located on Mezzanine A and include books about education and master's theses from all subjects).

Third Floor

■ The third floor is considered a "no talking" floor, though there are two reservable group study rooms.

■ The Department of Archives and Special Collections contains several original (primary) sources such as diaries, letters, scrapbooks, and financial records relating to Mississippi, the Blues, and other subjects. Because these materials are unique, they do not check out. Anyone can view these materials Mon. – Fri., 8:00 a.m. – 5:00 p.m.

■ Library Administration – turn in student job applications here.

■ Bike Room – try our fit desks while you study.

■ LCC call numbers A – H.

Finding Help in the J.D. Williams Library

You may have never used the LCC before, as school and public libraries use the Dewey Decimal System to classify much smaller collections. Our online resources also are more extensive than many other libraries, and academic libraries can even differ from one university to the next. The best way to get acquainted with your library is to go there and meet a librarian.

Our librarians are experts at research; they understand how to explore a myriad of information to find the best sources. They can help you find articles, books, websites, and other research sources for any type of class assignment. Just as Facebook helps you find information about your friends, or Siri helps you find information through your iPhone, a librarian helps you find what you need for your academic papers and projects. Because they are also professional educators, librarians understand the demands of your instructors. They can help you find, evaluate, and use proper sources that will allow you to meet your academic requirements.

QUESTION?

How can you contact a librarian?

1. E-mail
2. Instant message (chat)
3. Phone
4. Reference Desk
5. Personal consultation
6. "Ask a Librarian" link on website
7. Find subject librarian for your major on the library's website

Did you know?

Library hours can vary, so daily hours for the J.D. Williams and Science Libraries are posted on the website, along with the hours for Starbucks. The libraries are open 24 hours the week before and week of final exams each fall and spring.

We have a librarian for every major offered at Ole Miss. Use the "Ask A Librarian" link on the library's homepage to connect with the librarian assigned to your major and meet with him or her. If you do not have a major yet, you can ask questions through the online chat box. It is easy to connect with the librarians by calling, e-mailing, instant messaging, or coming to the Reference Desk on the first floor.

Whether you need a personal research consultation or have a quick question about a source, always ask a librarian. Whether you use the J.D. Williams Library to research, reflect, relax, study, sleep, or socialize, please know that it's your library to respectfully share with 20,000 friends. You are always welcome in the library; enrich your academic experience at Ole Miss by using it.

Glossary

Citations – Whenever you use someone else's words or ideas in your academic work, you need to properly cite them to distinguish where your thoughts end and their thoughts begin. Anything else is considered plagiarism, which can result in expulsion. There are several different types of citation styles (MLA, APA, Chicago, etc.) to cater to the needs of varying writing styles. You may be asked to use more than one style throughout college. Print and online citation guides are available in the library.

The Commons – located on the first floor of the J.D. Williams Library and serves as a place for conversation and computer work. The Reference Desk, staffed by a librarian from 9:00 a.m. – 9:00 p.m., is in the Commons where students can ask questions related to their assignments. Most of the library's computer stations are in the Commons, along with group study areas that contain a table, chairs, white board, and flat screen TV for practicing presentations. The Commons also holds reference books, atlases, a color printer, a black and white printer, copy machines, microform readers, scanners, VHS tapes, CDs, DVDs, a Scantron machine, STUDIOone, and vending machines.

Department of Archives and Special Collections – located on the third floor of the J.D. Williams Library and contains publications, photographs, recordings, and manuscript collections. The collecting focus is on the University of Mississippi, Mississippi in general, and the Blues. Anyone is welcome to use the materials inside Special Collections, Monday through Friday from 8:00 a.m. to 5:00 p.m. You can find items located in Special Collections by using "One Search" on the library's website. Digital photography (no flash) is allowed on most collections—just ask first, please.

Librarians – UM Libraries employ 27 librarians and 29 staff members to organize and maintain print and electronic collections and user facilities, while also educating users to properly find, evaluate, and use information throughout the research process. While holding a Ph.D. is optional for academic librarians, a Master's degree in Library Science is required.

Library of Congress Classification System (LCC) – An alphanumeric classification system that was first developed in the late nineteenth and early twentieth centuries to organize and arrange book collections of the Library of Congress. Because the system adequately organizes large collections, it has been adopted by several institutions, including ours. Use LCC call numbers to locate items in the library.

Stay Social:

Like "University of Mississippi Libraries" on Facebook, follow "UMLibraries" on Twitter and Instagram, and follow "UM Libraries Ole Miss" on Pinterest.

QUESTION?

Why do you need to cite sources?

Whenever you use someone else's words or ideas in your academic work, you need to properly cite them to distinguish where your thoughts end and their thoughts begin. Anything else is considered plagiarism, which can result in expulsion. Always give credit to the sources being used in your paper.

About the Author

Melissa Dennis, Head of Research and Instruction Services and Associate Professor

Ms. Dennis received her B.A. in English from the University of Mississippi and her M.L.I.S. from the University of Southern Mississippi. She promotes library resources and services on all UM campuses and throughout the community. Ms. Dennis also is a faculty advisor for the student organization, Library Ambassadors.

Cecelia Parks, Research and Instruction Librarian and Assistant Professor

Ms. Parks received her B.A. in History, Political Science, and Leadership Studies from Hollins University (Roanoke, VA) and her M.L.S. from the University of Maryland.

Chapter 8
Reading College Texts
by Stephen Monroe

"Reading is the route to intelligence."
Robert Scholes, *The Crafty Reader*

If you want to be smarter than other people, you simply need to read more than other people. There is no secret to knowledge. And knowledge has nothing to do with an ACT score. Right now, you should forget—leave behind—your ACT score, whether it was high or low or in between. It means nothing now. You are here, in college, and you can become anything you wish. Do you want to be a doctor? A journalist? A political scientist? An accountant? Read widely. Read books about your chosen profession and about everything else. If you read actively and selfishly, you will learn how to think. Your mind will grow full

and strong like the Catalpa tree outside the Union. If you don't read, or if you read minimally or lazily, you will gain nothing and your mind will become runny and soft like undercooked eggs.

Benefits of Reading

The benefits of reading are obvious. If you need proof, however, you should look to a landmark report from 2007.

To Read or Not to Read: A Question of National Consequence draws upon decades of scientific and statistical evidence to make a compelling, research-based argument for the benefits of reading.

The report finds that voluntary, regular reading correlates strongly with the following:

- ■ Gainful employment, promotions, and career satisfaction;
- ■ Active participation in social, cultural, and civic life;
- ■ Contributions through volunteer service and charity work;
- ■ Job security, even during economic downturns;
- ■ Freedom. (I'm not kidding: only three percent of adult prisoners read proficiently).

In America, reading will not only make you smarter, it will make it easier for you to build a successful, happy life.

Reading When You Don't Want to Read

My mom always said, "Sometimes in life you have to do things you don't want to do." As a kid, I hated this idea, and I was sure that she was wrong. Well, she was right.

In college, you will need to read books about subjects that don't immediately interest you. You also will need to read at times when you'd rather be doing something else. Maybe it's the first warm day of spring and Frisbees are flying in the Grove. The only problem: you have a test tomorrow in your least favorite subject. You have put off reading the textbook, which you know was a mistake, but you are now trying to rally. You want to do well on the test, but you dread the thought of reading all of those piled up pages. How do you motivate yourself to read in this scenario?

You have to find your own answer to that question. Each of you will be motivated by different thoughts and emotions. Some may be negative: the fear of a shameful return to your hometown and family at the end of this first semester. Some may be positive: the hope of a triumphant return to your hometown and family at the end of this first semester.

No matter where you find your motivation, you do need to find it. It takes energy and determination to read actively and effectively, especially when you are short on time or when there are seemingly better things to do.

You will, at times, need to read when you'd rather be doing something else.

Did you know?

Oxford resident and former Ole Miss student William Faulkner is generally regarded as the greatest novelist of the 20th Century. His fictitious Yoknapatawpha County is based on Lafayette County and Oxford. He won the Nobel and Pulitzer Prizes. James Franco adapted and directed Faulkner's *As I Lay Dying* and *The Sound and the Fury*.

The Practice of Reading

Dozens of researchers have "invented" various methods of reading school textbooks. The most famous of these methods may be SQ3R, which is shorthand for survey, question, read, recite, and review. You may have learned this method in high school. By breaking down the complicated process of reading into seemingly easy-to-follow steps, methods like SQ3R can be useful. Furthermore, they are designed to be straightforward and easy to learn. For details, you can look to the web, where many universities offer information on SQ3R and other reading methods. This module from Oregon State University is a good example:

success.oregonstate.edu/learning/
reading-strategies-tips

You also can take advantage of free workshops offered on our own campus by the Center for Student Success and First-Year Experience. Their DIY Learning Tools Workshops often cover reading strategies.

cssfye.olemiss.edu/diy-learning-tools/

Truth be known, you can memorize the best reading system in the world and still be a horrible reader. Reading, especially in college, is difficult work. It requires an active mind. If you feel relaxed while doing it, you are doing it wrong.

> **Reading is difficult work.**
> **If you feel relaxed while reading, you are doing it wrong.**

Reading Actively

"The process of reading is not a half sleep, but, in the highest sense, an exercise, a gymnast's struggle . . . the reader is to do something."

Walt Whitman, *Democratic Vistas*

Have you ever been reading along, only to suddenly realize that you've not been paying attention? You look back and see an entire page or two that you've "read" but that you can't remember? We've all done this, and we should all learn from our mistakes. Such listless reading is bad. It is the opposite of active, beneficial reading.

Did you know?

John Grisham (J.D. `84) is America's bestselling novelist. More than 250 million copies of his books are in print. Grisham has been generous to Ole Miss, funding programs in Creative Writing, Law, and Poverty.

Walt Whitman was right. Reading is an exercise. If you want to get your mind into shape, you must lift the heaviest ideas, struggling to understand them.

Walt Whitman was right. Real reading is not "a half sleep." It is, instead, "an exercise." If you want to get into shape, will you go to the Turner Center to gently roll a very light weight across the floor? Will you stand still on an unplugged treadmill? Will you take a nap by the swimming pool? No. Instead, you will push yourself. You will crush out serious reps in the weight room. You will go hard on the treadmill for forty minutes. You will swim laps until your arms hurt and your lungs burn. If you want to get into shape, you will exercise. The same is true with your reading. If you want benefits — if you want to get smarter — you will lift the heaviest ideas, struggling to understand them. You will keep your eyes wide open and your body tense as your mind races. You will pull yourself through the tough passages. You will go for at least forty minutes. You will yank and tug at the words on the page. You will agree. You will disagree. You will care. If you lose focus for a moment and miss a page, you will double back and read that page again until you've got it. You will not be relaxing, you will be exercising your mind. You will be reading.

Creating the Conditions for Active Reading

*"I find television very educational. Every time someone switches it on
I go into another room and read a good book."*

Groucho Marx

How to create the conditions for active, effective reading:

1. Read when well-rested and alert. Too tired to read? Take a twenty-minute nap followed by one shot of espresso.

2. Read in a quiet place. If you think you read best with the television on, you are lying to yourself. You cannot read actively or effectively while watching *The Walking Dead*. Turn off the television. If you need background noise, try downloading Mozart or Brahms. Even better, download an hour's worth of nature sounds. Try searching "rain" on iTunes.

3. Read in a comfortable, but not too comfortable, spot. Under the covers of your bed in your pajamas in a completely reclined position is too comfortable. In a

Did you know?

The late Barry Hannah, a long-time Ole Miss Writer-in-Residence, was called "the maddest writer in the USA" by Truman Capote. He was considered by many the finest short story writer of his time. His books include *Geronimo Rex, Bats Out of Hell* and *Yonder Stands Your Orphan.*

hard chair in a hot room in your fanciest Sunday clothes is not comfortable enough. Find something in between.

4. Read alone. Get away from everyone. Schedule around your roommate or get out of your room. Campus is huge. We have lots of nooks and crannies, and we even have a really cool place designed just for readers: the J.D. Williams Library.

Read in a comfortable — but not too comfortable — spot.

5. Read while disconnected from the world. This is not the time to post on Instagram or kid around on Snapchat. Turn everything off. Don't look at your cell phone. You just looked. Don't look at your cell phone.

Activity

Try this: go to the J.D. Williams Library and browse the shelves. Do not stop first at the online catalog. Go right to the stacks (the shelves) and browse the old fashioned way. Don't hurry, just look around. If a book looks interesting, for whatever reason, pull it down. Flip through it. What kind of book is this? When was it last checked out? Read the first few paragraphs. Now, put it back on the shelf. Wander around the library, browsing at your own pace. Don't hurry. Don't think about going someplace after the library. Just chill for a while in the library. It's one of the few places where you can really be alone and quiet and not bothered by anyone. Keep browsing. Pull down random books until you find one that makes you curious, until you find a book that you might like to read. Now, check out that book. Take it back to your room. Don't show it to anyone. Don't talk about it. Keep it to yourself. Within the week, find time to read your book. No, it doesn't have anything to do with your classes. No, it will not help your grades. Yes, you will have to skip doing something else in order to read it. How about not watching television tonight? Not playing Madden? How about skipping a party on Saturday by pretending that you are sick? Do whatever you need to do to read this book. Why? Because you found it. Because no one else is making you read it. Because no one else expects you to read it. Read it because you went into a library with a million books and you found this one book in particular. Read it selfishly; read it only for yourself.

Jackson native Richard Ford (former Ole Miss visiting professor of creative writing) is considered one of the finest living writers in America. His books include *The Sports Writer*, *Rock Springs*, and *Independence Day*, which won the Pulitzer Prize in 1995.

Marginalia

My mom always said, *Don't write in your books*. As a kid, I hated this idea. I wanted to write in my books, and I was sure that my mom was wrong. Well, on this point, she was wrong.

You should write in your books (as long as you own them). Highlighters can be helpful, but there is no better tool than a sharp pencil. Use the margins to write notes to yourself, to record your reactions to particular ideas or passages, and to underline unfamiliar words.

Perhaps because some people consider writing in books to be nearly criminal (my mother), it is somewhat difficult to find fully developed systems of marginalia. This really isn't a problem, however, because you can simply develop your own. I use an exclamation mark to note a passage that bothers or alarms me, a question mark to mark a passage that I don't understand, D to signal a word or term that I need to define — you get the idea.

Indeed, such marks can be extremely useful when you are reviewing a particular reading assignment. If you have read carefully and left yourself reminders of your thoughts, you can take a few minutes before class to refresh your memory and walk in ready to contribute to the discussion or to listen more intelligently to the lecture.

Conclusion

There are many good reasons to read actively and energetically. Perhaps the most important at the moment: succeeding in college and earning your degree. Between now and graduation, you will spend hundreds of hours reading. If you do it well, you will make good grades and accomplish your goals. You also will learn more about the world and about yourself than you can now imagine. Enjoy the exercise. Happy reading.

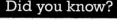

Did you know?

During the 1970s and 1980s, when Willie Morris was Ole Miss Writer-in-Residence, he would invite his writer friends to Oxford — William Styron, George Plimpton, Alex Haley — giving the town even more literary clout. His most notable works include *Good Ole Boy, North Toward Home,* and *My Dog Skip.*

Activity

Discuss active reading and personal systems of marginalia.
Read and discuss this poem by Billy Collins:

Marginalia
by Billy Collins

Sometimes the notes are ferocious,
skirmishes against the author
raging along the borders of every page
in tiny black script.
If I could just get my hands on you,
Kierkegaard, or Conor Cruise O'Brien,
they seem to say,
I would bolt the door and beat some logic into your head.
Other comments are more offhand, dismissive -
"Nonsense." "Please!" "HA!!" —
that kind of thing.
I remember once looking up from my reading,
my thumb as a bookmark,
trying to imagine what the person must look like
who wrote "Don't be a ninny"
alongside a paragraph in The Life of Emily Dickinson.
Students are more modest
needing to leave only their splayed footprints
along the shore of the page.
One scrawls "Metaphor" next to a stanza of Eliot's.
Another notes the presence of "Irony"
fifty times outside the paragraphs of A Modest Proposal.
Or they are fans who cheer from the empty bleachers,
Hands cupped around their mouths.
"Absolutely," they shout
to Duns Scotus and James Baldwin.
"Yes." "Bull's-eye." "My man!"
Check marks, asterisks, and exclamation points
rain down along the sidelines.
And if you have managed to graduate from college
without ever having written "Man vs. Nature"
in a margin, perhaps now

Did you know?

Ellen Douglas (real name Josephine Haxton) was a writer-in-residence at The University of Mississippi from 1979 to 1983. Her most famous student was the late Larry Brown. Brown said, "She taught me what it really means to write a story."

is the time to take one step forward.
We have all seized the white perimeter as our own
and reached for a pen if only to show
we did not just laze in an armchair turning pages;
we pressed a thought into the wayside,
planted an impression along the verge.
Even Irish monks in their cold scriptoria
jotted along the borders of the Gospels
brief asides about the pains of copying,
a bird singing near their window,
or the sunlight that illuminated their page-
anonymous men catching a ride into the future
on a vessel more lasting than themselves.
And you have not read Joshua Reynolds,
they say, until you have read him
enwreathed with Blake's furious scribbling.
Yet the one I think of most often,
the one that dangles from me like a locket,
was written in the copy of Catcher in the Rye
I borrowed from the local library
one slow, hot summer.
I was just beginning high school then,
reading books on a davenport in my parents' living room,
and I cannot tell you
how vastly my loneliness was deepened,
how poignant and amplified the world before me seemed,
when I found on one page
A few greasy looking smears
and next to them, written in soft pencil-
by a beautiful girl, I could tell,
whom I would never meet-
"Pardon the egg salad stains, but I'm in love."

REFERENCES

National Endowment for the Arts (2007). To Read or Not to Read: A Question of National Consequence. Washington, 2007. Retrieved from nea.gov/research/toread.pdf

About the Author

Stephen Monroe, *Chair and Assistant Professor of Writing and Rhetoric*

Stephen Monroe is Chair and Assistant Professor of Writing and Rhetoric.

Chapter 9
The University of Mississippi Writing and Speech Programs: The Department of Writing and Rhetoric

By Brad Campbell, Robert Cummings, JoAnn Edwards, Karen Forgette, Wendy Goldberg, Kate Hooper, Guy Krueger, and Alice Myatt

The **Department of Writing and Rhetoric (DWR)** is the home of the University's composition and rhetoric program and the speech program; its primary mission is to improve student writing and speaking. The DWR is part of the College of Liberal Arts, and DWR faculty and staff have offices in Lamar Hall. In addition to teaching writing and speech courses to most Ole Miss students (listed in the undergraduate catalog as WRIT or SPCH courses), the DWR also is the home of a writing minor and the University's Writing Centers, spaces that provide writing and composition peer consulting services for all disciplines on all campuses. The Oxford campus Writing Center is located in Suite C on the third floor of Lamar Hall. The Southaven and Tupelo campuses also have Writing Centers.

When it comes to successful academic and professional writing and oral presentations, experience proves that there is no one solution or magic key that automatically guarantees student writing/speaking projects will receive the highest possible grades. However, we do have some proven tips and strategies from our writing and speech instructors, and we share them with you in this chapter. Further, since much of the writing you do in your EDHE 105 or 305 classes will be reflective response essays, a brief guide on how to write effective reflective essays is included in this chapter (see Appendix A). Appendix B is an explanation of how to read and understand a writing assignment, and in Appendix C two Ole Miss students share letters of advice about writing assignments.

Tip 1: Develop your critical reading skills.

Here's what Keith Hjortshoj, author of *The Transition to College Writing*, says about the importance of reading:

Performance on examinations, problem sets, labs, research projects, and writing assignments depends heavily on knowledge acquired from texts of many kinds. As a consequence, effective reading probably represents the most crucial set of skills you can acquire in college, where reading everything thoroughly from beginning to end might not always be possible. Given a particular assignment, however, the question is not only "Should I read this?" Because if the answer is "yes," then you need to ask yourself other questions:

> *What am I reading?*
> *Why am I reading it?*
> *How can I read it most efficiently?*
> *How can I remember what I will need to know about it?*

These questions acknowledge that reading is not a single kind of activity. Reading can be done in many different styles, with different approaches and strategies, used for specific purposes and for particular kinds of tests (31).

Stated simply: your writing is only as good as your reading. In college, expect to read, read, and then read more. Understanding the what, why, and how of your reading will do much to ensure that your writing projects meet the goals of your assignments. You may find it helpful to read more of Hjortshoj's work, *The Transition to College Writing*; we include it in our list of resources. (Be sure to read "Reading College Texts" – Chapter Eight.)

The Writing Center
is located on the third floor of Lamar Hall.

Writing Center consultants are students much like you. It's easy to schedule an appointment for help, but don't wait until the last minute! To make an appointment for either face-to-face or online consultations, call 662-915-7689 or log onto **rhetoric.olemiss.edu/writing-centers/** Visit the Writing Center website for a schedule of operating hours.

Tip 2: Understand your audience.

Writing is communication, and knowing your audience is vital to your success. As you write, consider, "Who will be reading this? What is the best way to reach my audience? How can I get my point across in an interesting, thought-provoking way?"

Did you know?

Ole Miss alum Greg Iles has produced twelve *New York Times* bestselling novels. He received the Mississippi Author of the Year Award, as well as the Bertelsman Award for New Fiction for his novel *Black Cross*.

Tip 3: Talk with your professor.

Instructors are a valuable resource that students often overlook. Get in the habit of visiting them during their office hours, asking questions about anything that you don't understand. If you can't make it to their office hours, don't be shy about asking to set up an appointment.

Conferencing with your instructor when working on writing or speech assignments is one of the best strategies to understand what you need to do to improve. When you conference with your instructor, be sure to bring a full draft of your project. Also, it is a good idea to take notes when you conference with your instructor so you have a record of the meeting for later reference.

Tip 4: Use the Writing Center!

Many students find value in making regular visits to one of the University's Writing Centers. Located on the third floor of Lamar Hall, the peer consultants in the Writing Center are undergraduates who have experience in writing and in helping their peers. The writing consultants enjoy working with students during all stages of the writing process, from brainstorming ideas to the final revision. Many successful students begin going to the Writing Center with their first writing or speech assignment and continue making appointments with various consultants over the course of the semester and beyond. The goal of the Writing Center is to help students become better independent writers, so the consultants don't "proofread" papers or merely "correct" errors; they help you brainstorm, talk about research, explore resources, and answer your grammar and citation questions.

Consultations are available both online and face-to-face, and appointments may be made online at rhetoric.olemiss.edu/writing-centers/.

Here are some tips for using the Writing Center:

1. Make an appointment. The Writing Center can often accommodate walk-ins, but don't count on it. It's better (and easy) to make an appointment.

2. Be on time. Sometimes the Center is really busy. If you can't make it to your scheduled appointment, please call 662-915-7689 or visit the website to re-schedule.

3. Bring a copy of your assignment and your work at any stage. You can bring class assignments, paper assignments (both formal and informal), speeches, resumes,

> "Students who have brief questions or inquiries about making an appointment may use our online, real-time quick chat feature to talk with a consultation coordinator during the Writing Center's open hours." The Quick Chat is accessed from the DWR Writing Centers webpage, rhetoric.olemiss.edu/writing-centers/

Did you know?

Steve Yarbrough mines the Mississippi Delta — and Ole Miss — for his stories and novels. Yarbrough earned a B.A. and an M.A. at Ole Miss. His five novels and three collections of short stories have garnered critical acclaim.

personal statements, letters of application, and just about anything you want to work on. Bring a typed paper, if possible. Handwriting can be challenging to read, and a typed paper is much easier to read and review.

4. Bring a list of writing concerns you've had in the past or that your teachers have noticed. We can help you improve your understanding of those problems.

 Follow us on — **Twitter@OleMissWCenter** to keep up with special events or important messages concerning Writing Center services. (Note that we are unable to schedule appointments via Twitter.)

 Become a **Facebook fan of the Ole Miss Writing Center** and take a look at what's happening in the Writing Center.

Tip 5: Use a good writer's handbook.

While there is no official handbook for DWR first-year composition classes, a writing handbook helps you regardless of your academic major. Becoming familiar with any good writing handbook will be an asset as you work with various types of writing assignments.

Some recommended resources for writers:

The "For Students" web pages at the DWR website: *rhetoric.olemiss.edu/student/*

The Ole Miss Writing Center website: *rhetoric.olemiss.edu/writing-centers/*

The Norton Online Guide for Writers: *wwnorton.com/write*

The Online Writing Lab at Excelsior College: *owl.excelsior.edu/*

The Purdue Online Writing Lab: *owl.english.purdue.edu/*

Books you may find helpful:

Birkenstein, C. & Graff, G. (2014). *They Say, I Say: The Moves that Matter in Academic Writing*, 3rd ed. New York: W.W. Norton.

Hacker, D. et al. (2015). *A Writer's Reference*, 8th ed. Boston: Bedford/St. Martin's.

Hjortshoj, K. (2009). *The Transition to College Writing*, 2nd ed. Boston: Bedford/St. Martin's.

Weinstein, L. (2012). *Writing Doesn't Have to Be Lonely: 14 Ways to Get the Help of Other People When You Write.* Cambridge, MA: One of a Kind Books

Did you know?

Tom Franklin (Department of English) has been compared to Larry Brown, Barry Hannah and William Faulkner. His story, *Poachers*, was included in the anthology *Best Mystery Stories of the 20th Century*. His novel *Crooked Letter, Crooked Letter* was awarded the *Los Angeles Times* Book Award in 2011 and was selected as the University's Common Read for 2012.

APPENDIX A
Writing an Effective Reflective Essay Response
by Karen Forgette and Guy Krueger

Why Reflection?

Much of the writing you do in EDHE 105 or 305 is reflective response writing. Reflective response writing asks you to consider how campus events or experiences influence your beliefs, attitudes, values, and ideas. In reflective response assignments, you critically examine an event or experience, analyze the interaction between that event or experience and your own prior knowledge and assumptions, and make explicit connections between what you already know and what you are learning in college.

Reflection is important because it empowers you to take charge of your own learning. As you make connections between your ideas and the world around you, you begin to analyze how your thinking is shaped by your environment. You also begin to evaluate your intellectual growth. Although reflective writing is more personal than other kinds of academic writing, it is no less challenging. Reflective writing requires sophisticated critical thinking and self-analysis.

In some college courses, such as the first-year composition sequence, you are required to write reflective response assignments. Though reflective response writing may not be explicitly required in all of your college courses, the reflective skills you learn in EDHE serve as powerful tools to help you identify and examine your own learning throughout your college career.

The Nuts and Bolts of Reflection

Reflective writing may be new to many college students; however, the steps that lead to other successful writing projects work equally well with reflective response writing. The first step is to understand exactly what it is you are being asked to write about. Reflective writing does not ask you to restate what you have done; rather, the goal is to try to better understand what your classroom work and your college experiences mean to you as a student and a learner. This type of writing, too, can benefit from a process, the same process students use when composing an argument essay or a research paper.

Did you know?

Ole Miss Professor of English Beth Ann Fennelly is one of the best poets working today. She won a 2003 National Endowment for the Arts Award, as well as the prestigious 2006 United States Artists Grants. She has three books of poetry. She is the director of the MFA program in writing at Ole Miss.

The first step to any successful writing process is to understand and think about the assignment before you write. ***Being asked to reflect on an event includes preparing for the assignment that follows the event.*** One tip to help your chances of writing a successful reflection paper is to ask yourself a few questions before the event:

1. **What do I expect the event to be like?**

2. **Have I ever attended an event like this before? If so, what, and what was it like?**

3. **What do I hope to learn by attending this event?**

4. **Can I prepare for this event in any way (e.g., bring a pen and paper or a way to take notes, bring my phone to take a picture, etc.)?**

By asking yourself some questions and preparing before the event, you put yourself in a better position to later reflect on what you experienced and how it was significant to you as a learner. If there is time, making a few notes in response to these questions or others is a great idea.

The next step to consider is attending the event. The types of events you attend vary, so you should be aware of what, and how, you can record information. For example, if you are attending a speaking event, you can probably take notes or even record the event if allowed. This way, you could have access to direct quotes, or, at the least, be able to recall some of the more important points. If the event is more active, say, Rebel Run, you may reflect solely from your memory, or perhaps from a couple of pictures. Whatever the case, it is important to think about your assignment as you attend an event, to remember that your task is to make meaning out of the event. In other words, remember that your goal in reflective writing is to explore the significance to you of an event, not simply to restate or summarize what you did.

Then, you need to compose your reflection. Without thinking about the significance of the event, your temptation may be to sit down and describe what happened. To avoid this, try to again ask yourself some questions. Here are some ideas:

1. **Did the event change your thinking or outlook, even in a minor way(s)? How? Be specific.**

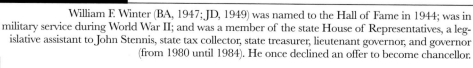

Did you know?

William F. Winter (BA, 1947; JD, 1949) was named to the Hall of Fame in 1944; was in military service during World War II; and was a member of the state House of Representatives, a legislative assistant to John Stennis, state tax collector, state treasurer, lieutenant governor, and governor (from 1980 until 1984). He once declined an offer to become chancellor.

2. Did you experience something that interested, inspired, and/or upset you or caught your attention? Explain.

3. Did you experience something that reminded you of or made you think about your own life in any way(s)? Explain.

4. Did you learn anything about yourself? Explain.

For example, you would not be writing a successful reflection paper if you attended Rebel Run and wrote about exactly what happened and ended by saying you had a good time. You could, however, write a successful paper by acknowledging that you were not looking forward to participating in an event with so many people you did not know but then realizing you had fun meeting new people and finding out about them. This type of reflection could allow you to explore how and why you interact with others and why you are nervous around new people. Of course, this is just one possibility of countless ways to construct a reflection.

In terms of structure, you should need no more than a few sentences, or, at most, a paragraph, to describe the event. The majority of your essay should be spent on more substantive ideas, such as what you learned and why that might be significant to you. Also, remember that reflection is often personal. Though you will turn in your work to your instructor, you should write to help yourself think about your own learning, no matter how small the impact on your knowledge or literacy might seem.

Finally, do not forget that your reflective responses are essays, though short ones. Thus, use the writing process to help you submit more polished and thoughtful work. Write at least one draft of your response and allow yourself time to read over your work to make sure you are addressing the idea(s) that has the most meaning to you and that the idea is clearly articulated. Also, leave time to edit and correct mistakes that may interfere with reading. Your final product should demonstrate not that you simply attended an event, but that you were able to make meaning of that event and reflect on the significance of that meaning.

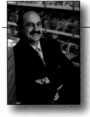

Did you know?

Samir Husni — aka "Mr. Magazine" — owns the world's largest collection of first edition magazines (more than 25,000 titles). A professor of journalism and director of Ole Miss' Magazine Innovation Center, Husni was called "The country's leading magazine expert" by *Forbes ASAP* magazine.

Below is a sample reflective response that demonstrates the use of at least some of the steps listed in this section:

I attended the concert by Rain on October 27, 2011. Rain is a touring act of performers that dress up like, impersonate, and play music by the Beatles. The show took place at the Ford Center and looked to be sold out.

I was interested in going to see Rain because my parents listened to the Beatles a lot when I was younger, so I grew up learning to like a lot of their music. I felt like I would have more fun at a concert when I knew the music. I have been to other concerts where I was not familiar with the music and still had fun, but that is because I was with my friends. Since I went to this show alone, I was more comfortable knowing the songs.

What surprised me most about this concert, though, was that I did not know some of the songs played by Rain. Having heard a lot of Beatles music growing up, I thought I would know everything that was played, but I didn't. I heard of lot of music I know, like "Twist and Shout" and "Hey Jude," but I was lost during some of the songs. Most of the crowd seemed to know everything that Rain played though. I was the youngest person I could see in all of the people around me.

I think the thing that was most interesting to me was watching some of the people in the crowd. I liked the music, but I also enjoy people-watching. Some of the people were dressed up very professionally, but seemed to be reliving their youth. People were dancing, singing, and smiling like they were back watching the Beatles years ago. People were also very moved by the video screens, which showed important events from the time the Beatles' music came out.

Watching the people got me thinking about growing older myself. The people at the Rain show seemed to be so happy when they listened to the music and watched the show. I wonder if I will look back on my years and college and think I didn't enjoy them as much as I could. I also wonder if I don't pay enough attention to important events like the first black president or Occupy Wall Street. Will I listen to Lady Gaga or Ke$ha and remember their songs as fondly as the people in the crowd remembered the Beatles?

Overall, I had a good time and the concert made me think about myself a little more. I also realized I don't know nearly as many Beatles songs as I thought I did.

Did you know?

Journalism students in the Meek School produce magazines and documentaries on current topics that are widely distributed. In recent years, they have won the Robert F. Kennedy Prize for College Journalism twice. (One is given per year in the national competition.)

APPENDIX B
Decoding a Writing Assignment

Sometimes an assignment can look like it is written in a foreign language. With patience and practice, you will become more confident with what an assignment is asking and, as a result, your papers will improve. Look over the assignment below and review the margin notes.

Assignment - Medical Ethics: Now and Then by Matt Saye

(A)
Read the article from *Wired Magazine* entitled "Seven Creepy Experiments That Could Teach Us So Much (If They Weren't So Wrong)" available at: **wired.com/magazine/2011/07/ff_swr/all/1**

(B)
1. Describe the position on medical ethics taken by both the *Wired* article and *The Immortal Life of Henrietta Lacks* and analyze both authors' positions *(C)* on medical ethics. Do the authors seem to have the same view of medical ethics? Are there any places where they disagree?

2. The article from *Wired* comes some 60 years after Henrietta Lacks' cells were taken from her without her knowledge. Using evidence from both *(E)* the article and Skloot's book, describe how medical ethics have changed in the intervening 60 years and analyze the consequences of these changes.

3. One of the main points made by Skloot in *The Immortal Life of Henrietta Lacks* is that Lacks' cells were taken without her knowledge or consent. Do *(F)* you think that any of the medical experiments described in the *Wired* article would be unethical if participants were willing subjects who had been properly informed of the dangers and consequences of the experiments, or is science bound by a "moral compass" regardless of consent?

Margin notes:

A) If an assignment asks you to read, then you should read actively.

B) Describe is one of the verbs professors often use in writing an assignment. Your response should be specific and include details.

C) This is another key verb. Analyze here means to break down the authors' positions to understand how and why their arguments are constructed.

D) Here, you are being asked for your opinion. When you give it, be sure to support your opinion with evidence from the text under question.

E) Using evidence means to give examples and citations from the texts to support what you say about the medical ethics and how they have changed. Be sure to provide titles and page numbers when you refer to those examples and use quotations from the texts.

F) Again, you are being asked for your opinion, and it is quite acceptable, in reflective response assignments, to begin a paragraph by writing, "I think" or "I believe." Just be sure to provide reasons and support for what you think or believe.

APPENDIX C
What First Year Students Say...

Dear College Writer,

Having a hectic, demanding, and stressful schedule is something nearly every college student must learn to balance. In order to be successful in your writing, I would make a few suggestions. First of all, I would plan. Plan out your day—know exactly when you will have time to work, study, eat, and write. Secondly, do not wait until the last minute. You will overly stress yourself and end up with a poor grade if you procrastinate for too long. Another important suggestion for writing is to make it gradual. Do your research, prepare, and write drafts so that when it is time to write the final, you will be ready. Remember to stay motivated and always keep a good attitude and you will go far. Good luck!

Sincerely,

Hannah Harpole

Dear College Writer,

There are lots of things that you'll have to prepare for when doing a research paper, or a paper of any kind for that matter. One of the first things that you should prepare for is procrastination. When you receive an assignment you should start working on it the night you get it or at least two days afterward. The reason for this is because if you don't start on the assignment as soon as possible you'll procrastinate and find yourself doing it the night before the due date. Normally papers are better formatted and understandable when they are gradually thought out. If you wait till the night before, things seem cluttered and your grade will suffer.

Allen Ball

APPENDIX D
A Few Presentation Basics

You are in the middle of a tough semester, and on top of all your other responsibilities you have been assigned a stand-and-deliver presentation in one of your classes. Whether you find the challenge exciting or you find yourself anxious and uncertain, the same physical reactions are at play. Adrenaline is pumping and priming you for the *extreme sport* of public speaking. If you are less than happy about the requirement to speak in public, you are not alone. Since the 1973 Bruskin Study in the London *Sunday Times*, public speaking has consistenly been reported as a top personal fear (Dweyer and Davidson 2012; Chapman University 2014-2016). No wonder employers continue to inform universities they need students who can verbally communicate well (NACE, 2011-2016). How can you learn to manage the physical and mental effects brought on by speaking in public? Take the time to make your presentations POP by planning, organizing, and practicing before you present.

PLAN your presentations around your strengths or the necessity of the situation. If you get to choose your topic, draw on your knowledge, interests, and passion. A solid command of your subject matter helps you speak with confidence and credibility. Even if your instructor or professor assigns your topic, find a way to relate to the subject and bring your unique talents to the experience.

Entrepreneur and marketing expert, Seth Godin, notes, "A presentation that doesn't seek to make change is a waste of time and energy. Before you start working on your presentation, the two-part question to answer is, 'who will be changed by this work, and what is the change I seek?'"(2013). The more you know your audience's attitudes and needs, the more likely you are to meet your speaking goal.

ORGANIZE everything in your presentation around a single focus, and send the audience home with one clear message. Organized presentations have an introduction, body, and conclusion – all supporting a thesis. Your thesis presents the main idea of your presentation in one clear sentence. Use the introduction to reveal your thesis, as well as orient your audience to the occasion. Develop the body around a series of points supporting your thesis. Finally, highlight why your thesis is relevant in the conclusion.

Increase the clarity of your message by arranging body points logically. Common ways to organize points are by topics, spaces, time spans, causes/effects, and problems/solutions. Bring points to life by offering examples, stories, explanations, and evidence. Making the point – *we are running out of water* – becomes far more interesting and engaging when you (1) explain the critical drought situation, (2) provide evidence showing water could run out within five years, and (3) demonstrate the effect of water shortage on food supplies.

Finally, use language with accuracy, expression, and style. Experiment with varied word choices, expand your vocabulary, and employ language your audience will understand. As you practice for your presentation, strive for fluency by banishing meaningless – like, you know – words. Every word should be a contributor.

PRACTICE your presentation to increase confidence and polish. Practice over time, not just over night. Cramming increases stress. Practice makes you more capable of delivering a confident, fluent, flexible presentation. Up to 90 percent of communication is nonverbal (Mehrabian, 1972). So practice actions and tone, as well as words.

Stand confidently by planting both feet on the ground, centering your weight, and making consistent eye contact. Make friends of mirrors and recording devices. Watch yourself objectively and analyze how you stand, the gestures you use, and what your face is saying. Full engagement of body language should make you feel less stiff and more naturally expressive. If you plan to move around the room, walk with purpose and avoid the temptation to pace.

Speak clearly by speaking in concise sentences and enunciating words.

> **"Ultimately, the presentation is about the message – not you. Once you have a topic, consider your speaking goal."**
>
> **Mary Kate Domino, Winner of 2014 Undergraduate Speaker's Edge**

Practice aloud, not silently to yourself. Time your presentation for a reasonable speaking rate. Project your voice, and breathe. Breathing helps you stay relaxed and supplies your brain with needed oxygen to recall the presentation you designed.

Connect to your audience with a sincere, expressive, conversational style. Avoid reading your speech. Limit speaking notes to key words and phrases. If you practice enough, you will know what you want to say. Standing in front of an audience with limited notes may be a bit unnerving at first, but the more you connect with your audience, the more empowered you will feel.

In general, audiences want you to succeed! When you deliver with confidence, audiences will react favorably. In fact, a study published by the Royal Statistical Society showed some people responded to confident delivery more than accuracy (Smith and Wooten, 2013). Of course, to maintain top credibility you need both. So build your confidence through preparation and rehearsal and give yourself permission to strive for connection instead of perfection during delivery.

Many people do not realize Dr. Martin Luther King, Jr. never planned to say "I have a dream" when he delivered his famous speech from the steps of the Lincoln Memorial in 1963 (Jones and Connelly, 2011). He added the refrain in response to a shout from the crowd, "Tell them about the dream, Martin. Tell them about the dream" (Jones, 2011). Dr. King moved his notes aside and reacted to the moment. "I have a dream," he shared. "I have a dream," he kept repeating. One of the most recognized speeches of the twentieth century followed.

Dr. King did not limit himself to the page; he transcended it.

You, too, can be inspired by the passion to connect your message to the audience. You simply need to be prepared for the moment. So, plan, organize, practice, and present your presentations with all the knowledge and passion you have to share. You can not only empower yourself and enliven your audience, but potentially gain an edge with employers one day when they see your ability and willingness to communicate well.

REFERENCES

Chapman University (2014-2016). Alphabetical list of fears by percentage. *Chapman Unviersity Survey on American Fears.*

Davies, D. (2011, January 17). Clarence B. Jones Interview (Radio Broadcast). *Fresh Air*, Washington, D.C.: National Public Radio.

Godin, S. (2013). *How to Listen*. Retrieved from sethgodin.typepad.com/seths_blog/2013/02/hot-to-listen.html.

Hjortshoj, K. (2009). The Transition to College Writing, 2nd ed. Boston: Bedford/St. Martin's.

Jones, C. and Connelly, S. (2011). *Behind the Dream: The Making of the Speech that Transformed a Nation* (pp. 104-125). New York: Palgrave McMillan.

Mehrabian, A. (1972). *Nonverbal Communication*. New Brunswick: Aldine Transaction.

National Association of Colleges and Employers (NACE) (2011-2014). *Job Outlook Survey*.

Smith, B. and Wooten, J. (2013). *Pundits: The Confidence Trick: Better confident than right?* Significance, 10 (4).

About the Authors

Brad Campbell, *Director of the Oxford Campus Writing Center*

Brad Campbell's research interests include writing center theory, composition theory, and cultural studies. Specifically, he is interested in the intersection between writing and culture and the formation of writerly identities. He received his B.A. in English and psychology from the University of Mississippi and his M.A. in English from Mississippi State University.

Robert Cummings, *Executive Director of Academic Innovation and Associate Professor of Writing and Rhetoric*

Robert Cummings received his Ph.D. in English from the University of Georgia, and he is the award-winning author of *Lazy Virtues: Teaching Writing in the Age of Wikipedia*.

JoAnn Edwards, *Director of Forensics*

JoAnn Edwards is the coordinator of Speaker's Edge, and she teaches Speech at the University of Mississippi. She received her M.A. in theatre from the University of Mississippi and a Graduate Certificate in communication education from Minnesota State University, Mankato.

Karen Forgette, *Core Lecturer with the Department of Writing and Rhetoric*

Karen Forgette's research interests include self-regulated learning, electronic portfolios, service learning, and learning communities. She serves as the coordinator of writing instruction for the FASTrack first-year cohort program at the University. She obtained her M.A. degree from the University of North Carolina – Chapel Hill.

About the Authors

Wendy Goldberg, *Core Instructor with the Department of Writing and Rhetoric*

Wendy Goldberg is the coordinator and chair of the Writing 102 committee and works closely with all Writing 102 instructors. Her research interests include integrating pop culture, including comics and manga, in the classroom. Ms. Goldberg taught for six years at the United States Coast Guard Academy before coming to the University of Mississippi. She received her M.A. from the University of Connecticut.

Kate Hooper, *Lecturer of Speech at the University of Mississippi*

Kate Hooper is a performance and vocal coach. She received her M.F.A. in theatre performance from the University of California Los Angeles and a Graduate Certificate in communication education from Minnesota State University, Mankato.

Guy Krueger, *Core Lecturer and the Writing 101 Curriculum Chair in the Department of Writing and Rhetoric*

Guy Krueger's research focuses on basic writing theory and praxis at institutions across America. Additionally, he is interested in assessment and placement in first-year composition (FYC) courses. Krueger has been at the University of Mississippi since 2010. Currently, he is ABD – English with a concentration in rhetoric and composition – Southern Illinois University – Carbondale.

Alice Myatt, *Assistant Chair of the Department of Writing and Rhetoric and Assistant Professor of Writing and Rhetoric*

Alice Myatt received her Ph.D. in English from Georgia State University with a concentration in visual rhetoric and composition pedagogy, to which she adds her research interests of learning in digital environments, writing pedagogy, and writing center studies.

The Gertrude Castellow Ford Center for the Performing Arts

"If art is to nourish the roots of our culture, society must set the artist free to follow his vision wherever it takes him. We must never forget that art is not a form of propaganda; it is a form of truth. … In serving his vision of the truth, the artist best serves his nation." – President John F. Kennedy, 1963

Chancellor Robert C. Khayat (1995-2010) envisioned an arts facility that would serve the University of Mississippi community by offering opportunities to attend performances by world-class artists and to express themselves through their own creative efforts. With an initial gift of $20 million from the Gertrude C. Ford Foundation in 1998, and an additional investment of $20 million from the State of Mississippi and the University of Mississippi, the Ford Center for the Performing Arts

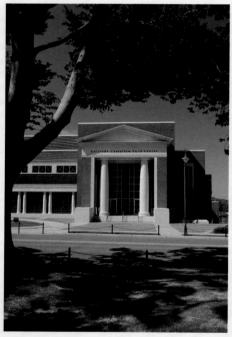

was completed in 2003. The 88,000 square foot, six story facility, houses two theatres, dressing rooms, a green room, large storage areas in the basement, and administrative offices. It officially opened on Friday, March 24, 2003 with an inaugural gala hosted by Chancellor Khayat and starring Morgan Freeman as master of ceremonies. A cast of University alumni appeared together with a dozen university ensembles from the departments of Music and Theatre.

The Ford Center is guided by its mission to "enrich the intellectual and cultural environment of the University of Mississippi and the region by providing a venue for programming in performing arts, public affairs and the humanities. The Ford Center will complement the University's commitment to excellence in education, research and service while celebrating imagination, innovation and creativity."

The University of Mississippi considers the social and communal nature of live performances to be an important part of a student's education. Interaction or communication between audience members and the performers provide a visual expressivity that extends beyond the end of the performance. As a touring house, the Ford Center presents national touring productions of Broadway musicals, plays, ballet, modern dance, opera, jazz ensembles, symphonies, choral groups, and international artists. As a producer, the Ford Center incubates and serves as a catalyst for collaborative projects between the University and the community. The facility also serves as a venue for campus and local productions, University functions, lectures, and meetings.

On September 26, 2008, the University of Mississippi hosted journalists from around the world as the site for a presidential debate. The first debate between Barack Obama, a Democratic senator from Illinois, and John McCain, a Republican senator from Arizona, was broadcast live from the Gertrude C. Ford Center for the Performing Arts. With more than 150 events annually, performances include Morgan Freeman, Hal Holbrook, Art Garfunkel, Mary Stuart, The Blind Boys of Alabama, B.B. King, and Lewis Black. Noted lecturers such as Prince Edward, the King of Jordan, Janet Reno, Cornell West, James Earl Jones, Thomas Friedman, John McCain, and Tom Brokaw are among a growing list of authors and noted intellectuals who have appeared in the Ford Center.

The UM Box Office handles ticket sales for all performances in the Ford Center. The main location is in the Student Union (except from 2017-2019 during renovation of the Student Union). The Ford Center Box Office is generally open only on days of a performance. **Students receive discounted prices for every show**. Check online (fordcenter.org or olemissboxoffice.com) for performance times and ticket order information.

The Ford Center welcomes all individuals to enjoy its beautiful atmosphere and the accouterments of an exceptional performing arts facility. As a student at the University of Mississippi, you have the opportunity to explore a variety of art forms and expand your understanding of the world around you. You might be surprised at how a live performance can reach you on an intellectual or emotional level that is new and exciting. Sharing those experiences with friends can create a special connection that you may discuss and remember for many years. Be a Rebel and take a chance. Attend something you have never seen before.

Theatre Etiquette

1. Arrive early. If you are late, you may be held out or reseated until an appropriate time for you to get to your assigned seat. People who arrive late disturb the performers on stage and audience members, and there is added risk trying to negotiate seating in the dark. It is best to arrive about 30 minutes early so that you have time to purchase concessions, find your seat, and read the program before the show starts

2. Take care of any personal needs, as you should not leave your seat until intermission or until the performance ends.

3. Please sit in the seat you are assigned so you do not cause confusion for other audience members.

4. Silence or turn off all electronic devices, including cell phones, beepers, and watch alarms. It's embarrassing if it goes off in the middle of a tense moment of the show and it will break the mood for everyone! Please refrain from sharing on social media or texting during performances; the glow from your device is distracting.

5. Most shows do not allow photography of any kind. Flash photography inside the theatre is never allowed - it is a distraction to those around you and a danger to the performers.

6. The overture is part of the performance. Please cease talking at this point.

7. Please refrain from talking, humming, or singing along with the show, except when encouraged to do so by the artist or show.

8. Please wait for an appropriate moment to dig something out of your pocket or bag.

9. Go easy with the perfume and cologne, as many people are highly allergic.

10. If you need assistance during the show, please go to your nearest volunteer usher. If additional assistance is needed the usher will contact the appropriate person to help you.

11. Leaving while the show is in progress or before the actors have taken their final bows is discourteous. Wait until it is over and then exit with the rest of the audience.

12. Food and beverages are not allowed in the theatre.

13. Be courteous and everyone will enjoy the show!

Chapter 10
Academic Dishonesty & Plagiarism
By Noel Wilkin

We are living in a time when information is more accessible and prolific than in any time in history. With a smartphone, computer, or tablet, people can find information on just about any topic or subject. This access generally is regarded as a good thing. It is important to realize, however, that while the information around us is wonderfully accessible, it is not ours. Credit for creating it belongs to someone else. My wife and I have a beautiful lithograph of a painting that hangs in our dining room. It is a painting of a farm; I see it every day. We bought it, and it belongs to us. Yet, that does not mean that I can lead people to believe that I painted it. In fact, I

do not have the skills, knowledge, tools, or capability to create anything quite that beautiful on a canvas. This painting resulted from the artist's vision, experiences, creativity, and perspectives. What he chose to represent in the painting of the farm was based on his knowledge of farms, a view of an actual farm, and knowledge of what belongs on a farm. He chose to leave some details in, and leave some out. He chose the colors and the perspective. There was a lot of time, effort, and personal perspective that went into this painting. With this example, it seems simple and would seem strange to claim credit for creating the original painting. It should seem just as strange and unusual to claim credit for thoughts, perspectives, and ideas that belong to someone else whether they appear in an image, a painting, an illustration, a poem, a book, or a paragraph.

An individual's ideas, perspectives, skill, and knowledge are reflected in every picture or illustration we see and every phrase that we read. The words used, the structure of the sentences, and the order of information are all the creations of the original author. As a result, by reading and processing the work of others, the information shapes our perspectives and shapes the way we work and live. It also shapes how we think and how we write. This influence on our thoughts, ideas, and perspectives by others is an essential part of education. We learn from the work and creativity of others. Yet, when it is time for us to create, for us to extol our perspectives, **the ideas, words, sentences, and creations must be our own.**

Why does it matter?

In the example of the painting, if I were to tell people that I painted it, who would care? While it would probably not have much direct impact, it would certainly change people's opinions of me. In addition to perhaps leading people to believe that I was delusional, it would be an outright lie. It would clearly indicate to others that I was dishonest, lacking of character, and not worthy of trust. The same outcomes result when people inappropriately use the work of others and claim credit by presenting it as their own. Let's assume that a class was given an assignment to paint a farm scene and the assignment was to be graded. Simply turning in someone else's work is clearly a shortcut and dishonest. At an obvious level, if this were not discouraged it would be unfair to the other students who put in the effort to complete the assignment on their own. Fairness is not only valued at a societal level, it is an important element of assigning grades within classes. Yet, at an academic institution, dishonesty is a more egregious violation.

Your ideas, words, and creations must be your own

While studying at the University, you are a member of a community that places tremendous value on getting things right, striving for truth, and being sincere (Horacek, 2009). Horacek (2009) argued that academic integrity is not simply a nice attribute of academic institutions, it is "absolutely necessary for getting difficult things done" (p. 12). Researchers at academic institutions struggle to discover the truth about our world and about our past, and make truthful predictions about our future. This new knowledge is not simply a blogger's opinion on reality. It is the foundational knowledge upon which people in our society base decisions, live our lives, and choose our actions. Asking and answering questions in principled and methodical ways (like the scientific method), are the hallmarks of this search for truth. Getting it right is critical. As a student at the University, you are not only receiving an education, you also are a participant or initiate into this community of researchers (Horacek, 2009). These perspectives of fairness, integrity, and academic honesty are represented in the University's creed:

Did you know?

An Ole Miss All-American, Olympic Gold Medalist, and the 1985 Basketball Athlete of the Year, Jennifer Gillom was a pioneer player in the Women's National Basketball Association. She is now one of the league's top coaches.

The University of Mississippi is a community of learning dedicated to nurturing excellence in intellectual inquiry and personal character in an open and diverse environment. As a voluntary member of this community:

> *I believe in respect for the dignity of each person*
> *I believe in fairness and civility*
> *I believe in personal and professional integrity*
> *I believe in academic honesty*
> *I believe in academic freedom*
> *I believe in good stewardship of our resources*
> *I pledge to uphold these values and encourage others to follow my example.*

> **the University of Mississippi creed emphasizes:**
> • **dignity**
> • **fairness**
> • **integrity**
> • **honesty**
> • **stewardship**

Standards and procedures

In addition to the Creed, which succinctly describes the University community's values and communicates to our community the ideals that we believe are fundamental to our success, we also have policies that outline what happens when academic honesty, fairness, and professional integrity are violated.

Standards of honesty • *The University is conducted on a basis of common honesty. Dishonesty, cheating, or plagiarism, or knowingly furnishing false information to the University are regarded as particularly serious offenses. Disruptive behavior in an academic situation or purposely harming academic facilities also is grounds for academic discipline (Student Academic Conduct and Discipline, 2010).*

This standard reflects the values of the community and is based on the premise that honesty is at the heart of our mission. Protecting it and ensuring it is a responsibility that is taken very seriously.

When violations occur, these policies guide appropriate discipline. The purpose of these policies and the associated discipline are to ensure preservation of a community that is conducive to the goals of the institution. As stated in the University's Academic Conduct and Discipline Policy, "The broad purpose underlying student discipline is to order University living in such a way that the interests of the student body as a whole and of the individual members are best served" (*Student Academic Conduct and Discipline*, 2010). This statement reinforces the fundamental philosophy regarding the discipline of students. Discipline is used to ensure that the interests of the institution are protected, and the interests of the student body and community as a whole hinge upon honesty.

Different universities will have similar expectations for academic honesty, although they might have different standards of discipline or processes by which cases of academic dishonesty are evaluated and sanctioned. Probably one of the most notable standards is that

Did you know?

Master playwright and actor John Maxwell is best known for his award-winning one-man show, *Oh, Mr. Faulkner Do You Write?* Maxwell has performed the play internationally to rave reviews. Maxwell earned his theatre degree from Ole Miss.

Standards of Honesty

The University is conducted on a basis of common honesty.

• • •

Dishonesty, cheating, or plagiarism, or knowingly furnishing false information to the University are regarded as particularly serious offenses.

• • •

Disruptive behavior in an academic situation or purposely harming academic facilities also is grounds for academic discipline.

• • •

("Student Academic Conduct and Discipline," 2010)

of the University of Virginia. Their honor code system dates back to 1842, and guilt results in expulsion from the university. "Any student found guilty of an Honor offense, or deemed to have admitted guilt after having left without requesting a trial, will be permanently dismissed from the University" (*Honor Code at UVa*, 2010).

Discipline of academic dishonesty at the University of Mississippi begins between the faculty member and the student. Upon discovery of academic dishonesty, faculty members will recommend a sanction after a discussion with the student. There are many possible sanctions that can be imposed or recommended. A few examples include failure on the work, failure in the course, grade reduction in the course, probation, suspension, and expulsion. If the faculty member is recommending a sanction of probation, suspension, or expulsion, then the Chair, the appropriate Dean, the Registrar, the Provost, and the Vice Chancellor for Student Affairs are notified. The Provost will notify the Registrar, who then will contact the student, if the sanction is probation or suspension. The Chancellor is notified by the Provost if the recommended sanction is expulsion. The Chancellor then contacts the Registrar, who then will contact the student (*Student Academic Conduct and Discipline*, 2010). The student has the right to challenge the sanction through a process of appeal. Some schools within the University of Mississippi maintain honor code systems with their own processes. These include the schools of Law, Pharmacy, and Engineering. For the other schools and the college, this process is handled by the Academic Discipline Committee. Students should refer to the policy for specifics on this process and the timeline requirements for filing an appeal.

Academic dishonesty

The University houses a wide variety of diverse subjects and disciplines. Each subject fosters the discovery of truth and advancement of knowledge in many different ways. The disciplines, or subject areas, rely upon different methods of helping students grasp new concepts, and each offers students the opportunity to learn different information, content,

Did you know?

Chris Offutt, associate professor of English, has written multiple screenplays including scripts for HBO's series *True Blood* and *Treme'* and Showtime's *Weeds*. He insists his students turn off the TV and pick up a book, believing that "the most important thing for any writer is to read."

and strategies of knowing. As a result, it is difficult to provide one definition that will encompass all examples of academic dishonesty. Definitions of academic dishonesty most often include two parameters: (1) "unauthorized assistance" and (2) "the work is graded" (Garavalia, Olson, Russell, & Christensen, 2007, p. 34). Examples of unauthorized assistance can include anything that is helpful in completing the assignment and forbidden by the instructor. It is easy to think of common examples like access to information during exams, looking on another's test during an exam, and obtaining the answers from others. Of course, this is differentiated from assistance that is commonly authorized such as the use of books in the library for the purpose of writing papers, appropriate assistance from team members in team-based assignments or work, a calculator in certain situations, etc. Therefore, the first step to understanding what is appropriate is to understand what assistance is authorized in given assignments. The second criterion involves the grading of the work. Assignments and exams help instructors to understand how a student is performing in a given course. They allow for the assignment of grades that are based on the student's performance and provide feedback to the students as to how well they are performing in the course. Use of unauthorized assistance affords the student an advantage that is not available to all students and violates the University's value of fairness. It also results in an inappropriate grading of the student's work and an inappropriate (i.e., unfair) assignment of a grade. As a result, instructors have a responsibility to the students they teach and to those who hire graduates to ensure that students are acquiring the knowledge and skills necessary to be successful; grade assignment is an indicator of successful acquisition of the knowledge and skills taught in the class. Assignments, papers, examinations, quizzes, and other assessment tools are essential to determine whether students are learning the material being taught and developing the skills commensurate with the grade assigned. This responsibility increases the importance of remaining vigilant in detecting, preventing, and disciplining cases of academic dishonesty by students.

> **Some schools within The University of Mississippi maintain honor code systems with their own processes. These include the schools of Law, Pharmacy, and Engineering.**

The University's standards of honesty specifically mention types of dishonest behaviors – cheating, plagiarism, or knowingly furnishing false information to the University. In each instance, these behaviors provide some form of unauthorized assistance and the information is used to grade or assess the student. In instances of cheating, such as doing someone else's homework, purchasing a paper written by someone else, and copying answers during a test, it is easy to see how these behaviors gain an individual an unfair ad-

Did you know?

Over the past decade, the health care sector has added many new jobs. Roughly one in ten college graduates now gets a health-related degree. Former Chancellor Dan Jones challenged students to consider a health profession. "The most important reason to consider: the personal fulfillment. It provides, in my view, the most tangible way for someone to live a life of service."

vantage and many can see why this is unauthorized assistance – thus making these examples of academic dishonesty. Similarly, providing false information to the University (e.g., giving inappropriate ACT scores, forging transcripts to provide false GPAs) seems reasonably straightforward as being dishonest and gaining unearned or inappropriate advantages. Other examples of academic dishonesty mentioned in the policy and other places (*Types of Plagiarism*, 2010; Garavalia, et. al, 2007) are included on the next page. Plagiarism, while in some instances may seem straightforward, can be more difficult to understand. Please note that academic dishonesty is not limited to these examples. However, this list is meant to describe the breadth of behaviors and activities that fall into the category of academic dishonesty. (See examples on next page.)

Plagiarism

Those in academia have a high standard of scrutiny towards plagiarism, and yet, different academic disciplines will have different standards and different expectations when it comes to citations (Anderson, 1998) and to defining and assessing plagiarism (Blum, 2009). Blum attributed this high standard to the need to link information and build upon the foundation of others. "Proper academic citation provides a way for authors to trace their influences, to situate themselves intellectually, to prove that they have done their background theoretical reading, to demonstrate engagement in an ongoing community of inquiry, and to provide sources for readers who want to consult earlier thinkers or data" (Blum, 2009, p. 14). While studying at the University, students should keep this in mind and realize their professors have this perspective when reviewing assignments and grading papers. As a professor, I expect students to provide that window into their reasoning when writing papers and completing projects. I also expect them to provide accurate citations of their sources. This allows me to fully assess the content of their work, the thought process that they had in completing the work, and the strategies used to assemble resources used to complete the work – hence it allows me to assess their ability.

A simple definition of plagiarism is, "the act of using the words of another without giving the originator credit" (Anderson, 1998, p. 1). Plagiarism "refers to appropriating any material – ideas, writings, images, or portions of those – and claiming to be the original creator" (Gilmore, 2008, p. 2). Like many offenses, there is a range of plagiarism that can take place. Blum (2009) proposed a range that stretches from "deceptive" to "uninformed" (p. 27). Deceptive plagiarism examples would include "buying a paper" or "using someone's freely given paper" (Blum, 2009, p. 27). On the other end of the spectrum is uninformed plagiarism that would include "imperfect mastery of citation conventions" (Blum, 2009, p. 27). It could be argued that at the college level, students should have a good idea as to what

Did you know?

Former Rebel great Eli Manning is a two-time Superbowl Most Valuable Player. In the off-season, Manning lives with his family in Oxford.

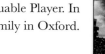

Some Specific Examples of Academic Dishonesty*

■ Plagiarism

■ Copying another's homework

■ Allowing someone to copy or use your homework

■ Copying answers to test questions

■ Allowing others to do your work or homework

■ Allowing someone to take your exam for you

■ Handing in a paper that was purchased

■ Handing in a paper written by someone else

■ Taking a test for someone else

■ Attempting to gain possession of a test prior to its administration

■ Accessing unauthorized computer files, reference materials, files, previously completed work, notes during exams

■ Stealing books or other University resources (from the library, museum, computer center, or other University facility)

■ Harming or causing damage to facilities that support the academic environment

■ Damage to books, laboratory equipment, computers, laboratories, or other facilities

■ Fabricating references or citations

■ Paraphrasing without acknowledgement

■ Accessing an office without authorization in an attempt to gain an advantage

■ Employing bribery, intimidation, or harassment in an attempt to gain an unfair advantage

■ Falsely attesting that work has been completed when it has not been completed

■ Falsely claiming attendance at functions or classes

■ Falsely claiming attendance of others at functions or classes

■ Altering grade reports

■ Changing grade forms or class rolls

■ Altering, falsifying, or misusing University documents

■ Falsifying research data

■ Disruptive behavior in class or at University functions

■ Physically or verbally harassing an instructor or fellow student

■ Interfering with an instructor's ability to teach or students' to learn

■ Copying from the Internet

Sources: (*Student Academic Conduct and Discipline*, 2010; *Types of Plagiarism*, 2010; and Garavalia, et. al, 2007)

* Academic dishonesty is not limited to the examples in this list.

Did you know?

Charlie Conerly astonished Ole Miss fans as a quarterback for the Rebels. He set three NCAA passing records while leading Ole Miss to the SEC Championship. He was Rookie of the Year the following season for the New York Giants. He later won NFL Player of the Year honors.

should be cited and the manner in which it should be cited, or have the ability and motivation to look it up or ask the instructor. Learning about how to appropriately cite is still taking place in college. Students should become familiar with the reference style appropriate for their disciplines to ensure proper citation strategies and notations when using other people's work (e.g., Lipson, 2006; Hacker, 2009).

If an instructor suspects that some of a student's work has been plagiarized, the policy dictates a meeting with the student. Without a full analysis of the situation, it is difficult for an instructor to know where on the continuum a particular offense might fall. It may be easy to assume that the student has had unauthorized assistance on graded work. The policy requires a discussion with the student for the purpose of assessing where the offense falls on the scale and whether it matches the criteria for being considered academic dishonesty.

Strategies to prevent or avoid plagiarism

Students are encouraged to take active steps to prevent inadvertent or unintentional plagiarism. The prolific amount of information and ease of access, in addition to the need to support one's arguments and assertions with foundational knowledge, raises the importance of knowing how to appropriately use the thoughts and words of others to do one's own work. In writing, there are three options when using the ideas of others to support your work – quote and cite the original authors, paraphrase and cite the original authors, and summarize and cite the original authors. The pivotal role that citation plays increases the importance of learning an appropriate citation style for the discipline of study. Some of the more commonly used citation styles are the American Psychological Association (APA) Style, the Modern Language Association (MLA) system of citations, the Chicago Manual of Style, and others. Two concise references on citation style include *A Writer's Reference* by Hacker and *Cite Right* by Lipson.

Discerning when it is most appropriate to quote, paraphrase, or summarize words and ideas is an important skill eclipsed only by the importance of knowing how to appropriately do each. Some inappropriately assume that only full sentences borrowed from another source need to be quoted (Howard, 1999). Even the act of copying phrases (three to five word sections of sentences) from other sources patched together with synonyms or abbreviated thoughts based on the original author's work is considered plagiarism. While there is some debate over this type of writing, which has been called "patchwriting," and its role in learning to write, it meets the criteria for plagiarism (Howard, 1999, p. 11). Writers' references and handbooks are good sources of learning strategies for appropriate paraphrasing and summarizing. "A summary condenses information; a paraphrase reports information in about the same number of words as the source" (Hacker, 2009, p. 420).

Did you know?

Archie Manning — the softspoken quarterback who inspired the song, *The Ballad of Archie Who* — was one of the most exciting college quarterbacks to ever play the game. In a single game against the University of Alabama, he accounted for 540 yards of offense. Ole Miss lost.

(Please note that Hacker [2009] is the reference used by the University's Center for Writing and Rhetoric.) These strategies espoused in writers' handbooks also assist in learning how to avoid this type of patchwriting when paraphrasing or summarizing. Because both should be in your own words, perhaps the most valuable recommendation is to "set the source aside, write from memory, and consult the source later for accuracy" (Hacker, 2009, p. 421). Additionally, the University's librarians have created a tutorial on plagiarism (*Research Help Tutorial: Plagiarism and Academic Honesty*, 2010).

Students are likely to improve their ability to appropriately cite supporting source information if they take the time to learn about plagiarism. There are no shortcuts to doing your own work; if it feels like a shortcut, then it probably is not appropriate. Allowing ample time to do the work correctly, cognitively reflecting on the body of information assembled, gathering all of the appropriate and authorized resources, and taking careful notes also are important strategies. Sloppiness and failure to take the time to appropriately reference materials as you take notes based on other sources can easily lead to inadvertent plagiarism. Once the information is extracted it is difficult to remember from where it came. As you take notes from sources and incorporate information, quotations and citations should be carefully noted. Finally, don't hesitate to ask the instructor to clarify the materials that are approved, what citation style is appropriate, or for assistance. Help is available from the instructor, from reference librarians, from the Writing Center, and from the Center for Writing and Rhetoric.

REFERENCES

Anderson, J. (1998). *Plagiarism, Copyright Violation and Other Thefts of Intellectual Property: An Annotated Bibliography with a Lengthy Introduction*. Jefferson, NC: McFarland & Company.

Blum, S. D. (2009). *My Word! Plagiarism and College Culture*. Ithaca, NY: Cornell University Press.

Garavalia, L., Olson, E., Russell, E., Christensen, L. (2007). How do students cheat? In: E. M. Anderman, & T. B. Murdock (Eds.), *Psychology of Academic Cheating* (pp. 33-55). San Francisco, CA: Elsevier.

Gilmore, B. (2008). *Plagiarism: Why it Happens, How to Prevent it*. Portsmouth, NH: Heinemann.

Hacker, D. (2009). *A Writer's Reference*, 6th ed. Boston, MA: Bedford/St. Martin's.

Honor Code at UVa. (2010). Retrieved from scps.virginia.edu/honor_code.htm

Horacek, D. (2009). Academic Integrity and Intellectual Autonomy. In: T. Twomey, H. White, & K. Sagendorf (Eds.), *Pedagogy, not Policing: Positive Approaches to Academic Integrity at the University* (pp.7-17). Syracuse, NY: The Graduate School Press of Syracuse University.

Howard, R. M. (1999). Standing in the Shadow of Giants: Plagiarists, Authors, Collaborators. Stamford, CT: Ablex Publishing Corporation.

Lipson, C. (2006). Cite Right: A Quick Guide to Citation Styles – MLA, APA, Chicago, the Sciences, Professions, and More. Chicago, IL: University of Chicago Press.

O'Hare, F., & Kline, E. A. (1996). *The Modern Writer's Handbook*, 4th ed. Boston, MA: Allyn and Bacon.

REFERENCES CONTINUED

Research Help Tutorial: Plagiarism and Academic Honesty. (2010). Retrieved from
olemiss.edu/depts/general_library/instruction/resources/plagiarism_ac_honest/plagiarism_academic_
honesty.html

Student Academic Conduct and Discipline (ACA.AR.600.001). (2010). Retrieved from
secure4.olemiss.edu/umpolicyopen/ShowDetails.jsp?istatPara=1&policyObjidPara=10817696

Types of Plagiarism. (2010, November). Retrieved from plagiarism.org/plag_article_types_of_plagiarism.html

University Creed. (2010). Retrieved from olemiss.edu/info/creed.html

What is Plagiarism? (2010, November). Retrieved from plagiarism.org

About the Author

Noel Wilkin, *Provost and Executive Vice Chancellor for Academic Affairs,
Professor in Pharmacy Administration, and
Research Professor in the Research Institute of Pharmaceutical Sciences.*

Noel Wilkin received his B.S. and Ph.D. from the University of Maryland.
Dr. Wilkin's areas of research include practical reasoning and its role in decision
making, mechanisms to enhance optimal drug therapy, pharmacy entrepreneurship and management, and issues facing professional education.

Chapter 11
Communication and Technology

By Kathy Gates, Nishanth Rodrigues, and Ryan Whittington

Students today live in a world of instant communication and immediate access to information. In fact, it is not unusual for students to be more comfortable with the use of technology than their instructors. After all, you were born into a world saturated with video games, personal computers, mobile devices, smart phones, and the World Wide Web, whereas previous generations began using these technologies as adults.

The EDUCAUSE Center for Applied Research (ECAR) National Study of Under-graduate Students and Information Technology is a comprehensive study of technology use among undergraduate students. The 2016 report noted that students believe tech-nology is critical to academic success and that they bring to campus a variety of small, portable, network-enabled de-vices. According to the study, 93 percent of students own laptops, 96 percent own smartphones, and 57 percent own tablets. Add to this e-readers and gam-ing devices and students typically bring two, three, or four networked devices to campus—or more! Among the technol-ogy-based tools that students use are the library website, learning management systems such as Blackboard, e-textbooks, productivity tools, and software to manage cita-tions and e-portfolios. In fact, the study found that most students (58 percent) said that learning works best for them when courses incorporate at least some online components. Technology is embedded in students' lives in all sorts of ways, such as to communicate with instructors and peers, access learning management systems, take notes in class, and much more. Patterns of technology use among UM students are similar to the national trends reported in the ECAR study.

What does this mean for you as a UM student? For one, it means that there are incredibly exciting new ways for you to learn, communicate with instructors and friends, and engage in campus life. However, it also means that you need to be cautious with technologies or services that are new and unfamiliar to you. This chapter offers information and advice on navigating the Internet in ways that are most beneficial to you.

Technology at Ole Miss

The "online" UM campus is rich with technology services for taking care of business and staying connected. The campus portal, myOleMiss (**my.olemiss.edu**), is a place where you can register for classes, accept financial aid awards, check midterm and final grades, order transcripts, and much more. Many UM instructors use Blackboard (**blackboard.olemiss.edu**) to post assignments and other class information. Some instructors use personal response systems or "clickers" in class to increase student engagement. OrgSync (**dos.orgsync.com**) is an interactive website that supports UM student organizations and helps students get involved. You can check your e-mail using UM Gmail (**mail.go.olemiss.edu**), and you can find out about campus news and events through UM Today, an online announcement board that includes messages relevant to you. UM Box (**olemiss.box.com**) is a cloud-based file storage and collaboration service where you can store documents, work with other students on group projects, and more. RebAlert is a notification system in which UM students receive text messages in cases of campus-wide class cancellations or emergencies. The Ole Miss News site (**news.olemiss.edu**) has the latest news and human interest stories from the University. Almost all of these services have mobile-friendly versions.

Technology beyond the Ole Miss campus

Countless communication services and tools are available outside of the campus intranet. Popular social media networking sites such as Facebook, Twitter, Pinterest, and Tumblr, allow members of the Ole Miss family to connect with individuals and communities around the world. Messaging applications such as SnapChat, WhatsApp, and Facebook Messenger allow for even more intrapersonal commentary. Wikipedia (wikipedia.org) is one of the most well-known "wikis," or networks of interrelated online documents and information. Instant messaging is a popular way to communicate in real time using text-based tools, whereas software applications such as Skype (skype.com) allow for voice conversations over the Internet.

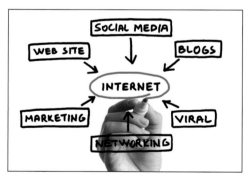

Privacy and personal safety

With the abundance of online interaction comes new and challenging concerns related to privacy and personal safety. Listed next are some practical suggestions for protecting yourself online. See also the IT Security website (**itsecurity.olemiss.edu**), which contains recent alerts, security basics, tools, and resources.

■ Use discretion when posting information.

Don't announce that you are alone or out of town even among Facebook friends. Don't post or e-mail anything that you wouldn't want to share with the public, including your parents, instructors, or potential employers. A common mistake is to inadvertently send a message to the wrong recipient, for example through automatic word-completion capabilities in e-mail programs. Information posted online can be immediately duplicated and forwarded, creating a lasting record that cannot be erased … ever.

■ Never give out private information.

Numerous "phishing" scams exist to try to extract personal information from you for the purpose of stealing your identity or your money. Often they are designed to direct you to a bogus website that looks very similar to the website for a legitimate institution. Never give out your social security number or password, and only give out your credit card information when you are absolutely sure that the site is trustworthy.

> With the abundance of online interaction comes new and challenging concerns related to privacy and personal safety.

■ Manage your privacy settings.

Most social networking sites such as Facebook allow you to control who has access to your information. Take the time to learn what these settings mean and then proactively manage them to help protect your identity. Even so, remember that technology is not flawless. Properly-controlled privacy settings can occasionally fail and are therefore no substitute for practicing good judgment about what should and should not be posted on the Internet. Occasionally "Google" yourself to see what information is posted for public viewing.

■ Think about the impact to your reputation.

It is not unusual for employers to "Google" applicants to gain insight into their personalities and values. Be especially careful with any photographs that you post, and think about the impression they create with viewers who may or may not know the circumstances or setting. Keep in mind that once information has been posted on the Internet, it is virtually impossible to delete. Read the accompanying section in this Chapter ("The Good, the Bad, and the Awful of Scoial Media") to see some real-world examples of poor reputation managment.

Did you know?

Frank "Bruiser" Kinard was the first Rebel selected as an All-American (1936). He spent nine years in professional football. He was the first Mississippian enshrined in the Pro Football Hall of Fame.

Being a good citizen online

Netiquette, or Network Etiquette, is a set of accepted practices that have evolved over the last 20 years defining good behavior on the Internet. There are many good books and articles that provide detailed netiquette guidelines. A few of the most important conventions for communicating in cyberspace are noted here.

Internet shorthand

When you send text messages or communicate online you will find a multitude of abbreviations and codes that serve as shorthand. There are several good sources for finding out what these mean, including NetLingo (netlingo.com). Common examples are *bff* for best friends forever, *lol* for laughing out loud, and *idk* for I don't know. Likewise, there is a convention in which writing in ALL CAPS means that you are SHOUTING.

Keep in mind that once information has been posted on the Internet, it is virtually impossible to delete. Party pictures you post today may well turn up in Google searches ten years from now.

Flame wars and spam

Be careful what you sign up for online. If you are faced with an enticing service that requests personal information and is not one that you went looking for, there may be a possibility that this service could 'sell' your information to other third parties and result in additional SPAM coming your way.

Stay informed!

Be sure to check your Ole Miss e-mail, including UM Today, daily. UM Today is used to communicate pertinent information about events on campus. Also, if you want to receive RebAlert emergency notifications, verify that your cell phone number is listed correctly in myOleMiss by going to Student -> My Profile and selecting Contact Information.

Respect others online

The UM Creed (**https://olemiss.edu/info/creed.html**) sets expectations for treating others with fairness, respect, and dignity. These expectations are just as relevant and important in the digital world as they are on the physical UM campus. Just as it is never acceptable in "real life" to threaten, harass, embarrass, or otherwise target another person, it

Did you know?

Beloved Rebel Deuce McAllister is the only player to have more than 1,000 all purpose yards for three straight seasons. He was selected as an All-Pro twice as a running back for the New Orleans Saints. He traveled to Central America the summer before his senior year (without the coach's permission) so he could graduate on time.

is absolutely unacceptable to do these things using the Internet, digital technologies, or mobile phones. The UM Creed also sets expectations for good stewardship of resources. These expectations apply to digital environments, especially as related to network bandwidth usage and data storage.

Illegal downloads and copyright infringement

Copyright law limits the right of a user to copy, download, distribute, edit, or transmit electronically another person's intellectual property, including written materials, images, videos, software, games, sounds, music, and performances, without permission. Violations of copyright law may include giving others unauthorized access to copyrighted materials by posting that material on social networking sites, or downloading from Internet websites or through Peer-to-Peer (P2P) file sharing any material owned by another without the owner's permission. Even if you do not intend to engage in infringing activity, installing P2P software on a computer easily can result in you unintentionally sharing files (copyrighted music, movies, or even sensitive documents) with other P2P users, and you may then be personally responsible for the legal and financial consequences.

> **When sending e-mail, always use a descriptive subject line to help the reader quickly assess the importance and relevance of the message.**

Protect your WebID and password

Your WebID and password give you access to myOleMiss, e-mail, Blackboard, the campus wireless network, and many other services. Never share your password with anyone else, and don't access the account of another person. A comprehensive list of restrictions and cautions is available in the IT Appropriate Use Policy **olemiss.edu/ause.html**.

Computer use and wellness

Social networking sites, video games, and other kinds of technology can be a fun way to stay connected with friends and entertain yourself, but when used excessively they can distract you from what is really important. Internet tools can enhance learning but when used in class independently from the instructor, e.g., to check BuzzFeed, read the *Daily Mississippian* online, or send and receive text messages, they can cause you to miss important concepts. It is easy to become overwhelmed with the amount of information that is being streamed to you. Finding a good balance between online communication and face-to-face relationships is essential, both personally and professionally. Learning to filter out the "noise" and even going "offline" periodically are critical to your personal productiv-

Did you know?

Wesley Walls was one of the last players to start on an Ole Miss football team on both offense and defense. He was an All-American selection at tight end his senior year. As a pro, he was selected five times to play in the Pro Bowl. In 2014, Walls was inducted into the College Football Hall of Fame.

ity and overall sense of well-being.

The University's commitment is also reflected in the work of the UM Energy Committee and Active Transportation Committee, as well as in the newly updated UM Master Plan, which provides guidelines for sustainable growth at the university.

LiveSafe App

In November 2016, the University partnered with LiveSafe, a mobile safety communications application. LiveSafe is a free mobile safety app that allows faculty, staff, students, parents, alumni, and even visitors at Ole Miss to report nonemergency or anonymous tips to the University Police Department (UPD). The app is available for free download for both iOS and Android devices. More information about the app is available at **olemiss.edu/livesafe.**

Glossary

UM Today – Important campus announcements sent as a daily e-mail message and also displayed in the campus portal, myOleMiss (my.olemiss.edu).

Blackboard – A web-based learning management system used by UM instructors to share important class information (blackboard.olemiss.edu).

RebAlert – The campus emergency notification system by which text messages are used to notify students and employees in campus emergency and alert situations (such as tornado watches).

Phishing – An attempt to fraudulently acquire confidential information for use in identity theft, e.g., by sending an e-mail or setting up a website that resembles a well-known organization.

Netiquette – A set of accepted practices that have evolved over the last twenty years defining good behavior on the Internet

Flame war - A hostile dispute conducted on a public electronic forum such as a message board.

Troll – Someone who initiates and encourages a flame war for the purpose of eliciting an emotional reaction.

Peer-to-Peer (P2P) File Sharing – A means for downloading files directly from other users on the Internet; often used to illegally download materials such as music and video without the owner's permission.

WebID – An account name that gives you access to many UM systems such as e-mail, myOleMiss, Blackboard, and the campus wireless network

Did you know?

William Eggleston was instrumental in giving legitimacy to color photography as an artistic medium. He developed an interest in photography while a student at Ole Miss. His show *14 Pictures* was the first one-person color photo exhibit at the Museum of Modern Art.

REFERENCES

Dahstrom, E., Walker, J.D., and Dziuban, C. (2013). ECAR Study of Undergraduate Students and Information Technology. Retrieved from www.educause.edu/ecar.

About the Authors

Kathy Gates, *former Chief Information Officer*

Kathy Gates served as the Chief Information Officer for the University of Mississippi from 2006-2017. She is retired.

Nishanth Rodrigues, *Chief Information Officer*

With more than 24 years of IT experience in academia, manufacturing, and professional health care, Rodrigues is an award-winning leader in information technology. Previously assistant vice president and chief technology officer at Michigan State University, he joined the University of Mississippi as Chief Information Officer in 2017. Rodrigues earned his Master of Business Administration degree from Michigan State University and his bachelor's degree in network engineering from Davenport University.

Ryan M. Whittington, *Director of Markeing and Brand Strategy*

Ryan Whittington, an early adopter of just about every social media platform (yes, even MySpace @rmwhitti), received both bachelor's and master's degrees in journalism from the University of Mississippi. He has worked in University Communications since 2012. In his spare time, you can catch him looking for his next half marathon to run with his wife, Beth.

The Good, the Bad, and the Awful of Social Media

Introduction

As an institution of higher education in the 21st century, we would be remiss if we did not talk about social media and the role it plays in dictating your personal and professional reputation. As members of Generation Z, you have all grown up using social media. In fact, a January 2018 Pew Research Center study found that 88 percent of online adults between the ages of 18-29 use Facebook, and 64% of all Internet users within that same age range use Instagram.

Thanks to smartphones and a world that has come to expect instant communication, your tweets, status updates, snaps, and Instagram stories can be shared across the Internet in a matter of seconds. While technology and social media have the ability to make our lives much easier in so many different ways, they also come with more than their fair share of pitfalls.

Social Media Crises on Campus

The University of Mississippi and its student body experienced the pitfalls of social media following election night in November 2012.

Shortly after 10 p.m. on the evening of November 6, Ole Miss students took to social media to share their thoughts on the election and to describe a verbal exchange between supporters of Gov. Mitt Romney and President Barack Obama. What began as political speech turned into ugly incidents of racially charged speech fed in part by students' use of social media. In fact, the political exchange was soon being described on social media as a "riot."

Student tweets exaggerating, even fictionalizing, what happened and the resulting media coverage reached millions of people around the world, creating a sense with many observers that a riot actually had occurred at Ole Miss. The situation could have been avoided if those involved had reminded themselves that you can not believe everything you read on Twitter, and you should not re-tweet information you don't know to be accurate.

> **"Going to watch the riot at Stockard!!"**
> – 11:18 p.m.—student tweet

The rise of anonymous social platforms such as *Yik Yak* also have proven problematic on many educational campuses. In 2014, more than a dozen high schools and colleges charged students with threats of violence after "yaks" were made on the app. Almost all of these incidents were pranks, but to administrators and the authorities, all were quite serious. Students who made these threats felt that they were unable to be traced. However, *Yik Yak* personnel were cooperative with school officials and turned over IP addresses and GPS locations of those individuals, which led to felony charges and arrests.

These events proved detrimental for students, faculty, staff, alumni, and fans at all institutions, and while these are only a handful of examples, the bottom line is that students should never make false comments online – no matter the platform.

Privacy and personal safety
Reputation management

Have you ever typed your name into a Google search? If not, now is a good time to do it. It is not uncommon for potential employers, graduate school admissions offices, scholarship committees, and yes, even your parents, to seek out information about you on the Internet.

A Google search of a person's name can return photographs, status updates, and biographical information posted to any number of different social networking profiles. An embarrassing photograph or distasteful video taken at a party and posted on social media could restrict you from future job interviews, promotions, and certain career fields.

Remember that screen grabs and other technologies have made it virtually impossible to remove anything from the Internet.

On the evening of March 7, 2015, members of the Sigma Alpha Epsilon fraternity at the University of Oklahoma learned firsthand just how disastrous their words could be for their organization, their university, and their fellow students. That night, members of the group were filmed singing a racist song on a bus. The nine-second video made its way to a number of different social media channels and quickly went viral. It sparked outrage nationwide and ultimately led to the closure of the University of Oklahoma SAE chapter and the expulsion of two fraternity members.

While both the university and the organization were swift to react to the heinous video, the long-term repercussions for the members of the fraternity and those targeted in the community remain.

According to the parents of one of the students expelled, their son "made a horrible mistake and will live with the consequences forever."

Plenty of stories exist about individuals who later regret what they post to their personal social media profiles. But keep in mind, just because you land that first job or internship doesn't mean you should get lazy on social media.

In February 2016, a daycare employee in Arizona was fired when a controversial Snapchat she sent made its way back to the business's owner. The 19-year-old employee took a photo of her middle finger extended in front of a small child's face with the caption, "swear I love kids." The owner later relieved the employee of her duties.

Best Practices on Social Media

There are several best practices that can be used on social media. While some apply to personal accounts and others more to professional accounts, a few are applicable to both and are important to keep in mind when posting to your followers.

Identify your views as your own. As members of the Ole Miss community, the things we say and do reflect directly upon the University. On your personal accounts, be clear to identify your views as your own if you have identified yourself as a member of the University community. A simple disclaimer in your profile is sufficient, such as, "Opinions are mine," or, "All views, posts, and opinions are my own."

Think before you post. Comments made on social media are not only a reflection on you, but also on any group or organization you represent. Remember, everything you post online is public, easily searchable, and will be online forever. Use good grammar when posting online. Mistakes are a reflection of you and your education.

Be respectful. Be constructive and respectful when discussing differing opinions online. Remember that even if your social profile is private, disparaging comments about others can often be traced to the original source. Do not engage in online arguments or debates. In other words, don't "feed the trolls."

Be accurate. Keep in mind that not everything you read on social media (or on the Internet) is true. Film director Spike Lee found out the hard way that misinformation can be commonplace on the Internet. In 2012, a man named Marcus D. Higgins used Twitter to inform celebrities of the address of George Zimmerman, a neighborhood watchman accused of shooting and killing teenager Trayvon Martin.

Lee re-tweeted Higgins' tweet to his 240,000-plus followers believing it was accurate. Instead, an elderly Florida couple with the same last name was forced into hiding when Lee shared their address with all of his followers (many of whom shared the address with their followers, and so on.)

Before your next post to your followers, just remember to think before you post, be respectful and honest, be accurate, and be kind.

Think Twice Before You Post

by Alex Hicks, Graduate Assistant, University Communications

Has someone ever told you to "clean up" your social media? If you answered yes, I am going to guess you probably did not listen. If you answered no, then let me be the one to tell you. Social media can decide your future. I know it sounds dramatic, but just hear me out. I interned for a company in South Carolina the summer before my senior year at Ole Miss. Of course, many of the people I met throughout the summer asked about my plans after college. We got into the subject of job searching, and I talked to a recruiter for a company in that area. He told me that one of the first things they do once they receive an application and resumé from a potential employee is look at his or her social media. He warned me to clean up my social media and begin using my best judgement before posting anything. Of course, I didn't think it was as big a deal as he made it sound, but I was still scared enough of the consequences to go through my social media accounts and delete a few things. From then on out, I thought through everything before I posted something on social media.

That fall, I applied to be a social media ambassador for Ole Miss. After I was offered the position, I was told that they looked me up on social media before even considering calling me for an interview. If I had not listened to the recruiter I talked to months before, I may not have ended up with my internship here.

Social media can make or break you. What I mean by that is when people see your social media, they immediately form an opinion of you. As unfair as it seems, it is actually what social media was designed for in the first place. It is supposed to be used for people to connect with others and share things about themselves. It was made so that people may share things about their lives with people all around the world. We all have opinions, and in many countries we enjoy free speech; we can say what we believe. So this is not me telling you what to say or not say. This is me urging you to use your best judgment.

Are your social media posts intelligent? Are they respectful?
Think before you post. You will thank me later.

Using LinkedIn

It is incumbent upon students and young professionals in today's ultra-competitive job market to evaluate how best to advertise their skills to potential employers. Whether it is an internship or full-time position you are seeking, social media can help to distinguish you as a top candidate. *LinkedIn* is one of the most powerful social networking tools available. The business-oriented social networking site launched in May 2003, and serves as a means for professional connections.

Creating a *LinkedIn* profile is simple and only requires a valid e-mail address. Your *LinkedIn* profile is a resume that you can customize and is searchable by others. Before creating a *LinkedIn* profile, make a list of all previous work experience, including the name of the organization, your role within the organization, dates during which you were employed, and skills you acquired during the work. Also list all awards and honors you have previously received, as well as your involvement in any clubs, organizations, or academic societies.

When you are ready to create your *LinkedIn* profile, keep in mind that potential employers often identify candidates for positions based on work experience, education, and endorsements and connections with other *LinkedIn* users. Make sure your profile is complete with all of the relevant information. Once you publish your *LinkedIn* profile, it is time to begin building professional connections. You should request to connect with those who will be beneficial to your job-search goals, such as past supervisors who can endorse your skills, instructors who can speak to your academic credentials, mentors, and other professionals in your intended career field. As you begin to make connections on *LinkedIn*, consider requesting endorsements from your connections for specific skills that you have mastered. This will help your profile stand out to potential employers.

Conclusion

In early 2016, Facebook reached more than 1.59 billion active users per month, while Instagram had 400 million and Twitter had 320 million. Studies show that close to 60 percent of all online adults use two or more social media sites. The widespread use of social media has made it even more necessary to have a heightened sense of awareness when posting personal information on the Internet. Be careful! As the online landscape continues to evolve, it is important to think about the long-term effects of your social media behavior. Be smart. Think before you post. Ask yourself, "Will this post embarrass someone? Will it embarrass me?" If the answer is maybe or yes, don't do it!

The Top 10 Social Media Accounts to Follow at Ole Miss

1. **@OleMissRebels** (Twitter) – The official Twitter account of the University of Mississippi.

2. **@RebAlert** (Twitter) – The campus-wide Emergency Alert System sends updates, warnings, and other pertinent information related to campus safety via Twitter.

3. **@UMchancellor** (Twitter) – Chancellor Jeffrey Vitter's Twitter account frequently shares his thoughts on Ole Miss and higher education.

4. **@CoachLuke** (Twitter) – Head football coach Matt Luke provides congratulatory messages to members of the Ole Miss family.

5. **@RossBjorkAD** (Twitter) – Director of Athletics Ross Bjork constantly interacts with fans and responds to inquiries from his "mentions" column.

6. **@ummc1** (Facebook) – The University of Mississippi Medical Center's official Facebook page allows followers an inside look at some of the hospital's outstanding healthcare and research stories.

7. **@olemiss** (Instagram) – What better way to capture the most beautiful campus in the country than through filtered images?

8. **@weareolemiss** (Snapchat) – The official Ole Miss Athletics Snapchat account provides followers with a behind-the-scenes perspective of your favorite Rebel athletic programs.

9. **@olemiss** (Pinterest) – Looking for your next tailgating recipe? This page has hundreds of delicious pins to satisfy your sweet tooth.

10. **@OleMissSports** (YouTube) – Catch up on the most recent episode of *The Season*, the Emmy Award-winning show produced by Ole Miss Athletics.

Chapter 12
Test-Taking Strategies

By Dewey Knight

Taking tests, quizzes, and final exams are an inescapable part of college. Strong, effective test-taking skills are crucial for college and career success.

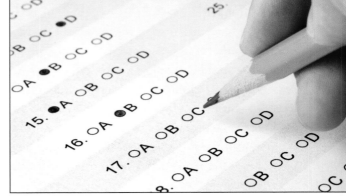

You may have noticed that test-taking is different at the University than it was in high school or in some community colleges. Typically, university courses have fewer tests than high school or community college courses. This may seem like good news, but the reality is that college tests cover more material, sometimes half of the course content, so preparing for tests requires more study hours over an extended period of time. **Test preparation cannot be accomplished in one night.**

Some professors award students' grades based solely on test score(s). Homework assignments and class participation will help you understand and apply what you are learning, but there are courses where your test score will be the primary or only factor in assessment. Look at the syllabus for each of your classes at the beginning of the semester and record all important dates (quiz, test, and exam dates are the most important). By recording important dates in your planner, cell phone, or computer, you can be prepared, and tests will not sneak up on you.

To effectively prepare for tests:

1. *Begin preparing on the first day of class.*
2. *Identify the days and times of all your exams for the whole term in your planner.*
3. *Find out exactly what material the test will cover.*

4.   *Understand that specific types of preparation are required for specific types of tests.*

5.   *Make a study schedule.*

6.   *Begin serious reviewing several days before the test.*

7.   *Maximize your memory.*

8.   *Get everything ready the night before the test.*

9.   *Manage your energy so that you're ready to focus and work quickly.*

10.   *Have a productive, positive attitude.*

11.   *Study with other students.*

12.   *Remind yourself of your long-term goals.*

13.   *Arrive at the classroom early, but not too early.*

14.   *Don't use drugs or energy drinks to stay awake.*

15.   *Don't let open-book or take home tests lull you into thinking the test will be easy!*

Test-Taking Anxiety

A serious issue that can arise because of taking a test is test-taking anxiety. Recognizing if you have this anxiety is the most important part of being able to control and conquer it. Some of the symptoms include perspiration, sweaty palms, headache, upset stomach, rapid heartbeat, and tense muscles. Anxiety can cause difficulty in organizing your thoughts, reading and understanding questions, and remembering key words. Anxiety also causes mental blocking. The best way to combat these anxiety symptoms is to avoid laziness, procrastination, and daydreaming. Build self-confidence by studying well in advance of the test. Procrastination only increases test anxiety. The Student Health Center and the University Counseling Center can help you if you believe you are suffering from test anxiety.

Preparing for Final Exams

First confirm your final exam schedule by going to the Registrar's website. Remember, your finals may be scheduled for days and times other than your regularly scheduled class times.

To avoid becoming overwhelmed by final exams, use time management skills to maximize your preparation for finals. Two or three weeks before exams, sit down and make a new calendar for the end of the semester. By plotting on a calendar all the specific assignments that need to be completed and lessons that need to be studied, you can better estimate how much time is needed to complete each task. Aim to have at least five days before exams to completely concentrate on finals. **Do not try to finish projects, write papers, and study for finals at the same time. It cannot be done!**

It is easy to lose momentum at the end of the semester and think the best thing to do

Did you know?

Shepard Smith, one of television's top news anchors, attended Ole Miss in the 1980s.
A rabid Rebel sports fan, Smith frequently mentions Ole Miss on-air while hosting
"Fox Report with Shepard Smith" and "Studio B."

is rest before a final exam. This is not true. The best thing to do is push through the last two weeks of school and prepare and study as much as possible. Set priorities by looking at where you stand in each class and calculating what score you need on each exam to succeed. The greatest effort should be put into any courses where you have a borderline grade because the final exam can make a major difference in the grade you earn for the course.

Some students allow the thought of final exams to cause them great anxiety; however, some anxiety is normal and can even be a motivator to study more. Ask your advisor, professor, or other students what you can expect on the exam so that it is not completely foreign to you when you walk into the classroom on exam day. By being mentally prepared for what to expect when coming into the classroom, you can reduce the amount of anxiety you are feeling.

Tips for Success on Final Exams:

1. Put academics first during exam week.

2. Use good time-management strategies.

3. Set priorities for study.

4. If you work, ask for time off if you need it.

5. Use the five-day study plan.

6. Stay healthy in order to do your best.

7. Plan rewards.

Make sure to stay motivated in the weeks leading up to exams. Choose to spend time with students who take their studies seriously and support and encourage you to study, too.

Types of Test Questions

There are a variety of test questions that can be used to test your knowledge of course content. Test questions can be categorized as objective or subjective questions. Objective questions require a lower level of thinking because they ask for facts and concepts that usually appear in the form of multiple choice, true/false, fill-in-the-blank, and short answer questions. Subjective questions ask for your opinion about the material or they challenge you to think of the material in a new way. Essay and critical thinking questions are subjective because there are numerous ways in which they can be answered.

Did you know?

Reuben Anderson has broken more legal barriers than any other Mississippian. Anderson was the first African-American graduate of the Ole Miss Law School. His impressive list of accomplishments was accented when he served as Presiding Judge for the Mississippi Supreme Court.

Here are some of the best ways to approach different types of test questions:

■ It is crucial to read all test questions carefully but especially when reading a multiple choice question. Mark special words that are found within the question such as "not," "always," and "only." Cross out answers that you know are definitely wrong, and if you are guessing, make sure to eliminate answers that are misspelled. Pay attention to "all of the above" and "none of the above" answer choices. If you can determine that two answers are correct, then "all of the above" is probably the correct answer. If two of the answers are not correct, the answer is probably "none of the above."

■ When answering matching questions, make sure to read through both columns and determine whether there are multiple matches to a word in the list. Review the list after you've answered to make sure that all letters are in their correct space.

■ True/False questions can be difficult even though there are only two possible answers. Read through the questions carefully and note words such as "frequently," "sometimes," and "a few" because these words usually indicate a true statement. Words such as "never," "only," and "always" usually indicate a false statement. If a true/false question is causing a lot of difficulty, go with your gut instinct.

■ Fill-in-the-blank and short answer questions require you to recall definitions, key terms, or items in a series. Read the question carefully, and spell terms correctly.

■ Problem-solving questions can be detailed, and it is important to mark the specific steps and directions in the question. Determine what information is needed to answer the question and break the question into parts. Also, write down each process or operation to be performed so you can more easily work through each step of the question. Once you believe you have come to an answer, re-check your work.

■ Essay questions are popular in college because their answers call for a deeper understanding of the material. Make sure to answer all parts of the question, and your answer should be the length the teacher suggests. Before writing, make an outline of what will be covered in the essay to make sure you do not leave anything out. Too often, students make the mistake of not providing enough details in their answers. Essay questions demand more, not less. Because essay questions are long and take extra time to grade, a well organized essay will stand out and make it easy for the professor to see that the key points have been discussed. Make every effort to write legibly too, so the professor doesn't have to struggle to read your work.

If you do not succeed on a test despite having spent adequate time preparing, schedule an appointment with the instructor, go over the test, and learn what and how you can improve for the next test. Always take the initiative to learn from past mistakes to improve in the future.

REFERENCES

Staley, Constance. "Test Taking." *Focus on College Success*. Second Edition. University of Colorado, Colorado Springs. Wadsworth Cengage Learning. 2011. 208-239.

Test Anxiety. Sharon Mitchell. University at Buffalo. 8 February 2012. ub-counseling.buffalo.edu/stresstestanxiety.php

Van Blerkom, Dianna L. "Preparing for Final Exams." *Orientation to College Learning*. 4th ed. Wadsworth Publishing Co. 2004. 323-340.

Baldwin, Amy. *The First-Generation College Experience*. Boston: Pearson Education, Inc., 2012. 193-197. Print.

About the Author

Dewey Knight, *Associate Director for the Center for Student Success and First-Year Experience*

Dewey Knight holds a Bachelor of Business Administration degree in advertising and a Master of Arts degree in higher education/student personnel. Both degrees are from the University of Mississippi. He is currently completing his Doctor of Philosophy degree in higher education at the University of Mississippi.

Chapter 13
Academic Advising and Registration

By Kyle Ellis, Travis Hitchcock,

Jennifer Phillips, Mariana Rangel, and Beth Whittington

College students have high expectations of academic advising and quickly learn that the personal relationship between academic advisors and students is important for their success.

Academic advisors and advising programs especially have a major impact on first-year students as they face the transition from high school to college or transfer from one institution to another. Academic advisors can serve as a primary support for new students, providing guidance in course selection, hold removal, and choosing a major, but academic advisors can offer much more than this to their advisees. Advisors have a wealth of knowledge regarding majors and campus resources; they are eager to help students achieve academic success.

Academic advising at Ole Miss

Although class selection is a major portion of academic advising, there is much more to the advising experience at Ole Miss. Advising is a partnership between the advisor and student regarding the student's classes, future plans, academic challenges and any issues outside of the classroom. Every University of Mississippi student is assigned an academic advisor based on major and must meet with his or her advisor at least once each semester. Some majors have faculty members within their department who serve as faculty mentors. The role of the faculty mentor is to assist students with more in-depth questions regarding internships, research, careers, or graduate school.

Freshman Advising

The majority of freshmen will have a professional advisor in the Center for Student

Success and First-Year Experience (CSSFYE), while others will be advised by either a faculty member or professional advisor within their department. Students with a declared major who are advised in the CSSFYE during their freshman year will be assigned an advisor within their major at the beginning of sophomore year. Please refer to the chart below to locate your advisor.

CSSFYE Advising

General Studies
Freshman Studies

College of Liberal Arts
Biology
Chemistry and Biochemistry
Economics
English
Mathematics
Modern Languages
Political Science
Public Policy Leadership
Psychology
Sociology and Anthropology
Southern Studies

School of Business
Banking and Finance
Entreprenuership
General Business
Management
Managerial Finance
Management Information Systems
Marketing
Marketing and Corporate Relations
Real Estate
Risk Management and Insurance

School of Applied Sciences
Communication Sciences and Disorders
Criminal Justice
Dietetics and Nutrition
Exercise Science
Hospitality Management
Paralegal Studies
Social Work
Sport and Recreation Administration

Patterson School of Accountancy
Accountancy

School of Engineering
Biomedical Engineering
Chemical Engineering
Civil Engineering
Computer Science

School of Engineering
Electrical Engineering
General Engineering
Geology
Geological Engineering
Mechanical Engineering

Departmental Advising

College of Liberal Arts
African American Studies
Art and Art History
Classics
History
International Studies
Liberal Studies
Music
Philosophy and Religion
Physics
Religious Studies
Theatre Arts

Meek School of Journalism and New Media
Integrated Marketing Communications
Journalism

School of Education
Elementary Education
English Education
Mathematics Education
Science Education
Social Studies Education
Special Education

School of Pharmacy
Pharmaceutical Sciences
Pharmacy

Health Related Professions
Dental Hygiene
Health Informatics and Information Management
Health Services
Histotechnology
Medical Technology
Medical Laboratory Sciences
Nursing
Radiological Sciences

Did you know?

Ole Miss alum Claude Wilkinson is one of the most respected young poets working today. His poetry — called a cross between Wordsworth and Frost — moved Barry Hannah to invite Wilkinson to serve as one of the first Grisham Writers-in-Residence at Ole Miss.

Before your advising appointment:

Now that you have learned a little bit about academic advising, you may be asking yourself, "Who is my academic advisor?" Your academic advisor is determined by your major and your classsification (freshman, sophomore, etc.). The easiest way to find information about your advisor is through your myOleMiss account. Start by searching for "Advisor" in the drop-down box on the right side of your screen. When you click on "My Advisors," you will see your advisor's name and contact information. As an undergraduate student at the University of Mississippi, you are required to meet with your advisor once every semester. Until you meet with your advisor, you will have an ADVISOR HOLD on your account, which will prevent you from registering for classes. Even though you are only required to meet with your advisor once a semester, you are encouraged to contact your advisor any time you have academic-related questions. Just as you expect your advisor to be knowledgeable about your degree plan, career options, University policies and campus resources, your advisor expects you to do your part as a student. Here are some things you should do BEFORE you meet with your advisor:

Stay connected: Get in the habit of checking your Ole Miss e-mail at least once a day. Advisors usually send e-mails concerning important University dates, upcoming events related to your major, and when and how to make your advising appointment. You also can ask your advisor questions via e-mail.

Do career-related research: As a new student, you may feel overwhelmed about the many major choices the University offers. Even though your advisor can give you information regarding different majors on campus, your advisor cannot make the decision for you. Remember, you are in charge and are the only one who truly knows what is best for you. Deciding on a major is an active process, which requires you to learn about yourself and about the field you are planning to study. Chapter 20 has some great tips on how to begin the process of career exploration.

Become familiar with the requirements for your major: The best resource for degree requirements is the official University catalog, which can be found at catalog.olemiss.edu. It may seem daunting at first, but the catalog is clearer than you might expect. Successful students take charge of their academic career and set goals for themselves. Even though your advisor is the expert, you should strive to become familiar with the academic requirements for your major.

Develop a list of questions: After looking at degree requirements for your major, you may have questions for your advisor. Make sure to write them down so you don't forget them!

Did you know?

At Ole Miss, Dan Goodgame served as editor of *The Daily Mississippian*. He then attended Oxford University as a Rhodes Scholar. He later served as White House correspondent, Washington Bureau chief, and top editor for *Time* magazine.

ACTIVITY:

Which of these are good questions to ask your academic advisor?

"I am struggling in my Math class. What campus resources do you recommend?"

"Which class is easier?"

"I am thinking about taking a class at the community college close to my home this summer. Will those hours transfer?"

"I heard Professor _____ is terrible! What do you think?"

"I am having trouble getting involved on campus. Do you have any suggestions for me?"

"These are the classes I am considering taking next semester. What are your thoughts?"

"Which classes would fulfill my social science requirement?"

"Can you get me into a class that is closed?"

During your advising appointment:

After following the steps listed in the previous section, you should feel confident and prepared for your advising appointment. Consider the scenarios below:
Can you pick out the strengths and weaknesses in these advising sessions?

Scenario 1:

Jane walks into her advisor's office three weeks before her registration window opens. She sits down in the chair and pulls a notebook from her backpack. She opens to a page on which she has many questions written down and a list of classes that she wishes to take. The advisor helps her work through her questions, and then they go over the classes together. Jane and her advisor leave the meeting feeling as though progress was made.

Scenario 2:

Bob walks into his advisor's office three days after his registration window has opened. He flops down in the chair and slumps down. He looks down at his feet as his advisor addresses him and tries to talk to him about his current grades and career aspirations. He tells his advisor to just give him some classes. The advisor tells Bob that this should be a collaboration between the two of them and he needs to help pick his classes. When asked about a major, he tells his advisor to pick a major that she thinks he should have. He continues to be nonverbal, noncommittal, and non-participatory. The advising session ends with Bob being advised toward a few classes but meaningful progress has not been made.

Confidentiality in advising:

College students over the age of 18 are protected by the Family Education Rights and Privacy Act (FERPA), a federal law that protects students' educational records. Without your consent the University cannot release information such as your grades, bursar bill, schedule, or financial aid. However, many students choose to give the University permission to release information to their parents or legal guardians. You can change your FERPA permissions on myOleMiss by selecting the link "Access for Relatives/Guardians" under "My Profile."

After your advising appointment:

Once you have met with your academic advisor, you have taken the first step towards registration. The next steps are checking your holds and your registration window on your myOleMiss account. Each semester you will be assigned a specific date and time when you will be allowed to register for classes, known as your "registration window." Holds prevent students from registering for classes. Some common holds you may encounter are:

TYPE OF HOLD	WHO TO CONTACT
Advisor Hold	Your academic advisor
Accounts Receivable Hold	Office of the Bursar (2nd Floor Martindale)
Bursar Hold	Office of the Bursar (2nd Floor Martindale)
Financial Aid Hold	Office of Financial Aid (2nd Floor Martindale)
Campus Clarity Hold	Health Promotion (Turner Center)
Student Conduct Hold	Conflict Resolution and Student Conduct (Somerville Hall)
Dean of Students Hold	Office of the Dean of Students (Minor Hall)
Library Hold	J.D. Williams Library

Once you have met with your advisor, cleared your holds, and your registration window has opened, you are ready for registration! Here is a refresher on registering for classes through myOleMiss. As you review this process, keep in mind that adding a class to "My Favorites" does not register you for the class. If you are ever in doubt, feel free to contact the Center for Student Success and First-Year Experience at 662-915-5970.

Did you know?

John T. Edge graduated with a degree from the Ole Miss Center for the Study of Southern Culture. He writes a monthly column, "United Tastes" for the *New York Times*. He contributes to *Garden & Gun* and *The Oxford American*.

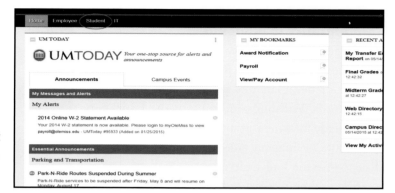

Select student tab from toolbar.

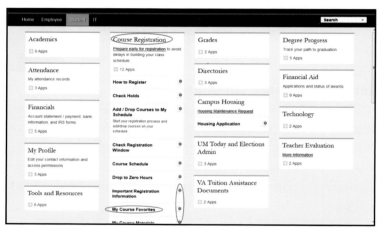

Under course registration section, select My Course Favorites. Students can click the green bookmark icon next to app to save to book-marks for easy access later.

Alternately, students can use the search function to search for My Course Favorites.

Click Add to My Favorites.

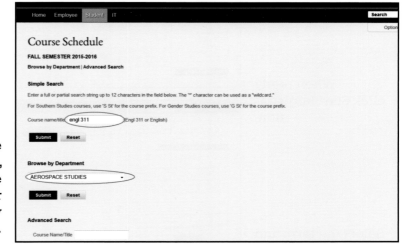

On the course schedule screen, insert course name/title or browse by department.

On the search results screen, select view all sections to see offered sections for the course.

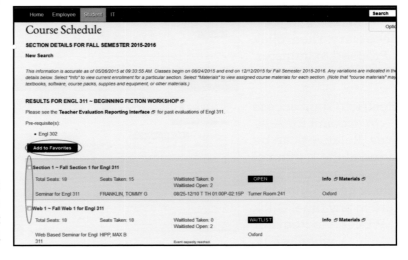

Check box(es) next to desired course sections and click on button to Add

Did you know?

Students can and do start businesses. The School of Business Administration's Gillespie Business Plan Competition and Insight Park, a high-tech research and business center, provide support and infrastructure to startup companies.

to Favorites.

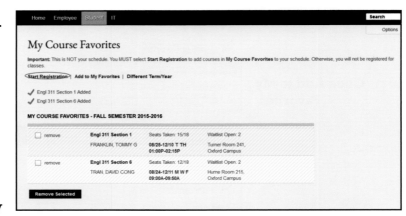

When ready click Start Registration.

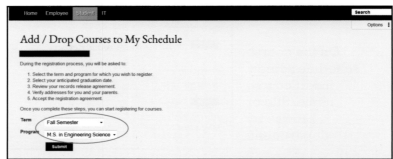

Select the term and program for which you are registering.

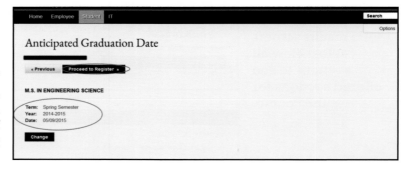

Review information for anticipated graduation date for accuracy and make changes if necessary. Then, click Proceed to Register.

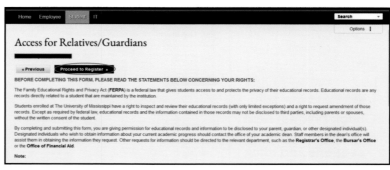

Restrict/Grant access to account for relatives. Relatives can be added at the bottom of the page and can have their information edited at any time. Click Proceed to Register when ready.

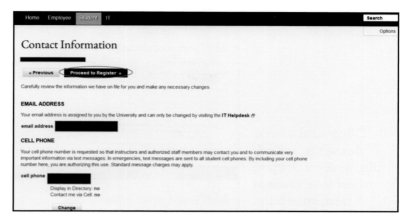

Make edits to your contact information (phone number, email address). Click Proceed to Register when ready.

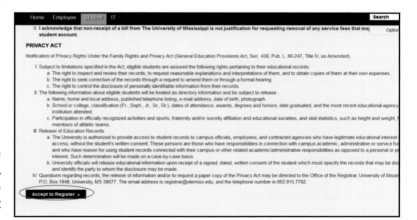

Be sure to carefully read the information about registration. Click Proceed to Register when finished.

After viewing the registration agreement, scroll to the bottom and click Accept to Register.

Allen Clark, assistant professor of modern languages, is responsible for the state of Mississippi's first Arabic language major. The program has brought national recognition to the University and offers a summer study abroad experience that immerses students into Arabic culture.

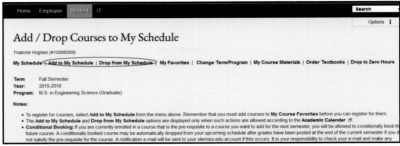

Click Add to add classes to schedule, and/or Drop to remove classes from schedule.

Check box(es) next to courses you wish to add and click Add to Schedule.

Calculating College Grade Point Average (GPA)

Trying to calculate and understand your college GPA can be difficult and confusing, especially since the calculations are done differently than in high school. The first thing you need to learn is that there are three different types of GPA calculated for college students: resident GPA, transfer GPA, and overall GPA. If you have transferred credits from another institution, the grades you have earned are reflected in your transfer GPA. Your resident GPA is your Ole Miss GPA and only takes into account classes you have taken at the Unviersity of Mississippi. Your overall GPA is a combination of your transfer and resident GPAs.

How is GPA calculated?

Your GPA is based on quality points. Quality points are grade points multiplied by the number of credit hours a course offers. You may remember grade points from high school, i.e., A = 4, A- = 3.7, B+ = 3.3, B = 3, B- = 2.7, C+ = 2.3, C = 2, C- = 1.7, D=1, and F=0. Let's say you take a biology lecture and biology lab and make an "A" in both courses. The lecture is worth three credit hours and the lab is worth one credit hour. First, convert both

On December 12, 2012, the UM choral ensemble performed at a White House reception.

"A"s to "4"s. Now multiply each "4" by the number of hours earned from the class. The biology lecture is worth 12 quality points and the biology lab is worth four quality points.

TABLE 1

Class	Grade	Grade Point	Hours	Quality Points
Bio. Lecture	A	4	3	12
Bio. Lab	A	4	1	4

I FIGURED OUT MY QUALITY POINTS. WHAT NOW?

Once you calculate how many total quality points you have earned, you need to divide that number by the total number of graded hours (the number of credit hours you are taking, excluding pass/fail coures). For example, during the summer after high school graduation, you completed six hours of English credit at a community college (two classes) and earned a "B" in both. Then, for your first college semester, you take a three-credit hour algebra course and earn a "C+," a three-credit hour music appreciation course and earn an "A-," and a four-credit hour chemistry course and earn a "B." What is your overall GPA after the first semester? Remember, divide the total number of quality points by the total number of graded hours.

TABLE 2

Class	Grade	Grade Point	Hours	Quality Points
English I	B	3	3	9
English II	B	3	3	9
Algebra	C+	2.3	3	6.9
Biology	B	3	4	12
Music App.	A-	3.7	3	11.1
French	B	3	6	18
Total			22	66

You should calculate an overall GPA of a 3.0.

What GPA do I need to maintain to be in good standing?

The general answer is 2.0 resident GPA. If your resident GPA falls below a 2.0 during your time as a student at Ole Miss, you will be placed on academic probation. During any semester that you are on academic probation, you must obtain a 2.0 semester GPA. Failure to do so could result in suspension from the University.

Did you know?

Noted sculptor and Ole Miss alumnus William Beckwith has created statues of William Faulkner, Jefferson Davis, B.B. King, and Elvis.

CONCLUSION

The relationship between an academic advisor and an advisee can be mutually beneficial. Students at the University of Mississippi should understand the basic components of the advising process, such as advising structure for their major, their assigned advisor, office location, and availability. Most importantly, you should be an active participant in the advising process. Have goals, plans, thoughts, and ideas about your ideal educational experience. Ask questions about your education plans. Take advantage of having an advisor available to provide information and guidance on a wide range of academic matters. Working with your advisor, registering for classes, and understanding your grade point average are just three of the many new responsibilities associated with being a college student. Take a moment now to schedule an appointment with your advisor.

Glossary

Academic Advising – collaboration between you and your advisor regarding your classes, your future, and any questions you have about academic or student life.

Academic Probation – academic standing that occurs when a student's resident GPA drops below what is allowed by the University for his or her class standing.

Faculty Mentor – Assists students with questions regarding internships, research, careers, or graduate school.

Favorites – Classes are placed in a queue before actually "registering" for the course.

Holds – Placed on a student's account that will not allow registration of courses. The student must contact the department from which the "hold" was placed to have it removed.

About the Authors

Kyle Ellis, *Director of the Center for Student Success and First-Year Experience*

Kyle Ellis came to the University of Mississippi in 2004 as an academic advisor. He received his B.S. in health and human performance and M.S. in education from the University of Tennessee at Martin. He earned his Ph.D. in higher education in 2011 from the University of Mississippi.

Travis Hitchcock, *Assistant Director for the Center for Student Success and First-Year Experience*

Travis Hitchcock received his Bachelor of Science in family and consumer sciences, Master of Arts in higher education/student personnel, and Doctorate of Philosophy in higher education from the University of Mississippi.

Jennifer Phillips, *Assistant Director for the Center for Student Success and First-Year Experience*

Jennifer Phillips received her B.A. in English and M.A. in higher education from the University of Mississippi. She is currently working on her doctoral dissertation in higher education. In her spare time she likes to read.

Mariana Rangel, *Academic Advisor/Instructor in the Center for Student Success and First-Year Experience*

Mariana Rangel earned her B.S. in psychology from Lipscomb University in 2010, M.Ed. in counseling from the University of Mississippi in 2012, and is currently pursuing a doctorate in higher education administration at Ole Miss.

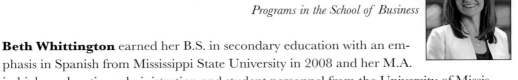

Beth Whittington, *Assistant to the Dean for Undergraduate Programs in the School of Business*

Beth Whittington earned her B.S. in secondary education with an emphasis in Spanish from Mississippi State University in 2008 and her M.A. in higher education administration and student personnel from the University of Mississippi in 2012.

REBELS Abroad

Since your first semester is full of new, exciting experiences in Oxford and at the University of Mississippi, you may think, "Why would I ever leave?" While we want to encourage you to take part in all that the University of Mississippi campus and Oxford have to offer during the school year, you should know about the amazing opportunities for international experiences available to all students that will help you become a global citizen.

What is study abroad?

Studying abroad is a life-changing experience. Not only do you step out of your comfort zone and experience a new way of life and a new culture, you learn so much about yourself. Seeing yourself through the lens of another culture allows you to reflect on your opinions and prejudices and evaluate your own culture in an unbiased manner. You'll increase your tolerance, independence, and empathy when exposed to another culture. You also gain life-long friends and experiences that will stay with you forever and mold your future academic, professional, and personal goals. The University of Mississippi Study Abroad Office offers study abroad programs in almost every country in the world. UM students can take courses overseas ranging from two weeks to two semesters. There are many types of programs available that appeal to a wide variety of students.

Faculty-led programs are those where a UM faculty member travels with a group of students and provides an experiential learning experience in an overseas location. Faculty-led programs are usually two to four weeks long in the wintersession or summer, and they are a good introduction to international travel and international education. It also is a great way to get to know a UM professor on a completely new and deeper level. You'll have someone who you can ask for a recommendation when the time comes!

Exchange programs are programs where you exchange places with a student from another country. While you are abroad experiencing life in Paris, eating "macarons" and learning French, a Parisian student would be attending UM football games and learning all about Southern hospitality! You pay UM tuition and fees to UM, so it is a cost effective way to study abroad for a semester or year. UM's affiliates and partner universities also offer ways to go abroad and pay the fees of the affiliate or partner. Sometimes these fees are more than what you might pay at UM, so you should talk with a Study Abroad staff member about options and scholarships.

International internships also are available through exchange programs and affiliate programs. You can gain valuable international work experience that will help with your future job prospects.

You can study abroad starting in the wintersession of your freshman year, and you can study abroad as many times as you like. The earlier you plan, the easier it will be to fit a study abroad experience into your academic plans. While all UM-sponsored programs will earn resident UM credit, it is your responsibility to ensure how those credits apply to your degree by completing the course approval form during the application process. While abroad, you are registered at the University of Mississippi, and any scholarships or aid that you receive generally will apply to your term abroad. Couple that with a semester exchange program, and you have no reason NOT to study abroad! Even if you have a very structured

degree program, most students will not get behind in their academic career with proper planning. Meet with the Study Abroad staff to learn more.

What can studying abroad do for me?

It isn't easy to describe what studying abroad is like and the way it changes you. Many students who study abroad find it difficult to return to their homes because everything has remained the same, except them. Reflecting on these feelings upon re-entry gives students even more perspective on the profound experiences they have had and how they have changed for the better. Most students find that their study abroad experience changes their priorities and professional goals, helps them realize what they are truly passionate about, and helps them gain career insight. So, how can you leverage your study abroad experience when you start looking for a job?

Talk with the Career Center on campus about how to integrate into your resume the skills you learned abroad and how to talk about your experience. Employers know that students who study abroad are more independent, require less supervision, have valuable cross-cultural communication skills, and are open-minded individuals. Also, if you focus on learning a language, you have a valuable skill to list on your resume. Studies have shown that students who study abroad make more money in their first jobs. Students who complete international internships learn how to be global leaders and enhance their resume with international workplace experience. All students build confidence as a result of studying abroad, which translates positively in interviews.

What if I just can't fit it in? How can I get involved on campus?

There are many programs on campus where you can meet new friends and experience other cultures. Take a look around your classrooms. You likely will have an international student or faculty member in at least one of your classes. Get to know them! You'll

Study Abroad Checklist

☐ Stay in good academic and disciplinary standing. Some programs require a 2.5 GPA or higher.

☐ Meet with your academic advisor and discuss the courses you need to take for your degree.

☐ Visit the Study Abroad Office website and meet with a Study Abroad Office staff member to discuss which locations would best serve your academic and personal needs, then narrow your options.

☐ Select a program!

☐ Apply and obtain approval for UM course equivalencies.

☐ Apply for a passport.

☐ Attend on-campus orientation to learn about culture shock, international health insurance, what to expect, policies, and rules.

☐ Apply for a visa, if required.

☐ Depart!

☐ Attend orientation at your host institution or with your faculty member to learn about the city, transportation, academics, policies, and expectations. Ask the international office at your host institution when you have questions.

☐ Have the time of your life!

☐ Return to UM, tell everyone about your experience.

☐ Repeat!

find their perspectives and experiences refreshing.

Interested in becoming a student mentor for exchange students?

Join the Global Ambassador program offered through the Study Abroad Office.

Interested in mingling in a social setting?

Join students and faculty for the Cultural Café at the Writing Center (Lamar Hall) on Friday afternoons, offered through the Office of International Programs.

Other Activities and Programs:

- Language Clubs through the Department of Modern Languages
- International Student Organization
- International Education Week
- See the Intensive English Program, the Office of International Programs, and the Study Abroad Office on campus for additional opportunities for global engagement on campus.

One of the most common things we hear from alumni and parents is how much they wish they had studied abroad. When you are in college, you are as unfettered as you will ever be in your life. Once you graduate, you immediately have responsibilities, be they a pet, a partner, or a job.

The Study Abroad Office tries to make it as easy as possible for you to study abroad and fund your experience. Now that you've decided to go abroad, go for as long as you can. Students who go for a summer often say they wish they had studied for a semester. Students who study for a semester say they wish they had studied for a year. Studying abroad for a year allows you to fully immerse yourself in a different culture. Your second semester is usually the time you feel like a local. There's not a better feeling in the world!

Resources:

Study Abroad Office: studyabroad.olemiss.edu

Facebook Page: facebook.com/rebelsabroad

Twitter: @rebelsabroad

Pinterest: pinterest.com/rebelsabroad

Instagram: @rebelsabroad

Snapchat: rebelsabroad

Student Blogs: rebelsabroad.com

Office of Global Engagement:
oge.olemiss.edu

Intensive English Program: iep.olemiss.edu

Office of International Programs:
international.olemiss.edu

Department of Modern Languages:
modernlanguages.olemiss.edu

Croft Institute for International Studies:
croft.olemiss.edu

Student Organizations (searchable): dos.orgsync.com/stuorgssearch

Career Center: career.olemiss.edu

Myths About Study Abroad

"I don't speak a foreign language, so I can't study abroad." FALSE!

You can take courses taught in English all over the world, from Ecuador to Sweden to Japan. Don't be intimidated by the host country's language. If you've always wanted to go to a specific place, we can get you there.

"Studying abroad is really expensive. I can't afford it." FALSE!

Some programs can be expensive; however, financial aid and scholarships will generally apply to a study abroad program. There are even specific scholarships available for studying abroad. If you choose an exchange program, you will be charged UM tuition and fees, which makes the experience cost effective. Some countries' costs of living are lower than the United States' so you may benefit from a good exchange rate and lower costs of everyday items. Meet with the Financial Aid Office to discuss how your aid applies to study abroad, and visit the Study Abroad Office for information on study abroad scholarships.

"I can't study abroad because I'll get behind in my classes." FALSE!

With proper planning, you can stay on track to graduate in four years.

Basic Packing List

- ☐ Passport! Everyone needs a passport to travel outside of your native country.

- ☐ Clothing that is easily layered. Don't pack everything – remember that you'll want to buy some local fashion.

- ☐ One or two suits if you are completing an internship abroad.

- ☐ Camera. You'll want to document everything. Consider writing a blog to share with your family and friends and for you to reflect on after you've returned.

- ☐ Guidebooks.

- ☐ Backpack for weekend traveling.

- ☐ Journal. Write down your experiences quickly. You think you will never forget something, but writing it down ensures you won't. You'll also be able to reflect on your feelings during your time abroad, which shows how much you grow while studying abroad.

- ☐ Computer, tablet, and/or smart phone. Wireless access will be your friend. Don't forget that you'll also have access to computer labs on campus and around the city if you prefer not to take your electronics.

About the Author

Blair McElroy, *Interim Chief International Officer and Director of Study Abroad*

Blair McElroy earned a Bachelor's degree in international studies, minoring in Chinese and French, and studied abroad in Beijing, China, for a semester. She then completed her Juris Doctorate from the University of Mississippi and studied abroad at Cambridge University during law school. In 2006 she joined the staff of the Study Abroad Office at the University of Mississippi and specializes in contracts, risk management, and social media in addition to advising students to study abroad in France, the Middle East, parts of Africa, and Asia.

Health Professions Advising Office

Mission Statement

The Health Professions Advising Office (HPAO) provides support to all current and prospective students who are interested in entering any type of health profession, including medicine, dentistry, nursing, physical therapy, dental hygiene, and much more. The office advises students about health-related professional schools, assists with school and course requirements, and provides application support. HPAO also hosts events, sponsors student organizations, and provides any support that helps students at the University of Mississippi succeed in their goal of becoming a health professional.

Health Professions at Ole Miss

The Health Professions Advising Office (HPAO) provides essential support to students interested in the health professions. HPAO provides information regarding course requirements, interviews, references, and other aspects of being a strong applicant for health-related professional schools.

The HPAO website, healthprofessions.olemiss.edu, provides a wealth of information about health professions.

Student Organizations

The Health Professions Advising Office (HPAO) houses several student organizations. These organizations provide leadership opportunities for students in the area of Health Professions.

Alpha Epsilon Delta (AED) is the pre-health profession Honors Society. The Mississippi Beta Chapter has been active on campus since its charter in 1937. It is the 24th oldest chapter in the nation. To be a member of AED, a student must achieve and maintain a 3.2 overall G.P.A. and a 3.2 Math and Science G.P.A.

American Medical Student Association (AMSA) is the student organization reserved for students planning to attend medical school. This organization offers many opportunities for students to hear guest speakers from various specialized fields of medicine. To be a member, students must be on the pre-medical curriculum track.

American Student Dental Association (ASDA) is the student organization reserved for students planning to attend dental school. To be a member, students must be on the pre-dental curriculum track.

How to sign up for HPAO

To receive information from the Health Professions Advising Office, go to
healthprofessions.olemiss.edu.
Step 1) Scroll to the **Current Students tab** and click on **Enroll in the HPAO**.
Step 2) Fill in **required fields** and **press Submit**.

How to sign up for an Advising Appointment with HPAO

Step 1) Click on the **Academic Advisors** tab.
Step 2) Click on **Schedule Your Appointment Now**
Step 3) Select **Advising Session** and **Staff Member**

Health Professions Advising Office
359 Martindale | 662-915-1674 | hpao@olemiss.edu

Section II: Wellness

PHYSICAL
The physical component is developed through a combination of beneficial physical activity, exercise and healthy eating habits.

SEXUAL
The sexual wellness component is a state of physical, emotional, mental and social well-being to sexuality.

EMOTIONAL
The emotional component recognizes awareness and acceptance of one's feelings.

FINANCIAL
The financial component involves taking steps to live within your financial means and living in, and planning for, future financial health.

wellness
WHEEL

Wellness is the responsibility of each individual to actively maintain a balance and integration of the 8 dimensions of wellness depicted in the image above. All of the dimensions work together and if one is lowered, then all others are impacted.

SOCIAL
The social component encourages participation in one's community, campus and environment.

ENVIRONMENTAL
The environmental component encourages us to recognize our own responsibility for the quality of the air, the water and the land that surrounds us.

INTELLECTUAL
The intellectual component measures the degree to which an individual engages in creative, critical thinking, mental activities.

SPIRITUAL
The spiritual component encourages individuals to increase their understanding of the beliefs, values and ethics, which can help guide a clear path in their lives.

Whether you realize it or not, we have just covered one of the eight dimensions of wellness. However, intellectual wellness should not be your only focus if you want to be a successful student at the University. All eight components of the wellness wheel are essential to having a balanced, healthy life. The rest of the chapters are identified by the dimension of the wellness wheel most closely associated with the chapter content. As you will learn, everything in your environment contributes to your sense of well-being.

8 DIMENSIONS OF WELLNESS

Wellness is the responsibility of each individual to actively maintain balance and integration of the eight dimensions of wellness depicted on the previous page. All of the dimensions work together and if one is lowered, then all others are impacted.

PHYSICAL

The physical component is developed through a combination of beneficial physical activity, exercise, and healthy eating habits. The ability to recognize that our behaviors have a significant impact on our wellness and adopt healthful habits (while avoiding destructive habits) leads to optimal Physical Wellness.

Characteristics:
- Safe and regular exercise
- Knowledge of nutritional information
- Balanced diet
- Maintain regular sleep patterns
- Manage stress with healthy strategies
- Practice healthy hygiene habits
- Avoid drugs, such as tobacco, that hinder physical health

EMOTIONAL

The emotional component recognizes awareness and acceptance of our feelings. This includes our ability to understand ourselves and cope with the challenges life brings. The ability to acknowledge and share feelings of anger, fear, sadness or stress; hope, love, joy, and happiness in a productive manner contributes to our Emotional Wellness.

Characteristics:
- Sensitive towards self and others
- Identify ways to cope with stress
- Independent, but seek help when needed
- Responsible for own actions
- Attend programs on stress management
- Attend programs to learn more about healthy relationships

SOCIAL

The social component encourages participation in our community, campus, and larger environment. This includes how we relate, connect, and communicate with the people around us.

Characteristics:
- Learn about all departments, services, and programs on campus
- Volunteer
- Serve on committees
- Actively participate in organizations
- Incorporate social or fun activities along with upholding obligations

INTELLECTUAL

The intellectual component measures the degree to which we engage in creative and critical thinking, and other mental activities. An intellectually healthy person uses the resources available to increase knowledge and skills.

Characteristics:
- Attend class
- Complete assignments
- Get adequate amount of sleep
- Communicate with professors and University staff
- Attend presentations, lectures, and other programs offered by the University
- Try new experiences
- Develop strong organizational skills

SPIRITUAL

The spiritual component encourages us to increase our understanding of the beliefs, values, and ethics that can guide us in our lives. This dimension helps us to establish personal peace and harmony.

Characteristics:
- Take time to reflect each day
- Relax without the distraction of technology
- Practice yoga/meditation
- Follow personal faith/religious traditions

ENVIRONMENTAL

The environmental component encourages us to recognize our own responsibility for the quality of the air, water, and land around us. The ability to make a positive impact on the quality of our environment, be it our homes, our communities, or our planet contributes to our environmental wellness.

Characteristics:
• Create a comfortable work environment
• Create a safe living environment (smoke free, violence free)

FINANCIAL

The financial component involves taking steps to live within our financial means and planning for our future financial health. Learning to think short-and-long-term about money is essential for financial well-being. Exploring various career options and finding a vocation will directly inform and impact financial decisions.

Characteristics:
• Plan financially
• Create a budget
• Be a good consumer
• Create a savings account
• Develop good credit
• Pay bills on time
• Understand student loans
• Explore career paths

SEXUAL

The sexual wellness component connects physical, emotional, mental, and social well-being to sexuality. It is not merely the absence of disease or dysfunction. The sexually well person accepts his or her sexual orientation, engages in sexual relationships that are consistent with his or her values and development, and refrains from using sex to manipulate or influence others.

Characteristics:
• Accept his or her sexual orientation
• Engage in sexual relationships that are consistent with values
  and development
• Refrain from using sex to manipulate others
• Minimize unwanted consequences through communication and protection

Chapter 14
Make a Difference — Get Involved!

By Bradley Baker

Getting involved is different for everyone. More often than not, how many organizations you are a part of is how student involvement is quantified. Thinking that way only scratches the surface of campus or community involvement. Registered Student Organizations (RSOs) are just one of the many resources the University and surrounding community provide to students. Your activities outside the classroom can help you develop and prepare for the profession that awaits you after your college experience. Create your involvement so that you not only enjoy what you are doing but also builds on what you learn in the classroom. The term for this is co-curricular activities.

Be intentional about your activities outside the classroom. Find the things that you enjoy doing. You will put more effort into activities and subjects that you enjoy and appeal to you. Do not choose your involvement for the wrong reasons such as social pressure or others' ideals. This chapter attempts to outline resources and opportunities on campus and in the Oxford community. It is up to you to take advantage of these offerings to increase your portfolio and skills, while enhancing your college experience. These skills and experiences will be with you long after you graduate.

Find out what being involved means to you: whether it is a Registered Student Organization, a campus job, Ole Miss Outdoors, or a community organization such as Leap Frog, your niche exists.

Become a part of the community: Get involved on campus and connect with other students, faculty, and staff. It will not take long for you to be comfortable and feel at home.

Make new friends: If you limit yourself to the classroom, a residence hall, or an apartment complex to meet people, you will miss the chance to participate in the diverse campus opportunities around you. Join organizations and meet people with similar interests or discover new interests to alleviate feelings of isolation that many new students experience.

Leadership and teamwork skills: In today's workforce, teamwork is a critical skill for success. Participating in student organizations where you have the opportunity to learn, grow, and reach your full potential is vital to your future success.

Life skills you cannot get behind a desk: Involvement in campus activities builds confidence and provides opportunities to perform in situations that are similar to those you may experience beyond the college years. College involvement is a great way to discover your interests, strengths, and abilities.

Have fun: Yes, the primary goal while at Ole Miss is to learn through studying, going to class, and reading your course materials, but it is also important to find interests and areas where you can enjoy yourself and relax.

Campus involvement helps you develop relationships.

Learn to manage your time: Campus involvement certainly keeps you busy, but it also helps you to be productive with your time. Students who are involved waste much less time than those who choose not to be involved.

Build relationships: Networking, networking, networking. Being involved in campus activities gives you the chance to fine tune your skills in making contacts and developing relationships.

Brief history of Registered Student Organizations

The University of Mississippi was chartered in 1844, and most likely the next day, students started forming groups and organizations of common interests and goals. College students have always looked for peers of like mind and involvement. Today, students gather in the coffee shop in the Union, at picnic tables in The Grove, and huddle around the Catalpa Tree to discuss various topics and enjoy each other's company.

Some of the first formal organizations were literary societies that met in secrecy. The first two literary societies were the Hermaean Society (1849-1946) and Phi Sigma Society (1849-1934).

Most literary societies' activity consisted of formal debates on topical issues of the day, but literary activity could include original essays, poetry, and music. As a part of their

Did you know?

Bradford Cobb (B.A. English '96), a partner with Direct Management Group in Los Angeles, manages one of the biggest names in music – Katy Perry. For Perry's first meeting with Cobb, she blew past the receptionist and did cartwheels down the hall, landing in the splits in his office. Katy Perry visited the UM campus in the fall of 2014 as a guest host for ESPN College Game Day.

literary work, many also collected and maintained their own libraries for the use of the society's members. College societies were the training grounds for men in public affairs in the nineteenth century (Harding, 2008).

> **"Divide your time properly between work and play. There is danger of you becoming either a 'book worm' or a 'rah-rah boy.'"**
>
> 1928-29
> *The M-Book*

These societies were the precursors to the modern Greek system. Delta Kappa Epsilon was founded in 1850 as the University's first fraternity. Chi Omega was founded in 1899 as the first sorority. Ole Miss's first traditionally African-American fraternity, Omega Psi Phi was founded in 1973 (Sansing, 1999). The Greek system at the University is still strong today; approximately one-third of undergraduate students are Greek.

Soon after the Civil War, the University of Mississippi began to publish *The M-Book*, which is still published today. *The M-Book* served as a guide to activities on campus. In the 1890s *The M-Book* was the first glimpse into student activity that did not include the literary societies or Greek organizations. The students were just as involved then as they are today with many different types of clubs and organizations. Honor societies and social clubs such as The Stag Club, comprised of seven members per class of the Law School, were prominent. Academic clubs such as the Press Club, Science Club, and Teachers Club, kept students focused on their topics of interest. Recreational clubs such as YMCA, Glee Club, and Racket Club were all outlets for students to have fun (Sansing, 1999). The Ole Miss chapter of the Black Student Union (BSU) began in 1968 as a lobbying organization for African-American students. Today, the BSU is one of the largest organizations on campus.

In the early 1900s Chancellor Kincannon created the Student Honor Council. This was an attempt to allow the students to work together. The Student Honor Council grew into the Associated Student Body (ASB) in 1917. Over the years, ASB has been integral in instituting change. In 1946, ASB ordered an investigation into outdated food services and regulations governing women (Sansing, 1999). As a result, the University lessened the regulations on women and improved the food services.

Role of Registered Student Organizations on campus

Registered Student Organizations serve many roles at the University of Mississippi. RSOs provide the opportunity to develop interests, build community, serve others, prepare for life after college, and provide a voice on current issues. Since the founding of the University of Mississippi, students have been finding ways to institute change and develop groups of similar interests. RSOs can play a vital role in the growth of the University and you as an individual and responsible community member.

Did you know?

Alum Florence L. Mars wrote a ground-breaking civil rights book, *Witness in Philadelphia*, about the 1964 killings of three civil rights workers in Neshoba County, Mississippi.

Types of student organizations

The University of Mississippi has more than 200 student organizations registered with the Office of Leadership and Advocacy. RSOs serve many purposes and interests. As a University, we place these organizations in categories so that it is easier for students to find organizations that meet their interests. RSOs can be tied to departments, colleges, specific majors, or just a group of students with a similar interest. You will be hard pressed not to find an RSO with which to get involved. If you have a cause, service project, or interest that is not represented at Ole Miss, you can work with the Office of Leadership and Advocacy to launch a new RSO.

Academic/Professional - Organizations designed for students interested in a particular career or academic field of study who want to establish networks and further develop their skills in that area.

> "Don't be too quick to tell people about your high school honors. They are all very commendable, but college students don't appreciate them so much as your home-town acquaintances did."
> 1928-29 *The M-Book*

Cultural/Multicultural - Organizations focused on providing support and fostering community within various cultures, races, religions, and orientations represented among the student body .

Fraternity/Sorority - Organizations represented under the National Panhellenic Conference, Inter-Fraternity Council, and National Pan-Hellenic Council.

Health/Wellness - Organizations focused on the improvement and betterment of all University members.

Honorary/Honors Society - Organizations, both local and national, that provide service and leadership opportunities as a well as recognition for students with academic honors.

Political - Organizations that encourage expressions, debate, and support of political issues, views, and/or candidates.

Religious/Spiritual - Organizations that provide spiritual and/or religious development and support.

Did you know?

Alum Ray Mabus currently serves as United States Secretary of the Navy. He also served as the Ambassador to the Kingdom of Saudi Arabia and Governor of Mississippi.

Service/Philanthropic - Organizations that provide volunteer or service opportunities for civic minded students eager to serve the campus and/or community.

Special Interest - Organizations that exist to enhance campus life and provide support to students through a variety of programs and events .

Sponsored - Organizations that have a designated and acknowledged partnership with a University, academic, or administrative unit.

Sport Clubs - Organizations sponsored through the Department of Campus Recreation that serve students, faculty, and staff members in different sports and recreational activities.

Student Governance - Organizations designed to support and represent University students.

MSync

To get involved on campus or in any of our Registered Student Organizations, login to this site with your Ole Miss username and password: orgsync.com/. MSync offers an online community management system that centralizes campus involvement. This web-based platform streamlines communication and helps build a stronger campus community. Not only will you find a profile for each RSO, there also are a calendar of events and an announcement feed that keep you up-to-date on what is happening on campus.

Getting involved outside of registered student organizations

The University, City of Oxford, and Lafayette County offer many ways to get involved in the community. Getting involved can often mean more than joining a club or RSO. It can mean getting out of your comfort zone and trying something different. Maybe you have never attended a theatre production or been to an art exhibit. During your time at Ole Miss, experience everything the area has to offer. To find something to do on campus, you do not have to look any farther than the Ole Miss Student Union. If you are

Did you know?

Ole Miss alum Lenore Prather (JD '55) was the first female elected to the Mississippi Supreme Court. She served as Chief Justice from 1998-2001.

> **"You can work with the Office of Leadership and Advocacy to launch new service projects."**

looking for opportunities in Oxford and Lafayette County, read the local paper or contact the Chamber of Commerce.

Involvement opportunities on campus

Take advantage of campus departments to develop skills or get guidance. There are so many offices that are dedicated to giving you a great experience at the University and to help you develop as a person. If you are interested in how to get an internship, develop a resume, or improve your interviewing skills, go to the Career Center. The Office of the Dean of Students has student involvement advising, leadership development programs, and volunteer opportunities. Visit the Center for Inclusion and Cross-Cultural Engagement to develop your multicultural competencies. The Study Abroad Office is a place on campus that provides cultural opportunities both in and out of the country in formats that range from full semesters abroad to experiences that last for just a few weeks. Develop your personal health and wellness at Campus Recreation, become a Student Ambassador or Orientation Leader through the Office of Admissions, or become an International Student Ambassador in the Office of International Programs. These are all ways that you can get involved and take advantage of leadership opportunities on campus.

Inside J.D. Williams Library is the largest blues archive in the world with thousands of recordings, videos, photographs, and more. Included within the archive is B.B. King's personal record collection, among other musical treasures. Throughout the year, the Department of Art sponsors exhibitions of both undergraduate and graduate student work in Gallery 130 of Meek Hall. The exhibitions also include work by visiting professional artists. The University Museum, located on the edge of campus, is home to several collections such as the Mississippi Folk Art Collection and Millington-Barnard Collection of Scientific Instruments. In addition to existing collections, the museum hosts several traveling exhibitions year-round.

And there is more! The University offers several entertainment options throughout the fall and spring semesters. The Student Activities Association (SAA), for example, sponsors more than 125 events each year. From concerts and movies in The Grove to the Miss University Pageant and Parade of Beauties, the SAA offers students opportunities to get involved with an organization or simply enjoy an event. The Gertrude C. Ford Center for the Performing Arts also serves as a premier entertainment venue in North Mississippi, featuring Broadway shows, concerts, and ballet, to name just a few. Built in 2003, the Ford

Did you know?

Howard Bahr came to study at Ole Miss after a career as a railroad worker. While a student, he served as curator of Rowan Oak, William Faulkner's home. His award-winning books include *The Black Flower*, *The Year of Jubilo*, and *Pelican Road*.

Center has hosted Morgan Freeman, Marty Stuart, James Earl Jones, and even the 2008 Presidential Debate. The University's Music Department provides opportunities for entertainment through visiting performers as well as faculty, staff, and student performances. Likewise, Ole Miss Theatre features student productions throughout the academic year that provide entertainment as well as artistic training for the students participating in the productions. Last, Ole Miss Outdoors (OMOD) provides students with once-in-a-lifetime opportunities to experience the outdoors across the southeast of the U.S. and beyond. Previous OMOD trips have included fly-fishing in Arkansas, white water rafting in Colorado, and dog sledding in Canada.

Involvement opportunities in Oxford

The Oxford area has a rich history in both the literary and musical arts. For example, Nobel Peace Prize winner, William Faulkner, made Oxford his home in the early 1900s. Faulkner is best known for penning popular novels including *As I Lay Dying* and *Absalom, Absalom*. Rowan Oak, home to Faulkner and his family for more than 40 years, is located just outside of our main campus. Faulkner's presence in Oxford attracts visitors each year to the Oxford Conference for the Book and the Faulkner and Yoknapatawpha Conference held on campus and at Rowan Oak. Thacker Mountain Radio is a free show held on the Square every Thursday night that features musical performances as well as author readings. The popular show is recorded and broadcast across the state on Saturday nights on Mississippi Public Radio. The area also offers a chance to take in the artistic abilities of others with Southside Gallery, Powerhouse Community Arts Center, and Taylor Arts in nearby Taylor. If you are looking for something to do outdoors, the City of Oxford sponsors the LOU Pathways project with walking and biking paths throughout the city. Additionally, the University has mountain biking trails that are free and open to the public.

Volunteer opportunities on campus and in the community

RSOs do not provide the only means for service opportunities within the community. There are several groups both on and off campus that provide students with a chance to get involved by volunteering. For example, The Big Event is held in the spring each year. The event is the University's largest student-led volunteer effort and a means for students to say thank you to the Lafayette, Oxford, and University communities through service to local residents. Volunteer Services within the Office of Leadership and Advocacy

provides students with the resources, connections, and advising they need to get involved with service and volunteering throughout local communities. Outside of the University, activities such as popular after-school programs at the Boys and Girls Club and Leapfrog afford students the chance to mentor school-age children from both Oxford and Lafayette County schools. Other service opportunities include the 9/11 Week of Services and Remembrance, Adopt a Basket, Make a Difference Day, Martin Luther King, Jr. Day of Service, National Volunteer Week, and RebelTHON.

Student involvement

The concept of getting involved while at Ole Miss differs from student to student as each person has different aspirations and goals. Getting involved means being intentional about your time at the University of Mississippi by taking advantage of the opportunities outside the classroom to gain experience, network, build your resume, and develop skills necessary to be successful when you jump into the real world. Whether you join an RSO, participate in volunteer work on or off campus, develop a relationship with a particular University office, or find an organization in the Oxford/Lafayette community, make your involvement your own and have a purpose. College is a fun time; make the most of your experience at the University of Mississippi.

"Sport clubs are competitive and range from cricket to hockey."

ONLINE RESOURCES

Get Involved Twitter Feed: @GetInvolvedUM

Career Center: career.olemiss.edu/

Campus Recreation: campusrec.olemiss.edu/

Office of Leadership and Advocacy: dos.olemiss.edu

Ford Center: fordcenter.org

Gallery 130: art.olemiss.edu

LOU Pathways: oxfordms.net/pathways-commission

MSync: orgsync.com

Ole Miss Big Event: olemissbigevent.com

Ole Miss Music Department: olemiss.edu/music

Ole Miss Outdoors: campusrec.olemiss.edu/ole-miss-outdoors/

Ole Miss Theatre: theatre.olemiss.edu

Rowan Oak: rowanoak.com

Student Activities Association: saa.olemiss.edu

Study Abroad: outreach.olemiss.edu/study_abroad/

Thacker Mountain Radio: thackermountain.com

University Museum: museum.olemiss.edu

Visit Oxford: visitoxfordms.net

Volunteer Oxford: volunteeroxford.org

About the Authors

Bradley Baker, *Director of the Ole Miss Student Union*

Bradley Baker has been with the University since 2005 and oversees the operations of the Student Union and advises the Student Activities Association and the Ole Miss Big Event. He received both this bachelor's and master's degrees from the University.

Overview of
Robert's Rules of Order

This is a condensed version of Robert's Rules of Order. It is intended to provide a basic background in parliamentary procedure to conduct business in as efficient and orderly a manner as possible.

Addressing the chair

All meetings should be conducted from the "chair" (usually president). Members addressing the chair should refer to the presiding officer as "Brother President."

Obtaining the floor

Before a member may make a motion or speak in debate, he or she must obtain the "floor." To claim the floor, a member raises his or her hand and waits to be "recognized" by the chair. The chair will recognize the member by announcing his or her name or title. This member then has the floor and can stand and speak until yielding the floor by sitting down. While a motion is open to debate, there are three situations where the floor should be assigned to a person who may not have been the first to rise and address the chair. These situations:

1. If the member who made the motion claims the floor and has not already spoken on the question, he or she is entitled to be recognized in preference to other members.

2. No one is entitled to the floor a second time as long as any other member who has not yet spoken to the pending motion requests the floor.

3. The chair should attempt to alternate opposing opinions on a question if he or she is aware of members requesting the floor who have opposing views.

Making a motion

1. First, a member makes a motion. Though he or she makes a motion, the member uses the word "move" to make the motion (for example: "I move to allocate...").

2. Another member seconds the motion by saying, "I second it" or simply, "Second." It should be noted that a second by a member merely implies that the motion should come before the meeting and not that he or she necessarily favors the motion. A member may second a motion because he or she would like to see the assembly go on record as rejecting the proposal, if the member believes a vote on the motion would have such a result.

3. The chair then states the "question" on the motion. Neither the making nor the seconding of a motion places it before the council; only the chair can do that by this

step (stating the question). When the chair has stated the question, the motion is pending and is then open to debate (providing it is a debatable motion). If the organization decides to do

what a motion proposes, it adopts a motion or it is carried. If it decides against the motion, it is rejected or lost.

Amending a motion

The motion to amend is a motion to modify the wording (within certain limits) of a pending motion before it is acted upon. An amendment must be germane; that is, it must be closely related to or have some bearing on the subject of the motion to be amended.

A motion to amend is handled the same way as a main motion and requires a second to be considered. An amendment is adopted by a majority vote even in cases where the motion to be amended requires a 2/3 vote for adoption.

Point of order

When a member thinks that the rules of the meeting are being violated, he or she may make a "point of order," calling upon the chair to make a ruling and enforce the regular rules. A point of order: can be applied to any breach of the meeting's rules; is in order when another has the floor; does

not require a second; and is not debatable unless the chair, being in doubt, submits the point to a vote of the meeting, in which case the rules governing its debatability are the same as for an appeal.

Previous question

The previous question is the motion used to bring the meeting to an immediate vote on one or more pending questions. The motion for the previous question: takes precedence over all debatable or amendable motions to which it is applied; can be applied to any immediately pending debatable or amendable motion; is out of order when another has the floor; must be seconded; is not debatable; is not amendable; and requires a 2/3 vote.

Postpone indefinitely

A motion to postpone indefinitely is a motion that the assembly declines to take a position on the main question. Its adoption kills the main motion, at least for the duration of the session, and avoids a direct vote on the question. It is useful in disposing of a badly chosen main motion that cannot be either adopted or expressly rejected without possibly undesirable consequences. The motion to postpone indefinitely: is out

Student Profile: Elam Miller

Hometown: Murfreesboro, Tennessee
Major: Public Policy Leadership

How do I get involved? Ole Miss has so many organizations that cater to a wide variety of interests and causes so every student has an opportunity to get involved on campus in whatever they like. Students have resources on campus that can help them get involved such as your advisors, EDHE instructors, fellow students, and even social media platforms where these organizations promote and push their missions. Another great resource is MSync. MSync is a website that has information on all of the registered student organizations at Ole Miss. Browse around the site, and you can even contact the leaders of those clubs or sign up to be on an organization's email list. Also be sure to check out the student activities fair at the beginning of the fall semester, I promise you that you won't regret it! But don't fret if you miss out on the organization fair because lots of student orgs actually let you join at any time during the year including ASB. There is a place for everyone here at Ole Miss, and while it might take a little time to find the right place, I know that you eventually will do it!

How soon should I get involved? Everyone is different, but for me, I think you should try to get involved from the very beginning of your first semester. Coming from out of state, I didn't know a lot of people when I first got here. I soon found that the best way to meet people was to get involved. I jumped in head first and got involved in as many things as I could, but don't be afraid to say no to some things. My biggest piece of advice I can give is to get involved in the things that seem interesting to you. Don't be afraid to join a club that your friends might not be a part of or start a new organization of your own. The Ole Miss experience is what you want to make of it, so use all of the resources that we have to make it happen!

What are the benefits of being involved? Involvement has allowed me to grow as a leader and gain experience that I will take with me for the rest of my life. It has helped me find what I was passionate about. For example, my freshman year I decided to become a Green Grove Ambassador and help clean up the Grove after game days. Green Grove has been an awesome organization that I joined because I thought what they were doing was really important for the school and for the environment, and I am always excited to volunteer every year. Most importantly, getting involved has given me my closest friends that I otherwise would have never met.

How has getting involved helped you as a student and prepared you for your career? Before getting involved, I can honestly say that I had no idea what I wanted to do for the rest of my life. The more I got involved on campus, the more I began to learn about myself and about what I am interested in. My freshman year I was the Community Council President of my residence hall, Brown Hall, and it really opened my eyes to the possibility of becoming a leader on campus. I learned that I enjoyed implementing initiatives and that real change is possible when you get a group of passionate individuals together. I've learned so much about confidence, communication, and relationship building from every other organization I've been a part of whether it is an honors society or a service project, and they have molded me into the person I am today.

What has been your favorite moment or experience you have had by getting involved on campus, in the Oxford community, or with a national opportunity? My favorite experience I have had while at Ole Miss has been being a McLean Mentor. I first learned about the McLean Institute for Public Service and Community Engagement in my EDHE class, I thought it sounded interesting and decided to give it a shot. When I met the children I would be mentoring, I learned so much from them, and they have helped me grow as a leader in the Ole Miss community. The students and I bonded as we worked on homework and played "hangman" with their weekly spelling words. My leadership work as a McLean Mentor has shown me that I do not have to be from the same background, state, or even the same age to build unbreakable bonds with someone. Despite our different situations and problems, we still can make connections. Those students and I worked together for an entire year, and we matured and became stronger people. I did not know when I became a McLean Mentor that I would change so much. The lessons I have learned from getting involved will serve me well for the rest of my life.

Is there such a thing as being too involved? Absolutely. I truly believe that getting involved on campus was one of the best decisions that I have ever made; however, at one point my sophomore year I realized that I probably hadn't slept in a couple of days. At that point I realized that it was time for me to decide what I liked the best. I was so excited with making sure that I dedicated myself to everything I was a part of, but I needed to really think about what was best for *me* moving forward. Like I mentioned earlier, get involved in the things that seem interesting to you, and don't worry about what other people are doing because you'll meet passionate and awesome people in every organization on campus. Your Ole Miss experience might look different from mine, and that's one of the awesome things about going to school here, we have such freedom and diversity to make all of our college experiences unique and worthwhile.

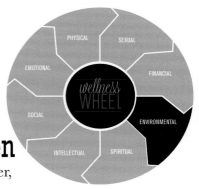

Chapter 15
Red, Blue, and Green

By Lindsey Abernathy, Ian Banner,
and Kendall McDonald

Sustainability (noun); [suh-stey-nuh-bil-i-tee]—Sustainability is a multi-disciplinary, problem-solving approach to creating a social system that meets the needs of the present generation without compromising the needs of future generations or the needs of the ecological systems in which humans exist.

Did you know that our campus generates more than 12 tons of trash each day? That's 4,380 tons of trash every year—just from the University of Mississippi campus. This means about 400 pounds of trash will be landfilled per person on this campus this year. You might be asking yourself, *"How could I possibly generate so much trash in a year?"* or, *"What can I do to reduce this number?"* or maybe even, *"Why should I care that I am producing this much landfill waste?"*

The purpose of this chapter is to equip you with the skills, knowledge, and resources to answer these types of questions. Applying concepts of sustainability to your life is smart—you'll save time and money, improve your health, and exemplify the UM Creed by being good stewards of our resources.

What is Sustainability and Why Should We Care?

"The scientific evidence is clear: global climate change caused by human activities is occurring now, and it is a growing threat to society." American Association for the Advancement of Science (2006)

Sustainability is all about solutions. It is a multi-disciplinary, problem-solving approach to creating a social system that meets the needs of the present generation without compromising the needs of future generations or the needs of the ecological systems in which humans exist. Simply put, sustainability focuses on "enough for all, forever". Right now, the needs of future generations, as well as ecological systems, are compromised. Ninety-seven percent of climate scientists agree that climate change is real and is primarily driven by human activity. The good news is that many sustainable lifestyle choices have tangible benefits for individuals. Living a low-carbon lifestyle has personal benefits that can impact your health in positive ways. Every time you opt to ride your bike or walk instead of driving, or eat a veggie wrap rather than a cheeseburger, you are helping the planet and creating healthy habits for your body that, if continued, will lead to a better quality of life over the long term.

Th University of Mississippi's Commitment to Sustainability

The University of Mississippi has been associated with the Climate Leadership Network, a national network of more than 600 college and university presidents, since 2008. The network was created because campus leaders across the country are "deeply con-

cerned" about **climate change** and its "potential for large-scale, adverse health, social, economic, and ecological effects." Higher education institutions in particular have an obligation to respond to these concerns through integrating sustainability in operations, academics, and research.

One major goal signatories in this network have is to develop a plan to become **climate neutral**, which entails eliminating or reducing the greenhouse gas emissions at universities as much as possible and mitigating the remaining emissions. The University of Mississippi conducts a **greenhouse gas inventory** to account for what we are responsible for releasing into the atmosphere both directly and indirectly by our operations. The University's commitment is also reflected in the work of the University of Mississippi Energy Committee and Active Transportation Committee, as well as in the newly updated UM Master Plan, which provides guidelines for sustainable growth at the university.

The Office of Sustainability

The Office of Sustainability was created to advance sustainable practices at the University. The mission of the office is to be a catalyst for environmentally positive change by educating, connecting, and empowering the members of our community for the well-being of people and our ecological systems.

The Office of Sustainability often identifies new ideas, designs programs, and imple-

Did you know?

Ole Miss alumnus William Dunlap is renowned for his extraordinary landscape paintings.

ments projects to bring those ideas to fruition. We also play a role in supporting others – such as UM departments, student groups, and community organizations— in their efforts to adopt the principles of sustainability by measuring the impact of and spreading the word about those efforts. We believe that our efforts to promote the principles of sustainability make the University a better place to study and work and ultimately have a positive impact on current and future generations

Renewable Energy and Green Buildings on Campus

Did you know that the largest roof-mounted solar power complex in the state is located on the UM campus? The Center for Manufacturing Excellence (CME) features 414 photovoltaic solar panels on the roof. This building generates enough electricity to run the lights and air conditioning for the entire building. CME is one of multiple buildings on campus to receive a Leadership in Energy and Environmental Design (LEED) certification by the U.S. Green Building Council. Visit CME, the Khayat Law Center, or the School of Pharmacy's Medicinal Plant Garden to see sustainable design in action.

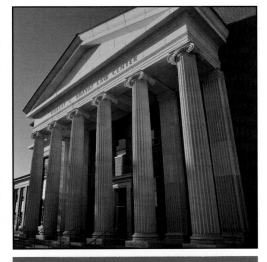

The Khayat Law School is LEED certified

In 2017, UM offset three percent of the institution's electricity use from the previous fiscal year by purchasing 3,835 kilowatt hours through **renewable energy certificates**. The purchase is estimated to be the equivalent of growing 69,848 trees per year for 10 years or not using 6,240 barrels of oil.

Students' Guide to Sustainability at Ole Miss

Sustainable Living in the Residence Halls

There are many actions students living on campus can take to contribute to campus sustainability efforts. In each residence hall, there are central recycling bins for plastics, aluminum, and paper. Residents can also help to save energy by turning off lights, unplugging appliances not in use, and using cold water to wash their clothes. Each residence hall has a Hydration Station that students can use to refill their reusable water bottles and

Did you know?

Ole Miss alum Mary Donnelly Haskell is a recording artist and actor whose credits include *Sisters* and *Touched by an Angel*.

avoid generating plastic waste. Residents can also utilize bike racks and the nearby O.U.T. bus stops to decrease emissions made by driving and make on-campus travel more efficient.

Students living in residence halls who are interested in getting more involved with sustainability, can serve as Eco Reps. Eco Reps serve as peer-to-peer leaders in sustainability by participating in activities such as CFL (Compact Fluorescent Lightbulb) swaps, Power-Down campaigns, recycling craft events, and other opportunities. These activities are facilitated by Eco Rep Leaders who are upperclassmen who serve as mentors to residential Eco Reps. Eco Rep Leader applications are open in late spring semester, and rising sophomores to seniors are eligible to apply.

Sustainable Transportation: Think Beyond Four Wheels

Relative to other college towns, Oxford is a compact city. On average, most people who commute to the University live less than three miles from campus. As a student at Ole Miss, you do not need a car to get around campus and Oxford. With the increasing mileage of bike lanes, sidewalks, and bus routes, Ole Miss students, faculty, and staff are finding new ways to commute.

Biking is a great way to burn calories instead of fuel. UM has been designated a Bicycle Friendly University by the League of American Bicyclists. The University offers bike rental, bike registration, and maintenance services at the Ole Miss Bike Shop, located across the street from the Turner Center. Parking and Transportation also provides students with the easy and affordable option of utilizing our campus bike-share. Simply download the Social Bicycles app on your phone, register your account, and find one of the many bike-share stations on campus. Students receive up to two hours of riding **free** per day!

Be sure to review the safety information included with each bike.

The City of Oxford also is a bicycle friendly community and has many miles of bike lanes and mountain bike trails. Ride solo or join the Ole Miss Cycling Club on their group rides on the trails.

Did you know?

Ole Miss alum Guy Hovis starred on *The Lawrence Welk Show*.

The Oxford University Transit (O.U.T.) bus system is an easy way to get around campus and the city. It is free to UM students—just make sure to show your Ole Miss ID. Every O.U.T. bus is equipped with a bike rack so you can split your commute between bus and bike.

You can borrow a car for a few hours or days through the University's partnership with Zipcar car-sharing service. Apply for your membership online at zipcar.com/olemiss to begin driving. The University also offers membership to Zimride, a service that helps students, faculty, and staff coordinate carpools either for everyday use or for special trips, such as spring break. If you commute to campus from Batesville or another surrounding area, you may also be interested in Zimride's Vanpool program. Sign up for Zimride's services at zimride.com/olemiss.

For complete information about transportation on the UM campus, visit parking.olemiss.edu.

Waste Reduction: Y'all Still Landfill?

According to the Environmental Protection Agency (EPA), the average American produces 4.3 pounds of waste daily—that would be more than 30,000 pounds of trash generated by residents of Stockard and Martin Halls in one week. Because more than half of this waste ends up in landfills, it is important to take steps to  reduce our waste contributions as individuals and as a university community. Four options to consider are recycling, reducing, reusing, and composting.

Recycling

Did you know that a plastic water bottle tossed in the trash ends up in a landfill, where it does not even begin to decompose for 700 years? Or that Americans throw away 2.5 million plastic bottles every hour? A simple way to reduce your **carbon footprint** is to recycle. It is easy—bins are located across campus in all academic buildings, residence hall lobbies, and the J.D. Williams Library.

You can recycle many things on campus including:

- Paper (including newspapers, notebook paper, magazines, and junk mail)
- Cardboard
- Plastics #1 and #2 (look on the bottom of the container for the number)
- Aluminum
- Printer ink and toner cartridges.

Did you know?

Kate Jackson, best known for her role on the original *Charlie's Angels*, attended Ole Miss in the mid-1960s.

Composting

If you have eaten food prepared at Rebel Market, the Marketplace in the Residential Colleges, Lenoir Dining, the Grill at 1810, Freshii, or Ole Miss Catering, you have indirectly contributed to the UM Compost Program. The program composts pre-consumer food waste from these dining facilities, converting eggshells, banana peels, and other kitchen scraps into soil for campus and community gardens.

Composting is important because food that is thrown in the trash eventually ends up in a landfill under layers and layers of waste. This blocks the flow of oxygen to decomposing food, resulting in the release of methane, a potent greenhouse gas that traps heat in the atmosphere. Food in a compost pile breaks down naturally, greatly reducing the environmental impact of your breakfast, lunch, and dinner.

Since the program's creation in 2013, the compost program has diverted more than 92,000 pounds of food waste from the landfill—that is more than 46 tons! The program was proposed by a student through the UM Green Fund and is operated by the Office of Sustainability.

Flip the Switch

Did you know that when you go to class and leave your cell phone charger plugged into the outlet, it is still using energy? An easy way to avoid "vampire energy" is to plug your electronics into a power strip, and flip it off when you are not using those electronics.

When purchasing electronics, look for ENERGY STAR-certified products. If you have a lamp in your room, be sure to use energy efficient bulbs such as LEDs or compact fluorescent bulbs (CFL). CFLs are 13 times more efficient than standard incandescent light bulbs.

Finally, be sure to turn off lights and electronics when you leave your room for long periods of time. This small action can have a big impact.

Did you know?

Noted artist Glennray Tutor received his MFA from Ole Miss in 1976.

Sustainable Food: Eat Real

You may have heard the term "real food" mentioned before, and at first, it can seem confusing. Isn't all food technically real?

It's not. The dictionary defines "food" as "something that nourishes, sustains, or supplies," and the term "real" as "true and actual; not artificial." When you take into account that nearly 70 percent of the average American's diet is made up of processed foods—that is, foods that are not in their true form or contain artificial ingredients—the term "real food" starts to make a whole lot more sense.

Eating local, fresh, real food is a win-win situation—nutritionally, it is healthier for your body, and it is also better for the land on which the food is grown. Also, consider eating more veggies and less meat. If all Americans went vegetarian for just one day, the U.S. would save 70 million gallons of gas and 100 billion gallons of water, according to the Huffington Post. Try out Freshii (located below Rebel Market) for lots of vegetarian options.

You can also learn how to grow your own produce right here on campus by joining the **UM Garden Club**. The garden, which is located behind Residential College South, acts as an educational tool for all levels of interested gardeners. Members grow produce for themselves and the UM Food Bank. E-mail the Garden Club at umgarden@olemiss.edu for more information on getting involved. No prior experience necessary! When grocery shopping in Oxford, visit the farmers' market or Chicory Market, a farm stand offering local goods. Visit sustain.olemiss.edu/food for more information.

The UM Green Fund

The UM Green Fund supports innovative sustainability projects on the Ole Miss campus. Since its launch, the Green Fund has financed projects ranging from the installation of hydration stations in UM buildings and the addition of native plant species on campus to the establishment of the UM Compost Program.

The Green Fund is managed by a committee students, faculty, and staff. The committee selects projects annually and evaluates them on visibility, feasibility, and impact. Any UM student, faculty, or staff member can propose a project.

In addition to a baseline donation from the University, the UM Green Fund relies on donations from students, faculty, and staff. The more donations to the fund, the more sustainability projects can be implemented on campus! The University matches by 50 percent every dollar donated by an Ole Miss student.

Did you know?

Noted poet, novelist, essayist, and dramatist Stark Young graduated from Ole Miss in 1901.

Seven Ways to Get Involved in Sustainability at UM

Take a Class - UM offers several sustainability-related courses, as well as a minor in environmental studies. This minor is interdisciplinary and is applicable to all majors.

Volunteer - Almost all volunteer work supports the principles of sustainability, whether you are working at the UM Food Bank or the Oxford Recycling Center. The Office of Sustainability can assist you in finding a volunteer opportunity.

Join a Student Group - The UM Garden Club and Ole Miss Cycling Club are sustainability-related student organizations.

Attend an Event – Attending an event on campus is a great way to learn about new topics and issues. UM hosts events including Food Day in the fall and Green Week in the spring.

Serve in a Leadership Role – EcoReps, Green Grove Ambassadors, the Green Fund Committee, and the Associated Student Body Sustainability Committee are all opportunities for students to play a larger role in UM sustainability efforts.

Intern – The Office of Sustainability's Green Student Intern Program provides opportunities for students to gain professional experience working on topics ranging from waste reduction to sustainable transportation.

Submit a Green Fund proposal – Do you have an idea for making the University more sustainable? Write a Green Fund proposal! The Office of Sustainability can guide you through this process.

An Ole Miss Student's Perspective

My name is Tyler Caple, and I am a member of the class of 2019. I'm majoring in International Studies and Chinese due to my passion for languages and travel. However, my goal has never been to be a translator or a linguist but to work with people from around the world to combat global issues. I believe climate change and pollution are two of the biggest challenges our world currently faces, and this belief has led me to be active in campus sustainability efforts.

It is easy for new college students to get bogged down from classwork and adjusting to a new environment. My freshman year it was hard to discover what extracurriculars I should devote my free time to, because I was looking for something that not only fit my interests but made me feel connected to campus. Thankfully, I tried volunteering with Green Grove, a game day recycling program run by the Office of Sustainability. My experience meeting other sustainability-minded people and interacting with Ole Miss fans was so positive that I searched for more ways to be involved.

After becoming aware of the Office of Sustainability, I joined the EcoRep Leader program the spring of my freshman year. EcoReps promote sustainable practices such as recycling and energy reduction in the residence halls, which is a great way to meet people you normally wouldn't otherwise meet. My sophomore year, I expanded upon my love for Green Grove as a Green Grove Ambassador. It was fun leading a group of volunteers around on game days and showing them that recycling does not have to be an afterthought.

Currently, I am a Green Student Intern with the Office of Sustainability. I help with planning and promoting events such as film screenings and Green Week, and help operate the UM Compost Program. I receive academic credit for my internship through the Environmental Studies minor program. With this minor, I have taken courses such as environmental geology and biology, but my favorite course so far has been Introduction to Environmental Studies in which our class visited the Magnolia Grove Monastery!

I truly believe that sustainability can be integrated into any field of study. From engineering to business to nutrition to philosophy, there are so many ways your studies can contribute to a cleaner, better world. One of the best ways to start getting involved is here on your college campus!

Did you know?

The retention rate for freshmen from first to second year was 85.1% in fall 2017.

Glossary

Carbon Footprint – The Environmental Protection Agency (EPA) defines a carbon footprint as "the total amount of greenhouse gases that are emitted into the atmosphere each year by a person, family, building, organization, or company." This includes emissions from riding in a car, electricity use, heating a home, and more.

Climate Change – According to the EPA, "climate change refers to any significant change in the measures of climate lasting for an extended period of time. In other words, climate change includes major changes in temperature, precipitation, or wind patterns, among other effects, that occur over several decades or longer."

Climate Neutrality is defined as having no net greenhouse gas (GHG) emissions, to be achieved by eliminating net GHG emissions, or by minimizing GHG emissions as much as possible, and using carbon offsets or other measures to mitigate the remaining emissions.

Climate-Neutral Campus – A campus has no net climate impact resulting from carbon or other greenhouse gases. This can best be achieved through a hierarchy of actions that include aggressive reduction of energy consumption, followed by conversion to low or no impact energy sources, and finally through carbon offsets.

Global Warming – According to the EPA, global warming "refers to the recent and ongoing rise in global average temperature near Earth's surface. It is caused mostly by increasing concentrations of greenhouse gases in the atmosphere. Global warming is causing climate patterns to change. However, global warming itself represents only one aspect of climate change."

Greenhouse Gas Inventory – An accounting of greenhouse gases (GHG) emitted to or removed from the atmosphere over a period of time. Policy makers use inventories to establish a baseline for tracking emission trends, developing mitigation strategies and policies, and assessing progress. An inventory is usually the first step taken by entities that want to reduce their GHG emissions.

Renewable Energy Certificates – When electricity is produced from a renewable generator, such as a wind turbine, two products are created: the energy, which is delivered to the grid and mixes with other forms of energy, and the REC. When renewable energy is delivered to the grid, it cannot be distinguished from the electrons in non-renewable sources. The REC is a way to track the renewable electricity and represents the environmental benefits associated with the generation of renewable energy. (Source: 3Degrees)

Sustainability – A multi-disciplinary, problem-solving approach to creating a social system that meets the needs of the present generation without compromising the needs of future generations or the needs of the ecological systems in which humans exist. By fostering education that encourages responsible and equitable management of our environmental, social, and economic resources, the sustainability framework challenges our University to consider the interdependent nature of our lives, the natural environment, our communities, and the economy and especially the improvement of these relationships.

About the Authors

Lindsey Abernathy, *Associate Director, Office of Sustainability*

Lindsey Abernathy joined the Office of Sustainability in 2014 as project manager and assumed the role of associate director in fall 2017. Lindsey works on operational projects involving energy and recycling on campus, as well as educational and outreach programs designed for students, faculty, and staff. She holds a bachelor's degree in journalism and an MBA from UM.

Ian Banner, Director, *Office of Sustainability;*
Director, Facilities Planning; University Architect

Ian Banner came to the University of Mississippi in 2005 after being in private practice and serving as associate professor in the School of Architecture at Mississippi State University. His areas of architectural expertise include energy efficient design and construction, daylighting, passive systems such as thermal buoyance "stack-effect" ventilation, and the environmental impact of building materials. Banner holds a B.A. in architecture from Plymouth University, a master of philosophy degree from the University of Cambridge, and is a member of the American Institute of Architects.

Kendall McDonald, *Project Manager, Office of Sustainability*

Kendall McDonald joined the Office of Sustainability in 2015 as a sustainability fellow and assumed the role of project manager in fall 2017. Kendall works extensively with the Green Student Intern Program, the Eco Reps Program, and other campus initiatives generating involvement in sustainability. She also facilitates the University's Active Transportation Advisory Committee. She holds a bachelor's degree in public policy leadership with minors in environmental studies and English.

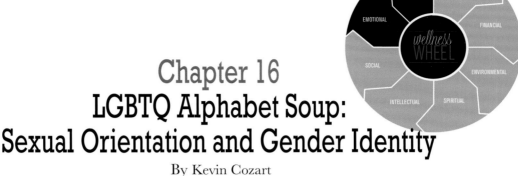

Chapter 16
LGBTQ Alphabet Soup:
Sexual Orientation and Gender Identity

By Kevin Cozart

"I'm gay."

Chances are that someone close to you, be it a sibling, cousin, parent, aunt/uncle, favorite celebrity, or even the person looking at you in the mirror, has said those words to you by this point in your life. If no one has said it directly to you, then you probably know someone who identifies as gay, lesbian, bisexual, or

transgender. While the visibility of openly LGBT individuals is increasing, and your generation is significantly more accepting, simply saying "I'm gay (or lesbian or bisexual or transgender)" is the hardest thing some of your fellow students may ever have to say, and telling friends or family can be even more difficult.

The point of this chapter is not to challenge your personal views on sexual orientation and/or gender expression, but to give you the knowledge necessary to operate in a diverse world that includes gay, lesbian, bisexual, and transgender people.

T is a good place to start. Understanding Sex and Gender:

You may be asking yourself, why start with T? The answer is because sexual orientation is often defined in terms of a person's gender identity or expression, therefore it is important that you understand those concepts first.

Most likely up to this point in your life, you have used the terms sex and gender interchangeably. However, there is a distinction that is important to understand. Biological sex is classified by genetic traits and the reproductive organs. There are three main designations of sex: male, female, and intersex. An intersex individual has reproductive organs that are not easily classified as either male or female, oftentimes a combination of male and female traits.

GENDER is an ideal constructed from societal perceptions of what is male or female, feminine or masculine. Within the concept of gender are two more concepts: gender identity and gender expression. Gender identity is a person's internal or private sense of gender. Gender expression is how people express or perform their gender. Gender can be broken down into two main categories: cisgender and transgender. A cisgender individual's biological sex and gender identity and expression are the same. A transgender individual's gender identity does not align with the sex assigned at birth.

Some subcategories of transgender people:

- **Trans*:** a catch-all term for people who don't identify with their sex assigned at birth.
- **Drag Queens/Kings:** most often gay men or lesbians who occasionally wear clothing and/or make-up usually reserved for the opposite gender.
- **Transsexual:** an individual whose gender identity is opposite of the sex assigned at birth; may take surgical and non-surgical steps to match gender expression with gender identity.
- **Two Spirit:** this concept comes from Native American tribes and describes individuals who either identify or express both genders.
- **Genderqueer:** a person who identifies as neither male nor female but somewhere outside of a gender binary.

* TRANSGENDER is an adjective and not a noun or verb; transgenders or transgendered are incorrect forms of the word.

Above, gender was defined as a social construct for what is masculine or feminine. Below are some examples of how gender is or has been constructed and is relative to an individual's subculture:

- For many males living in the United States, wearing a skirt would usually be considered in the realm of gender nonconforming behavior. However, in Scotland, Tonga, Uganda, and several other cultures (including western religious sects), wearing a skirt or robes is culturally accepted as masculine.
- During World War II, many women were forced to work outside the home in factories helping build the implements of war. Some even flew new airplanes from the factories to military bases. However within a decade after the war ended, this type of work was seen as unfeminine, and it took several more decades to be considered "acceptable" for women to work in heavy manufacturing plants or fly airplanes in the military.

■ Wearing make-up, getting manicures or pedicures, etc., are often seen as feminine, but heterosexual male actors, models, news anchors, and even the President of the United States do it on a daily basis without being seen as less manly because it is accepted as part of the job.

Scientists do not consider sexual orientation to be a conscious choice.

What's in a pronoun?

One of the issues that friends, acquaintances, and colleagues of transgender people often have difficulty with is pronouns, especially if the person is transitioning. Our common pronouns (he, she, his, hers, himself, herself) denote gender. They, their, and themselves are becoming more acceptable for use to denote a singular person because it avoids gendering the object of the pronoun. However, there are other pronouns that have been and are continuing to be created to serve as genderless alternatives to our current gendered options. The best practice is to ask people what pronouns they prefer.

S, G, or B: The trouble with the sexuality trinary - popular labels assigned when discussing sexual orientation are straight (heterosexual), gay (homosexual), or bisexual. However numerous studies have proven that sexuality is a spectrum that doesn't fit within three distinct labels. To help understand this concept, let's look at the definition of a few terms:

Sexual Behavior: a conscious decision regarding sexual relations with respect to gender. Examples: There are men who have sex with men (MSM) but don't consider themselves to be gay. There are individuals who are gay but choose to have sex with members of the opposite gender.

Sexual Orientation: an innate physical and romantic attraction to someone of the same or opposite gender or both. Sexual orientation can be denied or ignored, but it cannot be changed by an individual.

Did you know?

Charles Overby (1968) edited the state's largest newspaper, the *Clarion-Ledger*, which won a Pulitzer Prize under his leadership. He was named to the Alumni Hall of Fame in 1992 and is a recipient of the SilverEm. The Overby Center for Southern Journalism and Politics is named in his honor.

Types of Sexual Orientations:

Heterosexual: an individual who is emotionally, romantically, and sexually oriented towards individuals of the opposite gender.

Homosexual: an individual who is emotionally, romantically, and sexually oriented towards individuals of the same gender.

Bisexual: an individual who is emotionally, romantically, and sexually oriented towards individuals of both genders in varying degrees.

Pansexual: an individual who is emotionally, romantically, and sexually oriented towards individuals regardless of gender.

Asexual: an individual who experiences little or no sexual attraction to any gender. Those who consciously abstain or are celibate are not considered to be asexual.

Fluid: A relatively new concept that says that a person's emotional, romantic, and sexual attractions can and do fluctuate naturally over time.

The most definitive research on sexuality was completed by the Kinsey Institute in the middle of the twentieth century. Their research produced what has become known as the Kinsey Scale which ranges from 0 (completely heterosexual) to 6 (completely homosexual). Most individuals fall somewhere along the scale and not at either of the ends. Though some scientists have challenged their research methods over the years, subsequent researchers have been able to replicate their results.

I have a Q/Um you forgot the Q?

There are actually two "Qs": Queer and Questioning. Let's look at queer first.

For a long time, queer was used to describe people who didn't conform to society's norms of sexual behavior and/or gender expression, eventually evolving into a derogatory term. Recently members of the LGBT community have reclaimed queer as a positive term to describe themselves, especially those with multiple "labels." Another use is the term genderqueer that represents non-binary gender expression and non-heterosexual sexual orientation.

Questioning is the phase in almost every one's life where they question their sexual orientation and/or sexually experiment with members of the same gender. This is a natural process that often occurs during puberty and continues through the college years.

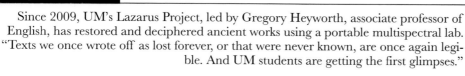

Did you know?

Since 2009, UM's Lazarus Project, led by Gregory Heyworth, associate professor of English, has restored and deciphered ancient works using a portable multispectral lab. "Texts we once wrote off as lost forever, or that were never known, are once again legible. And UM students are getting the first glimpses."

Coming Out

Coming out is the common term for when individuals tell people that they are LGBTQ. While this is correct, coming out is a lifelong process for members of the LGBTQ community, and it begins with coming out to one's self. There has been a significant push for individuals to come out publicly as a means to put a personal face on the LGBTQ community as a way of advancing LGBTQ rights. This contact hypothesis as described by social scientists makes it harder for people to discriminate against minorities or underrepresented populations if they know a member of a specific population. This push has been successful, but can also apply intense pressure to come out before a person is ready, especially for celebrities.

What to do if...

I'm coming out as LGBTQ...

You have begun a lifelong journey of discovering and expressing your true self. Although there are risks involved with coming out while still financially dependent on your parents or while living in a conservative state, the rewards are much greater. Remember, you have freedoms and resources available to you at the University of Mississippi that you probably didn't have in your home community.

Your next step when you are ready is to build a network of fellow LGBTQ individuals as well as allies. You may wish to receive counseling support from the University Counseling Center or join student organizations such as the UM Pride Network or LAMBDA. Remember, only you can decide when and how to come out to others.

Coming out as transgender on campus can present additional challenges. The Counseling Center is an important resource in helping negotiate coming out to friends and family, working with student housing, working with professors to go by another name, or in considering physical transitioning options.

A roommate or friend comes out...

First and foremost, if your roommate or friend comes out to you, you should feel honored. As coming out is a difficult decision with many potential risks for students, the decision to come out to you should be seen as a sign of respect and trust in you.

Taking that into account, it is understandable that you may need time to process your thoughts and feelings before having a full, open, and honest dialogue. If needed, reach out to your community assistant, staff at the Counseling Center, faith leaders, or others. Most important is maintaining your friend's privacy. Just because your friend told you, doesn't mean it's time for everyone else to know. Those mentioned above are bound legally to maintain privacy.

Consider becoming an ally, someone who is visibly and vocally supportive of gay members of our community. To learn more contact the Center for Inclusion and Cross-Cultural Engagement. While it probably doesn't need to be mentioned, your roommate or friend coming out to you probably doesn't reflect sexual or romantic interest in you. Do you approach members of the opposite gender and announce your sexual orientation as a pick-up line?

Did you know?

Founded in 1835, the town of Oxford was named for the British university city in hopes of attracting a fine university. Thirteen years later, in 1848, the University of Mississippi opened its doors to the first 80 University students.

The Law and the LGBTQ Community

In the United States - The 2003 U.S. Supreme Court decision in *Lawrence vs. Texas* that struck down laws that criminalized homosexuality is seen by many as the first real victory for the LGBTQ community at the federal level. The next significant victory was the inclusion of sexual orientation and gender expression in federal hate crimes legislation in 2009. In late 2010, the "Don't Ask, Don't Tell" policy that barred openly lesbian, gay, and bisexual members of the military from serving was repealed, and in June 2013, the United States Supreme Court issued their decision in *Windsor vs. the United States*, striking the federal definition of marriage. This allowed same-sex couples who live in and have been married in marriage equality states to receive more than 1,000 rights that had previously been denied. The *Obergefell vs. Hodges* decision by the Supreme Court on June 26, 2015, struck down all remaining bans on same sex marriage. While this was a momentous occasion, there are still no federal protections for members of the LGBTQ community as far as employment discrimination and public accommodations. What does this mean? If members of the LGBTQ community out themselves by marrying, they could potentially be fired from their jobs or kicked out of their rented house/apartment without any legal recourse at the federal level. Only about one quarter of states include these protections in their laws.

> **JUSTICE ANTHONY KENNEDY:**
> A Reagan appointee, Justice Kennedy is responsible for all three of the major decisions regarding LGBTQ rights over the last decade with each decision inevitably paving the way for the next. When he authored the Windsor decision in 2013, only nine states and the District of Columbia were performing same-sex marriages. Two years later, all states are now recognizing marriages between individuals of the same gender.

In Mississippi - While much progress has been made at the national level, Mississippi law allows for members of the LGBTQ community to be fired without cause or denied/kicked out of rental housing for no other reason than their status as LGBTQ. Mississippi's hate crimes law does not cover crimes of hate directed towards LGBTQ Mississippians. Prior to Executive Order 13672, Mississippi's public universities represented the patchwork nature of policies with regards to protections based on sexual orientation as we, the University of Southern Mississippi, and Mississippi State University (also includes Gender Identity) include sexual orientation in our non-discrimination policy while others do not. Because universities process federal fi-

---

Did you know?

After graduating from Ole Miss, Glen Ballard's first job was a gofer for Elton John. He went on to write and produce songs for Michael Jackson (*Man in the Mirror*) and Alanis Morissette (*Jagged Little Pill*). He's won several Grammy Awards.

nancial aid for the government, they are considered federal contractors and can no longer discriminate on the basis of sexual orientation and gender identity or expression under EO 13672.

Popular Culture, Mass Media, and the LGBTQ Community

For many LGBTQ youth growing up in small towns, there can be a sense of loneliness and isolation, that you are the only one like you. The Internet, television, and movies are for many youth their only real connection to other LGBTQ people. In the last year, several popular YouTubers came out, proving mass media can be a powerful tool to educate people about the LGBTQ community, but it has some drawbacks as well.

- ■ THE GOOD - Allows LGBTQ youth to know that other queer people exist and gives them a glimpse into a world where LGBTQ people can be out and proud.

- ■ THE BAD - Many depictions of queer people tend to be white-centric and often male dominated. While YouTube and other user-generated content mediums have helped, you still have to work to find examples of LGBTQ women and others from underrepresented populations.

- ■ THE UGLY - Popular culture, especially commercial media, tend to perpetuate and not challenge stereotypes about the LGBTQ community. This can lead many, including LGBTQ youth and anti-LGBTQ forces, to develop distorted, incorrect, and often negative impressions of the LGBTQ community. Also, the Internet facilitates bullying, allowing people to harass others anonymously. This bullying often touches on the actual or perceived sexual orientation and/or gender identity/expression of the victim. This phenomena has gotten so bad that the term bullycide has been coined to label instances where individuals have been bullied to the point of committing or attempting suicide.

Did you know?

Donna Tartt studied creative writing at Ole Miss under Willie Morris and Barry Hannah. A Greenwood, Mississippi, native, Tartt's most famous work, *The Secret History*, has sold millions of copies. Recently, *Goldfinch,* won the 2014 Pulitzer Prize for Fiction.

LOCAL LGBTQ ORGANIZATIONS

- **Parents and Friends of Lesbians And Gays** (PFLAG) Oxford/North Mississippi meets the third Thursday of every month in the Sarah Isom Center on campus. pflagoxfordnorthmiss@gmail.com

- **Center for Inclusion and Cross-Cultural Engagement** — inclusion.olemiss.edu

- **ALLIES** —Faculty and staff who have experienced the ALLIES program are trained to serve as mentors and advocates for gay, lesbian, and bisexual students in need. Look for a placard with rainbow columns either on their window, door, or outside office wall. For more information, contact The Center for Inclusion and Cross-Cultural Engagement or allies.olemiss.edu

- **Sarah Isom Center for Women and Gender Studies** — sarahisomcenter.org

- **UM PRIDE Network** — twitter.com/umpridenetwork

- **OUTlaw** — law.olemiss.edu/programs/outlaw.html

Did you know?

The Lyceum, our first academic building, is the oldest building for higher education in the state and has been in continuous use since it opened in 1848 for both educational purposes and, for four years (!861-1865), as a military hospital.

FAMOUS LGBTQ People

Tate Taylor - Actor (*Winter's Bone*), Director (*The Help*), and UM Alumnus

Tom Daley - Olympic Medalist (Diving)

Robbie Rogers - Professional Soccer Player (MLS)

Matt Dallas - Actor (*Kyle XY*)

Wentworth Miller - Actor (*Prison Break*)

Michael Sam - Former SEC Defensive Player of the Year and Professional Football Player

Maria Bello - Actress (*Coyote Ugly*)

Jodie Foster - Actress (*Silence of the Lambs*)

Raven-Symoné - Actress (*That's So Raven*)

Matt Bomer - Actor (*White Collar*)

Chris Hughes - Facebook Co-founder

Frank Ocean - Singer/Songwriter

Jane Lynch - Actress (*Glee*)

Tim Cook - Apple CEO

Annise Parker - Former Mayor (Houston, TX)

Bryan Singer - Director/Writer/Producer (*X-men*)

Laverne Cox - Actress (*Orange is the New Black*)

Leslie Feinberg - Writer, Activist

Lana Wachowski - Director, Screenwriter, Producer (*Sense8, The Matrix, V for Vendetta*)

Jim Parsons - Actor (*Big Bang Theory*)

Brittney Griner- Professional Basketball Player (WNBA)

Eddie Izzard - Comedian and Actor

Aydian Dowling - Fitness Model and Transgender Activist

Ingrid Nilsen - YouTube Content Creator

Tyler Perry - Actor and Drag Performer (*Madea*)

Brendan O'Carroll - Irish Comedian and Drag Performer (*Mrs. Brown's Boys*)

Nyle DiMarco - Model and Activist for the Hearing-Impaired

Israel Gutierrez - Journalist and ESPN Sports Reporter

Gus Kenworthy – World Champion Free skier and Olympic Silver Medalist

Patricia Velasquez – Supermodel

Glossary

Heterosexual: an individual who is sexually oriented towards individuals of the opposite gender

Homosexual: an individual who is sexually oriented towards individuals of the same gender

Bisexual: an individual who is sexually oriented towards individuals of both genders

Pansexual: an individual who is sexually oriented towards individuals of any gender

Asexual: an individual who experiences little or no sexual attraction to any gender. Those who consciously abstain or are celibate are not considered to be asexual.

For LGBTQ individuals experiencing depression or suicidal thoughts, call the Trevor Helpline 24 hours a day, 7 days a week at **(866) 488-7386.** Or call the University Counseling Center at **(662) 915-3784**, or after hours, contact the University Police Department at **(662) 915-7234.**

About the Author

Kevin Cozart, *Coordinator of Operations for the Sarah Isom Center for Women and Gender Studies*

A native Mississippian, **Kevin Cozart** holds a master's degree in journalism with an emphasis in integrated marketing communications and a bachelor's degree in liberal studies with minors in political science, mass media, and marketing from the University of Mississippi. He has served as advisor to the UM Pride Network, administrator for the Allies Program, and as a member of the Chancellor's LGBTQ Advisory Committee as well as various other University committees and organizations. He received a Master's degree in higher education and student personnel from UM in May 2017.

Chapter 17
Relationships
By Marc Showalter

Talking, Hanging Out, Hooking Up, Seeing Somebody, Dating: What does it all mean?

Much of our success in college has to do with the quality of our relationships. Whether it's the new relationships we develop once we get to campus or hanging onto the relationships we had when we left home, relationships have a huge impact on our level of contentment and satisfaction with life

While every relationship is different and has its own unique set of concerns, there are three characteristics that are typically part of any healthy relationship.

Respect

Mutual respect is essential for any healthy relationship. This begins with respect for yourself and extends to respect for the other person. It means having respect for the relationship and believing that what you want in a relationship matters. It also means respecting that the other person's thoughts and feelings are important.

People in healthy relationships have respect for the differences someone else brings to the relationship and are open to learning about the other person and his or her life experiences. Respect means not trying to control or coerce the other person to be and do what we want. Respect for your boundaries and the boundaries of the other person shows that you understand that without care and respect, the relationship is in jeopardy.

Trust

When we trust the other person, both people feel safe to share their thoughts and feelings without fear of rejection, judgment, or ridicule. Trusting yourself and feeling free to be yourself, and allowing the other person to do the same, is another indication of a healthy relationship.

Trust means being reliable and consistent in your actions and doing what you say you will do. It means demonstrating that you will not intentionally hurt the other person and having confidence that he or she will not intentionally hurt you.

Setting boundaries and knowing that it is okay to say "no" is another example that there is trust in the relationship. We build trust by giving the other person the benefit of the doubt and believing that we are all doing the best we can at the time.

Open and Honest Communication

Telling the truth. Speaking up, even if your voice is shaking. Saying what you are feeling instead of holding onto it. Being honest about what you want and need. These are all examples of open and honest communication. We should not expect the other person to be able to guess what we are thinking, nor should we decide what the other person thinks, feels, or meant without first listening and trying to understand what happened. Ask. Be clear. Deal with conflicts as soon as possible. Do not expect things to get better on their own. Most people do not like conflicts, but part of becoming a mature person is developing the ability to face challenges rather than avoid them. Try to understand where the other person is coming from before you try to make your point. Try to see things from the other's perspective. Be willing to set boundaries honestly and openly even when it is scary. Brené Brown said it very well, "Daring to set boundaries is about having the courage to love ourselves, even when we risk disappointing others. We can't base our own worthiness on others' approval. Only when we believe, deep down, that we are enough can we say "Enough!"

Family

Relationships with our family often change when we head off to college. We are not the same and yet, our families may want to believe we have not changed at all. Working on a healthy relationship with your family can make the transition to college easier. Here are a few ideas to consider:

Did you know?

Ole Miss alum Jeanne Shaheen has served as Governor of New Hampshire, as Director of the Harvard Institute of Politics and, most recently, as United States Senator from New Hampshire.

■ **Try to see things from your family's perspective.** Treating them as you want to be treated is a great place to start. How do you speak with them? How do you honor their commitment to your family? Do you expect them to do whatever you want without considering how they might see things? Do you realize you still have things to learn from them? The respect you show to them will continue to build the respect they have for you.

■ **Learn to disagree in a respectful way.** You will not always agree with your family, and you probably shouldn't. Learning how to communicate adult-to-adult with your family is the beginning of moving to healthy and more mature relationships. You do not want the relationship to stay as it was in high school, so you have to be willing to be part of the change. Your families will be working on this, too.

■ **Be respectful when you go home for a visit.** Remember that home is not your residence hall or apartment, and your family deserves to know something about your plans for the night. Taking a look at yourself and your expectations may help you see yourself and your parents in a different light, and it might make the time at home more pleasant.

■ **Use your freedom responsibly.** If you make poor choices, it will be tougher for your family to trust you, and they may not be as willing to respect your wishes. Your family believes in you and wants you to be successful. When you do what you say you will do and take care of your responsibilities, their trust in you grows, and it is easier for them to recognize your ability to manage college life.

■ **Do not just tell them what they want to hear.** There is often pressure to live up to others' expectations, and the fear of disappointing people we love is powerful. You will experience lots of different feelings during this time, some good and some difficult. Sharing all your feelings, even if you are afraid they won't be understood, helps to let everyone know that it is okay to tell your truth.

■ **This is not going to go over well.** It is possible that you will become involved in a relationship that is not what your family expects or wants for you. It could be a friendship with someone of a different race, religion, sexual orientation, or culture. It might be a new romance that is a surprise for the same reasons. Being able to communicate about these relationships might not be comfortable, and it may require a lot of courage, but this kind of honesty can help to strengthen respect and trust between you and your family.

■ **Tell your family when you mess up.** We all make mistakes, and it is tough to tell family members that we have done something we should not have done. Going to the people who love you the most is usually the best choice in difficult times. They may not be happy to hear the news, and the first reaction might be unpleasant, but hearing it from you is much better than them finding out via social media.

Roommates

"I don't even know this person, and I'm sharing a space that's not as big as my closet at home!" Welcome to college life. It may be that you have never shared a room with any-one before, but most college students have the opportunity to live with a roommate. This is a chance to develop skills that will last a lifetime.

On campus housing staff are great resources for helping you navigate life with a room-mate. They are your first and best place to go when you need help or have difficulties. Housing staff, including your CA, are trained and experienced, and they want you to be happy and successful. Get to know your CA, and ask for help when you need it.

To help you have a healthy relationship with your roommate, here are a few things to keep in mind:

Treat others the way you want to be treated. Turns out the Golden Rule is still golden. It is easy to place blame on the other person and expect the perfect roommate. What kind of roommate do you want? Are you willing to be that kind of roommate? Would your mother approve of how you treat your roommate? Have you tried to under-stand the problem from your roommate's perspective? Ask yourself these questions, and take responsibility for your role in the conflict.

Watch out for each other. Tell your roommate where you are going and when to expect you. Call if your plans change. If your roommate seems to be struggling with something, reach out and help. This is the kind of person you want to be, right?) You do not have to be best friends with your roommate, even though that would be nice, but learning to get along and trust each other makes life much easier. If you tell your roommate that you will do something, follow through. Do not talk about your room-mate in ways that would undermine trust. In your room and in life, learning to get along with others is among the most important skills you need for happiness and success.

Communicate early and often. The more clearly your expectations and con-cerns are expressed, the easier it will be to manage problems when they occur. Some of these things are not easy to talk about, but that is part of learning to be an adult. When a problem arises, address it as directly and as soon as possible, and face-to-face, not by text or social media. Let your roommate know what the issue is and work on a solution to-gether. Fixing the problem is much more important than fixing the blame. Respecting each other and your differences will help you learn to get along and maybe even develop

Did you know?

A graduate of the Class of 1931, Jamie Lloyd Whitten set a record for the longest serving member of the U.S. House of Representatives. He served as congressman continuously from 1941 to 1995.

a better friendship. Holding on to concerns and hurt feelings often leads to resentment and frustrations and does not help the relationship.

New Friends

One great thing about coming to college is the opportunity to meet people, students and faculty who are from different parts of the United States and the world. Some students have grown up in one town, gone to the same school, and never had to worry about making new friends. Others have moved and met new people many times. Whatever your experience, here are a few things to keep in mind as you make new friendships:

Be yourself. When you come to a new environment, it can be tempting to do whatever it takes to belong. Resist changing who you are to be what others seem to want you to be. You can be adaptable to different personalities and open to new things without compromising who you are and what you believe. Respect yourself and that will carry through any situation. Someone said "Be yourself. Everyone else is already taken."

Be open to making friends who are different from you. Take the risk and make friends with someone who is not just like you. Get to know people who are different from you to gain a new perspective on the world. You may find that you enjoy something you have never considered or make a friend who has a lot to learn from you and vice versa. These friendships are one of the greatest benefits of the college experience.

Choose people who will help you accomplish your goals. The people you spend time with not only reveal things about yourself, they also influence the direction you take. Think about the people with whom you spend your time. Will these relationships get you closer to your goals or take you farther away?

"But if I do that, she may not like me." Be willing to tell your friends what you want. Set boundaries and be consistent. If you respect yourself and trust your relationships, you can tell the truth about what you really think and feel, and it will strengthen your friendships. If friends do not respect you enough to accept who you really are, the relationship might not be good for you.

Romantic relationships

Talking, hanging out, dating, hooking up…What does it all mean? Do you like me? Check one: yes, no, maybe. Are we "a thing?" You have been trying to figure this out since middle school, and it only gets more complicated in college. Romantic relationships are one of the most important things on the minds of most college students. It can be the best of times and the worst of times, all in the course of 24 hours or less.

Did you know?

Bill Parsons (Class of '79) served as Director of NASA's Kennedy Space Center.

You are crushed out on someone, and he or she likes you, too. Now what? "This is just what I've been waiting for. This is the real thing. We are so in love. I think." To help you have positive and healthy romantic relationships, consider these suggestions:

Respect for your values and beliefs. Does your new "main squeeze" respect your values? Is what you want in the relationship important to the other person? Do you have enough respect for yourself and the potential relationship to set boundaries and stick to them? Does the other person respect your limits? If your new partner pressures you for more physical intimacy than you want and refuses to respect your boundaries, this may not be the "thing" you hoped it would be.

Do you feel safe to fully be yourself with your new partner? Can you express whatever you think and feel and know that you will be accepted and valued? Can you allow yourself to be vulnerable with those parts of yourself that you do not easily share? Sometimes we jump into physical intimacy before we know if we can trust our partner with our emotional intimacy. If you cannot trust your new love to know all of you, then you might want to think about just how trustworthy this person is for you.

Jealousy is not love.

Some people think jealousy is a sign of love, but that is not true. In fact, rather than love, jealousy is an indication of insecurity, poor self-esteem, dependence, feelings of inadequacy, and lack of trust. A partner who gets upset if you do not tell him or her where you are, or does not want you spend time with your friends or have a life outside the relationship, is not demonstrating love but expressing insecurity and distrust.

Effective communication is critical to a healthy romantic relationship. To be fully known and to fully know a partner requires open and honest communication. What we say to our partner is important, but how well we listen is even more important. As we struggle to understand the difference between talking and hanging out, is it any wonder how difficult it is to express more complex things, especially our emotions?

Use "I" messages rather than "you" messages to reduce defensiveness and blame in communication. Rather than saying, "You broke your promise," own your feelings by saying, "I felt let down." Instead of casting blame or putting your partner on the defense, "I" statements create a dialogue in which both partners can express what they are experiencing more freely and honestly.

Respecting yourself and the other person helps develop trust. When we trust someone, it is easier to communicate in an open and honest way. It takes courage to do things that are difficult or new to us. None of us are perfect, and our relationships certainly are not perfect. Being human is not about perfection, but if we care about ourselves and the people in our lives, we can do the things to make our relationships healthier, and isn't that what most of us want?

Characteristics of a Healthy Relationship

Think about these characteristics and decide how they apply to you. This can be a great topic of conversation with that special person in your life.

1. Respect for each other
2. Free to be yourself
3. Honest and open communication — primarily face to face
4. Best friends
5. Don't abuse alcohol or drugs
6. Don't control or manipulate
7. Feel secure, safe, and comfortable
8. Trust — don't cheat
9. Resolve conflicts effectively
10. No violence
11. Have fun together — enjoy the same things
12. Maintain separate interests and activities — each supports the other's separate pursuits
13. No pressure for sex
14. Proud of each other
15. Friends and family are happy about the relationship
16. More good times than bad
17. Have close friends outside the relationship
18. Share values

Unfortunately, many students end up in relationships that are not good for them. When you are in the middle of a poor relationship, it can be difficult to see things objectively. On the next page is a list to consider if you or a friend is in an unhealthy relationship. Do you see anything that looks familiar?

Did you know?

Chef Kelly English studied family and consumer sciences at UM. He paid his way through college as a cook in local kitchens. He continued to pursue his passion for food by graduating from the Culinary Institute of America at the top of his class in 2004. Winning numerous awards and being featured in several food magazines, he now is executive chef/owner of restaurants in Oxford, Memphis, and Biloxi.

Characteristics of an Unhealthy Relationship

1. Controlled or manipulated
2. Makes you feel bad about yourself
3. Abuses alcohol or drugs
4. Criticizes you and puts you down
5. Physically abusive
6. Doesn't have other friends
7. Not trustworthy — cheats
8. Pressure for sex
9. You and the relationship aren't a priority
10. Doesn't listen — interrupts
11. Friends and family are unhappy about the relationship
12. Feel scared or uncomfortable
13. Afraid of his or her temper
14. Unhappy most of the time
15. Tries to distance you from other friends, relationships (family), or activities

If you think you or a friend might be in an unhealthy relationship, here are a few suggestions of what you can do. It can be hard to acknowledge that this might be going on, and you might even be in denial. No matter what, please consider these things:

1. Realize that you deserve better.
2. Ask for help from family and friends.
3. Do not keep secrets.
4. End a relationship you feel is unhealthy or wrong for you.
5. If you feel the relationship is unhealthy, but you feel unable or scared to end it, seek support from Housing Staff, the Office of Violence Prevention, the University Counseling Center, or other support services on campus or at home. If you are worried about a friend, get help from any of these places. It may be the most loving thing you can do.

REFERENCES

Brown, B., (2014) Brene Brown: 3 Ways to Set Boundaries. Retrieve

from oprah.com/spirit/how-to-set-boundaries-brene-browns-advice

About the Author

Marc Showalter, *Clinical Assistant Professor in Leadership and Counselor Education*

Marc Showalter has been working with college students and teaching freshmen for more than twenty years. A former Director of the University Counseling Center, he teaches full time in the School of Education.

Suicide: A Preventable Condition

By Bud Edwards, Ph.D., Director of the University Counseling Center

Every fall I participate in a number of campus welcoming events as we celebrate the arrival of new students, and each spring I attend other celebration ceremonies to mark the completion of the college experience, graduation. In between those events is a year where students face a great of deal stress that can lead to a variety of mental health issues. One of those issues is suicide. Suicide is an extreme response to life circumstances that includes a variety of contributing factors. These factors manifest themselves differently in different people and may have been present over a long period of time or arise in a short period of time with a high level of intensity. Suicide as a singular act is difficult to predict, but the good news is that it is preventable.

Suicide prevention is rooted in several domains. One domain is an accepting community that cares for its members and wants the best for each other within that community. This type of community is reflected in The Creed, where we pledge to respect the dignity of each other and to treat each other with fairness and civility. Another domain is for that community to be knowledgeable about good mental health and to practice good mental health by promoting self-care with ourselves and with each other. It is important to know all of the resources on campus that support good physical and mental health and to use those resources appropriately. A third domain is to connect with each other and to value those relationships enough to have productive conversations about good mental health. In other words, our relationships are important enough to speak to each other if/when we see something wrong. We care enough about each other to accept that a community member may be struggling, to address our concerns with that person, to direct him or her to the appropriate resources, and to provide support while he or she works to get to a better, healthier place.

At Ole Miss we enjoy a sense of family that is the essence of the university. As family, we hold each other close and lift each other up during our time here on campus and after we graduate and move on to the next chapter of our lives. Please review the following information and allow this moment to be the start of our commitment. While we are here, join me in pledging to make our campus suicide free. Let's demonstrate our dedication to The Creed by applying its principles daily to meet this goal of no suicides in our community.

THE NUMBERS:

Among all suicides, **33.4%** of those deaths involved alcohol; **23.8%** tested positive for anti-depressants; **20%** involved opiates, both legal and illegal forms.

Among high school students who were surveyed, **17%** had seriously considered attempting suicide. Female students in this sub-population were twice as likely to seriously consider suicide (22.4% to 11.6%).

Among adults age 18-22 in college who were surveyed, **8%** had suicidal thoughts and **2.4%** made a suicide plan.
cdc.gov/violenceprevention/

A national survey of university/college students reported in the last 12 months:
• **46.4%** of respondents reported feeling hopeless
• **32.6%** of respondents reported feeling so depressed that it was difficult to function
• **6.4%** had intentionally harmed themselves
• **8.1%** had seriously considered suicide
• **1.3%** had attempted suicide
acha-ncha.org/docs/ACHA-NCHA-II_ReferenceGroup_ExecutiveSummary_Spring2014.pdf

DEFINITIONS

Suicide-death caused by self-directed injurious behavior with an intent to die as a result of the behavior
Suicide attempt-a non-fatal, self-directed, potentially injurious behavior with an intent to die as a result of the behavior; might not result in injury
Suicidal ideation-thinking about, considering, or planning suicide
cdc.gov/violenceprevention/suicide/definitions.html

Tips for talking with someone who might be considering suicide

Be honest and direct about your concerns.

    People may feel isolated and hopeless, and letting them know that you care can be helpful.

Ask if they are thinking of harming themselves.

    This can be done directly (Have you had thoughts of killing yourself?) or indirectly (Have you had thoughts of hurting yourself?). Either way is valid and may depend on your comfort level and/or your relationship with the other person. It is important to ask this question. **If you cannot ask this question, please find someone who can.**

Remind them that they are not alone and that there is plenty of help for them on campus; something can be done to help them feel better. Again, try to decrease the feelings of isolation and/or hopelessness.

Make a connection with one of the campus resources.

    Help them talk about their concerns with the University Counseling Center (UCC); an advisor; or someone in Student Affairs, such as a Housing staff member, a physician, or nurse practitioner at Student Health Services; a UPD officer; or some other trusted professional. The goal is to get them to the UCC to speak with a clinical staff member. Reaching out to any of the above individuals can help achieve that goal.

Suicide is preventable.

    For most people, there is a window of vulnerability that we can intervene in and work to help them make a different choice. Do not underestimate your ability to help save a life.

Talking about wanting to die or to kill oneself

Talking about feeling hopeless or having no reason to live

Looking for a way to kill oneself, such as searching online or buying a gun

Talking about being a burden to others and that others would be better off if one was gone

Warning Signs

According to the National Institute for Mental Health, there are several warning signs that may indicate someone might be considering suicide:

Talking about feeling trapped or in unbearable pain

Showing rage or talking about seeking revenge

Withdrawing or feeling isolated

Increasing the use of alcohol, drugs, or both

Giving away prized possessions

Acting anxious or agitated; behaving recklessly

Sleeping too little or too much

Displaying extreme mood swings

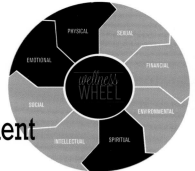

Chapter 18
Mindfulness for Stress Management

By Camp Best

mind full
or
mindful?

What is Stress?

Stress is your body's physical and emotional responses to some form of change in your environment. There can be good stress surrounding positive events such as graduation, getting married, getting a job, riding a rollercoaster, or participating in a competitive sporting event. However, in today's world, the word stress most often is used as a synonym for our negative feelings of anxiety, worry, uneasiness, nervousness, or pressure in response to change, and most of us are all too familiar with the harmful effects of experiencing too much negative stress, both physically and emotionally. As various forms of stress-related illnesses become more common on our college campuses due to economic, cultural, and technological factors in our society, it is important for our well-being to be aware of what causes our stress, how it affects us, and most importantly, what we can do to counter or alleviate it.

Fight, Flight, or Freeze Syndrome

Unfortunately, we cannot discern between good stress and bad stress because of the way we are physiologically constructed, and because we are still reacting in an automatic, primitive way to what is known as the "fight, flight, or freeze syndrome." This term came into popular use in the early part of the 20th century, and refers to the dramatic physiological changes that an animal goes through when threatened and then mobilizes for either fighting, freezing, or fleeing, much like a cat reacting to a barking dog.

In prehistoric times, when our ancestors encountered a life-threatening situation such as being attacked by a lion, their

bodies reacted to this emergency in much the same way as a protective, survival mechanism. Interestingly, we still react this way today because our brains are being stimulated in the same place.

My Amygdala Made Me Do It! — Brain Science 101

It's pure brain science. The "fight, flight, or freeze syndrome" triggers an immediate animal-like hyper-arousal on our part by stimulating what is known as our Sympathetic Nervous System (SNS). The control center in our brain for this automatic reaction is the amygdala.

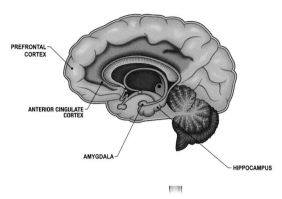

When our amygdala lights up or comes "online," it is like pushing the gas pedal on a car, and this triggers some of the following familiar responses that we actually have no control over:

■ the firing and release of a flood of certain strength-inducing and energizing hormones, including epinephrine (adrenalin) and cortisol, preparing our bodies for action

■ the dilation of our pupils to let more light in so that we can see "the enemy" better

■ the hair raising up on our body like little antennae so that we can be more sensitive to the vibrations around us; we know this as chill bumps or goose bumps

■ a rapid increase in our heart rate and breathing so that more blood and energy can flow to the muscles of our arms and legs (if we need to run from the enemy)

■ a shutting down of the blood flow to the digestive system so that the blood can be better used elsewhere in our defense system (no need to digest food if you are going to be eaten by a predator); we feel this as "butterflies" in our stomach. (Kabat-Zinn, 1990).

Test Anxiety

In addition to these physiological changes in our bodies, there also are some major activities going on in our brain. What is important for us to know as new college students is that the amygdala does not act alone. The hippocampus is the part of our brain responsible for storing and recalling information . . . like test answers. **When the amygdala lights up, the hippocampus grows dim! This is what happens when we experience classic test anxiety.** We have studied and studied and are sure that we know the answers, but when we sit down to actually take the test, the answers are no longer there, because they are in the dark. Our unnecessary worry and anxiety about the test has turned the amygdala on, and as a result it is lights out in the hippocampus.

Did you know?

Ole Miss quarterback Parker Hall was the first professional football player to complete over 100 passes in a single season.

The prefrontal cortex or PFC is our most evolved part of the brain and is used for our highest levels of functioning in the world. The PFC is the executive control center of our brains – it's our "smart" brain, and we use this part of our brain for learning things deeply, for making decisions, for reasoning, and for intuition and wisdom. So, when the amygdala is on fire and doing its thing, and we are actively in stress mode, unfortunately the light in our PFC grows dim, and we are not able to readily access this part of our brain. Often the result is that we react automatically to situations without thinking, we don't make the best decisions, and many times act irrationally. Again, blame it on the amygdala!

Our Old Cow Paths

If you grew up or travelled through rural areas in your earlier life, you may have noticed something interesting about the fields and pastures that stretch along the sides of the road. When cattle are being raised and tended to in these fields, you often will see clearly defined and well-worn paths that cut through the grass and lead from the pasture to the barn. Cows create these paths by travelling along them over and over, day after day, always taking the same route from the field to their barn at night. The cows never question whether there is a better way once a path has been created, and they automatically take the same route home each time without thinking.

It's the same way for humans. Our repeating behaviors and automatic reactions to stressful events and circumstances in our lives are learned in our childhood and are deeply engrained by the time we are young adults entering college. We actually create neural circuits or pathways in our brains by repeating these reactions; they are our well-worn cow paths. These paths are sticky and magnetic. When we are in stress mode and our prefrontal cortex is dark, we find ourselves heading blindly right down the same old cow path before we can blink an eye. Often this results in our doing or saying something that we later regret.

What are some of your old cow paths?

Helpful hint: Many students readily identify their struggles with time management and the distractions that come from overusing social media and their cell phones as good subject material for recognizing their old cow paths.

Did you know?

Gene Hickerson (Class of '58) enjoyed a 15-year career with the Cleveland Browns. Before he joined the team, the NFL had a total of seven men who rushed for more than 1,000 yards in a season. Behind Hickerson's blocks, the Browns had a 1,000-yard rusher for 10 consecutive seasons.

Chronic Stress − **When our lives get out of whack.**

When our amygdala is lit up on a regular basis due to stressful situations, and we continuously internalize and not manage these occurrences properly, our emotional, social, spiritual, and physical lives really get out of balance. This can happen to any of us and for many reasons, but it is generally the result of a slow accumulation of the effects from numerous small events or the "amazing dose of daily hassles" that occur for everyone over time, without giving ourselves the opportunity for an appropriate release.

Thankfully, life is vastly different in the 21st century than it was ages ago when predators were roaming the land. While we seldom face the threat of an actual attack by a predator, most of our stressful stimulators are social, psychological, and technologically induced situations, and fight, flight, or freeze usually are not acceptable or helpful responses. Our amygdala still doesn't know the difference between an angry lion and a full parking lot when you are late for class, or between a stampeding elephant and a difficult final exam, or between a hissing snake and being made fun of on social media.

Since we are unable to find the full release that fighting or running from these situations would bring us, our systems become over-burdened with internalized stress reactions. To add even more stress, our culture encourages us to pretend that we are not stirred up, and we commonly hide our reactions from others and ourselves, storing them deep inside our minds and bodies. Sometimes, when we are exposed to more stress-provoking lifestyles on a regular basis, such as going to college for the first time, we move into a perpetual state of hyper-arousal without even knowing it, because we begin to think of this feeling as "normal."

Although college is traditionally viewed as "the time of your life" with lots of fun and excitement, the truth is that stressful situations are inevitable during this time. One of the more typical causes for stress occurs during the early part of your first-year experience on campus. Moving away from home and coming to Ole Miss to live independently without parents and family to help manage your daily affairs is a major transition and a significant life change for most students. Consequently, stress and anxiety often occur as you attempt to manage and adjust to this important phase of your life. Your internalized response to this "threat" or change in your life might be that slightly nauseous feeling in your stomach when you have to say goodbye to someone you love or when you meet someone new. It also can be that irritating headache you get when you can't find a parking place or the bookstore is out of scantrons, or that tongue-tying dry mouth and racing heartbeat when you have to speak for the first time in class.

> **Stress and anxiety often occur for students as they attempt to manage and adjust to this important phase in their lives.**

Truthfully, living "stress-free" on a college campus today, even one as beautiful and laid back as Ole Miss, is impossible. College is highly competitive from the get-go, and students are asked to immediately cope with the pressure to succeed and excel academically. Typically, the greatest stress from academic pressures occurs during mid-term tests, final exams, and when final papers and projects are due, because all of this takes place within a short period of time when everything seems to be due at once.

Each student's response to accumulated stress is personal and can vary considerably. Everybody comes to this point in life with a history of events in their childhood and adolescence that forms the basis for how they will react to new stressors. Additionally, there may be sudden, acute events or traumas that occur in a student's life, such as the serious illness or death of a parent or friend, that when added to our everyday stressors can create an emotional crisis. At times this combination of things can lead to serious anxiety, panic attacks, depression, and in the worst case scenario, thoughts of suicide. When left unchecked, chronic stress also can begin to take a physical toll on someone, even at a young age. Research suggests that many of our familiar diseases, including heart disease, high blood pressure, diabetes, respiratory ailments, chronic ulcers and other digestive tract disorders, and even some forms of cancer might have their early roots in unchecked chronic stress. Compounded stress has been shown to aggravate or even be a causal factor in other physical conditions, such as recurring headaches, backaches, stomach aches, indigestion, diarrhea, skin disorders, insomnia, and excessive fatigue.

That's the Big Bad News . . .

Now that we have acknowledged the big bad news about stress, let's summarize by reviewing ten key points before moving on:

- Stress, both good and bad, is common to all animals and human beings.
- Human beings are still responding to bad stress by going into fight, flight or freeze, just as they have for thousands of years.
- The fight, flight, or freeze syndrome is a result of our sympathetic nervous system kicking in, and there are automatic physiological responses that take place in the human body when this happens.
- The control center for all of this is in the most primitive part of our brain known as the amygdala.
- When the amygdala lights up or comes online, other parts of our brain respond automatically. Specifically, our hippocampus where we store answers to tests goes off-line, and our prefrontal cortex where we make thoughtful, rational decisions also goes off-line.
- We are all "creatures of habit" even as early as our college years, and we have created certain neural pathways engrained in our brains, based upon repeated childhood experiences, that are just like old cow paths.
- When we find ourselves in stress mode, we are much more likely to automatically head down these well-worn and familiar cow paths without thinking because our amygdala is on (fight, flight or freeze), and we don't have access to our prefrontal cortex (rational and reasoned thinking).
- College life is filled with many stressful situations every day, and our body's and mind's natural response to these stressors can build up over time without us knowing.
- We all respond differently, but sometimes this accumulation of stress can build to a chronic level and may even become extremely threatening to our physical and emotional health.
- There are certain common behavioral signs that show up when we are suffering from chronic stress, and we should be aware of these so that we might seek help or offer help to our friends and classmates when these symptoms occur.

And now for the **GOOD NEWS . . .**

There is an amazing lifestyle practice that can bring us greater calm in the midst of all of this chaos and that can serve as a natural antidote to some of the stress that we deal with on a daily basis. This is called the practice of **MINDFULNESS.**

So, what exactly is this Mindfulness thing?

Mindfulness is intentionally bringing a focused attention to all of our experiences in the present moment with wonder and curiosity and without judgment. (Kabat – Zinn, 1990).

Mindfulness is being consciously aware of what is going on in our minds and bodies in the present moment and not going around sleep-walking on automatic pilot. (Kabat – Zinn, 1990).

Present Moment Thinking

Mindfulness is "reminding" ourselves to be fully awake in the here and now: not lost in our thoughts or daydreams and not spending lots of brain time on rehashing the past or rehearsing for the future. It has been said that the average human being has between 50,000 and 75,000 thoughts per day. And guess what? Ninety percent of these thoughts are repeats! Worse than that, 80 percent of our past thoughts usually have some kind of negativity attached to them. Once again, we can blame this on our amygdala, because due to its prominent presence, it is the natural inclination of our mind, primitive as it may be, to look for dangerous or threatening situations.

Mindfulness is a conscious mental shift in our thinking in which we fully appreciate and accept the present moment for all that it is. We do this rather than allowing our minds to be constantly focusing on the past and wishing that things could have turned out differently from the way they did, which is impossible, or worrying about the future and fretting over how things might or should be, as if we can control this by our thoughts, which also is impossible. In reality, neither the past nor the future exist, or rather, they only exist in our wandering minds. The past is remembered and the future is imagined, and the majority of the time, it is these past and future thoughts that cause our stress and anxiety.

Taking a Sacred Pause

Being mindful means being fully aware and conscious so that we can respond to stressful situations in our life with reasoned choice rather than reacting as semi-awake zombies on automatic pilot. By utilizing this practice on a regular basis, we can counter the negative effects of our aggressive and overactive amygdalas and actually turn the light off in our old lizard brain and light up our prefrontal cortex. **In this way we are able to pause and create a space for ourselves in which we actually have a choice in the way we respond rather than heading straight down our old cow path again.** By practicing mindfulness, we can counter the ill effects of test anxiety in the same way, darkening the amygdala and turning the light on in our hippocampus, so that we can access or "see" information and test answers more readily.

Paying Attention!

Monkey mind—Our minds are so active and busy all the time that we might think of them like wild monkeys in the jungle swinging from tree to tree, chattering and screeching and always looking for a better place to land. Or, you might think of the mind like a new puppy, jumping from place to place, never resting in one spot, and always getting into something. Sadly, this "monkey mind syndrome" has been intensified by all of the distractions prevalent today due to the increased use of social media and technology.

In 2009, humans could pay attention for an average of 13 seconds. In 2013, it was eight seconds; goldfish can focus for nine seconds (Rasmus Hougaard, The Potential Project).

Waking Up and Paying Attention—Mindfulness is about developing the ability to "wake up" and be fully attentive to all the moments of your life, reducing the amount of time you spend worrying about the future or fretting about the past. But, paying close attention to the present moment and keeping our minds focused on the task at hand are not easy things to do, especially in our highly charged and distraction-oriented culture in which so many things are vying for our attention at the same time. Paying attention and sharpening our focus really are skills that we have to learn, just like learning how to do a math problem or learning how to shoot a basketball. But, it has often been taken for granted that students automatically know how to successfully do this. Not necessarily so. Fortunately, mindfulness practices can teach us how to build and strengthen the muscle of paying attention. You might think of it as "cognitive weight-lifting."

So, all of this sounds wonderful right, but how do we do this?

Practicing Mindfulness in your daily life . . .
one breath at a time.
STOP | BREATHE | BE MINDFUL

In its simplest form, the anwer has been "right under our nose" the whole time. **The breath is the key to practicing mindfulness, and therefore can be instrumental in reducing stress and anxiety.** We can use our breath in two important ways to accomplish this:

First, we can use the breath as an intentional object or anchor for our attention. Our busy minds are constantly jumping around looking for some past memory or future idea to attach to, energize, and head down the old cow path. Remember, it is the natural inclination of our minds to do this, especially when the amygdala is turned on. Also remember, that it is these past or future thoughts that are more highly charged with negative, stressful energy. Consciously raising awareness of our breath, whether this is done while sitting in meditation or walking across campus between classes, can give our busy minds a place to rest and settle in the present moment. **When we are able to rest our mind's attention on the breath in the present moment, we experience far fewer feelings of stress and anxiety.**

Second, we can use the breath in a more physiological and scientific way. By taking a deep, full belly breath, breathing in through the nose and out through the mouth, we can actually stimulate what is known as our Parasympathetic Nervous System (PNS). Deep breathing pushes the diaphragm in our lungs against the vagus nerve stimulating the PNS. Earlier in this chapter, we described the Sympathetic Nervous System (SNS) which goes into action in response to stressful situations. Thankfully, we are an intelligently designed piece of machinery, and when the Sympathetic Nervous System floods our bodies with highly charged endorphins and other stress hormones, we can turn on the Parasympathetic Nervous System with deep breathing, which releases relaxing chemicals into our nervous system causing our heart rate to slow down and our bodies and minds to eventually come back into greater balance. And most importantly, when we use the breath to stimulate the PNS, we are shutting the amygdala down and bringing the hippocampus and prefrontal cortex back online allowing us to access calmer and more rational approaches or responses to challenging situations in our lives.

Diaphragmatic or Belly Breathing

If you start paying closer attention to your breathing during the day, by practicing mindfulness, you often will notice that you only take short, shallow, half-breaths from the chest up. By doing so you are continuously depriving your brain of life-giving and stress-reducing oxygen and retaining too much carbon-dioxide waste. Don't try to save the planet by not breathing fully. Your diaphragm is located down near your belly, so this is where your breathing needs to start. The deeper and more thoroughly you breathe "diaphrag-matically" on a consistent basis, the healthier your heart, body, and mind will be and the less stressful you will feel. The beauty of our breath is that it is consistently and reliably available to each of us . . . we do not have to buy it or get a prescription for it. Also, our breath can only be in the present moment. Our minds can be a thousand miles away in past or future thought, but awareness of each breath can only happen in the present. The breath is like a mighty oak tree in The Grove, deeply rooted, calming, like your oldest and dearest friend. It is fundamentally connected to the amazing experience of being alive and can be your most trustworthy (but underrated) weapon to fight off all of the lions,

tigers, and bears in the daily jungle of college life.

Your breath is your greatest ally, always there, right under your nose, especially when this awareness is made part of a regular practice, called ***mindfulness***.

Mindfulness is not...

Mindfulness is not a religious prac-tice or faith. It is completely secular and does not require ad-herence to any particular doctrine, dogma, or set of beliefs – Christians, Buddhists, Jews, Hindus, Muslims, Republicans, Democrats, Libertarians, rich and poor, gays and straights, young and old . . . people from all faiths, backgrounds, and be-

lief systems are practicing mindfulness today. Many people say that practicing mindful-ness actually enhances and deepens their existing faith. Mindfulness is not about mind control, hypnosis, or transcending reality either. To the contrary, it is about waking up, pay-ing attention, and being fully alive and accepting of whatever our reality is in the present moment.   Also, "It does not involve becoming some kind of zombie, vegetable, self-ab-sorbed narcissist, navel gazer, space cadet, cultist, devotee, mystic, or Eastern philosopher" (Kabat-Zinn, 1990).

So you see, you don't have to shave your head and dance in a circle chanting special songs under a full moon to be mindful. **You simply have to breathe.**

BREAKING NEWS!

Mindful Consumption of Technology – There is no doubt that the 24-7, continuous news cycling, cyber-saturated world that we live in today is extraordinary and has dramatically changed how we learn and communicate, in many ways for the better. **BUT**, it also can be disruptive, abusive, and stress-inducing unless properly managed with occasional breaks from this tsunami of information. Think of this in the same manner as mindfully moderating your food intake or how you manage the quality of water you drink and the air you breathe. We might expand our concept of being mindful of our overall human diet to include the news, information, sounds, sights, and images that we are immersed in and are subconsciously absorbing into our psyches day in and day out. Unfortunately, to be competitive and grab our attention today, our news sources favor an imbalanced focus upon trauma and doom, and we are constantly taking in the details of violent and disturbing news. We consume this information diet just as we do food and water, and the bombardment to our nervous systems with these images, without relief, can overwhelm our brains and be extremely distressing over time. Most days it is more than we can adequately digest, but we don't consciously know this, so we just stuff it inside. It also can become addictive, just like certain foods, alcohol, and drugs, as our systems become accustomed to this steady diet of highly-charged sensational information. Though the benefits of the Internet, cellular devices, and social media are tremendous, we might consider that we are being slowly sucked into a mode of living that is draining us of our freedom, privacy, and valuable down time, which only adds to our daily stressors.

The mindful challenge is to occasionally turn off your computer and stop taking it to bed with you. Don't make it, your cell phone, a video game, or the television the first thing you connect with every morning. Instead, connect with yourself first. Eat breakfast, read,

meditate, or exercise first. Resist the impulse to go to your cell phone the first moment you leave class. Take a few moments to breathe, look around, and see that life is going on successfully without your constant connection to some kind of media. It certainly did for the hour or hour and fifteen minutes that you were just in class. See if you can extend that refreshing media-free down time between classes; maybe you can even do it for a whole morning. The earth will keep turning, and life will continue. Facebook, Twitter, Pinterest, Snapchat, Instagram, and all the blogs you read will be there the next time you check in, and so will your friends and classmates. Take the extraordinary opportunity to be fully present in the moments before, between, and after class. Gradually, you will feel yourself begin to relax more and more, and you will be amazed at the inner peace that is available to you and what you might have been missing in the world around you.

Suggested books for further reading on mindfulness:

Mindfulness, A Practical Guide to Awakening, Joseph Goldstein, Sounds True, Inc., 2013

A Mindfulness-Based Stress Reduction Workbook, Bob Stahl and Elisha Goldstein, New Harbinger Publications, Inc., 2010.

Wherever You Go, There You Are, Jon Kabat-Zinn, Hyperion, 1994.

Heal Thy Self: Lessons on Mindfulness in Medicine, Saki Santorelli, Three Rivers Press, 1999.

The Mindful Brain, Daniel J. Siegel, Norton and Company, 2007.

Mindfulness in Plain English, Bhante Henepola Gunaratana, Wisdom Publications, 2002.

The Way of Mindful Education, Cultivating Well-Being in Teachers and Students, Daniel Rechtschaffen, Norton and Company, 2014.

Mindfulness on the Go, Simple Meditation Practices You Can Do Anywhere, Jan Chozen Bays, Shambala, 2014.

Full Catastrophe Living, Jon Kavat-Zinn, Delta Trade Paperbacks, 2009.

Please contact the University Counseling Center (662-915-3784) or go to their website at counseling.olemiss.edu/outreach/ for more information on the current offerings of classes and groups.

Glossary

Stress – Your body's physical and emotional response to some form of change in your environment.

Fight, Flight, or Freeze Syndrome – A term referring to the dramatic physiological changes that we go through in our minds and bodies when threatened or stimulated by a stressful event.

Amygdala – The most primitive part of our brain which is responsible for sending out the signals to our nervous system to go into the fight, flight, or freeze syndrome.

Hippocampus – The part of our brain which is responsible for storing and recalling information. This part of the brain loses its effectiveness when the amygdala is on.

Prefrontal Cortex - The part of our brain which is responsible for our highest levels of thinking, including decision-making, reasoning, and rationalizing. This part of our brain also loses its effectiveness when the amygdala is on.

Sympathetic Nervous System – The part of our nervous system which receives the fight, flight, or freeze signals from the amygdala and sends our bodies and minds into stress mode.

Parasympathetic Nervous System - The part of our nervous system which can respond to the fight, flight, or freeze syndrome when stimulated by the breath and assists in relaxing our bodies and minds.

Old Cow Path – A metaphor for the neural pathways that we have created in our brains through repeated behaviors since childhood that cause us to automatically react in certain ways under stressful conditions.

Mindfulness – Intentionally bringing a focused attention to all of our experiences in the present moment with wonder and curiosity and without judgment.

Meditation – The ancient practice of sitting and quietly bringing your awareness, concentration, and attention to your breath and to your body in a relaxing manner, which often calms the mind and reduces stress and anxiety. Meditation is one form of practicing mindfulness.

About the Author

Camp Best, *Academic Mentor and Instructor, FASTrack Program, College of Liberal Arts*

Camp Best received his B. A. degree in history from Millsaps College and holds master's degrees in urban and regional planning, southern studies, and mental health counseling from Ole Miss. He is keenly interested in meditation, mindfulness, and other contemplative practices and how these can be used to promote the wellness of our campus community.

Chapter 19
Financial Literacy

By Laura Diven-Brown and Natasa Novicevic

Many new college students are challenged with the balancing act of independence and responsibilities. This is not an easy task, and many students feel overwhelmed, especially when it comes to managing their finances.

The purpose of this chapter is to help you manage one aspect of this new freedom – your financial habits. In fact, financial literacy has become an important topic on college campuses, both inside and outside the classroom.

We understand that talking about money can be boring, but maybe you have noticed how the cost of a cup of coffee or soda a day adds up, right? If you get in the habit of thinking about your spending now, it will help you in the long run when you are making bigger decisions than whether to buy coffee. So, we will cover a few topics that are useful right now but also later in life:

- The cost of college

- Understanding financial aid

- Living within a budget

- A few thoughts about credit/debit cards and debt

- Having fun in college without overspending

- The power of education and saving

You're still not convinced that this chapter is relevant to you? That could be because you are not too worried about money at this moment. We know that you may not have many (if any) monthly bills this year – and for some of you, your parents may be taking care of all your educational expenses. But this won't be the case forever. If you live in an apartment now or plan to move off campus as soon as next year, you need to budget for rent, utilities, and trips to the grocery store. You will probably want to have Internet in your apartment and TV channels too. These are all monthly expenses. Even if your parents help you, it is a good idea to understand what they have to do to manage these costs.

Your participation in the following exercises will help you learn about personal finance. We want you to be aware of your college expenses, to talk with your family about how you are paying for college, and to be knowledgeable about your financing options. Knowing this information is the first step toward creating a budget and learning to live within your means.

THE COST OF COLLEGE

What is your budget? It is the estimated cost of attending college for one academic year. Realistically, it is not just about tuition - it is a lot more. Your budget includes both direct costs (the charges you see on your Bursar bill such as tuition and fees, on-campus, housing, and meal plan) and indirect costs (not charged to your Bursar account, but things that must be paid for nonetheless: books, gas for your car, trips back home, and other personal expenses). FYI - The terms "budget" and "cost of attendance" can be used interchangeably.

So, how much do you think your first year at Ole Miss costs? After you have taken a few minutes to add things up, look at the numbers below.

Estimated Student Budget

Based on the 2017-2018 Academic Year (Also known as your Cost of Attendance)

Expense	Undergraduate
Tuition	$8,190
Capital Improvements Fee	$100
On-campus Housing	$6,080
Food	$4,422
Books/Supplies	$1,200
Personal/Travel	$4,820
Total for Residents	**$24,812**
Additional Fee for Nonresidents	$15,264
Total for Nonresidents	**$40,076**

Were you close? Or are you thousands of dollars off in your calculations? How are you or your parents paying for this? (And did you even consider things such as football tickets, eating out, or fees for extracurricular activities?)

This is a perfect example of what we want you to begin noticing. Although you may not feel the direct effect of spending money on your education, either because of financial aid awards or because your family is helping you, we hope that you will learn how important it is to be aware of the flow of money.

UNDERSTANDING FINANCIAL AID

Yes, we expect all of you read this section, even if you do not use financial aid – and even if you are quick to say "my parents handle this stuff." Did you know that 87% of our freshmen receive some form of financial assistance?

What is on your award letter? Here are a few terms to understand.

Grants and Scholarships: Grants and scholarships are considered "gift aid" because they do not have to be repaid. Grants are typically need-based (meaning that you have to demonstrate financial need to qualify), and the funds usually come from governmental sources. Scholarships are typically merit-based. Ole Miss offers many institutional scholarships, particularly to entering freshmen and community college transfer students, but there are private scholarship dollars available as well. Never turn down a grant or scholarship unless you cannot comply with the award requirements and conditions. It is free money!

Loans: Institutional, federal, and non-federal loans are awards that must be repaid. Some are need-based, some are not, and they usually have a set annual loan limit.

Work-Study: The Federal Work-Study program is a need-based employment opportunity on campus. If you are eligible, it is your responsibility to contact prospective supervisors and interview for a position. The Office of Financial Aid can provide job leads.

Estimated awards: These awards are indicators of what you may be eligible for depending on requirements and/or appropriate applications submitted.

Before you accept anything and everything that has been offered to you on your financial aid award letter, stop and question what it is you are agreeing to take on. Is it a grant, scholarship, or loan? Does it have to be paid back later? What do you have to do to keep receiving the award? Or, is award amount for one or two semesters?

Where do I start? Federal aid is the largest single source of funding for students. To qualify, students must complete the *Free Application for Federal Student Aid (FAFSA)*. This application also is used to determine eligibility for state and institutional need-based awards. It must be submitted every year. This is the first step you should take.

Remember these two things: file your FAFSA early and provide accurate information. The FAFSA application for the upcoming school year goes live October 1. Here are some reasons to file early:

1. To receive your aid on the earliest date: Some applications are selected for "verification" by the U.S. Department of Education. This is a process to confirm the accuracy of the information submitted on the FAFSA. During peak season (typically summer through the first two months of classes), processing can take three or more weeks. Make sure you check your Student Aid Report after filing the FAFSA or contact the Office of Financial Aid to find out if your FAFSA has been selected for verification.

2. To gain access to better loans and other aid: Funding is often available in limited allocations. Some need-based student loans and aid programs such as Federal Work-Study only are available in specific amounts and are awarded on a first-come, first-served basis. The earlier you file, the more likely you are to receive them, if eligible.

3. To avoid penalties for late fees: You know that fall semester bill that was due mid-August? If you still have not paid it by the end of October, the balance starts to accrue interest (1.5% per month). This may not seem like much, but if you wait until the end of the semester, you could wind up paying an additional several hundred dollars in interest. There are better things to do with all that money than pay interest fees! That's why you need to have your financial aid package and financial plan in place before you arrive for school.

After you have filed your FAFSA, you need to be diligent and **FOLLOW UP**. Do not wait for someone to contact you about the next steps; take action in finding out if the Office of Financial Aid needs additional information from you. Always read the e-mails you receive through your University e-mail address because that is how Financial Aid attempts to reach you.

If you receive an e-mail and are not sure what it is telling you to do, **VISIT THE OFFICE**. You are already on campus, so just walk over! Do it sooner rather than later. You will find that taking care of these kinds of matters can be considerably easier when you are proactive. There are advisors on duty at the front desk in the lobby who are more than happy to assist you. Or, if you prefer to speak to an advisor in private, this can easily be arranged with or without an appointment. Get to know the staff member who helps you, so later you can follow up with questions directly if needed – without having to tell your story again.

Never stop looking for financial aid options. While it is true that much of the scholarship aid available through the University of Mississippi is in the form of four-year scholarships for incoming freshmen only, these scholarships are certainly not the only ones out there. All students should consult their academic departments for major-specific scholarship opportunities. Participating in University-related activities or organizations, such as band, choirs, or ROTC may sometimes yield performance-based scholarships as well.

Did you know?

The Patterson School of Accountancy is known for its tradition of teaching excellence and commitment to students. This commitment is alive and well today, and several current Accountancy faculty have won the University-wide Outstanding Teacher Award.

Another often overlooked place to hunt for scholarship aid is in your local community. A few potential sources are civic organizations, churches, alumni association chapters, and parent employers. You also can visit national scholarship search engines such as *fast-web.com* and *bigfuture.collegeboard.org/scholarship-search*.

If you have already secured scholarships that you are satisfied with, be sure that you are aware of the terms and conditions you must meet to keep them. If, for some reason, you find yourself in the unfortunate situation of failing to meet those terms (or if you are concerned that you won't), you should always check with the scholarship provider or the Office of Financial Aid. In many cases, you will have the opportunity to appeal the loss of your scholarship and continue to receive it under probationary status until you are back in good standing.

Mississippi residents also should remember to apply for state grants every year. Do not pass up this opportunity. The application deadline for the Mississippi Tuition Assistance Grant (MTAG) and Mississippi Eminent Scholars Grant (MESG) is September 15 each year, and the deadline for the Higher Education Legislative Plan for Needy Students (HELP Grant) is March 1 each year.

Understand student loans: Although everyone wants grants and scholarships - and we understand why – there is not always enough of them to go around. More than 50% of our undergraduates use loans to fill the gap in funding.

It is important to remember that borrowing loans is a serious financial decision. These loans are typically the first credit you have in your own name. This obligation will most likely play a role in your life for years after college.

When borrowing is necessary (as it is for many of us), here are some important questions to ask yourself:

■ *What kind of a loan should I borrow first?* Borrow Federal Direct Student Loans first before turning to non-federal private loans. Federal loans typically have better terms and conditions.

■ *Which loan is better?* A subsidized loan has more favorable terms than an unsubsidized loan. The interest that accrues on a subsidized loan while you are in school is paid by the government (and not by you!). The interest on the unsubsidized loans begins to accrue from the very first disbursement and you are responsible. We suggest that you at least make payments on the interest that is accruing on these loans while still in school – it may not be much per month, but it will make a huge difference after a few years, saving you hundreds of dollars in the long run.

> Having an unpaid Bursar balance or any kind of hold on your University account, such as an advisor or library hold, prevents you from registering for the next term's classes. Take care of any holds before your registration window opens so you have the best chance to get the course sections you want for your schedule.

■ *How much assistance do I need?* Do not accept the maximum offered to you if you don't need it. Remember that loans are DEBT. You must pay them back. Do not saddle yourself with a heavy burden that will cause you real financial pain later. Instead, strate-

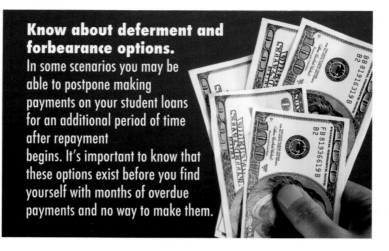

Know about deferment and forbearance options.
In some scenarios you may be able to postpone making payments on your student loans for an additional period of time after repayment begins. It's important to know that these options exist before you find yourself with months of overdue payments and no way to make them.

gize when you will use this money. For example, you may want to use loan funds during a year when you have especially difficult classes and won't be able to maintain a job. Or, you may opt to save some of your annual loan eligibility for summer classes when funding is limited.

■ *When do I have to start repaying these loans?* Most federal and institutional loans have grace periods, which are set periods of time after you graduate (or drop below half time enrollment) when payment is not yet due. For Federal Direct Loans, for example, the grace period is six months. The idea is to give you the opportunity to get a job before payments begin.

■ *Who is the lender of my loans and how much have I borrowed so far?* You can access your federal loan borrower history by creating an account on the National Student Loan Data System online at *nslds.gov*. If you have borrowed a non-federal private loan, make sure you know who the lender is and how to get in touch.

■ *Do I have the option to postpone making payments after graduation?* In some cases, yes – based on your circumstances. A **deferment** is a period of time when your payments are postponed and any interest accrued on a subsidized loan is paid by the government. A **forbearance** is a period of time when your payments are either postponed or reduced, but interest continues to accrue on both subsidized and unsubsidized loans. It is important to be aware of these options, particularly if you are experiencing financial hardships. You do not want to find yourself with overdue payments and no way to get caught up. In either case, your lender can advise you. No one wants to see you default – it is in everyone's best interest for you to pay back the loan funds.

■ *Will my first salary make it possible for me to start paying back my loans?* This is a smart question. Definitely research this further, but below are some figures to get you started.

The Office of Financial Aid sees as many as 900 students during the first week of classes! Try to take care of any concerns before the first day of classes so you can avoid a long wait to see a financial aid advisor.

BORROW WISELY

Investing in your education is smart. Borrowing more than you can pay back invites disaster. Listed below are some average starting salaries for various undergraduate degrees. A loan repayment chart accompanies the list. Evaluate your potential earnings and factor it into your calculations for borrowing and repayment.

A GOOD RULE: Don't borrow more than your annual starting salary.

AVERAGE STARTING SALARIES
BY DISCIPLINE/BACHELOR'S DEGREES
Southeast Region (AL, AR, FL, GA KY, LA, MS, NC, SC, TN, VA, WV)

Major	Mean Salary	Major	Mean Salary
Accounting	$50,715	Foreign Languages, Literatures, and Linguistics	$37,104
Special Education and Teaching	$38,150	Health Professions and Related Programs	$46,394
Biology	$32,270	History	$36,164
Biomedical/Medical Engineering	$62,470	Hospitality Administration/Management	$35,367
Business Administration, Management	$50,200	Journalism	$37,996
Economics	$51,674	Family Consumer Sciences/ Human Sciences	$30,307
Chemical Engineering	$67,726	Management Information Systems	$55,848
Chemistry	$44,261	Marketing	$47,276
Civil Engineering	$57,096	Mathematics	$44,854
Philosophy and Religious Studies	$33,553	Visual and Performing Arts	$36,803
Health and Physical Education/ Fitness	$36,315	Parks, Recreation, and Leisure Facilities Management	$33,764
Pharmacy, Pharmaceutical Sciences, and Administration	$47,300	Physics	$48,143
Building/Construction Finishing, Management, and Inspection	$58,511	Political Science and Government	$38,031
Homeland Security, Law Enforcement, Firefighting, and Related Protective Services	$43,677	Psychology	$32,226
Teacher Education, Specific Subject Areas	$43,114	Registered Nursing	$54,542
English Language and Literature/Letters	$35,921	Social Work	$34,323
Finance	$53,216	Sociology	$28,583
Computer Science	$78,877		

Source: NACE Salary Survey Fall 2017

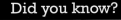

Did you know?

The Patterson School of Accountancy offers a CPA review course, which gives students a structured environment to study and sit for the exam during their last semester in the graduate program. Recent participants in this program have won gold, silver, and bronze medals for their performance on the CPA exam.

LOAN REPAYMENT CHART

AMOUNT BORROWED	# OF PAYMENTS	MONTHLY PAYMENT	ANNUAL PAYMENT
$10,000	120	$106	$1,272
$20,000	120	$212	$2,544
$30,000	120	$318	$3,816
$40,000	120	$424	$5,088
$50,000	120	$530	$6,360
$60,000	120	$636	$7,632

Based on 5% interest

We hope this information has made you a little more comfortable with your cost of attendance, award letter, and your understanding of student loans. Let's move on to managing your daily budget.

LIVING WITHIN A BUDGET

Basically, you must get in the habit of tracking where your money goes and making sure you do not overspend.

■ This means learning to differentiate between what is truly necessary and what is not (acknowledging your "needs" versus "wants").

■ It is also a matter of examining your expenses and knowing which are "fixed" (the same amount each month, such as rent) and which are "variable" (varying from month to month, such as groceries).

Budgeting can sometimes be frustrating because it is difficult to do. It is almost impossible for every week to be the same, so budgeting takes time and work each week. When unexpected expenses occur, such as a visit to the doctor or a higher than expected electricity bill, many people give up on budgeting. But, this is exactly when you need to stick to it because that is how you learn to plan for these challenges. Getting a head start now will make you more comfortable later when budgeting is even more important to you and your family.

The national average monthly student loan payment (for borrowers age 20-30 years old) is $351 (studentloanhero.com/student-loan-debt-statistics/). At the University of Mississippi, students who began as freshmen and took loans for school, graduated with about $30,000 debt.

Some students come to college with a new car and new clothes, and do not have to worry about money. Other students rely on their financial aid disbursement to pay for books and tuition and are looking for a job to cover other costs. Each person is different, and every budget plan is different. Even if you fall into the category of not having to worry about your finances at this time, we encourage you to recognize that living within a budget is a healthy habit to form. Your tasks in this section are to focus on thinking about your money and how it is spent.

One of the first steps to reaching your short-term and long-term financial goals is to practice budgeting. According to Federal Student Aid, an Office of the U.S. Department of Education, creating and following a budget can help with planning ahead for purchasing your textbooks, buying a laptop, as well as paying off your student loans after graduation and saving for an emergency fund. When you know where your money is going, you can find ways to reduce spending and stay on top of avoiding debt. Creating a successful budgeting plan starts with tracking your money for a while until you get familiar with your spending habits. See Activities Two and Three on page 357 of your text to get started and refer to the Glossary and Resources page at the end of this chapter for more reading on budgeting.

Do some investigation: Do you actually *know* if your semester bill has been paid in full with the Bursar yet? If not, then this should be the first conversation you have with your parents or with a financial aid advisor. It is important to have a financial plan in place for each semester (and summer!) and be aware of payment deadlines. Any unpaid balance means a hold on your account that could prevent you from registering for upcoming terms. To help you continually monitor the status of your Bursar bill, remember that you can view it online through myOleMiss, 24/7, and you can authorize your parent to access this information, too.

Have you ever thought about how much just one three-credit class costs? If you are a Mississippi resident, it is approximately $1,024, and, if you are a nonresident, the cost is approximately $2,932. This may put things in perspective when you decide to sleep instead of attending class. Each time you miss a Tuesday/Thursday class, that comes to about $37 for Mississippi residents, or $105 for nonresidents! Think about it. Thirty-five dollars is about three pizzas or a tank of gas! Skipping class is like buying an expensive concert ticket and then choosing to take a nap instead of going to the concert. You have paid for the class — go!

One more thing to check out. Do you (or should you) have any direct responsibility for helping with your own college expenses? Consider this: for most financial aid, you must maintain full-time enrollment and good grades to stay eligible; you definitely have the major responsibility for keeping your financial aid. Loss of funding could jeopardize everything.

On a different note, you may be able to contribute to the cause by finding a job. That could be a huge help (and it will give you an opportunity to make more connections on campus or in Oxford)! Most employers in Oxford will work around your class schedule because they know you have academic obligations. Jobs to consider: pizza delivery, babysitting, campus office work, lifeguarding, library assistant, or residence hall Community Assistant. Once you start earning your own money, you will find that you think more about how you spend it.

ACTIVITY ONE – Your Costs and Financial Aid

Now let's try out this activity to connect your costs and financial aid awards to your budget:

1) Go online to find *your individual* costs associated with going to school. Make sure to include all the direct and indirect components we mentioned earlier: tuition, nonresident fee (if applicable), course fees, residence hall rent, meal plan, text books, athletic tickets, school supplies, organizational dues (fraternity, sorority, sport clubs), gas, laundry, going out with friends, grocery shopping, parking pass, and any other costs you can think to include.

2) Visit the Office of Financial Aid, and find out how much you receive in financial aid (grants, scholarships, work-study, and loans). Once you know your total award package for the semester, subtract that figure from your costs. If you can do this online, that is fine, but remember that a financial aid advisor may know about additional money for which you are eligible.

3) Determine the amount of money you have to pay for the semester, and talk with your family or financial aid advisor about how you will manage paying for these expenses. Here are some possible conversation starters to have with your parents:

"I'm reading this chapter about financial literacy for my class. I found out how much it costs to go here, and compared it with the amount of financial aid I am getting. I have determined that college costs $_____ per semester. I got that figure by adding the fixed costs and personal expenses and then subtracting my financial aid. Do my figures sound about right to you?"

"How are you/we paying for this? Do I have a lump sum of money to manage this semester for my personal spending money, or will I get a monthly allotment in my checking account?"

"At this rate, it looks like I will owe $_____ in loans when I graduate, and I know that repaying them is my responsibility. I wonder if there might be another way to pay for college that doesn't put the burden on me later. What do you think about me getting a part-time job to help with these expenses?"

"I planned on being Greek (or participating on a club sports team). I found out it costs about $_____ per month for about nine months a year. I also hear there are other costs for pictures, t-shirts, travel, formals, etc. Are you okay with these costs?"

After the completion of this assignment, you should feel differently about your financial situation. You now have a working knowledge of the financial capital it will take to get you through college, and you are ready to continue assessing your daily financial habits while you are here.

> **Go to Class!** For federal aid purposes, your enrollment will be "locked in" on the Mandatory Drop Date of each term. If your attendance is not confirmed, you may be dropped from your class, and you may be required to pay back some of the financial aid that you have already received.

ACTIVITY TWO – Track Your Spending

Keep track of your daily spending beginning on a Friday. At the end of the week, it will be interesting to look back and see how you feel about your spending habits. List all purchases you made (or bills you paid) during this period.

Be sure to include Ole Miss Express charges, too. Although it seems like they are "free" when all you have to do is swipe your ID card, there really is an associated cost! If you used your meal plan, estimate $8.00 per meal, and do the same for any meals you had at a Greek house.

Date	What was Purchased?	Fixed Cost or Variable Cost	Need or Want	Amount	Reason – If this purchase was a "want," why did you buy it?
Friday					
Saturday					
Sunday					
Monday					
Tuesday					
Wednesday					
Thursday					
TOTAL					

So, how did you do? Did you spend money the way you thought you would? If not, that is ok! Things can and will get in the way sometimes. This is your first attempt, and it is OK to feel frustrated with the outcome. Remember: as important as it is to budget, it is just as important to forgive yourself if you happen to spend too much in any given week. Dwelling on it will only discourage your efforts.

Of course, do not make a habit of over-spending *every* week! You might try a smart phone application to help you track your spending. Some to explore are: Mint, Left to Spend, Toshl Finance, and Level Money.

ACTIVITY THREE – Cash Budget

In addition to managing your budget through an app, here is another option. Take a plain envelope and place $50 inside (or a reasonable amount that you decide). That is your budget for the weekend. Once you run out of money in your envelope, stop buying things. Report back, and let your classmates know how this activity went. Did you stay within your budget? Did you secretly add to the envelope as the weekend went on? Or say, "whatever!" – and use plastic instead? For some people, this is the best way to see just how quickly money can go when you do not plan ahead.

ACTIVITY FOUR – Apartment Living

Break into small groups. In this exercise, you are going to be roommates next year. Find out how much you would spend each month on rent, utilities, and personal expenses living off-campus in an apartment complex assigned to you by your instructor. Consider the following costs: rent, cable, internet, electricity, gas, cell phone, laundry, and gas for your car. Do some research around town on the prices offered from different companies, and try to come up with the best deals. For electricity and gas costs, you could talk to a manager of the apartment complex for monthly estimates. Be prepared to share your findings with the class. Each group member will turn in an individual reflection paper about his or her experience.

A FEW THOUGHTS ABOUT CREDIT/DEBIT CARDS AND DEBT

Some people buy everything with credit cards, while others stay as far away from them as possible. You will decide the best approach for you. It is not necessarily the case that you need to avoid credit cards like the plague, but you do need to be careful.

It's important to shop around when applying for credit cards. The Federal Trade Commission, which is the nation's consumer protection agency, has some helpful hints on what to look for when selecting a credit card.

First up – what is the annual percentage rate (APR) that was offered to you? The APR is a measure of the cost of credit, expressed as a yearly interest rate. It must be disclosed to you prior to your account being activated and is a good way for you to compare the credit card offers that you are considering. Remember - if you don't pay your bill on time or in full when it's due, you will owe a charge in addition to the amount of your purchase. Knowing the APR (and how it works) is essential because it can quickly have an impact on how much you have to pay back.

Other questions to ask before you take the plunge: Is there an annual fee or an individual transaction fee? There could be a fee just for having the card, and you should also know if an additional fee will be tacked on to each purchase you make. Is there a fee for late payments? Can you call customer service 24/7? What happens if the card is stolen? Does the card have a "cash back" feature? How does it all work?

Every time you make a purchase with a credit card, you should be prepared to make payments on the balance right away to prevent the monthly interest from accruing for too long. If you are able to do this, and you continue to make payments until your balance is down to zero again, it is a great way to start building your credit history. You will be glad for it later in life when you make bigger purchasing decisions such as renting an apartment, buying a car, borrowing a credit-based loan, or even buying a home. A strong credit history places you in a better position to support yourself when your parents or relatives may not be able to help you. That's why, as you begin to build credit, you should keep track of your credit history.

There are three primary organizations, or credit bureaus, that compile this information for consumers – Equifax, Experian, and TransUnion - and they look for trends in your financial activity to create what is called your credit report. According to Experian, factors such as on-time bill payments, how much debt there is to your name, and the length of time you have managed your credit accounts are taken into consideration. In other words, this is a report card on how you handle your finances. And, it's very important because it is the basis for your credit score, which is used to predict a borrower's ability to repay a debt and may have a big impact on every future financial decision.

Reviewing your credit report regularly is a good way to stay aware and catch any fraudulent or inaccurate activity on your accounts that may negatively impact your credit score. Did you know that you can get your credit report for free once every 12 months from each of above-mentioned credit reporting companies? Visit annualcreditreport.com for more information.

However, you must decide if having a credit card is a good option for you. It is always better to forgo a big purchase if you really cannot afford it (and definitely if you don't need it). The interest on credit cards is typically very high. If you do the math and realize that you cannot make the monthly payments on time, think twice before you use the card. Or, at least ask yourself: why do I think I will have more money in the near future to pay off this debt than I do now?

Let's now consider **good debt versus bad debt**. The main difference is the long-term value that you may or may not gain from these debts. For example, if you choose to go on a shopping spree and buy $300 worth of clothes, this would not be considered good debt because this purchase is setting you back financially and is not going to increase in value in the future. Borrowing loans for your educational expenses, however, is considered a good debt because you are investing in your education and in your long term success. Be careful, though, because loan debt also can definitely be bad debt if you borrow for the wrong reasons. This is why we warned against borrowing the maximum loans offered to you; be sure you have a reason to borrow.

Bottom line: If you do not have a reliable income and cannot discipline yourself to pay for your purchases as you go, a credit card will lead to economic disaster. If possible, avoid using your student loans and credit cards for clothing, spring break trips, going out, car payments, or Greek dues. It can be dangerous to rely on loans and credit cards on a daily basis and get accustomed to a standard of living that you really cannot sustain without going heavily into debt. Trust us, it is not fun to graduate and be stuck with having to pay on debt with your first paycheck!

Managing a Checking/Debit Card Account

Although most students use debit cards, there are times when writing a check is necessary. To establish online payments from Amazon.com, PayPal, or iTunes, a checking account is generally required.

5. Never lend your checks to anyone, even if your name and number are scratched off.

6. Immediately deposit or cash checks you receive, since checks held too long may be refused.

1. Keep a careful record of your checks (and related ATM/debit card transactions) to prevent overdrawing your account. Record in your ledger the amount, date, and to whom the check is made payable. Then subtract the amount from your previous balance.

2. Do not sign a check until you are sure the information is correct and complete. Void a check that is not usable. An altered check looks suspicious and might not be cashed.

3. To avoid risking forgery, notify your bank as soon as you discover that your checks have been lost or stolen. Otherwise, your bank's computer might process your checks and charge your account, no matter who has signed the checks.

4. Always use a pen, typewriter, or check-writing machine to make out a check. Never use a pencil.

7. If you mail a check for deposit, write "for deposit only" immediately above your signature endorsement on the back of the check.

8. Managing a checking account (like any other form of financial management) can be confusing. Ask your bank for help. Build a relationship with an individual at your bank.

Periodically, you will receive a statement of your account. It is important that your checkbook and the bank statement agree. Check to see if all debits (withdrawals) to your account are yours and match with your checkbook record. Remember that the actual amount of money remaining in your account may be less than that shown on the account statement if some checks you have written have not yet been cashed, or if you have made recent debit card transactions.

Debit Cards:

A Debit card doubles as an ATM card and an automatic checkbook, enabling you to get cash and make purchases from your checking account quickly and easily. Using a debit card is the most convenient way to shop, but you should take some precautions.

KEEP YOUR RECEIPTS: It is easy to forget how much you have spent, and if you do not use your receipts to keep track of the amount of money in your account, you may quickly become overdrawn. If you overdraw your account (meaning you have spent more money than you have), the bank charges you hefty fees (usually $20 to $30 for every purchase made after your balance hits zero).

PROTECT YOUR CARD: If someone steals your debit card, he or she could spend all the money in your account before you realize the card is gone. Check with your bank to see if you are liable for fraudulent charges.

RESERVATIONS: Be careful when using a debit card to reserve a car or a hotel room. Many companies charge the full amount to your card up front or even charge an excess amount for incidentals (such as room service). These charges could freeze your assets for the duration of your stay, leaving you without available cash. For hotels and car rentals, use a credit card if you have one.

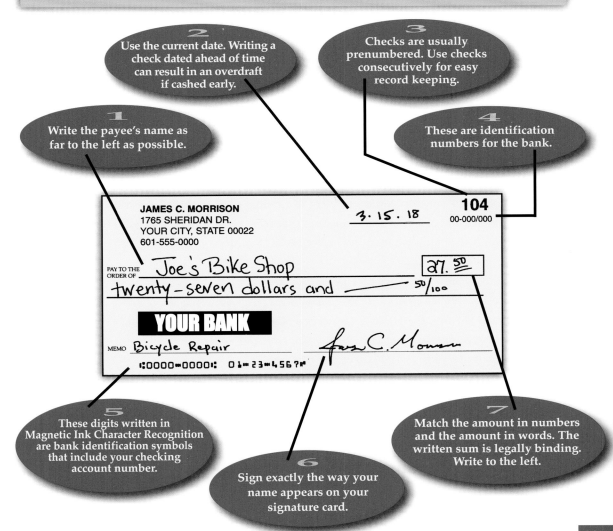

2 Use the current date. Writing a check dated ahead of time can result in an overdraft if cashed early.

3 Checks are usually prenumbered. Use checks consecutively for easy record keeping.

1 Write the payee's name as far to the left as possible.

4 These are identification numbers for the bank.

5 These digits written in Magnetic Ink Character Recognition are bank identification symbols that include your checking account number.

6 Sign exactly the way your name appears on your signature card.

7 Match the amount in numbers and the amount in words. The written sum is legally binding. Write to the left.

> **"We buy things we don't need with the money we don't have to impress people we don't like."**
>
> **– Dave Ramsey**

HAVING FUN IN COLLEGE WITHOUT OVERSPENDING

In this section, we want to share some advice with you about how to be a smart consumer.

Some easy ways to save on every day pick-me-ups: In a typical day, you might purchase a small café mocha ($3.95), peanut M&M's from a vending machine ($1.25), an Ole Miss sweatshirt from the campus bookstore (about $40 with tax), and Tylenol ($3.99 for a bottle of 24 capsules). So, in one day you just spent $49.19. Is there a way to spend less?

Consider this: a cup of coffee brewed in your room (same caffeine, a lot less money), a bag of M&M's you stashed after a grocery store run (you can buy in bulk), a sweatshirt bought from a store that sells more than just Ole Miss apparel, and generic brand headache medicine. You can save a bundle by planning ahead.

Learn to say "no": This is a tough one for a lot of people, especially when you find yourself in a new setting where it is important to make friends and feel like you belong. Standing out or not being included is a common fear of new students. There are ways to be included even if you do not participate in every single event. If someone asks, "Do you want to go hang out with us?" think before you say yes. Hanging out typically means spending money. If you are not in a position to go out, but you do not feel like telling your friends the reason why every time, consider some of these polite answers that were proposed by past EDHE students. The question was, "Hey, we're going to Wendy's. Want to come along?"

Thanks, but I am not hungry right now; maybe next time.

Thanks, but I just ate a little while ago. I don't mind going and keeping you company, though.

Oh, man, I just don't like Wendy's, but you guys have fun.

I would love to, but I'm trying to cut back on fast food.

I'm really tired right now, but please ask me next time.

No, I have to study for a _____ test right now. Y'all have fun.

No thanks, but I appreciate it.

All these responses are perfectly fine. You may even have a better way of answering. But just know that it is OK to say "no" because you should not need to spend money to impress people who probably do not care one bit about how much money you have and what you do with it.

It is sometimes harder, though, to say no to yourself. Next time you come across something that costs $40 or more, make a deal with yourself. If you are still thinking about that item the next day, go back and buy it. But you might find that once you are out of the store, the item is forgotten.

If you are better prepared for the kinds of spending opportunities that have caught you off guard in the past, you can choose responsibly and save yourself a lot of worry. Of course, you can always remember that something simply is not in your budget for that week and maybe that will encourage you to save up for next time.

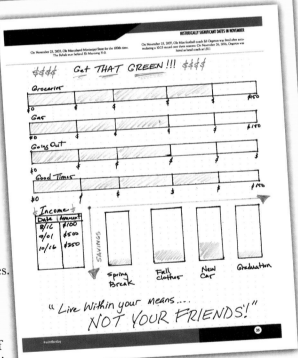

Top Tips from fellow Ole Miss Students:

1. Make a budget!
2. Never go shopping for groceries, clothes, etc., without a list.
3. Always buy necessities first, such as food, gas, toiletries, and school supplies.
4. Think twice before using a credit card!
5. Save money for emergencies.
6. Take advantage of all the free ways to have fun on campus and in town.
7. Don't spend impulsively...if you know you don't need it, don't buy it.
8. Get a part time job...in addition to earning money, it's a great way to get involved and meet people.
9. Track your debit card expenses online to see how much you're spending and where you're spending it.
10. We all have different financial situations. Live within YOUR means, not your friends'.

Real Life Reasons to Manage Your Money at Ole Miss
- You can't have just one pair of Nike shorts...or rain boots.

- So you won't be sitting at home while your friends are at the beach for Spring Break.

- To avoid angry phone calls from your parents!

- To prevent a heart attack when you realize you can't register for the upcoming semester because you owe money (that you don't have) for parking tickets.

- You may not purchase a meal plan for every year you're here...but you will never stop wanting to buy pizza sticks.

- Concerts at The Lyric aren't free.

- Because there's a t-shirt for everything, and you need ALL OF THEM.

How the Little Things Add Up

1 Venti Caramel Frappuccino per week:
$4.95 x 15 weeks = $74.25

3 Tall Lattes per week:
$2.95 (x3) x 15 weeks = $132.75

5 Tall regular coffees per week:
$1.95 (x5) x 15 weeks = $146.25

Common Sense Money Management
- **Set a cap** on the number of times you eat off campus per week or month.
- **Use an online banking or budgeting app** for your account, and check it EVERY DAY to keep tabs on your spending/catch any false charges.
- **If you have a credit card, do not carry it with you** when you might be tempted to use it for things you don't need!
- **Use OUT public transit to get around town!** It's free for students and saves gas money...and parking ticket fees when you return and are unable to find a legal spot.
- **Learn to say NO.** You don't have to go out to eat/go shopping/go on a road trip every time you are asked.

THE POWER OF EDUCATION AND SAVING

Your education is critical to your future financial strength and saving opportunities. The higher the educational level, the higher income earned over time. So, stay in school and get your degree.

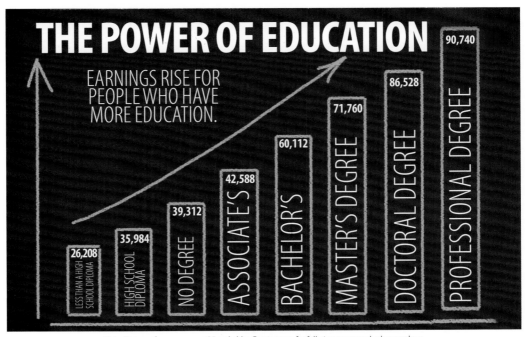

Note: Data are for persons age 25 and older. Earnings are for full-time wage and salary workers.
Source: U.S. Bureau of Labor Statistics, Current Population Survey 2016.

Also consider this example of starting to save and invest earlier rather than later in life.

Age	SCENARIO ONE Fred Invests Later From Age 30 - 65 (36 Years)		SCENARIO TWO Fred Invests Early From Age 19-54 (36 years)	
19	$0	$0	$300	$309
20	$0	$0	$300	$627
21	$0	$0	$300	$955
22	$0	$0	$300	$1,293
23	$0	$0	$300	$1,641
24	$0	$0	$300	$1,999
25	$0	$0	$300	$2,368
26	$0	$0	$300	$2,748
27	$0	$0	$300	$3,139
28	$0	$0	$300	$3,542
29	$0	$0	$300	$3,958
30	$300	$309	$300	$4,385
31	$300	$627	$300	$4,826
32	$300	$955	$300	$5,280
33	$300	$1,293	$300	$5,747
34	$300	$1,641	$300	$6,228
35	$300	$1,999	$300	$6,724
36	$300	$2,368	$300	$7,235
37	$300	$2,748	$300	$7,761
38	$300	$3,139	$300	$8,303
39	$300	$3,542	$300	$8,861
40	$300	$3,958	$300	$9,436
41	$300	$4,385	$300	$10,028
42	$300	$4,826	$300	$10,638
43	$300	$5,280	$300	$11,266
44	$300	$5,747	$300	$11,913
45	$300	$6,228	$300	$12,579
46	$300	$6,724	$300	$13,266
47	$300	$7,235	$300	$13,973
48	$300	$7,761	$300	$14,701
49	$300	$8,303	$300	$15,451
50	$300	$8,861	$300	$16,223
51	$300	$9,436	$300	$17,019
52	$300	$10,028	$300	$17,839
53	$300	$10,638	$300	$18,683
54	$300	$11,266	$300	$19,552
55	$300	$11,913	$-	$20,139
56	$300	$12,579	$-	$20,743
57	$300	$13,266	$-	$21,365
58	$300	$13,973	$-	$22,006
59	$300	$14,701	$-	$22,666
60	$300	$15,451	$-	$23,346
61	$300	$16,223	$-	$24,047
62	$300	$17,019	$-	$24,768
63	$300	$17,839	$-	$25,511
64	$300	$18,683	$-	$26,277
65	$300	$19,552	$-	$27,065
	$10,800		$10,800	

Think of a snowball rolling downhill – the earlier it starts to roll, the bigger it gets. Do not wait until middle age! Believe it or not, you could start saving right after college – or maybe even start now.

Let's talk about Fred. For 36 years, Fred put $300 into his savings account that yielded an annual interest rate of 3%, and he started doing this at age 30. So, from age 30 to 65, he managed to gain a net amount of $8,752. (The amount in his savings account at age 65 minus the total amount of money he invested during those 36 years.) What Fred didn't know is that had he started saving earlier in life, at age 19 for example, he would have gained more money over the same number of years. Take a look at this comparison – had Fred started putting $300 into his savings at age 19 and did that for 36 years, he would have had a net gain of $16,265. That is almost twice as much as he gained by starting at age 30.

IT IS UP TO YOU

We hope the information in this chapter, along with the assignments, has given you a better understanding of your finances. Financial literacy will continue to be an important part of your college education because this is the perfect time to strengthen your independence and form healthy financial habits. Even if money is not a concern for you at this time, it is a good idea to have the tools handy when the time comes for you to manage your resources.

There are many things you can do to help yourself manage money. You can budget and plan. You can think about situations before they occur and act rather than react. You can learn to say no. You can save and earn.

BUDGET APPS

Need an easy way to keep up with your budget? There are plenty of apps for smart phones that do just that: you can input your expenses, create categories with set expense amounts, and track how much you are spending on all the aspects of your college life.

Mint (iPhone and Android): free, syncs with bank account
Easy Envelope Budget Aid (iPhone and Android): free

Ace Budget 3 (iPhone): $1.99 (with a Lite version available for free)
My Weekly Budget (iPhone): $0.99

Expense Manager (Android): free
Financisto Personal Finance Tracker (Android): free

Glossary and Resources

FAFSA: Free Application for Federal Student Aid. This is the single application for federal aid and must be filed yearly by visiting *fafsa.gov*.

Grace period: A short time period after graduation during which the borrower is not required to begin repaying his or her student loans. The grace period also may kick in if the borrower leaves school for a reason other than graduation or drops below half-time enrollment. Depending on the type of loan, you will have a grace period of six months (Direct Loans) or 12 months (Health Professions Student Loans) before you must start making payments on student loans. The PLUS Loans do not have a grace period.

Pell Grant: A federal grant that provides funds up to a specific amount (determined annually) based on the student's financial need.

Private loan: Education loan programs established by private lenders to supplement the student and parent education loan programs available from federal and state governments.

Subsidized loan: With a subsidized loan, the government pays the interest on the loan while the student is in school, during the six-month grace period, and during any deferment periods. Subsidized loans are awarded based on financial need.

Unsubsidized loan: A loan for which the government does not pay the interest. The borrower is responsible for the interest on an unsubsidized loan from the date the loan is disbursed, even while the student is still in school. Students may avoid paying the interest while they are in school by capitalizing the interest, which increases the loan amount. Unsubsidized loans are not based on financial need.

Verification: Verification is an important process created by the Department of Education that helps confirm the accuracy of information submitted on the FAFSA. This review process ensures fair and accurate distribution of federal funds during the financial aid awarding process. Examples of documentation collected during the process include the verification worksheet (accessible through myOleMiss), student and parent IRS Tax Return Transcripts, and W2 forms.

For more reading on budgeting: Federal Student Aid, U.S. Department of Education. Budgeting. Retrieved from: studentaid.ed.gov/sa/prepare-for-college/budgeting

For more reading on credit, identity theft, and buying a car – and how they can impact your personal finances:Federal Trade Commission. (2013). *Focus on finances: Preparing for your future*. Retrieved from: consumer.ftc.gov/articles/pdf-0054-focus-on-finances.pdf

About the Authors

Laura Diven-Brown, *Director of Financial Aid*

Laura Diven-Brown is originally from the Chicago suburbs but now calls Oxford her home. She earned a B.S. in psychology from the University of Illinois, and a M.Ed. in higher education from the University of Mississippi. In her role as the Director of Financial Aid, she oversees management of student financial assistance programs totaling $290 million annually. She also served as an EDHE 105 instructor for four years.

Natasa Novicevic, *Assistant Director of Financial Aid*

Originally from Belgrade, Serbia, **Natasa Novicevic** has lived in the U.S. since 1993. She earned both a B.A. degree in business and marketing and a M.A. in higher education from the University of Mississippi. She taught EDHE 105 while serving as a graduate assistant in the Office of Financial Aid.

Chapter 20
Finding Your Way: Career Exploration

by Casey Cockrell-Stuart and Wesley Dickens

You may be thinking, "Why do I have to think about the job search and careers now? Graduation is such a long time away! I just got here, and I want to enjoy my first year at Ole Miss!"

Yes, you do have a lot going on right now. You have classes, extracurricular activities, hanging out with friends, and, of course, cheering on the Rebs! But you want to squeeze in a little time to make yourself an attractive candidate for your first job or for a graduate program. And you want to start now.

Don't get overwhelmed. Preparing for your career is not that difficult if you start early. By participating in activities such as internships, volunteer work, and job shadowing, you will not only develop important skills that look great on your resume, but you will understand more about whether a job is the right fit for you. Also, you will gain experiences which will make you much more competitive than the friend who took naps between classes.

The best part is you don't have to figure out any of this stuff on your own. The Career Center is available as a resource to help you–from deciding what you want to do all the way to securing that first job. We can help you choose a major and find part time employment while in school. We can also assist you in developing your resume and interview skills so that you can secure internships and jobs. The most successful students are the ones who visit us early and often. Be one of those students.

Choosing A Major

The first step to a dream career is finding your dream major. Some students may know exactly what they want to study when they get to Ole Miss, while others may not be so sure. However, even the students who seem most confident may change their minds. And by the way, it is OK not to know exactly what you want to do the minute you set foot on campus. College is a time to explore and to allow yourself to grow. Choosing a major is a part of that growth.

Make an appointment today.
The University of Mississippi Career Center
303 Martindale | Student Services | 915-7174
Hours: Monday – Friday | 8:00 a.m. – 5:00 p.m. | career.olemiss.edu

We understand that committing at 19 or 20 or even 25 to what you want to do for the rest of your life can be intimidating. How do you know if you will still like the career path you choose now when you are 35? At the Career Center, we have advisors to guide you through the process and to help you make a choice that fits you.

Getting help choosing a major is easy. All you need to do is make an appointment with a career advisor. During the appointment, your advisor helps you begin the process of selecting a major by asking you a few career and academic questions. Your advisor also may ask you exploratory questions that are similar to the ones located in the box below. These questions are aimed at digging deeper into your passions and interests. Remember that all answers you share with your advisor remain confidential.

Depending on what you and the advisor discuss, he or she might suggest that you take the Strong Interest Inventory or use TypeFocus. These are career assessments that find out your values, interests, personality, and skills to determine how they fit into a major or career. Read on to see how the Strong Interest Inventory and TypeFocus can help you discover your dream major!

Did you know

that the Myers Briggs Type Indicator can be helpful in choosing a major or career? With the results from your MBTI, a career professional can help you determine what majors or careers align with your personality type. These results can be especially useful when combined with the results from the Strong Interest Inventory.

EXPLORATORY QUESTIONS

■ Who were the people you admired when you were growing up? (Keep in mind that role models can be either real persons or fictional characters.) How are you like each person? How are you different from each person?

■ What magazines do you read regularly? What do you like about these magazines? What television shows do you watch regularly? What do you like about these shows? What websites do you visit regularly? What do you like about these websites? What keeps drawing you back to these?

■ What is your all-time favorite story, either from a book or movie? What do you like about this story?

■ What do you like to do with your free time? What are your hobbies? What do you enjoy about these hobbies?

■ What were your three favorite subjects in middle or high school? What three subjects did you hate? Why did you love or hate these subjects?

Strong Interest Inventory

You are going to spend much of your adult life working, so wouldn't you like to choose a major and career that you find interesting? That is what the Strong Interest Inventory is all about: determining your career interests. This career assessment compares your interests to various occupations to determine what you might find to be the most appealing. The assessment gives you an in-depth list of occupations and majors that might be a match for you. Once you take the assessment and have your list, you and your advisor discuss which options seem like the best fit and what steps to take next.

How does the Strong Interest Inventory work? The results work something like this: Imagine you walk into a room full of people. You notice that these people are split into six different groups, and each group is discussing a different topic (see box below). Naturally you are interested in certain topics more than others, so you are more drawn to those groups. Which group do you go to first? Second? Third? Believe it or not, the groups to which you are naturally drawn are a good indication of your career interests. The career advisor at the Career Center uses these interest areas to help you in selecting an academic major that excites you. For more information about the different categories, visit discoveryourpersonality.com/aboutstrong.html.

Strong Interest Inventory
Holland Categories and Sample Associated Activities

Realistic: participating in intramural sports at the Turner Center; working on the latest Habitat for Humanity project.

Investigative: attending open house at Kennon Observatory; assisting a professor in a research lab.

Artistic: going to the Buie-Skipwith Museum or the Gertrude C. Ford Center. Performing in a theatre group; photographing various sites on the Ole Miss campus.

Social: volunteering for The Big Event or other campus organization; organizing activities for Greek Recruitment.

Enterprising: running for president or a leadership position in a campus organization; competing in an entrepreneur competition.

Conventional: keeping the books for Associated Student Body; building model airplanes.

TypeFocus

TypeFocus is another tool available to you through the Career Center that may help you in making career decisions. Like the Strong Interest Inventory, the results of your Type-Focus inventory serve as a guide to your interests but on a more limited level. This assessment also allows you to learn about your workplace values and personality type and how they relate to choosing an academic major and career. Unlike the Strong Interest Inventory, you can take Typefocus without making an appointment with the Career Center.

> To access the TypeFocus assessment just login to your
> Career Center EmployUM account at hireolemissrebs.com
> Username: Ole Miss e-mail address | Password: Student ID number

The Strong Interest Inventory and TypeFocus are great tools to help you get started in the career and major search, but the only way to truly know what is the right fit for you is to get out there and explore! There are several ways to do this....

"As a freshman coming to Ole Miss, I wish I would have known that it is okay to not have every step of my next four years figured out. Four years is a long time to learn and grow with the idea of what you want to do with your life, and that choice of a major does not come overnight. I would say to take a semester to take the basic Freshmen courses (you'll need them anyway), and see if you like the classes in what you are thinking about majoring in before you commit."

-Ashley Noblin, Biology Major
Ocean Springs, MS, May 2016

EXPLORING YOUR MAJOR

Classes

As a new student, you have a lot of classes ahead of you during your time at Ole Miss. Why not use these classes to help you choose a potential major and career? You can "try on" majors before committing to them by selecting electives based on your interests. Also, ask your friends what they are taking. Read course descriptions to see if a class sounds interesting to you, and if it does, take it! Many students find their majors or minors this way. Educating yourself on all the opportunities that are available to you by taking a variety of classes is an effective approach in finding your career path at Ole Miss.

Job Shadowing

Would you like to do a quick test drive of a profession before committing to it? Of course you would, who wouldn't? Why commit to something when you are not really sure you will enjoy it? Job shadowing is a great way to gain access to a career without having to be hired into it. While a job shadowing experience is not as in-depth as an internship, you get some exposure to a field which helps you determine if that is the direction for you. Also, job shadowing experience is something you want on your resume because it shows you took the initiative to find out more about your future profession.

In a job shadowing experience, you learn what someone does on a day-to-day basis. You are exposed to some of the challenges, trends, and rewards of the field. If you are interested in shadowing, do not be afraid to reach out! Think of professionals you admire and ask to follow them for a short period of time. Most professionals love talking to students. If you are still nervous about contacting someone for job shadowing, come by the Career Center, and we will help you develop a strategy for reaching out.

Volunteering

You will learn about the value of volunteering in another chapter of the text, but have you ever considered how volunteering can help you choose a major? When you volunteer you are not only helping the community but also experiencing activities that can potentially turn into a career.

Volunteering also expands your experience section of your resume. If you volunteer, you are taking on responsibilities that transfer into job skills. Think about it: communication, leadership, and teamwork, just to name a few. You are picking up all these skills as a volunteer. You also can volunteer in a professional setting. For example, if you are a journalism major with a public relations emphasis, you could volunteer to do press releases and campaigns for a community organization. This type of volunteer experience helps you have examples of your work to discuss and showcase when you are searching for a job. Employers do not care if the experience is paid or unpaid. Experience is experience, whether it is a volunteer or paid internship.

> "When I decided to attend the University of Mississippi I had no idea what I wanted to do. I kind of had an idea but I wasn't for sure. I really wish I would have known more about the development of my major and volunteer work that I could have possibly participated in so that I could have gotten more experience with my career development."
>
> -Christopher Buford, Exercise Science
> New Albany, Mississippi, May 2016

Informational Interviewing

A few years ago, three students were about to graduate and did not know what they were going to do next. Instead of just getting any job, they went on a road trip. This road trip was one with a purpose: to meet people and hear their stories. The trip was the ultimate example of informational interviewing and was actually turned into a documentary series, "RoadTrip Nation." Since that initial trip, RoadTrip Nation has sent many students on similar expeditions to allow them the same opportunity.

The purpose is to visit a variety of people who love what they are doing. Hopefully, through the process, students gain insight on what their passion is in life. However, you do not have to be a part of a documentary to gain this valuable information. You can conduct an informational interviewing session anywhere, including Oxford or in your hometown.

By going on your own "RoadTrip," you are exposed to professions that could end up being your dream job. Once you identify people you find interesting, just reach out and set up an interview to learn more about them and their careers. This can be anyone – fellow students, professors, family, community members, business leaders, and Ole Miss staff. Follow these few steps to conduct a successful (and fun) informational interview:

1. Schedule an appointment with the person.
2. Choose either professional or business casual attire.
3. Arrive on time.
4. You direct the interview. Have some questions prepared that you would like to ask.
5. Thank the interviewee.
6. Send a thank you note.
7. Stay in touch with the interviewee in the future. You are developing a strong network base.

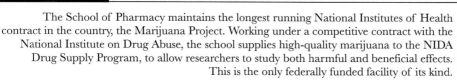

If you are feeling adventurous in your search to determine your career path, then audition for the documentary series by going to roadtripnation.com

Internships

Did you know that today employers not only like to see one, but multiple, internships on your resume? Interning is one of the most effective ways to show that you have taken initiative outside of the classroom to get experience in a potential career. Through interning you learn if this type of work is a good match for you while simultaneously developing networking contacts and getting to add experience to your resume.

You can start interning as early as the summer after your freshman year. If you are going to spend your summers interning, then you want something good, right? In that case, you need to come see us as early as this fall. Yes, that means now. The most competitive internships have deadlines as early as November through February. We can help you find internships to apply for, prepare your application materials, and practice your interview skills.

Getting any internship is not terribly hard, but being offered a great internship is a little more difficult. Here are a couple of tips to follow:

Did you know?

The School of Pharmacy maintains the longest running National Institutes of Health contract in the country, the Marijuana Project. Working under a competitive contract with the National Institute on Drug Abuse, the school supplies high-quality marijuana to the NIDA Drug Supply Program, to allow researchers to study both harmful and beneficial effects. This is the only federally funded facility of its kind.

Start early. Freshmen may not qualify for some of the internship opportunities available; however, it is never too early to gain knowledge about what is to come in the next year. By seeing what opportunities are available and the criteria for selection, you will know what you need to do to be selected.

Do your research. A great candidate does more than just look over the company website. A smart candidate does a simple Google search to also find recent press releases, company reviews, and industry journals. You want to know how the company is performing as well as identify their competitors. You will be an informed candidate by also knowing their recent successes and what is unique about the company. You will be successful if you not only know the company product but use it and are passionate about the product. Find the answers to all of the above to be the really informed (and most attractive) candidate (Bridges, 2012).

> "As a freshman, I was very overwhelmed with decisions I had to make. I knew what I wanted to do, but I didn't know how to get there. I wish I had known about the Career Center earlier in my time at college because I could have avoided a lot of stress! I could have learned more about where to look for internship opportunities as well as leadership positions on campus to bolster my resume."
>
> - Katherine Farese, Political Science Ashland, MS, May 2016

Stand out. Do something that helps you stand out from your competition. The harsh reality is your high school accomplishments are what got you to college. However, the moment you become a college student, those achievements start to fade. You have to replace them with new achievements. It is time to get involved with an organization you love, and do not be afraid to be a leader. Volunteer in the community. Excel in your classes. There are a variety of ways to stand out, so choose a few that fit you so you have something to put on your college resume when the time comes to apply for internships.

Resources

You can find internships in a lot of different places from networking to websites. Some of our favorite and most effective are:

Internships.com

Idealist.org (for internships in the non-profit sector)

Mediabistro.com (for social media internships)

Internqueen.com

Hireolemissrebs.com

Career Fairs

Did you know?

The UM School of Pharmacy has been a leader in professional education for many years, and nearly 100 percent of Doctor of Pharmacy graduates pass the national licensure exam on their first attempt. Also, the vast majority of graduates have job offers before they graduate or are employed within weeks of commencement.

Consider these resources and next steps if you are ready to apply for an internship. Remember to start looking as early as possible to avoid missing deadlines!

Websites: Internships.com, InternQueen.com, EmployUM (Ole Miss's online job and internship search database. Access through career.olemiss.edu)

Other ideas: Career Center's Internship Fair (usually held in the fall). Make an appointment with an advisor at the Career Center.

Follow the Career Center on Twitter @HireOleMissRebs
Like us on Facebook: University of Mississippi Career Center

You have taken the assessments which gave you an idea of which career options to explore. You researched these options by job shadowing, conducting informational interviews, gaining experience through interning, and taking a variety of classes. You have a great amount of information to help you commit to a major you love. You are on your way to your dream career! Your relationship with the Career Center does not stop now; we have more work to do to turn you into a competitive candidate. This work starts now.

What You Can Do Now

By participating in the exploratory activities we have discussed, you are well on your way to becoming a competitive candidate for employers and graduate schools. Although it is a little more work now, you will be glad you did it rather than wait until later to start gaining experience.

There are other ways to begin putting yourself ahead of the pack.

"I wish I had used the Career Center early. Yes, going to the Career Center your freshman year can help you. They have programs and pamphlets about choosing and preparing for your major. Also, if I had gone early I would have thought more about volunteering and leadership opportunities that would build my resume."

- Jordan Knight
Communicative Sciences Disorders
Sarasota, FL, May 2017

Information Sessions

One way to gain valuable career information is to attend employer information sessions in the Career Center. The Career Center hosts several employers from a variety of fields every semester to speak on the different positions their companies offer. While you may not be applying for these jobs right away, you can get information on what they are looking for in a candidate so you will be ready when it does come time for you to apply. If you wait until your senior year to attend these sessions you may not have time to pick up the needed qualifications. Go to the information sessions often and start now.

Career Fairs

You also can understand what employers and graduate schools are looking for in candidates by attending career fairs early in your college experience. The Career Center hosts several fairs every year. These fairs include events for all majors, internships, and specialty major fairs. You can attend these fairs to talk to employers for after graduation or even secure an internship for next summer. The career fairs are a helpful way to gain understanding of what you need to be doing now.

> "As a freshman, I wish I would've known about networking. Growing up I have been in professional settings and had the opportunity to gain knowledge about my future but talked about other topics instead. I wish I had taken the opportunity to learn more from the doctors, lawyers, and nurses that I have met."
>
> -Maegan Williams, B.S. Exercise Science
> Pascagoula, MS, August 2016

Networking

College life is designed for networking. There are activities and events going on every day of the week. So many activities in fact that you have to choose which ones you go to and which ones you have to miss. All of these events allow you to meet other college students, faculty, staff, alumni, professionals, and community members. Each interaction holds the possibility of being a contact that can help you in the future. Remember to keep in touch with people over the years. Once you meet a good contact or acquaintance, make sure to reach out to the person at least once per semester.

Two words about Facebook, Instagram, Twitter, Pinterest and Linked In – use them (appropriately)! Google is your new resume. While these sites are a convenient way to keep in touch with all of your new contacts, remember that future employers, professors, and staff can see your profiles, so keep them PG. And trust me, you will be "Googled." Simple rule to follow– if you would not want your *family* to know something then it probably should not be on the Internet. If you stay close to that rule, you can enjoy the sites without endangering your future professional chances.

From an Intern's Perspective

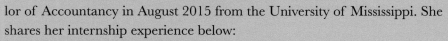

Maryilyn R. Berestain is a graduate student working on her Master of Accountancy at the University of Mississippi. Originally, from Belmont, MS, Marilyn received her Bachelor of Accountancy in August 2015 from the University of Mississippi. She shares her internship experience below:

Where did you do your internship?
Audit Intern at KPMG LLP in Orlando, FL (Jan. 2015 - Mar. 2015)

Why did you decide to do an internship?
Doing an internship gave me a chance to get a better understanding of what I would be doing after graduation and provide me a sliver of experience. When you start looking for a job, having done an internship gives you a leg up over everyone else.

How did you find the internship?
I knew the Patterson School of Accountancy worked very closely with the Career Center regarding job and internship opportunities for accountancy students. The faculty and staff of the accountancy school were adamant about informing students of the various firms and companies that came to visit the University, and the Career Center facilitated those visits for interviews with firms. I applied on EmployUM to interview with various accounting firms and secured some interviews. One of my interviews was with KPMG.

Describe the duties you had as an intern.
- Worked in a team-based environment to perform audit-related tasks
- Produced clear, well-structured, and effective audit documentation
- Applied KPMG's Professional Judgment Framework when completing work and documenting audit conclusions
- Demonstrated a quality service mindset
- Demonstrated a continuous learning mindset
- Assisted to ensure the integrity and transparency of financial information
- Collected supporting documentation from client

How did the internship differ from your expectations?

I knew I would be working long hours, but I was surprised at the fact that I was working 55 to 63 hour weeks. I also had a week of training prior to fully participating in audits, but it did not prepare me nearly enough for the level of complexity during the engagements. At most jobs, you eventually begin to understand your job, but in my experience, I felt like I never fully comprehended one task before I was asked to do another.

How did it help you decide what to do next in your career?

The audit field is definitely fast-paced and very stressful. My internship helped me realize that the audit field in public accounting was not for me. After my internship, I knew that I still wanted to work in public accounting; but instead of working in audit, I wanted to work in the tax department.

What are some tips for success as an intern?

- Always ask for feedback on all of your assignments.
- Learn to take criticism and use it to better your performance.
- Show initiative. Volunteer for projects or assignments. This will make you stand out.
- Network with your co-workers, managers, and mentors to build potential contacts.
- Send proper goodbye e-mails or notes to people you worked with closely or who mentored you.
- Absorb and learn as much as you can.
- Relax! Be confident!

What would you say to students who are just starting out at Ole Miss and considering an internship?

I would definitely advise students looking for internships to start early and do as many internships as possible.

Prepare a resume. Practice interviewing. Invest in proper business professional clothing. Get assistance from the Career Center!

Career developement — a life-long process

So, you get everything figured out — the perfect career path and the perfect academic major — to support your decision. Your work is done, right? If only it were that simple. Your professional development is a lifelong process.

Once you commit to an academic major and move through your education at Ole Miss, you are well on your way to launching your career. However, that is not enough. Developing your career and yourself as a professional is a process, meaning you work on it most of your life. Do not be discouraged by this, however. Attending to your career development can be exciting and rewarding. Continual career development may take you places professionally you have only dreamed of going.

Every once in a while:

- Re-evaluate your career plans
- Re-envision yourself
- Set new goals
- Consider additional education

Dream Job Questionnaire

Though the Career Center has several assessments that can assist you in making smart career choices, there are always more questions to ask to help you make the best decision. After you have identified some possible career choices, ask:

- What would I be doing on a daily basis?

- What would be my main responsibilities?

- Do I naturally gravitate to shows, books, or activities that are related to my career option?

- Do I find the people already in my chosen field to be interesting?

- Have I taken courses in this field? If so, is the material engaging to me?

- Do I know where the majority of jobs are located geographically?

- What are the typical salaries?

My Personal Career Building Checklist

❑ I have taken the Strong Interest Inventory.

❑ I have taken the MBTI.

❑ I have worked with a career professional at the Ole Miss Career Center.

❑ I have spoken with the internship specialist at the Ole Miss Career Center.

❑ I have shadowed someone who is working in an occupational field in which I am interested.

❑ I have participated in service learning projects and/or community service.

❑ I have conducted one or more informational interviews with individuals who are working in career fields in which I am interested.

❑ I have spoken to my professors to learn more about careers in their areas of expertise.

❑ I have attended one or more information sessions at the Ole Miss Career Center.

❑ I have attended an Ole Miss Career Fair.

❑ I have formulated short-term and long-term goals for my future.

Glossary

Career Fair – a networking event on specific days set aside each semester where students have the opportunity to meet with potential employers and learn about career paths and employment opportunities.

Career Professional – a person skilled in collaborating with and assisting students in determining a career path and selecting an academic major to support the chosen career path. Career professionals are skilled, also, in coaching students for upcoming interviews and in providing job search resources.

Information Session – an event where students can gain in-depth knowledge about employers, companies, federal agencies, etc. Information sessions usually are held at the Ole Miss Career Center, although some are at other locations on campus.

Informational Interview – a short interview conducted with someone who works in a particular field to learn more about the realities of specific occupational choices.

Internship – a work immersion experience that allows students to gain first-hand experience of how a particular occupational choice will fit with their interests and personality. Internships may be paid or unpaid.

Job Shadowing – the act of spending time (usually a day or so) with and observing an employee in his or her workplace to learn more about the tasks and responsibilities attached to a particular occupation or career.

TypeFocus – a free, online career planning tool that provides assistance to students who are attempting to make career choices. The TypeFocus program includes assessments and resources that students can use to make informed career decisions.

REFERENCES

Bridges, F. (2012). *How to get an awesome internship.* Forbes. Retrieved from
  forbes.com/sites/francesbridges/2012/05/31/how-to-get-an-awesome-internship/#5bfdd1494378

About the Authors

Casey Cockrell-Stuart, Ph.D., *Assistant Director of Employer Services, instructor in the Career Center*

Casey Cockrell-Stuart coordinates Career and Graduate School Days, Internship Fair, Teacher Recruitment Day, Engineering Career Day, and Pharmacy Recruitment Day. Dr. Cockrell serves as the liaison between the Career Center and the School of Education, Graduate School, and the College of Liberal Arts. She also teaches Career and Life Planning, an elective course for juniors and seniors, as well as advises students on a variety of career issues in the Career Center.

Wesley Dickens, *M.A., Coordinator of Career Preparation and Internships for the School of Business Administration*

Wesley Dickens came to the University of Mississippi in 2011. He earned his Master of Arts in Higher Education/Student Personnel from the University of Mississippi.

Chapter 21
Sex and Sexual Health

By Erin Cromeans

S-E-X is a mysterious three-letter word that we are all curious about at some point in our lives. Common questions students have include: What *exactly* is sex? How do you know it's okay to have sex? Does "hooking up" count as sex? Is sex ever bad? What makes sex great? Can I be sexual without having sex? These are all valid, honest, and appropriate questions to ask. Before we get started in this section on sex and sexuality, take a minute to think about three things:

Questions to consider

1. Where did you first learn about sex? What did you learn?
2. In your life, who talked with you about sex? Was the overarching message positive or negative?
3. What questions do you have about sex? Write them down and see if you find the answers by the end of this chapter.

College Culture

In each part of the world, there are social norms that help shape the customs and actions of the people living there. Sex does not escape this phenomenon. When thinking about how you learned about sex or who in your life has talked with you about sex, it probably comes down to the culture, religion, and values of your family.

It is important for you to remember who you are and the family culture you come from as we begin to explore the college culture. Please recognize that there  may be vast differences, and we each experience the culture in our own way. If you ask students across campus what the following terms mean, we guarantee you'll get different answers, especially among men and women: dating, hooking up, hanging out with, and talking to. However, even with our differing interpretations of culture, experience, and language, there are a few things we need to be clear about before we can move on.

Let's be clear

Let's be clear… good sex is not something to research in the magazine aisle at the grocery store, but is a healthy part of many relationships. It is natural and perfectly okay to be attracted to other people. These are biologically and physiologically-based feelings for both men and women. Let's be clear on one more thing: good sex requires mutual consent. For more information on consent, what it is, how to get it, how to give it, and what to do with a "yes" or "no," see Chapter 26.

What is sex?

What is sex? What is sexual health? Sex refers to the biological characteristics that define humans as female or male, but the general use of the term often is perceived to mean sexual activity. For the purposes of this chapter we will use the term sex when referring to sexual activity.

According to the World Health Organization (WHO) sexual health is: "…a state of physical, emotional, mental, and social well-being in relation to sexuality; it is not merely the absence of disease, dysfunction, or infirmity. Sexual health requires a positive and respectful approach to sexuality and sexual relationships, as well as the possibility of having pleasurable and safe sexual experiences, free of coercion, discrimination, and violence. For sexual health to be attained and maintained, the sexual rights of all persons must be respected, protected, and fulfilled." (WHO, 2014)

What's not sex? Who's having sex?

So, what's not sex? Abstinence, kissing, hugging, snuggling, cuddling, touching, and feeling. One can be sexual and enjoy these things without having sex. It is not true that "everyone's doing it." In fact, our perception is often much different than reality. At the University of Mississippi, we periodically conduct the American College Health Association - National College Health Assessment. In 2015, 65 percent of students reported having 0-1 sexual partners within the last 12 months. That's pretty compelling data to tell us that students are not "doing it" every night, and they are not on a quest to have sex with as many other students as possible in their college career.

Abstinence

Abstinence is always a healthy choice, even if you have had sex before. It does not matter what others are doing, what others will think, or what others will say. What matters is that you take care of yourself and do what you feel comfortable doing. Abstinence prevents disease and pregnancy for as long as you actually practice it.

Did you know?

The University of Mississippi is home to a federally-funded Chinese Language Flagship program, one of only 22 institutions of higher education across the United States for undergraduate students in critical languages such as Arabic, Chinese, Hindi Urdu, Korean, Persian, Portuguese, Russian, Swahili, and Turkish.

Safe Sex: What does that mean?

- Reducing your risk of contracting a sexually transmitted infection (STI)
- Using condoms makes intercourse safer sex
- Using condoms or other barriers makes oral sex safer sex
- Having sex play without intercourse can be even safer sex
- Safer sex can be pleasurable and exciting

To have safer sexual experiences you must understand how to protect yourself during sexual activities. During sex, there is skin-to-skin contact, and body fluids are often exchanged which can pass infections from one person to another. The body fluids by which infections can pass are blood, semen, pre-ejaculate, vaginal fluids and, in the case of HIV, breast milk. Also, any sex that allows the possibility of semen reaching the vagina could lead to pregnancy. Contraception can help prevent your chances of acquiring an STI or unexpected pregnancy.

Contraception

Becoming infected with an STI is not the only concern when considering practicing safer sex. There also is the risk of an unplanned pregnancy. What does contraception mean? Contraception is a method of preventing conception; it is any method or procedure that prevents fertilization. This includes three types of contraception:

1. **Intrauterine contraception**
    a. Device inserted in the uterus to prevent pregnancy
    b. May be kept in place five to ten years
2. **Hormonal methods**
    a. Implant
        i. A thin rod (device) placed under skin
        ii. Can last for up to three years
    b. Shots
    c. Patch, vaginal ring, progestin pill, combined estrogen/progestin, emergency contraception (plan B)
3. **Barrier methods**
    a. Male Condom (most common)
    b. Female Condom
    c. Diaphragm/Cervical Cap

Did you know?

Alumnus and long-time Ole Miss public relations director Ed Meek founded the Tupelo Furniture Market (now the largest in the U.S.). He also built a Las Vegas hospitality event — known simply as "the Show" — that is the largest of its kind in the western hemisphere.

A closer look

Using a condom is a simple and effective way to protect you and your partner when having sex. Women and men typically like condoms because they are inexpensive and easy to acquire. They help prevent pregnancy and sexually transmitted infections, unlike hormonal and intrauterine methods that only protect against pregnancy. Condoms do not require a prescription, and they can be used with other forms of birth control methods, except with another condom (you cannot use a male and female condom at the same time). Condoms also have no side-effects unless you are allergic to latex, in which case you can use non-latex condoms.

Communication

A whole book could be written on the importance of communication, both verbal and nonverbal, within the context of sexual relationships. However, for brevity, we'll look at three things in particular:

1. Determine what you want (or don't want) from sex and communicate those wants and needs effectively. Sure, that sounds easy enough, but in the moment, how do you do it?

Our advice: don't wait until "the moment" – have the conversation well before that time. Sex does not happen automatically once you start kissing, touching, or drinking. Each individual is constantly communicating; pay attention to your partner's words, actions, and body language. Ask questions, provide clear responses, and respect both your and your partner's boundaries.

2. Communicate consent. Please remember that the absence of "no" is not the presence of "yes." (See Violence Prevention chapter for more information.)

3. Negotiate the use of contraceptives or disease prevention techniques. To some, this may seem like a no-brainer, but it's not always the woman's responsibility to take a pill and the man's responsibility to bring a condom. The responsibility, conversation, and negotiation belong to anyone wishing to have sex. Ask these questions: "What would you like us to do for birth control?" and "How about disease prevention?" There are many reasons people give for not wanting to use preventive measures such as condoms. Listen to your partner's concerns and work out any possible alternatives, but in the end make the healthiest decision for both of you, and that might mean not having sex.

Talking about using condoms

Communication about the use of condoms with your partner is important. Though you may be nervous, telling your partner about an STI or unexpected pregnancy will be far more difficult. Practice what you might say beforehand, then choose the right time to talk. Don't be shy; be direct and honest about what you want and don't want. If you cannot talk to your partner about sex, it may not be the right time to become sexually active with this person.

Planned Parenthood has some great examples of ways to start the conversation with your partner.

If Your Boyfriend/Girlfriend Says: It doesn't feel as good with a condom.
You Can Say: I'll feel more relaxed. If I'm more relaxed, it will be better for both of us.

If Your Boyfriend/Girlfriend Says: Don't you trust me?
You Can Say: Trust isn't the point. People can carry sexually transmitted infections without knowing it.

If Your Boyfriend Says: I'll pull out in time.
You Can Say: I want to feel relaxed and enjoy this and pulling out is just too risky. There's a chance I could get pregnant, or we might get too excited to stop. And pulling out won't prevent sexually transmitted infections.

If Your Boyfriend/Girlfriend Says: Putting it on interrupts everything.
You Can Say: Not if I help put it on.

If Your Boyfriend/Girlfriend Says: But I love you.
You Can Say: Then you'll help me protect myself.

If Your Boyfriend/Girlfriend Says: I guess you don't really love me.
You Can Say: I'm not going to "prove my love" by risking my health. If you really love me, you would want me to feel safe.

Disease prevention

Formerly called sexually transmitted disease (STD), Sexually Transmitted Infections (STIs) are infections that are passed from one person to another during sexual contact. The reason for the name change is that, medically, infections are only considered diseases when they cause symptoms (NIH, 2014). Since many sexually transmitted infections are "silent" (meaning no symptoms), NIH has broadened the term to include all infections. There are many types of STIs, and they are also very common. According to the CDC, 110 million individuals are infected with an STI in the nation (CDC, 2014).

Practicing safer sex enables individuals to reduce their risk of getting an STI. Before we discuss protection from STIs — what infections are out there? There are more than 20 types of STIs, but we will discuss the following: chlamydia, gonorrhea, herpes, syphilis, genital herpes, HPV, and HIV.

BACTERIAL	CONTRACTED	SYMPTOMS	HEALTH RISKS
Chlamydia	Unprotected vaginal sex Unprotected anal sex Unprotected oral sex	"Silent disease" **Women** may have slight vaginal discharge, pain during urination, pain during sex, frequent urination. **Men** may have discharge or itchy feeling, mild pain on urination, infection of anus or throat.	**Women** may have infertility, infected cervix, pelvic pain, Pelvic Inflammatory Disease, ectopic pregnancy, arthritis. Can be passed to infant during labor/delivery. **Men** may have infertility, arthritis, eye infections, urinary infections.
Gonorrhea	Unprotected vaginal sex Unprotected anal sex Unprotected oral sex Mother to unborn	**Women** may have vaginal discharge, pain on urination, increase in urination. **Men** may have thick yellow/green discharge from penis, pain on urination, pain in penis. **Both men and women** may have rectal bleeding and discharge.	Infection of genital tract or area; lip, mouth, or anus of both men and women. Pelvic Inflammatory Disease, problems with pregnancy and infertility.
Syphilis	Unprotected vaginal sex Unprotected anal sex Unprotected oral sex Direct touch Close body contact Kissing Mother to unborn	**Both men and women** may have painless sores, swollen glands, skin rashes, flu-like symptoms, brain infection.	Skin, bone, heart disease, brain disease, dementia, blindness if left untreated, fatal if untreated.

VIRAL	CONTRACTED	SYMPTOMS	HEALTH RISKS
Genital Herpes	Unprotected vaginal sex Unprotected anal sex Unprotected oral sex Direct contact skin to skin	**Both men and women** may have fatigue and fever, painful blisters, itching, red skin formed into groups of sores; sores may crust and heal with scarring.	Virus hides in nerve endings and reoccurs.
HPV (Genital Warts)	Unprotected vaginal sex Unprotected anal sex Unprotected oral sex	**Both men and women** may have soft, moist, pink growths either on penis or in female genitals and around anus; growths may be cauliflower in shape.	Invasive cervical cancer and bladder cancers.
HIV	Unprotected vaginal sex Unprotected anal sex Unprotected oral sex Sharing needles	**Both men and women** may have swollen glands, flu-like symptoms.	Damages body's immune system, AIDS, can be fatal.

Vaccinations

Vaccinations are available for a few STIs including Hepatitis A and B and HPV. Hepatitis A is most frequently transmitted through sexual contact, particularly among men who have sex with men. Exposure to Hepatitis B may be common in certain high-risk groups, including heterosexuals with multiple partners and men who have sex with men. HPV vaccinations are used to prevent the most common strands of the virus; however, being vaccinated for HPV does not mean that an individual will not contract the disease. It is still possible to contract HPV with viral strands not included in the immunization.

Am I Ready for Sex?

We have discussed sex, sexual health, sexually transmitted infections, and contraception, but how do you know when you are ready to have sex? The majority of people have sexual feelings, but they do not always act on those feelings. When to have sex is a personal choice and will continue to be one the rest of your life. Whenever a sexual situation develops, no matter your age, you make a choice about whether or not to engage in sex.

If you are considering having sex ask yourself these questions:
- How clear can you be with your partner about what you do and do not want to happen?
- How will having sex make you feel about yourself?
- How will sex affect you physically and emotionally?
- Are you considering having sex because you want to or because someone is pressuring you?
- Will sex change your relationship with your partner?

It may help to talk to someone you trust and who cares about you when you need to make such a decision.

Sex and Consent

Healthy sex includes consent. Consent is an enthusiastic yes, not forcing someone to say no. Understand how your partner is feeling and what he or she wants before having sex. Consent can be withdrawn at any time in any relationship, even if you have had sex before. Remember that both partners are equally free to stop at any time you are having sex. If you aren't sure, ask.

Consent empowers people, and failure to get consent has serious consequences. If your partner is drunk or high, he or she cannot give consent. It can be confusing or hard to tell sometimes if someone can give consent. If you have to think about it, then you should wait before having sex. Coercing someone or pressuring someone to have sex is never consent. (See Violence Prevention chapter for more information on this topic.)

Campus and Community Resources

If you are seeking advice about contraceptives or devices, you may contact your physician, the Student Health Center, the Lafayette County Health Department, or Planned Parenthood. There are several places you can go to be tested for any or all STIs. On campus: the Student Health Center. Off campus: Lafayette County Health Department, Planned Parenthood, or a physician.

Testing Centers

Student Health Center
662-915-7274
V.B. Harrison Health Center
Mon-Thurs.: 8:00 a.m. - 5:00 p.m.
Fri.: 9:00 a.m. - 5:00 p.m.

Lafayette Co. Health Dept.
662-234-5231
101 Veterans Drive, Oxford, MS
Open Mon.-Fri.

Planned Parenthood
901-725-1717
2430 Poplar Avenue, Ste. 100
Memphis, TN 38112
Mon., Tues., Thurs.:
9:00 a.m. - 6:00 p.m.
Wed., Fri.: 8:00 a.m. - 4:00 p.m.,
Sat.: 8:00 a.m. - noon

Glossary

HIV – Human Immunodeficiency Virus, virus that causes AIDS

AIDS – Acquired Immune Deficiency Syndrome, a disease

HPV – Human Papilloma Virus, also known as genital warts

REFERENCES

Sexual transmitted infections. National Institute of Health (NIH): National Institute of Allergy and Infectious Diseases retrieved on 01.24.14 from www.nlm.nih.gov/medlineplus/sexuallytransmitteddiseases.html

Talking about condoms. Planned Parenthood. Retrieved on 01.24.14 from plannedparenthood.org/health-topics/sex-101/understanding-sexual-activity-23973.htm

Talking to your partner. Retrieved on 01.24.14 from plannedparenthood.org/health-topics/sex-101/understanding-sexual-activity-23973.htm

Talking about using a condom. Retrieved on 01.24.14 from plannedparenthood.org/health-topics/sex-101/understanding-sexual-activity-23973.htm

World Health Organization (WHO) retrieved 01.24.2014 from who.int/reproductivehealth/topics/sexual_health/sh_definitions/en/

About the Author

Erin Murphy Cromeans, *Assistant Director for Wellness Education, Department of Campus Recreation*

Erin Murphy Cromeans is currently pursuing a doctorate in health behavior. She received a Master of Science in nutrition and hospitality management degree at the University of Mississippi in 2011, a Master of Science in health promotion at the University of Mississippi in 2009, and a Bachelor of Science in exercise science at the University of Mississippi in 2007. Ms. Cromeans is a Certified Health Education Specialist (CHES) through the National Commission for Health Education and credentialing. She is currently working toward becoming a Certified Prevention Specialist through the Mississippi Association of Addiction Professionals. Ms. Cromeans has been a part of the Ole Miss Family for more than ten years and loves Oxford more and more each day! Hotty Toddy!

Chapter 22
Substance Use and Misuse: Alcohol and Other Drugs
By Erin Cromeans and Joseph Dikum

For Ole Miss freshmen: My son William's story. A new freshman class started at Ole Miss this week and I wish I could tell them all this story.

It's about my oldest son, William, who was a freshman in 2008. He would gladly tell them himself, if only he were alive.

With a quick wit and a big, friendly smile, William was an A student in the Honors College and Croft Institute at Ole Miss. He was fluent in Spanish, a member of Sigma Nu fraternity, and ran track for the Rebels his freshman and sophomore years.

The 400 hurdles is considered by many one of the most difficult in sports, and William had the courage to walk on and do it in the SEC. He lettered at Ole Miss his sophomore year and was rewarded by participation in the SEC Outdoor Track and Field Championships in 2010.

The Ole Miss letterman's jacket he earned is one of our most prized possessions. That and the plaque he received for making the SEC's all-academic team in 2010. It was quite an achievement considering he managed the Honors College, Croft Institute, fraternity, and track at the same time and came out on top.

"Making any kind of all-SEC team is a big deal," I told him the year he worked to excel in track and academics for the Rebels. "It will be an achievement that will always mark who you are and what you can do."

I still remember the pride in his voice the night he called me after receiving the plaque for the SEC academic honor on the floor of Ole Miss' Tad Smith Coliseum during half-time of a Rebel basketball game.

"I was out there with the football players," he said. "It was so cool." William met a beautiful, smart girl at Ole Miss who became his girlfriend for four years in college that we loved, and hoped that he would one day marry. He had friends who shared his joy of music and laughter and traveling the world. He was the same sweet, smart competitive young man who sang in the church choir and camped at Alpine in summers during his youth.

In college those first two years he appeared to be all-everything, and track practice kept him in check most weekdays his freshman and sophomore years. The season ran both fall and spring semesters with early morning weightlifting and afternoon workouts.

Enough to keep anybody straight. On the weekends, when the music cranked up and the lights turned low, he partied, with so many other students.

It was all contextualized into a good collegiate reason as opposed to abuse or a problem. It's the fraternity Christmas party, it's Double Decker, it's the night before the Alabama game, the Grove, a music festival. It was alcohol, it was ecstasy, marijuana, and Xanax, lots of Xanax.

We had talked before his freshman year at Ole Miss about the perils of viewing alcohol abuse and recreational drug use as something of a rite of passage in college.

"Some people get in so deep in college they can never get out of it," I told him. "I've seen it happen too many times. Be careful."

William suffered from anxiety and low self esteem. He tried to medicate with alcohol and drugs, like so many others. He was comforted that substances like alcohol brought him closer to the conversation in social situations.

He was considered a square more than a partier, and William hid his habit from many friends, but privately drawing the line was hard and one drug led to another over time as so often happens, sometimes by accident.

I had warned him that drug dealers can't be trusted, that drug dealers know tricks, like mixing heroin with cocaine to make it doubly addictive before a user knows what hit them. And it is easier to succumb when the dealer is a fraternity brother or the guy down the hall at the dorm who looks a lot like you.

"I know," he said, brushing off my warning. "Everybody knows that."

William was a senior at Ole Miss by the time we recognized the depths of his troubles. He graduated, another proud moment, but he was frail. He had wanted to go to law school but instead checked into rehabilitation once he realized the addiction had advanced to the point that he was no longer the person he once was.

William was scared. The drugs had taken over.

Dropping our firstborn off at a rehabilitation facility that cool fall day wasn't easy. We hoped the 30-day stay in an inpatient treatment center would get this problem under control and his life back on track, then we could all get back to normal.

We were naïve, or maybe just hopeful, as parents tend to be. William bounced between several rehabilitation facilities around the country for the next year. He was kicked out of one in Colorado because he purchased a bottle of cough syrup from a drugstore and drank it to get high. He was kicked out of another because he and a friend found a way to purchase one pain killer pill each from the outside world. They took it, for old times sake, and William confessed the misdeed to the counselor, asking for another chance, thinking his admission might make a difference.

"You were right," William told me. "My plan was to grad-uate (from Ole Miss) and quit. But it's harder (to quit) than I thought. I'm not sure how to get out of this."

We got William back into a rehab facility in Nashville, and finally, progress. He graduated to a halfway house. With a col-lege degree, he got a job at a Mac computer store. They put him in charge of training. His coworkers bragged about his sales skills and said he was a joy to work with.

"Sweetest young man," they said. Yes, and so very smart.

I quit my job and took another to be closer to him, visiting weekly and having daily phone conversations, anything to try and help. So I was alarmed one Friday night when I kept calling and he did not answer. By the next morning, when he still did not answer, I knew. The drive to Nashville took two hours but it felt like 22. I could not feel my hands on the wheel and my stomach churned. Once there, I found him dead from an acciden-tal drug overdose.

William had gotten off work that Friday and gone to a Widespread Panic concert, where he ingested alcohol and most every drug imaginable for hours. When he got home from the concert he texted a dealer and bought more drugs.

That cocaine, ingested just before midnight, combined with the other drugs in his sys-tem and took his life. The body can only take so much, after all. Eventually, it shuts down.

Three years plus a few months later we have made peace with William's addiction and tragic death, as much as parents can. We were blessed beyond measure to have been given this son to have in our lives for 23 years. Blessed beyond measure. And that is enough. We have memories of laughter and warm hugs, plus a hard-earned letter jacket from Ole Miss and so much more to cling to. But we don't want other students to suffer like he did, or other families to suffer like we have. That's why I wish I could reach out and touch every freshman to tell them William's story, to tell them that alcohol and drug bing-ing and abuse isn't a collegiate rite of passage, or a contextual excuse.

It can be a dangerous if not deadly path that is hard to escape.

David Magee is Publisher of *The Oxford Eagle*

ALCOHOL

Alcohol can affect you in many different ways and will vary person to person based on:

- How much you drink
- How often you drink
- Your age
- Your health status
- Your family history

Research indicates that people who drink moderately may be less likely to experience dependency. Moderate means:

For men: *no more than 4 standard drinks in one day AND*
no more than 14 standard drinks per week

For women*: no more than 3 standard drinks in one day AND*
no more than 7 standard drinks per week

Even though they come in different sizes, the drinks below are examples of **ONE** standard drink:

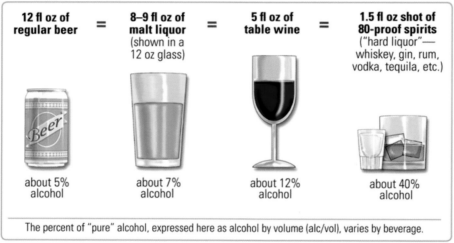

| 12 fl oz of regular beer | = | 8–9 fl oz of malt liquor (shown in a 12 oz glass) | = | 5 fl oz of table wine | = | 1.5 fl oz shot of 80-proof spirits ("hard liquor"— whiskey, gin, rum, vodka, tequila, etc.) |

| about 5% alcohol | about 7% alcohol | about 12% alcohol | about 40% alcohol |

The percent of "pure" alcohol, expressed here as alcohol by volume (alc/vol), varies by beverage.

National Institute on Alcohol Abuse and Alcoholism (NIAAA)

ZERO TOLERANCE LAW

If an individual, under the age of 21, is driving with a Blood Alcohol Content (BAC) at or above 0.02 percent, the individual will receive a DUI under Mississippi state law. This information surprises many students. The legal limit for people over the age of 21 is 0.08 percent, and that is probably the most common number you have heard. The key is if you are under 21, and you are driving with a BAC of 0.02 or more, you are liable for a DUI; for many students that could mean just one drink.

Critical Thinking: Why is the limit for under 21 years old set at 0.02 and not 0.00?

What is a standard drink?

Many are surprised to learn what constitutes a standard drink. The amount of liquid in your can, bottle, or glass does not match how much alcohol is actually in your drink. Different types can have varying amounts of alcohol.

If you choose to use alcohol, you should be well informed so you can make responsible choices. Remember, if you are under 21, drinking alcohol is against the law. So, the first question you need to answer: "Is drinking worth the risk of breaking the law?"

Critical Thinking: What are the immediate and long-term risks of underage drinking — choosing to break the law?

Protective Behaviors

Plan ahead and set limits (know how much you want to consume before the drinking begins).

- Avoid drinking games.
- Stay with the same group of friends the entire night.
- Use bystander intervention techniques.
- Monitor Blood Alcohol Content (BAC). Keep track of time and pace of consumption.
- Alternate alcohol and non-alcoholic drinks. (Stay hydrated.)
- Include food.
- Use a designated driver, taxi service, Uber, or safe ride option.
- Know your NO. In the event you are offered a drink when you do not want one, have a polite and convincing "no, thanks" ready.

DID YOU KNOW? Alcohol is a drug

Bystander intervention techniques

What is a Bystander?
A bystander is someone who is present but not involved; an onlooker.

What is Bystander Intervention?
An intervention is when those around an individual or group who are engaging in risky or dangerous behavior step up and intervene in an attempt to prevent harm.

What are the barriers that keep bystanders from acting?
1. Social Impact: being influenced by others in a social situation.
2. Fear of Embarrassment: not wanting to call attention to yourself or be singled out by speaking up.
3. Diffusion of Responsibility: believing that someone else will do something.
4. Retaliation Anxiety: being afraid of emotional or physical harm as a result of intervening.
5. Pluralistic Ignorance: thinking you must be the only one feeling this way.

Techniques for intervening:
- Notice the problem.
  Problem or emergency?
- Assume responsibility.
  Thoughts to overcome:
  "I am scared of what might happen," or
  "No one else is doing anything, it must not be a problem," or
  "It's not my job, someone else will do it."
- Know how to help.
- Take action.

Class Discussion: Discuss potential scenarios and work through the bystander intervention barriers and techniques.

When the above strategies and techniques are not used, risky behavior occurs. Typically, on our campus, we see the following negative consequences:

Negative Consequences of Risky Student Drinking

Social
1. Arguments and fights
2. Embarrassment of own behavior*
3. Regretting own behavior
4. Waking or disturbing roommate
5. Damaging property
6. Trouble with police and University authorities.

*In our world of widespread social media, let's remember that everything we do and say can easily be seen by thousands with the click of a button.

Physical

1. Hangover
2. Blackout/memory loss
3. Nausea/vomiting
4. Physical injury.

Academic

1. Missing class or work
2. Performing poorly on a test or assignment
3. Getting behind.

Sexual

1. Unwanted sexual experience
2. Sexual aggression.

Drunk Driving

1. Riding with a driver who has been drinking
2. Driving after drinking
3. DUI, DWI arrest
4. Seriously injuring or killing yourself or someone else.

PRESCRIPTION DRUGS

Higher education is currently faced with an epidemic of prescription drug abuse by college age students. Nearly 41 percent of surveyed teens agreed that prescription drugs are safer to use than illegal drugs, even if a doctor does not prescribe them. (drugfree.org retrieved Jan. 2015) Also, about one-third of teens believe that there is "nothing wrong" with using prescription drugs without a prescription "once in a while." (theantidrug.com, retrieved Jan. 2015)

Why do college students sometimes choose to misuse or abuse prescription drugs? Research has discovered some common reasons include self-treating, to get high, to help them study, or to fit in (theantidrug.com, retrieved Jan. 2015).

This risky behavior is dangerous, and the consequences can be deadly. In fact, about 100 people die every day in the U.S. from unintentional drug overdoses. This equates to about one death every 15 minutes. Also, every year more people die from prescription painkiller overdoses than from those due to heroin or cocaine combined – and the rate of overdose death from prescription painkillers has more than tripled since 1999. (CDC, 2015).

STIMULANTS

While the abuse of several kinds of prescription medications is seen on college campuses, one class of medications – stimulants – has been on the rise. Stimulants such as Adderall® are used to treat Attention Deficit Hyperactivity Disorder (ADHD) and also are known to have addictive potential, especially when they are being used without medical supervision.

ADHD is a complex behavioral disorder characterized by symptoms such as difficulty paying attention, hyperactivity, and/or impulsivity that are distractive and inappropriate for one's developmental level. ADHD is a chronic condition characterized by significant impairment at school, work, or in social functioning. In 2009, the Substance Abuse and Mental Health Services Administration (SAMSHA) reported that the non-medical use of Adderall® among 18-22 year olds was twice as high for full-time college students than for non-students. This is an alarming statistic, but unfortunately, few students are surprised to hear that college students are more prone to misusing these so-called "cognitive enhancers."

A recent study of students at The Ohio State University found a vast disparity (approximately eight-fold) between self-reported non-medical use of prescription stimulants and perceptions of what other students were doing. This inaccurate assessment of the social norm on college campuses can create a feeling that "everyone is doing it," when they actually are not. Students may use this perception as a rationalization for their experimentation with prescription stimulants, or it may provide an impetus to do so.

Here are some healthy alternatives:

- Do not skip class! This is one of the biggest mistakes students make in terms of academic success.

- Stay current with class material and review a little every day.

- Establish good study habits and a regular study schedule. Set aside extra time before important tests or deadlines.

- Use healthier "stimulants" – snacks, exercise, light, and even caffeine in moderation.

- Use your available resources (TAs, professors, tutors, friends, etc.) to get help when needed.

- Establish a study group to reinforce your learning.

Other Drugs

College students across the country frequently use drugs such as marijuana, cocaine, and hallucinogens. The following is a chart of illegal drugs that may be found on college campuses with a brief description of some of their effects and health risks.

SUBSTANCES	INTOXICATION EFFECTS	HEALTH RISKS
Marijuana/Hashish	Increased appetite, impaired learning, distorted sensory perception, panic attacks	Respiratory infections, possible mental health decline
Stimulants (Cocaine, Amphetamine, and Methamphetamine)	Increased energy, reduced appetite, anxiety, paranoia	Seizure, stroke, cardiovascular complications, insomnia
MDMA (Ecstasy, Molly)	Chills, sweating, muscle cramping, mild hallucinogenic effects	Sleep disturbance, depression, impaired memory
GHB (Date rape drug)	Drowsiness, disorientation, loss of memory, loss of coordination	Unconsciousness, seizures, coma
Hallucinogens (LSD, Acid, Mushrooms)	Panic, nervousness, paranoia, impulsive behavior, sleeplessness, increased heart rate	Hallucinogen persisting perception disorder, flashbacks
Inhalants (Dust it, Whipits)	Headache, wheezing, slurred speech, loss of motor coordination	Memory impairment, unconsciousness, sudden death
DXM (Robo, Triple C, found in some cough and cold medications)	Confusion, dizziness, distorted visual perceptions	Anxiety, numbness, tremors, memory loss, nausea
Synthetic Cannabinoids (Spice, K2)	Extreme anxiety, paranoia, hallucinations	Rapid heart rate, vomiting, agitation, increased blood pressure
Steroids	No intoxication effects	Blood clotting and cholesterol changes, hepatitis, hypertension, hostility, aggression, acne
Opioids (opium, heroin)	Euphoria, nausea, sedation, slowed or arrested breathing	Constipation, endocarditis, HIV, fatal overdose

*Note: All substances or a mixture of substances can lead to addiction.

Risk Factors and Addiction

It is not uncommon to associate risky behavior with being in college, but what risk factors do you think specifically relate to the misuse and abuse of prescription medications in the 18-25 year old population? Perhaps one of the biggest factors is that you have grown up in a drug-taking society. In the United States, we use more medications than any other country. We are one of only two countries (United States and New Zealand) that allows direct-to-consumer advertising of prescription drugs. We expect "quick fixes," and all of this may tend to normalize the use of medications.

It also is possible for students who abuse alcohol or drugs to become dependent on those substances. Dependence may be physical, psychological, or both. Dependence often is accompanied by tolerance, or the need to use more of a substance to receive the same effect. Dependence and increased tolerance may lead to addiction.

Some risk factors associated with addiction include: genetic predisposition, use of substances at an early age, psychological factors such as depression, environmental influences such as history of addiction in the family, and substance use among peers (CASA, 2013). Susceptibility to addiction differs with each individual, and no single factor determines whether a person will develop an addiction.

If you see the following signs or symptoms, reach out:

The following symptoms are associated with alcohol abuse:

- Temporary blackouts or memory loss
- Recurrent arguments or fights with family members or friends as well as irritability, depression, or mood swings
- Continuing use of alcohol to relax, to cheer up, to sleep, to deal with problems, or to feel "normal"
- Headache, anxiety, insomnia, nausea, or other unpleasant symptoms when one stops drinking
- Flushed skin and broken capillaries on the face; a husky voice; trembling hands; bloody or black/tarry stools or vomiting blood; chronic diarrhea
- Drinking alone, in the mornings, or in secret

Signs of addiction include the following:

- **Loss of Control**: Drinking or drugging more than a person wants to or intended

- **Neglecting Other Activities**: Spending less time on activities that used to be important, or a drop in attendance and performance at work or school
- **Risk Taking**: More likely to take serious risks to obtain one's drug of choice
- **Relationship Issues**: People struggling with addiction are known to act out against those closest to them, particularly if someone is attempting to address their substance problems; complaints from co-workers, supervisors, teachers, or classmates
- **Secrecy**: Going out of the way to hide the amount of drugs or alcohol consumed
- **Changing Appearance**: Serious changes or deterioration in hygiene or physical appearance
- **Family History**: A family history of addiction can dramatically increase predisposition to substance abuse
- **Tolerance**: Over time, a person's body adapts to a substance to the point that he or she needs more and more of it to have the same reaction
- **Withdrawal**: As the effect of the alcohol or drugs wears off the person may experience symptoms such as anxiety or jumpiness, shakiness or trembling, sweating, nausea, vomiting, insomnia, depression, irritability, fatigue, loss of appetite, and headaches
- **Continued Use Despite Negative Consequences**: Even though it is causing problems (work, school, relationships, health), a person continues drinking and drugging.

(National Council on Alcoholism and Drug Dependence, 2016)

Recognizing the signs and symptoms of substance abuse **early** is important to help prevent dependence and serious life-threatening consequences.

Who to contact:

Emergency: (911)

University Counseling Center (662-915-3784)

Campus Recreation: Wellness Education (662-915-6543)

University Police Department (662-915-7234)

Community Assistant (Residence Halls)

House Mother, Chapter President (Greek Life)

Friends and Family

When a student is ready to enter or resume college life in recovery, it can be extremely challenging. For UM students, the best resource is our Collegiate Recovery Community.

The Collegiate Recovery Community at the University of Mississippi was established to help students in recovery achieve their academic goals. Academic and social support are provided through a network of peers, faculty, and staff who understand the unique challenges recovering students face in a collegiate environment. The benefits of student involvement in the Collegiate Recovery Community are sober events and activities, volunteer opportunities, scholarships, and peer-led meetings on campus where students can support each other in their journey of recovery. For more information about the Collegiate Recovery Community, visit recovery.olemiss.edu or e-mail recovery@olemiss.edu.

The University of Mississippi is a smoke-free campus.

Brief Smoke-Free History at UM

In the fall of 2007, the University adopted the Tobacco Use Policy, limiting the use of tobacco products on the Ole Miss campus to "designated tobacco-use areas." Over time it became evident that this policy was not effective, and amidst growing concerns on campus over continued exposure to second-hand smoke, discussions among students, faculty, and staff about becoming a completely smoke free campus began to re-emerge. In the early fall of 2011, the Vice Chancellor's Office for Student Affairs began to solicit feedback from various constituencies on campus to determine whether or not there was broad support for such an effort. A proposal for a smoke-free campus received support from the Provost's Office, the Academic Deans, all 14 departments within the Division of Student Affairs, the Executive Director of the Alumni Association, the ASB Senate, and the ASB.

With such campus-wide support evident, Chancellor Dan Jones asked that a Smoke-Free Campus Policy Implementation Committee be developed. This broad-based committee was chaired by Ms. Leslie Banahan, Assistant Vice Chancellor for Student Affairs, and Dr. Shannon Richardson, Assistant Director of Campus Recreation. By the end of July 2012, the committee had revised the policy to its current form and presented it to the Chancellor for his approval, which was granted. The University's new Smoke-Free policy began with soft implementation on August 1, 2012, without citations for infractions, and included an aggressive public information campaign as well as introducing cessation support programs for students and employees. On January 1, 2013, the policy entered its full-enforcement stage with penalties for non-compliance.

Smoke-Free Policy (CHA.AM.100.108)

Nicotine and Addiction

In its pure form, nicotine (the additive chemical in tobacco) is a poison, an insecticide. In fact, in 1988, the Surgeon General asserted that nicotine is more addictive than heroin (U.S. department of Health and Human Services, 1988.) "Whether they are smoking cigarettes or chewing tobacco, most users quickly develop a tolerance for nicotine and need greater amounts to produce desired effects. When you consider a pack-a-day smoker takes 200-300 hits of nicotine daily, it is no surprise that addiction occurs" (Human Relations

Media 2002). As with any addiction, when tobacco users try quitting, they often suffer withdrawal symptoms. Many of the physical symptoms of dependency are a major reason why quitting tobacco is considered difficult.

Quitting

If you or someone you know has tried to quit smoking, then you know that it is a challenge. Most people make more than one attempt to quit; you may have to try many times before quitting for good, but with each effort you learn more about yourself and your addiction. According to the U.S. Department of Health and Human Services (2000), there are five keys to help you make a successful quit attempt:

1. Get ready. Set a quit date and change your environment.
2. Get support and encouragement. You have a better chance of being successful if you have help.
3. Learn new skills and behaviors. Practice stress reduction techniques, watch your diet, and drink plenty of water.
4. Get medication, and use it correctly. Ask your heath care provider for advice about which options are best for you. Some examples of medications that could help your chances of quitting for good include Chantix and Nicotine gum/inhaler/nasal spray/patch. Some are available by prescription, while others you can buy over-the-counter.
5. Be prepared for relapse or difficult situations. Many tobacco users relapse; do not be discouraged. Remember, it may take several attempts before you finally quit. Some difficult situations to watch out for include alcohol, other smokers, weight gain, and depression. If you are having problems with any of these situations, talk to your doctor before you start smoking again.

Note: the physicians and nurse practitioners in the Student Health Center, or the Wellness Education Team, can help you plan your quit attempt. They can provide access to counseling, prescriptions to appropriate medication, and follow up with you as time goes on. The Student Health Center Pharmacy also carries medications, often at reduced or no cost to students.

CAMPUS RESOURCES

Department of Campus Recreation: Wellness Education
Wellness Suites, Turner Center
Phone: 662-915-3459
E-mail: healthpromotion@olemiss.edu
healthpromotion.olemiss.edu
Contact: Erin Cromeans, Assistant Director for Health Promotion

University Police Department
Kinard Hall, Wing C
Non-emergency number: 662-915-7234
E-mail: upd@olemiss.edu
upd.olemiss.edu
Community safety, emergency response, and outreach

University Counseling Center
Lester Hall
Phone: 662-915-3784
counseling.olemiss.edu
Confidential individual and group counseling

Collegiate Recovery Community
(Housed within Wellness Education)
662-915-3459
recovery.olemiss.edu

Glossary

Dependence – A strong need to continue using a particular substance.

Physical Dependence – The need to continue substance use behaviors to avoid withdrawal.

Psychological Dependence – The need to continue substance use behaviors because of cravings for the pleasurable effects.

Withdrawal – Symptoms that are opposite to the effects the substance originally had on the body.

Tolerance – The need to continuously increase the amount of a substance used to gain the desired effect.

Recovery – A voluntarily maintained lifestyle characterized by sobriety, personal health, and citizenship.

BAC – Blood Alcohol Content or Blood Alcohol Concentration.

Stimulants – Drugs used to treat narcolepsy, ADD/ADHD, and other conditions.

Opiates – Drugs used to treat moderate to severe pain; may be prescribed after surgery.

REFERENCES

American Psychiatric Association. (2013). Diagnostic and Statistical Manual of Mental Disorders (5th ed.). Arlington, VA: American Psychiatric Publishing.

American Society of Addiction Medicine. (2011, April). Public Policy Statement: Definition of Addiction. Retrieved from: www.asam.org/for-the-public/definition-of-addiction.

www.cdc.gov/Features/VitalSigns/PainkillerOverdoses/ (Retrieved Jan, 2015)

Centers for Disease Control, (2014). Smoking and Tobacco Use: Disease to Death Fact Sheet. Retrieved from: www.cdc.gov/tobacco/data_statistics/fact_sheets/fast_facts/index.htm

drugfree.org/wp-content/uploads/2011/04/Full-Report-FINAL-PATS-Teens-2008_updated.pdf (Retrieved Jan, 2015)

Generation Rx: How Prescription Drugs are Altering American Lives, Minds, and Bodies (2005, New York: Houghton Mifflin Co.)National Center on Addiction and Substance Abuse. (2013, November). Who Develops Addiction? Retrieved from: www.casacolumbia.org/addiction/addiction-risk-factors.

National Institute on Drug Abuse. (2011, October). Commonly Abused Prescription Drug Chart. Retrieved from: www.drugabuse.gov/drugs-abuse/commonly-abused-drugs/commonly-abused-prescription-drugs-chart

National Institute on Drug Abuse. (2010, August). Drugs, Brains, and Behavior: The Science of Addiction. Retrieved from: www.drugabuse.gov/publications/drugs-brains-behavior-science-addiction/drug-abuse-addiction

ncadd.org/learn-about-drugs/signs-and-symptoms , (Retrieved Jan, 2015)

Quintero, G., Peterson, J., and Young, B. (2006). An exploratory study of socio-cultural factors contributing to prescription drug misuse among college students. Journal of Drug Abuse, 22, 903-926.

Recovery Research Institute. (2014) Seeking Recovery. Retrieved from: www.recoveryanswers.org/who-are-you/seeking-recovery/

samhsa.gov/data/2k9/adderall/adderall.pdf, (Retrieved Jan, 2015)

samhsa.gov/data/nsduh/2k10NSDUH/tabs/Sect1peTabs1to46.htm (Retrieved Jan, 2015)

samhsa.gov/data/2k9/adderall/adderall.pdf (Retrieved Jan, 2015)

Substance abuse and Mental Health Services Administration (SAMHSA, 2009), Office of Applied Studies. (February 5, 2009). The NSDUH report: Trends in Nonmedical Use of Prescription Pain Relievers: 2002 to 2007. Rockville, MD. Retrieved from www.oas.samhsa.gov/2k9/painRelievers/nonmedicalTrends.pdf

Substance Abuse and Mental Health Services Administration. (2012). Working Definition of Recovery. Retrieved from: store.samhsa.gov/shin/content//PEP12-RECDEF/PEP12-RECDEF.pdf

theantidrug.com/pdfs/TEENS_AND_PRESCRIPTION_DRUGS.pdf (Retrieved Jan, 2015)

theantidrug.com/pdfs/prescription_report.pdf (Retrieved Jan, 2015)

About the Authors

Erin Murphy Cromeans, *Assistant Director for Wellness Education*

Erin Murphy Cromeans is currently pursuing a doctorate in health and ki-
nesiology with a focus in Health Behavior. She received a Master of Science in
nutrition and hospitality management degree at the University of Mississippi in
2011, a Master of Science in health promotion at the University of Mississippi
in 2009, and a Bachelor of Science in exercise science at the University of Mississippi in 2007. Ms. Cromeans is a Certified Health Education Specialist (CHES) through the National Commission for Health Education and Credentialing. Ms. Cromeans has been a part of the
Ole Miss Family for more than ten years and loves Oxford more and more each day! Hotty Toddy!

Joseph Dikun, *Graduate Assistant in Pharmacy Administration*

Joseph Aaron Dikun, Pharm.D., received his B.S. in biology from Youngstown
State University in 2007 and his Pharm.D. from the Northeast Ohio Medical
University in 2011. Dr. Dikun is pursuing his Ph.D. in pharmaceutical sciences.
He also serves as an advisor for the University of Mississippi American Pharmacists Association-Academy of Student Pharmacists. He works with student pharmacists to implement professional development programs to address health and wellness issues on campus and in
the Oxford community.

Chapter 23
Physical Fitness

By Shannon Richardson

What is Physical Fitness?

Physical fitness is an important dimension of overall wellness, and it is one of the most visible signs of overall health.

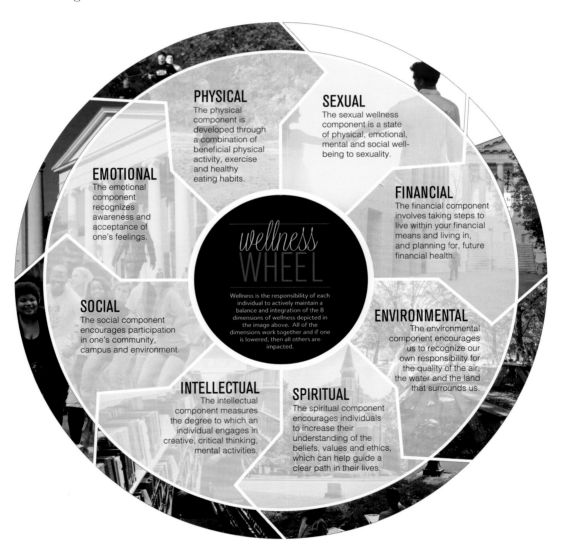

PHYSICAL
The physical component is developed through a combination of beneficial physical activity, exercise and healthy eating habits.

SEXUAL
The sexual wellness component is a state of physical, emotional, mental and social well-being to sexuality.

EMOTIONAL
The emotional component recognizes awareness and acceptance of one's feelings.

FINANCIAL
The financial component involves taking steps to live within your financial means and living in, and planning for, future financial health.

wellness WHEEL
Wellness is the responsibility of each individual to actively maintain a balance and integration of the 8 dimensions of wellness depicted in the image above. All of the dimensions work together and if one is lowered, then all others are impacted.

SOCIAL
The social component encourages participation in one's community, campus and environment.

ENVIRONMENTAL
The environmental component encourages us to recognize our own responsibility for the quality of the air, the water and the land that surrounds us.

INTELLECTUAL
The intellectual component measures the degree to which an individual engages in creative, critical thinking, mental activities.

SPIRITUAL
The spiritual component encourages individuals to increase their understanding of the beliefs, values and ethics, which can help guide a clear path in their lives.

You know that going to class, making notes, studying, and earning good grades are essential to receive your diploma, but did you know there are other things vital to your education? To enjoy a healthy life as a college student, you must consider all dimensions of wellness, including physical fitness.

While being a good student is critical to your success in college, you also must take care of your body. This chapter provides you with the knowledge and resources you need to achieve a top level of physical fitness while you are an Ole Miss student and to maintain a healthy lifestyle after you graduate.

"He who has health, has hope; and he who has hope, has everything."

– Thomas Carlyle

What is Physical Fitness?

The American College of Sports Medicine (ACSM) defines *physical fitness* as "a set of attributes or characteristics that people have or achieve that relates to the ability to perform physical activity" (American College of Sports Medicine, 2010, p. 2). In layman's terms, physical fitness is a task-specific term used to describe an individual's ability to perform physical activity. What makes it task specific?

Let's look at two former Ole Miss athletes to find the answer.

First consider Sam Kendricks, U.S.A., NCAA, and SEC pole vault champion of 2014, and the first person in school history to win the U.S.A. pole vault title as well as an Olympic medal for that event. Kendricks is 6'1" and 170 pounds. Now consider Marquis Haynes, the 2017 starting defensive end for the football team who is the Rebels' modern-era sacks leader (since 1983) with 32 and holds the modern-era career tackles for loss record with 47.5. Haynes is 6'3" and weighs 230 pounds. His strength, power, and agility make him fit for his position on the football team, but he would not be successful at the pole vault in which Kendricks competes. Conversely, Kendricks probably would not fare very well as an offensive lineman on the football team. Both athletes are fit, but that fitness is specific to their tasks.

Did you know?

Ole Miss alumnus Markeeva Morgan served as NASA's Space Launch System Program Stages avionics hardware subsystems manager. The SLS is the largest, most powerful rocket built for deep space missions, including to asteroids and eventually to Mars.

Fitness as a part of total wellness

Not everyone is going to be a collegiate or professional athlete. For those who are not, physical fitness sometimes is not as high on the priority list as maybe it should be. Adjusting to the collegiate lifestyle, balancing academic assignments, studying, employment, and a social life can leave little room for **exercise**, which is purposeful, structured physical activity designed to improve physical fitness. Nevertheless, physical fitness is no more or less important than any other aspect of **wellness**, and neglecting physical fitness in college can lead to potential health problems in the future, and can negatively impact your collegiate experience as well. With that in mind, here are a few tips to assist in maximizing the benefits of your exercise and physical activity. It is important to note that physical activity and exercise are often used interchangeably, but by definition, there is a difference so each term is used separately in this section.

> **Lifting weights does not make women "big."**

To Improve Fitness, You Have to Exercise

The **overload principle** states that a body must be subjected to a stimulus that requires effort outside its current capacity to elicit adaptation. In this case, the stimulus is physical activity or exercise, and the desired adaptation is improved fitness. Whether it is running, biking, swimming, or resistance training, if it feels easy to you, you likely are not getting enough change-causing stimuli to elicit adaptation. At best, you are just burning calories, but that is better than doing nothing.

Resistance Training is Important

The most common myth about resistance training is that if women lift weights they will get "big." Not true. Unless women use performance enhancing substances, they have a much different hormonal profile than men and do not get as big as men from resistance training. The way an individual performs resistance training can affect muscle size as well (see Strength vs. Hypertrophy vs. Endurance).

There are too many benefits to resistance training for women not to lift weights. Some of these benefits include increased metabolism, more favorable body composition, improved performance in physical activity, and protection against the development of osteoporosis. Adding resistance training exercises to your workout two to three days per week will help you realize these benefits.

Did you know?

University of Mississippi adjunct education professor, Susan McPhail, had roles in two film screenings at the 2015 Sundance Film Festival. She played supporting characters alongside Nick Nolte and Ryan Reynolds.

Strength vs. Hypertrophy vs. Endurance

Lifting weights to improve muscular strength, muscular endurance, and muscle size is similar, but there are a few differences. Those differences most easily are seen in the variations of the number of sets performed for each exercise, the number of repetitions performed in each set, and the rest periods between exercise sets. Use the chart below as a guide. The take home point is that you do not have to be big to be strong, and the biggest person in the gym is not always the strongest.

TRAINING SPECIFICITY

Training Goal	% 1RM	# of Sets	Rep Range	Rest b/w Sets
Muscular Endurance	<70	1-3	12-20	20-30 seconds
Hypertrophy	70-80	1-6	8-12	30-120 seconds
Muscular Strength	80-100	1-8	1-5+	2-5 minutes

(American Council on Exercise, 2003, p. 268)

Doing Anything is Better Than Doing Nothing

Thirty minutes of accumulated physical activity per day at a moderate intensity has significant health benefits (American College of Sports Medicine, 2010). This does not have to be vigorous exercise; physical activity such as walking the dog, gardening, or throwing a Frisbee in The Grove can be beneficial. Exercise does not have to be 30 continuous minutes to make a difference in your health. As long as at least 30 minutes of physical activity are accumulated throughout the day, health benefits are present.

Listen to Your Body

Recovery from exercise is just as important, if not more important than performing the actual exercise. Exercise creates micro tears in muscle fibers, and recovery time between workouts is when the fibers repair themselves, becoming stronger in the process. It is common for people to drastically increase their exercise volume as a result of a New Year's resolution or an attempt to get the perfect "beach body" for Spring Break. This commonly leads to fatigue and burnout, and a lack of results. Reaching physical fitness goals requires a long term outlook and specific plan. You do not need to crash diet or starve to achieve results; consistency is the key to success.

> It is common for people to drastically increase their exercise volume as a result of a New Year's resolution or an attempt to get that "beach body" for Spring Break. As a result of the increased physical activity, bodies get worn down.

Did you know?

Horizons is an educational enrichment program serving elementary school age students who might not otherwise have such opportunities. For six weeks each summer, Horizons students are brought to the Oxford campus to improve their reading and math skills, learn how to swim at the campus pool, and take art lessons at the UM Museum. The program's goal is to eliminate summer learning loss.

Always listen to what your body is trying to tell you. If you are thirsty, drink water. Reserve sports drinks for vigorous and extended activities; water is sufficient for a 20-minute run. Dehydration negatively affects a person's ability to exercise; combat this by regularly drinking water throughout the day, not just when you feel thirsty. Six to eight ounces of water every 15-20 minutes during exercise is recommended; longer exercise periods require more fluids. Let hunger tell you when to eat. Use food to fuel exercise and activity; match food intake to activity levels. Freshmen often are concerned about additional weight gain during the first year, but fad diets and severely reducing caloric intake are not healthy or viable options. Focus on eating a variety of nutrient-dense, whole foods and maintaining a consistent, structured exercise routine for a physically fit first year at Ole Miss.

How can you be physically fit and maintain your fitness?
Utilize the resources around you.

The Department of Campus Recreation

The University of Mississippi Department of Campus Recreation provides a variety of opportunities for physical activity and exercise. Its offerings are vast and are able to help satisfy not only physical fitness, but two of the other components of wellness, social and emotional wellness.

Campus Recreation is housed in the Thomas N. Turner Health, Physical Education, and Recreation building, affectionately and simply known as the Turner Center. The Health, Exercise Science, and Recreation Administration academic department also is housed in the Turner Center, so it is a busy place from early morning until late evening. Campus Recreation is divided into six program areas: Fitness, Intramural Sports and Sport Clubs, Informal Recreation, Aquatics, Outdoors, and Health Promotion.

Fitness

The fitness center is a 9,000 square foot facility located on the third floor of Turner Center. Home to the resistance and cardiovascular equipment, this is where many students choose to exercise. If more guidance is needed, 60 group fitness classes are offered each week, suitable to all fitness levels. Dance classes such as Zumba and Hip Hop are offered,

Did you know?

The School of Law placed 14th in the nation in the final moot court rankings for 2014. With three national championship teams and two other squads finishing as national semifinalists and quarterfinalists, the law school expected a strong finish. With a top 15 ranking among approximately 175 law schools with moot court programs, the School of Law earned an invitation to the Moot Court National Championship.

as well as more traditional fitness classes. These include: TRX, Hardcore Abs, HIIT Bootcamp, Strictly Strength, Cardio Kickboxing, and more. Mind/body classes are offered in four different formats with yoga for beginners and one for the more experienced. Classes are free during the first week of each semester and then cost $20 for unlimited classes during the semester. Students have the opportunity to hire a personal trainer for a more focused and individual fitness program.

Intramural Sports and Sport Clubs

If lifting weights and cardio machines are not your favorite activities, Intramural and Sport Clubs may be the perfect way to help you stay fit. Flag football, sand volleyball, basketball, and softball are just some of the standard sports offered. More adventurous students can register for some of the unique tournaments such as: Battleship (in canoes!), spikeball, dodgeball, wheelchair basketball, or inner tube water polo. Sport Clubs are a more competitive option and often compete against other schools within and outside of Mississippi. These vary from badminton, baseball, and soccer to bass fishing, paintball, or wakeboarding. With 20 sport clubs and a constantly increasing number of intramural sports, there are options for everyone to be active and fit through sport.

Informal Recreation

Campus Recreation also offers opportunities to engage in less formal sports competition. Three basketball courts are available for pick-up games or a casual shoot around. These courts also are able to be transformed to accommodate badminton or volleyball courts. Racquetball and squash courts are located on the lower level for open play. Also on the lower level is a game room containing ping pong tables and a study lounge. These areas are available to rent for group events. Any equipment needed for these activities can be checked-out or purchased from the front desk.

Outdoors

Ole Miss Outdoors, affectionately called OMOD (oh-mod), is located on the first floor of the Turner Center and is one of the best outdoor recreation programs in the country. OMOD is not a club but rather an inclusive program open to all students, faculty, staff, and community members – and it is for people of all abilities. Most outdoor recreation programs offer adventure trips or gear rental programs; OMOD offers both. Students lead these adventure trips after completing an academic course and becoming certified Wilderness First Responders. OMOD offers a variety of organized outdoor trips each year including kayaking, rafting, rock climbing, backpacking, skiing, hang gliding, fishing, caving, and more. The price of these trips includes gear rentals necessary to outfit these trips. Gear options include tents, sleeping bags, backpacks, camping stoves, water purifiers, canoes, kayaks, and much more. Additionally, OMOD operates the Rebel Challenge Course, a high and low ropes course located near the intramural fields. The challenge course is designed for groups to foster teambuilding, increase communication skills, and sharpen their problem-solving abilities. Groups can reserve the course online from the Campus Recreation website. OMOD also supervises the South Campus Rail Trail, which is a nature trail open to the Oxford and Ole Miss communities. You can walk, jog, and bike on this trail – check it out, take a friend, or walk your dog. It is a really pretty setting! The trailhead is located just south of Highway 6 on Chucky Mullins Drive.

Aquatics

The Olympic-size natatorium is located on the first floor of the Turner Center. During the hours the pool is open, at least one section is open for lap swim. The natatorium hosts events throughout the year, ranging from swimming lessons to triathlons to birthday parties. Aquatics also hosts a variety of events and resources, including a Master's swim program, water aerobics, and a free swim lesson program for students called Swim to Live. Visit the aquatics office on the first floor of the Turner Center to register for any of these events or to get more information.

Wellness Education

Wellness Education, located in 214 Turner Center, is a resource center for Ole Miss students looking for information or needing help with a variety of health-related topics and issues. Students are welcome to stop in or make appointments with any of the staff to address topics of interest. Our mission is twofold: to advocate for well-informed and healthful choices and to encourage striving for wellness in a positive, empowering, and open environment.

South Campus Recreation Center

The Department of Campus Recreation is also looking forward to opening our new facility, the South Campus Recreation Center. This facility, slated to open in 2019, will provide outstanding opportunities for the University community to pursue lifelong well-being and will serve as a transformational space in providing University of Mississippi students a premiere collegiate experience. The South Campus Recreation Center will be located at the former Whirlpool property. The 98,000 SF facility will include several innovative elements, including one of the nation's only collegiate recreation indoor high-ropes courses and a 6000 SF functional training zone (4000 SF inside, 2000 SF outside). The centerpiece of the facility will be north Mississippi's only indoor climbing wall. There will be abundant fitness space (25,000 SF), three fitness studios, two basketball courts, a multi-activity court, walking/jogging track, classroom with demonstration kitchen, and a convenience store. For more information, please visit campusrec.olemiss.edu.

Student Employment

In addition to numerous opportunities for recreation, Campus Recreation is one of the largest employers of students on campus, with the number of student employees reaching 200+ at certain times of the year. Students are hired to work in facilities, the fitness center, and as life guards, personal trainers, trip leaders, challenge course facilitators, and intramural officials. Please visit the website for more information: campusrec.olemiss.edu.

THE DEPARTMENT OF CAMPUS RECREATION
FACILITIES AND AMENITIES

Indoor Facility (Turner Center)

Cycling Studio

Group Fitness Studio

Olympic Natatorium

Racquetball Courts (7 courts)

Table Tennis Tables (3 tables)

Equipment Check-out (basketballs, racquets, etc.)

Ole Miss Outdoors Office

Locker Rooms

Department of Campus Recreation Main Office

Health Promotion

Intramural Sports and Sport Clubs Office

Fitness Center (~9,000 sq. ft.)

Group Fitness/Multipurpose Room (~8,000 sq. ft.)

Group Fitness Studio

4 Basketball Courts

Indoor Track (200m)

Outdoor Facilities (on campus)

Turner Tennis Courts (6 lighted courts) Behind Turner Center

Intramural and Sport Clubs Fields (~10 acres) Blackburn-McMurray Outdoor Sports Complex

(OSC)-Behind Women's Soccer Complex

Disc Golf Course (23 holes) OSC-Holes located along Insight Park Drive

Rebel Challenge Course (high and low ropes course) OSC-Along Insight Park

Drive just before the fields

South Campus Rail Trail (Chucky Mullins Drive, just south of Hwy. 6)

Glossary

Dehydration – condition of having less than optimum level of body water

Exercise – purposeful physical activity, designed to improve some aspect of physical fitness

Hypertrophy – increased muscle size

Metabolism– a measure of the number of calories a body expends per some unit of time

Natatorium– an indoor swimming pool

Overload Principle – a principle of human performance that states that beneficial adaptations occur in response to demands applied to the body at levels beyond a certain threshold (overload), but within the limits of tolerance and safety

Physical Activity – any task involving physical movement

Physical Fitness – a task-specific term used to describe an individual's ability to perform physical activity

Wellness – quality or state of being in good health

REFERENCES

Photos of Kendricks and Haynes taken by UM Communications Photography.

American College of Sports Medicine. (2010). ACSM's guidelines for exercise testing and prescription (8th ed.). Philadelphia, PA: Wolters Kluwer Health/Lippincott Williams & Wilkins.

American Council on Exercise. (2003). ACE personal trainer manual (3rd ed.). San Diego, CA: American Council on Exercise

About the Author

Shannon Richardson, *Assistant Director of Campus Recreation*

Shannon Richardson has more than 15 years of experience in campus recreation and student affairs. She holds a bachelor's degree in exercise physiology from North Georgia University, a master's degree in public administration from Georgia State University, and a doctorate degree in higher education administration from the University of Mississippi. Dr. Richardson resides in Oxford with her husband Hunter, and their daughters, Emma and Meg.

Spirituality: Taking Care of the Soul

At the core of every human being lives a beautiful and sacred center that historically benefits and grows best when it is nurtured. And so it is with young adult women and men who enter the new life of higher education at The University of Mississippi. Amidst University life essentials (studying, eating and drinking for nourishment, sleeping, working, building relationships), non-stop adjustments, and the challenges that come with the freshman experience, individual wellness includes taking care of the soul. To take care of the soul is to focus on spirituality, something that every human being possesses. The essence of spirituality is the search by an individual to know her or his true self, to tap into the Holy which lives at the sacred center.

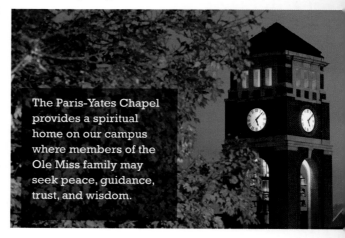

The Paris-Yates Chapel provides a spiritual home on our campus where members of the Ole Miss family may seek peace, guidance, trust, and wisdom.

For five years, I had the privilege to serve as one of several campus ministers at the University. It was powerful and humbling to experience the intentional involvement of freshmen in the nourishment of their spiritual lives. (I wish I had been so intentional when I was a freshman more than twenty years ago at a small liberal arts college in Mississippi!)

Daily, weekly, term after term, it was both joyful and encouraging to witness and hear about the rewards experienced by a variety of students who sought advice and settings that would help them take care of their souls. From their energy, I too increasingly improved my spiritual quest and practices, which included going away for retreats, reading, engaging holy conversation, and more to take care of my soul. Such focused choices were then – and are today – central to the wellness promoted for freshmen, as well as all members of the university community. As I reflect fondly and gratefully on my time at Ole Miss, I offer to all who might listen: to take care of the soul is to get the most from and bring good balance to the freshman experience.

Thanks to the intentional offerings and programs of the Student Religious Organizations at The University of Mississippi, an environment for spiritual growth and development is provided for those who might wish to go deeper – individually and in community with others. Not limited to the three Abrahamic religions (Judaism, Christianity, Islam) about which our local society tends to hear and know the most, spirituality reminds us that the Holy existed long before any religion evolved. Nonetheless, these and other religions, philosophies and practices, in one way or another, can benefit the care of the soul, namely when the individual approaches the quest with intention and openness. And if you are wondering about the possibility of having additional organizations, associations, or circles to nurture your spirit while enrolled at the University, consult with the Office of the Dean of Students for help.

Recently, during a rich and insightful conversation with an alumna of the University, I was asked what advice I would give to current students at the University – especially freshmen who were entering such a new and rich experience. After long contemplation of what I learned during my years in Oxford, I respond with the following four opportunities that can assist an individual with caring for her or his soul.

Embrace nature. Take a moment each day simply to look, hear, touch, and even smell the mystery and beauty of creation and of all that lives and grows in it; maybe even find time to be still, move slowly from place to place, or exercise in whatever way might allow some time in nature. It can be as easy as opening or looking out from a window or door, finding a non-climate controlled space that feels different from your normal environment, listening to the rain or staring at the sky. Give thanks for any and all of it as a gift. Worship and take care of it. Remember that nature, like us, is sacred.

Observe silence. Take at least five minutes at the start of each day to be still, quiet, and removed from the countless noises, sounds, gadgets, things, and even people that often distract us from necessary moments to hear and know the sacred center living within us. Depending on where you live, this may take some creativity. Use this time simply to wake up, give thanks for life and its endless blessings, process problems, clear the mind, open the heart, and provide some clarity to make for a better day ahead. If it does not happen at the start of the day, find a moment between or after classes.

Take a moment each day to enter any kind of conversation with the sacred center.

Pray. Take a moment each day to enter any kind of conversation with the sacred center; with or without words, with eyes open or closed, with hands clasped or palms open, by standing, kneeling, sitting, or even stretching. Be still and try to raise all that is on your mind and in your heart that might need processing, releasing, answers, and ultimately peace; maybe even do so by journaling. Find a faith community in which to pray and worship with others or a setting where spiritual things can be discussed and practiced. Daily and weekly spiritual practices typically make for better days and weeks. If you don't know how to pray or worship, you're not alone; ask someone, find a book about either, show up where others are gathered.

Serve. Take advantage of the community service and volunteer opportunities organized

by the University, local non-profits, or faith-based organizations as ways to extend your sacred center and gifts to others; spirituality helps us to know the true self by looking inward as well as by outwardly engaging others who, like us, are sacred. When we serve others, especially the poor, sick, needy, and lonely, it never fails that we too are served and rewarded. The Oxford-University community has an impressive variety of ways to serve, to bless, and be blessed by others.

Not limited to the three Abrahamic religions (Judaism, Christianity, Islam) about which our local society tends to hear and know the most, spirituality reminds us that the Holy existed long before any religion evolved.

These four opportunities (embrace nature, observe silence, pray, serve) through good intention and work can deepen the journey to discover the nature of our innermost essence – and search for the Holy within whom we "live and move and have our being." Through such practices, I personally have learned and heard from countless others that the inner life becomes increasingly developed. And most often, the individual is led to an experience of connectedness with the larger core reality, yielding a more comprehensive self – a better self, a balanced self.

As the realities and challenges of university life unfold, may you stay in touch with your sacred center and keep its care as a priority – don't ignore it, nourish it – and most of all, celebrate it. Your wellness includes taking care of the soul, which is to focus on your spirituality. May your freshman experience be extraordinary and become increasingly better through your encounter with the Holy.

About the Author

Rev. Ollie Rencher, *Rector of St. Peter's Episcopal Church in Charlotte, North Carolina*

The Rev. Ollie V. Rencher served the University of Mississippi from 2003 until 2008 as Campus Minister for The Episcopal Church at Ole Miss (ECOM) and Assistant Rector of St. Peter's Episcopal Church, Oxford. Passionate about ministry that cares for and connects people more deeply to God and one another, he serves in a variety of ways in his local community. A native of Clarksdale, alumnus of Millsaps College and The General Theological Seminary of the Episcopal Church (Manhattan), Rencher deeply enjoys his ministry and quality time with his wife, and continues to give thanks for his years of service in Oxford.

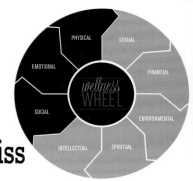

Chapter 24
Eating Healthy at Ole Miss

By Mariana A. Jurss

Eating Healthy at College

While college life introduces exciting new experiences, there are also challenges. Eating healthy can be one of those challenges. You may find yourself in stressful situations, eating on the run, bogged down with late night study sessions, and navigating all-you-can-eat dining facilities. These situations, along with tight budgets, lack of (or limited) cooking supplies, and hectic schedules make it difficult to make healthy eating choices. It takes time to adjust and adapt to new habits in your new environment, but it is important to know that it is possible to follow a healthy diet on campus with the right tools and motivation.

This chapter is a guide to help you make the healthiest food choices in the college environment. The key is balance, not perfection. Healthy eating does not mean starving yourself, being unrealistically thin, or eliminating foods you love. Instead, it is about feeling energized, finding balance, and feeling good about your body. Do not deprive yourself, or you are likely to binge later. Make simple goals and work toward those goals to achieve healthier eating habits, keeping in mind that healthy eating takes planning and practice.

Nutrition Basics and Building a Healthy Meal

Once you understand the fundamentals of nutrition, it is easier to comprehend the why and the how of healthy eating. We need food to provide us with energy and nutrients that our bodies require to function and keep us alive. There are six classes of ***essential nutrients***:

- carbohydrates
- lipids (fats)
- proteins
- vitamins
- minerals
- water

Ole Miss staff talk to FYE students about the importance of diet and exercise during a healthy eating walking tour of the campus.
Photo by Robert Jordan/Ole Miss Communications

These nutrients come from the food we eat. Our food is divided into *five main food groups*:

- ■ proteins
- ■ grains
- ■ vegetables
- ■ fruits
- ■ dairy

Each food group contains a key nutrient that is fundamental for good health and body function.

In 2011, the U.S. Department of Agriculture (USDA) launched MyPlate, an education tool designed to help U.S. consumers create healthy balanced meals. MyPlate focuses on providing a visual portion guide- without having to measure food from the five main food groups- to create a balanced meal.

Begin by filling **half of your plate with fruits and vegetables**. Key nutrients in vegetables and fruits are vitamins and minerals. Each vitamin and mineral has a specific role and is required for healthy skin, hair, nails, immune system, and overall proper function. Your goal when selecting fruits and vegetables is variety. You want to obtain a range of vitamins and minerals. Choose red, orange, and dark leafy greens such as tomatoes, sweet potatoes, and spinach. These protect from chronic disease, and most are low in fat, sodium, and calories.

Next, fill a fourth of your plate with a **lean protein**, such as fish, poultry without skin, beans, tofu, nuts, and seeds. The key nutrient in this food group is protein. Protein provides the body with energy, and it helps maintain muscle and replace hormones, blood cells, and other essential components in the body. Most people consume enough protein, so the goal is to choose leaner options and vary your choices to maximize nutrient intake and health benefits. For example, choose cooked seafood as your protein choice at least twice per week. Also, limit your intake of processed meats such as sausages, pepperoni, hot dogs, and even chicken nuggets as these are usually high in fat and sodium.

1 small steak = deck of cards	4 cheese cubes or 1 slice = 4 dice	1 cup of milk	1 whole egg	2 Tbsp of peanut butter = golf ball	½ cup beans = light bulb
3 oz. equivalent	1 oz. equivalent	1 oz. equivalent	1 oz. equivalent	2 oz. equivalent	2 oz. equivalent

Fill the last fourth of your plate with **grains**. The key nutrient in this food group is carbohydrates. Carbohydrates are the primary energy source for our body, particularly our brain and muscles; therefore, we need carbohydrates to have the energy to move and to think. The grain food group includes bread, pasta, rice, oatmeal, grits, crackers, cereals, popcorn, and tortillas. There are two types of grains, whole grains and refined grains. Whole grains provide you with more nutrients and fiber compared to the refined grains. Choose whole grains at least 50% of the time. Whole grains include oats, whole wheat bread, brown rice, and whole grain cereals.

Dairy is separated from the plate to emphasize that dairy does not need to be part of every meal, and your needs are dependent on your age. The key nutrient in this food group is the mineral calcium, which is the primary mineral of our bones and also plays a role in muscle contraction and blood clotting. The dairy group is made up of milk products that retain their calcium content. Calcium fortified soymilk is also part of the dairy group. Choose non-fat or low-fat dairy varieties of milk, cheese, and yogurt.

What about **fats**? The human body requires fat for optimal health. A well-balanced diet requires at least some fat, and getting enough fat is typically not a concern. Most of us get enough oil/fat in the foods we eat regularly, such as cooking oil, fish, nuts, salad dressings, meats, and dairy. People are more likely to over-consume fat versus not getting enough. Therefore, the general recommendation is to limit fat intake.

With this information in mind, MyPlate can serve as a guide to help you design balanced meals. Having a healthy understanding of what should go on your plate will assist you in making healthy choices. Another key ingredient to making healthy choices is to know what is in your food by reading food labels. Food labels can provide you with the information to make healthy choices. Learn more about reading food labels from the supplemental handout "What is in your food? Read the label."

Adapted from MyPlate *choosemyplate.gov/MyPlate*

The Busy College Student

You have probably heard the phrase "You are what you eat." This phrase reminds us that the food we choose to eat does something in our bodies. Food provides us with nutrients that help us stay alive, and depending on what foods we choose to eat, our bodies will feel energized and strong (healthy) or tired and sluggish (less healthy). Most of us want to feel good, and what we choose to eat plays a big role. Right now, you are probably thinking "Healthy!?!? Whatever, pass me the pizza and wings!" However, the habits you create in your college years will likely transfer to lifelong habits. Having unhealthy eating habits can lead to weight gain or the "freshman 15." Gaining weight is uncomfortable for anyone; even a few pounds can make your clothing fit tighter and lead to uncomfortable aches and pain. In addition, there is increased risk to develop high blood pressure, diabetes, cardiovascular disease, and certain forms of cancer associated with being overweight. However, having a good plan and creating a routine helps you make healthier food choices and develop healthy meal patterns that work for you. Maintaining a healthy lifestyle should be one of your goals in college.

General Healthy Eating Habits, Creating Structure, and Having a Plan

Healthy eating habits require planning. The first weeks of college are chaotic and perhaps even overwhelming, but once you get used to your class schedule you can figure out a routine that allows you to eat healthy. Your meal times may vary from day to day depending on your classes, but creating a plan or routine helps you avoid eating on the run or skipping meals. Here are some tips to get started:

■ Make time for meals a priority, especially breakfast.

This may be the first time you are on your own and planning your meals. Making scheduled meals a priority helps you avoid making unhealthy food selections on the run or skipping meals all together, especially breakfast. You probably have heard the phrase "Breakfast is the most important meal of the day." This is because breakfast, along with sleeping and exercise, provides you the energy you need to get through the day. If you are interested in doing well on an exam, eat a healthy breakfast. Research shows eating a healthy breakfast improves brain function, attention span, and concentration. Particularly, it improves memory and recall which are key to absorbing new information and utilizing it later during an exam. If you are concerned about your weight, start eating breakfast! Research shows that those who skip breakfast tend to weigh more compared to breakfast eaters. Also, eating breakfast helps you make healthier food choices throughout the day. Aim to have three meals per day - plus one or two snacks between meals if you get hungry.

*Adapted from "5 Reasons your teen needs breakfast"
eatright.org/resource/food/nutrition/healthy-eating/5-reasons-your-teen-needs-breakfast

■ Know your food options.

Know all of your food options. If you are on a meal plan, Ole Miss has three dining facilities, the Rebel Market, The Marketplace at the RC, and The Grill at 1810, in addition to multiple P.O.D. locations (Grab and Go food options) and restaurants located at the Union and other locations across campus. Lenoir Dining also is a great option, a restaurant on campus run exclusively by the Department of Nutrition and Hospitality Management students. The dining facilities have a variety of healthy food options such as grilled chicken, soups, salad bar, and a fruit bar. Also, for those with a gluten allergy or intolerance, the Rebel Market has a gluten free station. To get a full list and map of all the facilities on campus visit *olemiss.campusdish.com*.

■ **Find healthy options you enjoy.**

With so many on-campus dining options to choose from, it can be hard to differenti-ate what is healthy from what is not. Most dining facilities display nutrition information next to each food item. Take these opportunities to read about your food in order to know what is in your food! Make sure you survey all the stations at the dining facility to see your options. You can also download the CampusDish app to access nutrition infor-mation for the dining facilities at Ole Miss. Fast-food restau-rants such as Chick-fil-A or Panda Express make nutrition

information available online. To select healthy options, remember to use MyPlate as a guide. It is important to be conscious of what you are putting in your body. This does not mean you can never have fried items or dessert; it just means you know the nutrition con-tent of each food item to make informed choices of what you are putting in your body. It is okay to occasionally have empty calorie food items such as cookies and ice cream; the key is being conscious of the portion and how often you are eating it. Remember that healthy eating is about balance, enjoying your food while taking care of your body.

■ **Select healthy food options most of the time**

Once you have found healthy options you enjoy, you can select those healthy choices most of the time. Having a plan keeps you on a healthy track. If you focus on making healthy choices most of the time, enjoying an occasional treat can easily fit into a healthy lifestyle. Make sure you only add one or two treats occasionally. For some, it may help to create a routine for treats. For example, if you like fried food, you can make "Fried Fridays" the day you select the fried item you enjoy. Or maybe Saturday is the day you enjoy a frozen yogurt or other sweet treat. You have to create a system that works for you; re-member that we are all different, with different preferences, with different circumstances. The goal is to find what will work for you!

Healthy Food Choice at Ole Miss

Navigating the Dining Facilities

To make healthy choices at the dining hall we are going to go back to the basics, My-Plate. If you recall, the goal of my plate is to fill half the plate with vegetables and/or fruit, one-fourth with a grain, one-fourth with a protein, and don't forget your dairy. We are going to use MyPlate and other tips to make healthy choices at the dining facilities.

1. **Plan ahead and know what you are eating**
   - ■ Look at the menu before hitting the dining facilities. Planning your meals is a smart way to make healthy, balanced choices. You are more likely to splurge and choose unhealthy options at the last minute when you are hungry or in a rush, so plan ahead.
   - ■ Read the posted nutrition information. Remember that Ole Miss Dining posts their nutrition information at most locations and/or online.

2. **Make half of your plate fruits and vegetables**
   - ■ Select fruit and low-fat yogurt for a quick grab-and-go breakfast.
   - ■ Start with salad or soup a few days a week.
   - ■ Choose a cooked vegetable or salad as a side.
   - ■ Hit the fruit bar for dessert.

3. **Pick a lean protein**
   - ■ An omelet is a great choice for breakfast. Add veggies to your omelet, and pair it with whole wheat bread for a balanced meal.
   - ■ Grilled chicken and fish are good choices.
   - ■ Add bean, eggs, tofu, cottage cheese, or seeds to your salad.
   - ■ Decode the menu, and look for proteins that are labeled baked, grilled, roasted, sautéed, or in stews. These are usually significantly lower in fat compared to proteins labeled fried, crispy, crunchy, crusted, tempura, breaded, and battered.

4. **Make half of your grains whole grains**
   - ■ Choose oatmeal for breakfast.
   - ■ Select whole wheat bread for sandwiches. Create a balanced meal by adding a slice of low-fat cheese, veggies, and a lean protein to your sandwich.
   - ■ Choose whole grain pasta at the pasta bar.
   - ■ Select 100 percent whole grains when available, such as whole-wheat bread, whole-grain cereals, oatmeal, whole-grain pasta, brown rice, whole-grain tortillas, and quinoa.

5. **Remember to enjoy your food, but eat less**

   ■ Resist the temptation of eating too much at the all-you-can-eat dining facilities. Make sure you survey each station, and select food that you really want to eat. If available, choose smaller plates/bowls or stick to single food servings to help with portion control. Do not worry about going hungry; you can always go back for more.

   ■ Be mindful of your hunger cues. Wait at least 20 minutes before you go back for seconds. If you are still hungry, then your body needs a little more.

   ■ Do not linger! Enjoy eating with friends, but avoid staying for long periods of time to reduce the temptation to continue eating.

6. **Make it your own: Do not be afraid to mix and match plates**

   ■ Be proactive and creative when it comes to creating your meals. Take advantage of the "make it your own" stations. Dining facilities are on a cycle menu meaning that options repeat, and you can easily become bored.

7. **Slow down on sauces**

   ■ Sauces, gravies, and dressings tend to be high in fat and sodium.

   ■ Entrees with teriyaki, BBQ, glazed, and honey sauces are higher in sugar.

   ■ Watch out for foods prepared with a lot of oil, butter, or topped with heavy condiments such as mayonnaise, cream, or cheese.

   ■ You do not have to do away with sauces and condiments all together; just ask for less or put them on the side. Reducing extras help you control how much fat, sugar, and sodium you put in your body.

8. **Be on your guard at the Salad Bar**

   ■ Salads are a great way to add vegetables to your meals, but not all salads are healthy!

   ■ Most veggies get the green light, as they are filled with nutrients and most are naturally low in calories – romaine lettuce, spinach, tomato, cucumber, carrots, bell peppers, broccoli, red onion, mushrooms, etc.

   ■ Be cautious of foods high in fat and sodium – olives, bacon bits, fried noodles, croutons, and pastas and potato salad made with mayonnaise and oil.

   ■ Ask for dressing on the side, stick to one serving, and choose dressings that are light, low-fat, or fat-free. Balsamic vinaigrette and Lite Italian dressing are low-calorie options offered on campus.

9. Make dessert and fried food special occasion treats

■ Save dessert for the weekend or for special occasions. If you cannot resist, choose a nutrient-rich option such as fruit or yogurt parfait.

■ Skip the fried food on most days – save it for Fried Fridays! If you cannot resist, have one small piece or small side of the fried item and add a salad or a side vegetable.

10. Re-think your drink

■ Americans drink about 400 calories every day. Consider how often you drink sugary beverages such as sweet tea, sodas, sports drinks, energy drinks, fruit juices, and coffee beverages with sugar. A 20 ounce soda contains about 250 calories.

■ Choose water, unsweetened tea with a splash of sweet tea, or infused water which are available at all the dining facilities on campus.

We realize that dining facilities may not always be ideal, so if you are a vegan or vegetarian, have food allergies or intolerances, do not be afraid to speak up. Dining staff and a dietitian are available to help and give you information on ingredients and options available to you. We want you to have the best experience at the University of Mississippi, and we are working hard to offer healthy options tailored to your needs. We are here to serve you! (Adapted from "10 Tips for Healthy Eating at the Dining Halls' from the USDA ChooseMyPlate.gov at choosemyplate.gov/ten-tips-be-choosy-in-the-dining-hall.)

Keeping it Healthy while Eating Out

When eating out, follow the same MyPlate principles previously discussed – one-half plate of vegetables, one-fourth grains, one-fourth protein, and dairy. In addition, make sure you limit fried items and sugary beverages. Fast-food restaurants are convenient and can easily become an unhealthy habit. Be sure to make smart choices if you eat out more than once a week. Plan ahead, and check out the nutrition information online before you arrive. Similarly to eating on campus, if you plan ahead it is less likely that you will splurge and make last minute unhealthy selections. Here are some tips to help you make healthy choices when eating out:

■ Look over the menu carefully. Some restaurants have sections for "Healthy" or "Light" choices.

■ Look for words that may mean lower calorie or healthy cooking preparation: baked, braised, broiled, grilled, lightly sautéed, poached, roasted, and steamed.

■ Also look for words that indicate more added fat: batter-fried, pan-fried, buttered, creamed, crispy, and breaded. Choose these food options less often.

■ Order the small or child-sized portion if possible. Many restaurants serve more food than one person needs at one meal. If smaller portions are not available, or if it is more economical to get a main dish, split it with a friend or take half home.

■ It is OK to make special requests; just keep them simple. For example, ask for a side salad or baked potato instead of french fries; no mayonnaise or bacon on your sandwich; salad dressing or other sauces on the side.

■ As a beverage choice, choose water with lemon for added flavor, unsweetened tea, or other drinks without added sugar.

■ Avoid having an appetizer and dessert in addition to your main course. If you are tempted to get a dessert or appetizer, order one for the table to share.

■ At fast-food restaurants, anything that says super, big, or double adds a lot of calories and fat to your meal. If you are selecting a value meal at a fast-food restaurant, make sure that you keep your sides small and you choose a non-sugary beverage. A large order of fries and sugary beverage alone can add ~800-950 calories to your meal. Choose wisely!

■ For healthy eating options at fast-food venues on campus refer to the "Healthier Eating at Ole Miss" handout at RebelWell.olemiss.edu/eating-healthier-on-campus

Snacks to Keep in your Room, Apartment, or Mini Fridge

Snacks can be an important part of a nutritious eating plan if the foods you choose are healthy and contribute to a well-balanced diet. You want to choose nutrient-dense foods, and keep away from processed foods with added sugar and fat. Also, if you are watching your calorie intake, remember that snack calories count in your total calories for the day, so make sure to pick healthy, low-calorie snacks, and skip junk food and vending machines.

So how can we make our snack choices healthy? Think about whole foods in their natural form. If you are looking for something crunchy, grab a handful of almonds instead of reaching for a bag of chips. Nuts are rich in heart-healthy fats and are a good source of protein and fiber. If you are craving something sweet and salty, make some homemade trail mix (seeds, dried fruit, nuts, whole-grain cereals) and portion it out for the rest of the week. You can also include two food groups in your snacks. For example, an apple and string cheese, celery sticks with peanut butter, light yogurt with fresh berries, or carrots with hummus. These are all easy grab-and-go options that fit into a well-balanced diet!

Snack ideas:

Fruits, such as apples, bananas, pears, grapes, and peaches all are healthy snacks. You can select fresh, frozen, canned, and dried fruit. Just make sure you watch out for varieties with added sugar or syrup.

■ **Vegetables**, such as baby carrots, celery, broccoli florets, grape tomatoes, and bell peppers are all great options. Pre-washed and pre-cut veggies are convenient, and you can pair them with a healthy dip, such as salsa, hummus, nut butters, or enjoy them by themselves. Broth-based vegetable soups are also a great option; make sure you select low-sodium versions.

■ **Dairy**, such as low-fat yogurt, low-fat string cheese, low-fat cottage cheese, low-fat milk.

■ **Grains** – unsalted pretzels, brown rice cakes, oatmeal packets, whole grain crackers, whole-wheat bread, granola bars (Make sure these have less than 10 grams of sugar, and more than three grams of fiber.)

■ **Protein** – nuts and nut butters, eggs, tuna pouches, canned chicken, pre-cooked chicken.

■ **Water** - keep water handy! Invest in a water filter pitcher; it is a convenient and economical way to store water in your room or apartment.

Stay Hydrated

Hydration is important year round, especially during the summer and fall when temperatures are high. Your body depends on water to survive, from the lubrication of joints, to cell development, to removing waste. We get water from the food and beverages that we eat and drink, such as fruits, vegetables, soups, juices, and milk. However, drinking water is the best source of water for the body. The recommended daily fluid intake is about 91 ounces for females and 125 ounces for males. Generally, 20 percent of fluids come from food, therefore aim to have about 9 cups of fluids for women and 13 cups of fluids for men. It is important to listen to your body to keep adequately hydrated, i.e. your sense of thirst. Follow these tips to help you stay hydrated throughout the day:

1. Start your day by drinking a glass of water.
2. Keep a bottle of water with you during the day and refill it throughout the day. Take advantage of the various Hotty Toddy hydration stations located throughout campus. To get a complete list of all the locations where you can find a hydration station, visit the Office of Sustainability website at green.olemiss.edu/hydration-station
3. If you do not care for the taste of plain water, add lemon, lime, or berries to add flavor to your water.
4. Drink a glass of water with all of your meals.
5. Drink water before, during, and after exercise.
6. Listen to your body and drink water when you are thirsty.

Also, do not let beverages with the word "water" fool you. Check the nutrition label and ingredients if you are buying flavored water. Tonic water contains calories, sugar, and more sodium compared to sparkling and seltzer water, which are calorie-free and contain small amounts of sodium. Let water be your go-to beverage, because it is calorie-free, sugar-free, sodium-free, and low cost.

Drink Responsibly

Drinking has become a part of many social events in college, from parties to sporting events. Nutritionally, alcoholic beverages are one of the top contributors to caloric intake with minimal nutrition value. If you are of legal drinking age, drink in moderation if you decide to drink. Moderate intake for women is one drink per day and two drinks per day for men. What counts as one drink?

- 12 ounces beer, 150 calories
- 5 ounces table wine, 100 calories
- 1.5 ounces of 80 percent proof liquor, 100 calories

When choosing to consume alcohol, alternate your alcoholic beverages with water to keep your calorie-count down and stay hydrated.

Outsmart Emotional Eating

College life is full of emotions, and many times we turn to food to soothe our feelings. When feeling anxious, stressed, homesick, or tired, make sure you ask yourself if you are truly hungry before you reach for that extra snack. Pay attention to what you are eating when you are stressed. Having a regular meal schedule can prevent emotional eating. Also, be sure you get enough sleep as a lack of sleep can directly affect your weight, eating habits, and stress level. When you are studying for an exam or working late on a project, keep healthy snacks available if you need an energy boost. If you realize you are not hungry, have a list of three things you can do to prevent over eating, such as playing a short game on your phone, painting your nails, drinking a glass of water, taking a shower, or doing a few stretch exercises. To prevent emotional eating, you need to find an alternative to food to satisfy yourself emotionally. Recognizing that you turn to food to soothe your emotions is the first step, now you need to plan how to soothe those emotions. Here is a list of activities that can help with emotional management:

- **If you are depressed, lonely, or homesick** call a friend or someone who always makes you feel better, play with your dog or cat, or look into joining a club/organization on campus.
- **If you are anxious**, expend your nervous energy doing your favorite exercise routine, dancing to your favorite song, squeezing a stress ball, or taking a brisk walk.
- **If you are exhausted,** treat yourself with a hot cup of tea, warm shower, or nap.
- **If you are bored,** read a good book, watch a comedy show, explore the outdoors, or turn to an activity you enjoy (playing an instrument, shooting hoops, scrapbooking, etc.)

*Adapted and excerpt from the HELPGUIDE.ORG – Emotional Eating – How to Recognize and Stop Emotional Eating.

Still have nutrition questions?

This chapter includes only a few of many helpful tips for healthy eating in college. With all the nutrition information you read online or see on TV, it may seem like eating right is impossible. Claims that promote the new power food that will slim you down or easy solutions to your dietary needs may seem like good solutions; however, your best bet is a personalized visit with a registered dietitian. If you want to address your food intolerances, find healthy options on campus, eat for performance, or simply eat healthier, a registered dietitian can help you decipher all of the confusing information and provide you with nutrition advice that is catered to your goals. A registered dietitian is a food and nutrition expert who has gone through extensive nutrition training and education in addition to passing the examination requirements set forth by the Commission on Dietetic Registration. Visit rebelwell.olemiss.edu for more information and available resources.

Glossary

Calorie – (food energy) a measure of the energy used by the body and of the energy that foods supply to the body.

Carbohydrates – essential nutrients that are the body's main source of energy. These are found in breads, cereals, and rice.

Complex Carbohydrates – carbohydrates such as whole-grain breads and cereals, starchy vegetables, and legumes. Many of the complex carbohydrates are good sources of fiber.

Fad Diets - a diet plan that makes promises of quick weight loss with minimal to no science background. These diets typically restrict one or more of the essential food groups, or recommend consumption of one type of food in excess at the expense of other foods. These diets typically do not result in long-term weight loss, can potentially be dangerous to your health, and are generally not endorsed by the medical profession.

Fats – a nutrient that supplies energy, promotes healthy skin and growth, and is a carrier of certain vitamins. Found in oils, butter, and lard.

Fiber – plant material that cannot be digested. It assists with digestion and bowel movements. There are two types: soluble and insoluble.

Gluten - gluten is a protein found in wheat, rye, and barley. It can also be in products such as vitamin and nutrient supplements, lip balms, and certain medicines.

Minerals – nutrients such as calcium, iron, and zinc; some regulate body processes while others become part of body tissues.

MyPlate – the current nutrition guide developed by the U. S. Department of Agriculture to guide healthful eating. MyPlate depicts a plate and glass divided into five food groups. It replaced the USDA's MyPyramid guide.

Nutrients – substances in food that the body needs to function properly, to grow, to repair itself, and to supply energy.

Protein – an essential nutrient that helps your body grow, repair itself, and fight disease; it can also provide energy if needed. We get proteins in our diet from meat, dairy products, beans, nuts, and grains.

Registered Dietitian (RD) – an expert in human nutrition and the regulation of diet.

Saturated Fat – fats that are solid at room temperature and are typically found in animal products, such as meats, poultry skin, and foods made from whole milk. These fats increase the risk for heart disease.

Simple Carbohydrates – carbohydrates that are digested quickly and include sugars found naturally in foods such as fruits, vegetables, milk, and milk products. They also include sugars added during food processing and refining.

Trans Fat – trans fats are formed when liquid oils are made into solid fats like shortening and hard margarines. Trans fats can be found in processed foods such as crackers, cookies, snack foods, fried foods, and baked goods. It increases blood cholesterol levels and risk for heart disease.

USDA - the United States Department of Agriculture (USDA), also known as the Agriculture Department, is the U.S. federal executive department responsible for developing and executing federal government policy on farming, agriculture, forestry, and food.

Vegan – a diet that excludes all meat and animal by-products, such as milk and eggs.

Vegetarian – a diet that excludes meat and sometimes other animal products.

Vitamins – nutrients that do not provide energy but help regulate body processes. These are essential for normal growth and are required in small quantities in the diet because they cannot be synthesized by the body.

Whole Grain – whole grains contain the entire grain kernel – the bran, germ, and endosperm. Examples of whole grains include whole-wheat flour, oatmeal, and brown rice.

About the Author

Mariana A. Jurss, *RebelWell Registered Dietician*

Mariana A. Jurss joined RebelWell in July 2014. Prior to moving to Oxford, Mariana worked for a pediatric weight management program at a Children's Hospital in California working to prevent and treat childhood obesity and related illnesses, such as diabetes, heart disease, and high blood pressure. She is a registered dietitian and holds a Master's degree in public health from the University of California, Berkeley.

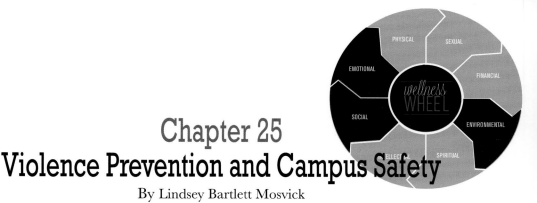

Chapter 25
Violence Prevention and Campus Safety

By Lindsey Bartlett Mosvick

Violence on college campuses continues to garner attention in the media recently. When we talk about violence in this chapter, we are referring to three specific areas: relationship violence, sexual assault, and stalking. One common thread ties all of these together: control. The perpetrators of these types of violence are seeking to exert power and control over their victims. Perpetrators and victims of violence can be any gender, socio-economic status, religion, or ethnicity. Here at the University of Mississippi, it is okay to talk about these issues; we recognize that our community is affected by them everyday. If you or someone you know has experienced violence, know that you are not alone.

Relationship Violence

Relationship violence is defined as a pattern of abusive behavior in any relationship that is used by one partner to gain or maintain power and control over another intimate partner. Relationship violence is also know as dating or domestic violence. Relationship violence can be physical, sexual, emotional, economic, or psychological actions or threats of actions that influence another person. This includes any behaviors that intimidate, manipulate, humiliate, isolate, frighten, terrorize, coerce, threaten, blame, hurt, injure, or wound someone.

Domestic/dating violence does not include only physical abuse. Perpetrators often use other methods to control the other person. This violence happens in a cycle; beginning with a honeymoon period, then tension-building stage, until something triggers the perpetrator to exert control. The cycle repeats, so it is difficult for victims to leave. Have you ever known someone in a relationship like the one just described? Do you have a friend whose boyfriend or girlfriend uses words to intimidate or humiliate him or her? Maybe you've noticed a friend has become isolated since he or she started dating someone? Familiarize yourself with the definition of relationship violence. One day you may be able to help a friend by being a proactive bystander.

Did you know?
- Females who are 20-24 years of age are at the greatest risk of nonfatal intimate partner violence.
- One in every four women and one in every seven men will experience domestic violence in her or his lifetime.

Sexual Assault

Sexual assault is defined as any type of sexual contact or behavior that occurs without the explicit consent of the recipient of the unwanted sexual activity. Falling under the definition of sexual assault is sexual activity such as forced sexual intercourse, sodomy, child molestation, incest, fondling, and attempted rape. (www.ovw.usdoj.gov/ovw-fs.htm)

The key word here is **consent**. What does it mean to give consent? Consent is basically giving someone permission to have some type of sexual contact with you. Consent must be clearly communicated and can be withdrawn at any time. For example, if you are "hooking up" with someone, you must be absolutely sure he or she is giving you consent at every stage of the hook-up. If someone says to you directly, "I want to have sex with you," then at a later time during the sexual interaction communicates that he or she no longer wishes to have sex, you MUST stop at this point. Going forward becomes a violation of our campus sexual misconduct policy.

Consent can be verbal or non-verbal and does not have to be legalistic or kill the moment. There are many ways to clearly communicate consent using words or actions that can be fun and even enhance the experience. The goal is to be sure you are both giving and receiving clear consent for each action.

What could make someone unable to give consent? A person who is mentally or physically incapacitated is not capable of giving consent. If a person is under the influence of drugs or alcohol, he or she cannot give consent. Signs that someone may be beyond the point of legal consent are: slurred speech, inability to walk/stand normally, vomiting, or being partially or totally unconscious. If someone is incapacitated by drugs and/or alcohol, even verbal consent is no longer valid. In other words, even if someone consents while sober, once he or she is incapacitated, the consent goes away.

According to the Rape, Abuse, and Incest National Network (RAINN), drug-facilitated sexual assault is when drugs or alcohol are used to compromise an individual's ability to consent to sexual activity. In addition, drugs and alcohol often are used to minimize the resistance and memory of the victim of a sexual assault. The most commonly used drug in this type of assault is alcohol; however many others are used such as Xanax, Vyvanse, and Rohypnol (Roofies), and even some over-the-counter medications. The victim is never at fault for sexual assault, even when alcohol or other drugs are involved.

Did you know?

John "Kayo" Dottley (class of 1950) is still the only Ole Miss player to rush for more than 1,000 yards in two consecutive seasons. He was also the first rookie to ever be selected to play in the Pro Bowl.

Did you know?

- ☐ 1 in 6 women and 1 in 33 men will be victims of sexual assault in their lifetime.
- ☐ Around 80 percent of sexual assaults that happen in college are not reported.
- ☐ The vast majority (90 percent) of sexual assaults are committed by someone known to the victim. (rainn.org/statistics)

Stalking

Stalking can be defined as a pattern of repeated and unwanted attention, harassment, contact, or any other course of conduct directed at a specific person that would cause a reasonable person to feel fear. Stalkers frequently use technology, and those behaviors are called cyberstalking

While many people believe that stalkers are harmless and best left alone, stalking is a serious crime that can, and often does, escalate to physical violence and/or sexual assault. Stalking is not a joke and does not just involve strangers.

Ways people might experience stalking:
- ■ Telephone (incessant calls and texts)
- ■ Follow or monitor location
- ■ Send letters or e-mails
- ■ Show up uninvited or send unwelcome gifts
- ■ Posts on social media (Twitter, Snapchat, Facebook, Instagram, Groupons)

Most of these behaviors, on their own, would be considered harmless. What makes stalking different is the repetitive pattern and the fear these behaviors cause in the victim. It is important to report stalking before behavior escalates, and it is okay to be scared. There are resources on campus to support victims of stalking.

Did you know?
- ☐ 80% of college stalking victims knew their stalker.
- ☐ People age 18-24 experience the highest rates of stalking (violenceprevention.olemiss.edu)

Did you know?

Larry Grantham (Class of '65) was a five-time All-Pro during his 13-year NFL career.

Green Dot

The Green Dot Strategy is a bystander intervention program developed by Dr. Dorothy J. Edwards, Executive Director of Green Dot, Inc. Dr. Edwards works with a variety of organizations spreading the word about Green Dot and working to end power-based personal violence. Here is an explanation of Green Dot in her words:

Visualize for a moment that unforgettable image of small red dots spreading across a computer generated map of the U.S., symbolizing the spread of some terrible epidemic — each tiny red dot representing an individual case. With disturbing speed, the three or four single dots multiply and spread until the whole map emits a red glow comprised of a zillion tiny dots.

Now imagine for a moment a map of [Ole Miss]. Each red dot on this map represents an act of power-based personal violence (partner violence, sexual violence, stalking, bullying, child abuse, or elder abuse) — or a choice to tolerate, justify or perpetuate this violence. A red dot is a rape — a red dot is a hit — a red dot is a threat — a red dot is an individual choice to do nothing in the face of a potentially high risk situation. Power-based personal violence is not a huge, solid mass that can simply be removed with one swift action or policy. Rather, it is the accumulation of individual decisions, moments, values, and actions made by the men and women from every corner of our world. It's hard to know exactly how many red dots are on our map at any given moment — but we do know there have been enough red dots to create a culture that promotes bystander inaction and sustains a rate of nearly a quarter of women becoming victims of violence during their lifetimes and an untold number of men experiencing similar trauma.

Now imagine adding a green dot in the middle of all those red dots on your map. A green dot is any behavior, choice, word, or attitude that promotes safety for all our citizens and communicates utter intolerance for violence. A green dot is pulling a friend out of a high risk situation — a green dot is donating a few dollars to your local service provider — a green dot is displaying an awareness poster in your room or office — a green dot is putting a green dot message on your facebook page — a green dot is striking up a conversation with a friend or family member about how much this issue matters to you. A green dot is simply your individual choice at any given moment to make our world safer.

How many green dots will it take to begin reducing power-based personal violence? How many of us need to add 2 or 3 or 7 or 50 dots to this map to begin to make a difference and begin to outnumber and displace those red dots? We cannot know the exact number, but we do know this: if most of us choose inaction — if most of us choose to close our eyes to this issue — if most of us choose apathy and indifference — then the red dots stand! If we do not begin replacing moments of violence with moments of support and safety, then we will surely continue to have more than 1 in 4 women and countless men become victims of violence. That is not OK. That must not be OK with any of us.

The power of Green Dot is simple: Red dots bad. Green dots good. You decide. (www.livethegreendot.com/gd_strategy.html)

University of Mississippi Sexual Misconduct and Relationship Violence Policies and Support

The M-Book contains policies that specifically address the issues of sexual assault and relationship violence and stalking. When students report on campus, they meet with the Title IV Coordinator. Students who experience violence while drinking have amnesty from alcohol violations. To view the policies in full, please consult your *M-Book* or go on-line to *conflictresolution.olemiss.edu*.

The University Counseling Center offers free, confidential counseling services, and the Violence Intervention and Prevention Office provides advocacy, support, and accommodations for victims of violence.

University Police Department

The safety and security of all students, faculty, staff, and visitors are of great concern to the University. The University Police Department (UPD) is a full-service, State Accredited and CALEA recognized agency operating 24 hours a day, seven days a week. UPD is responsible for campus police and security-related measures.

UPD officers possess arrest powers and are armed. They routinely conduct vehicle, bicycle, motorcycle, and foot patrols on campus, and they enforce state laws as well as University policies and regulations. UPD works closely with other community law enforcement agencies such as the Oxford Police Department and the Lafayette County Sheriff's Department in investigations of shared concern. UPD maintains formal agreements with those agencies to receive reports of criminal activity at off-campus events where participants are University students. UPD runs an active crime prevention program that strives to eliminate or minimize criminal opportunities when possible, and encourages faculty, staff, and students to be responsible for their own security and the security of others.

Did you know?
- Rebels Against Sexual Assault (RASA) is a student group dedicated to awareness and prevention of violence. Follow them on social media @olemissrasa, and join them on MSync.
- The University has a social event safety program designed to create safe party environments in our community.

RAINN's top safety tips for safe drinking:
- Don't leave your drink unattended while talking, dancing, using the [restroom,] or making a phone call.
- At parties, don't drink from punch bowls or other large, common, open containers.
- If someone offers to get you a drink from the bar at the club or party, go with that person to the bar to order it, watch it being poured, and carry it yourself.

■ Watch out for your friends, and vice versa. Always leave the party or bar together. If a friend seems out of it, is way too drunk for the amount of liquor he or she's had, or is acting out of character, get your friend to a safe place immediately.

■ If you think you or a friend has been drugged, call 911, and be honest and explicit with doctors so they'll give you the right tests (you'll need a urine test and possibly others).

Campus Safety Tips

University of Mississippi students are just as likely to be victims of crimes as anyone else. Use of simple safety precautions can greatly reduce your chance of becoming a victim of crime. Download the LifeSafe mobile app to your phone now! It is a free, real-time security communication app for members of the Ole Miss community.

■ **Lock the door** to your home and vehicle, even when you intend to return shortly.

■ **Program emergency numbers** into your cell phone. UPD's number is 662-915-4911.

■ **Do not** leave messages on your door or on social media indicating you are away or when you will return.

■ **Do not** allow strangers to "tailgate" behind you as you enter your residence hall or gated apartment complex.

■ **Do not** prop open outer doors to residence halls.

■ **Call** 662-915-7234 to report suspicious activity or persons on campus. Off campus, call 911.

■ **Protect your student ID**. If it is lost or stolen, immediately report loss to UPD at 662-915-7234.

■ **If you find yourself in immediate danger**, call 911 or 4911 in your residence hall; try to stay calm and get away at your first opportunity.

Protect yourself when walking, biking, or driving.

■ **Avoid** walking alone at night. Call UPD for Rebel Patrol assistance.

■ If possible, **carry a cell phone** and have it easily accessible.

■ Walk or bike along well lit, commonly traveled routes and **avoid** dark, isolated areas.

■ **Walk purposefully**, know where you are going, and project a no-nonsense image.

■ **Have your keys ready** for your home or vehicle; carry them in your pocket, not buried in a purse or backpack.

■ **Lock bikes to bike racks** with hardened alloy locks and chains or u-shaped locks to prevent theft.

■ **Know your location** when using cell phones. Some areas do not have emergency services readily available. Never text and drive!

■ **Drive to a police or fire station**, or **open place of business** if you feel you are being followed.

Resources on and off campus

UMSAFE
Support • Awareness • Facts • Empowerment

University of Mississippi Office of Violence Intervention and Prevention
University Counseling Center
662-915-1059| vpo@olemiss.edu
violenceprevention.olemiss.edu/ | umsafe.olemiss.edu/

Reporting violence or sexual assault on campus?
Title IX Coordinator
270-D Martindale Student Services Center
662-915-7045
olemiss.edu/depts/affirmative_action/tix.html

University of Mississippi Department of Police and Campus Safety (UPD)
Kinard Hall - Wing C, Floors 2 & 3
University, MS 38677
662-915-7234 | upd@olemiss.edu

Oxford Police Department
715 Molly Barr Road
Oxford, MS 38655
662-232-2400 | oxfordpolice.net

Family Crisis Services of Northwest Mississippi
662-234-9929
503 Heritage Drive
Oxford, MS 38655

Glossary

Relationship violence is defined as a pattern of abusive behavior in any relationship that is used by one partner to gain or maintain power and control over another intimate partner.

Sexual assault is defined as any type of sexual contact or behavior that occurs without the explicit consent of the recipient of the unwanted sexual activity.

Stalking is defined as a pattern of repeated and unwanted attention, harassment, contact, or any other course of conduct directed at a specific person that would cause a reasonable person to feel fear.

Drug-facilitated sexual assault is when drugs or alcohol are used to compromise an individual's ability to consent to sexual activity.

Consent requires a clearly communicated verbal or non-verbal agreement to engage in sexual activity. The individual consenting must act freely and voluntarily and have knowledge of the nature of the act involved.

A Green Dot is any behavior, choice, word, or attitude that counters or displaces a red-dot of violence. Green dots can be reactive (intervening in a high risk situation) or proactive (telling friends about Green Dot).

REFERENCES

Dating Violence. (2011). Retrieved from http://www.ovw.usdoj.gov/datingviolence.html

Sexual Assault. (2011). Retrieved from http://www.ovw.usdoj.gov/sexassault.htm

The Green Dot Strategy. (2010). Retrieved from http://www.livethegreendot.com/gd_strategy.html

University of Tennessee at Knoxville. "Research finds link between alcohol use, not pot, and domestic violence." *Science Daily,* 27 January 2014. Retrieved from www.sciencedaily.com/releases/2014/01/140127112733.htm

About the Author

Lindsey Bartlett, *Assistant Director for Violence Intervention and Prevention*

Lindsey Bartlett Mosvick has spent her career addressing the needs of survivors of relationship violence and sexual assault. Prior to joining the University of Mississippi, she served as Senior Policy Attorney at the D.C. Coalition Against Domestic Violence. She received her J.D. from the University of Virginia School of Law in 2010 and her B.A. in political science from the University of Florida in 2007.

Campus Resources

Quick Reference Guide
Student Support Resources at Ole Miss

Career Center

career.olemiss.edu • 303 Martindale • 915-7174

The Career Center assists students in making a successful transition from college life to the professional world. The Center provides educational services and activities that support the career development needs of students from the first year of college through graduation and beyond, including one-on-one career counseling and assessment. The Center offers two career courses for academic elective credit (EDHE 201 and EDHE 301).

Center for Excellence in Teaching and Learning

olemiss.edu/depts/cetl/ • 105 Hill Hall • 915-1391

The purpose of this unit is to promote exemplary teaching and effective learning at the University of Mississippi. The Center provides Academic Success Training (AST) workshops for students: olemiss.edu/depts/cetl/AST.html.

Center for Inclusion and Cross-Cultural Engagement

inclusion.olemiss.edu/ • Stewart Hall

The Center emphasizes inclusion and broad cultural educational opportunities for all students and provides programs and services that encourage cross cultural interactions among Ole Miss community members. The Center is a physical space that is both nurturing and welcoming for students with diverse backgrounds.

Center for Student Success and First-Year Experience (CSSFYE)

cssfye.olemiss.edu • 350 Martindale • 915-5970

The Center for Student Success and First-Year Experience (CSSFYE) assists a wide variety of students through five primary units: Academic Advising, First-Year Experience, Student Retention, Academic Support Programs, and Veterans' and Military Services. Professional academic advisors work with students who have yet to declare a major and freshmen in the Schools of Accountancy, Applied Sciences, Business Administration, and Engineering, and several departments in the College of Liberal Arts. First-year experience (including this course), academic support programs and classes, and student retention initiatives that support student success and persistence are housed in the CSSFYE. Additionally, the Center is home to Veterans' and Military Services.

Clinic for Outreach and Personal Enrichment (COPE)

cope@olemiss.edu • 850 Insight Park, Suite 163A • 915-7197

The UM Counselor Education Clinic for Outreach and Personal Enrichment (COPE) provides counseling services to children, adolescents, college students, and adults. Services are provided by UM faculty members and graduate students enrolled in a counselor education program at the University of Mississippi.

Department of Campus Recreation and Ole Miss Outdoors (OMOD)

olemiss.edu/campusrec/ • Turner Center – Room 214 • 915-5591

Campus Recreation strives to provide outstanding services, programs, and facilities for the University of Mississippi community that promote the development and maintenance of healthy lifestyles. Campus Recreation exemplifies the University's mission by fostering leadership and excellence, offering high-impact co-curricular programs in active, inclusive, and student-focused environments that provide an outlet for competition, exploration, play, and social interaction.

OMOD is a multifaceted program offered through the Department of Campus Recreation that exposes participants to the great outdoors. OMOD emphasizes adventure, environmental awareness, challenge, education, personal development, safety, and fun with a variety of exciting outdoor activities.

Department of Parking and Transportation

olemiss.edu/parking/ • Lester Hall – Room 120 • 915-7235

The Department of Parking and Transportation provides accessible parking, transit, and travel to students, faculty/staff, and visitors to the Ole Miss campus. The Department oversees day-to-day operations, parking enforcement, and other transportation-related programs and needs. Staff members strive to enforce regulations in a fair and consistent manner.

Equal Opportunity and Regulatory Compliance (EORC)

olemiss.edu/depts/affirmative_action/ • 217 Martindale • 915-7735

The mission of this office is to ensure the University's compliance with federal regulations regarding fair treatment of faculty, staff, and students; to ensure equal employment opportunity, and to ensure equal access to a quality education for students. EORC is also responsible for investigating complaints of discrimination including any complaints of discrimination filed under Title IX and serves as a liaison between the University and federal enforcement agencies concerned with equal opportunity and non-discrimination. The University of Mississippi is an EEO/AA/TITLE VI/TITLE IX/SECTION 504/ADA/ADEA employer.

ID Center

130.74.148.25/auxsvcs/idcenter/index.php

Johnson Commons • 915-7423

The Ole Miss ID Center produces identification cards for University of Mississippi students, faculty, staff, and community members. The Center's website has information about the Ole Miss One Card, the University of Mississippi's official identification card. There is also a link to the Ole Miss Express home page at olemissexpress.ugrydnetwork.com/.

IT Helpdesk

olemiss.edu/helpdesk • Weir Hall • 915-5222

IT (Information Technology) supports e-mail, web pages, and other applications that run on the University's campus-wide systems. Staff at the Helpdesk are available to assist students regarding software, hardware, and networking.

J.D. Williams Library

olemiss.edu/libraries • 1 Library Loop • 915-5858

This is the main and centrally located library on campus. Click ASK LIBRARIAN on the library home page to IM with a librarian about any questions you have regarding research topics, subject guides, or library databases.

Office of the Bursar

olemiss.edu/depts/bursar/ • 202 Martindale • 800-891-4596

The Bursar acts as the University's banker. Responsibilities include receipting and depositing University funds; assessing student tuition and other charges; preparing, mailing, and safekeeping student loan promissory notes; and disbursing student financial aid refund direct deposits and checks.

Office of Campus Sustainability and Ole Miss Green Initiative

olemiss.edu/green/ • 915-2074

The Office integrates sustainability principles throughout the University and collaborates with sustainability education and research programs across the campus. Contact the Office to learn about volunteer and internship opportunities.

Office of Conflict Resolution and Student Conduct

conduct.olemiss.edu • Somerville Hall • 915-1387

The Office of Conflict Resolution and Student Conduct provides a comprehensive array of approaches to support the University of Mississippi values of civility, respect for human dignity, and the honoring of community standards. Our purpose is to:

• Support students as they overcome mistakes
• Engage in character development with an emphasis on ethical decision-making and integrity
• Resolve conflict at the lowest level possible through education, facilitation, and support
• Foster a safe and welcoming community.

Office of Financial Aid

olemiss.edu/depts/financial_aid • 257 Martindale • 1-800-891-4596

The Office of Financial Aid is committed to helping students and their families obtain all available resources for financing the costs of attending the University. These resources include four basic types of student financial aid: scholarships, grants, loans, and part-time employment.

Office of Fraternal Leadership and Learning

greeks.olemiss.edu • Minor Hall • 915-7609

With nearly 7500 affiliated students, representing individuals from across the country and around the world, we are a robust community of engaged scholars, leaders and community servants. Comprising 33 organizations within the Interfraternity Council, National Pan-Hellenic Council, and College Panhellenic Association, we are proud to offer a variety of membership opportunities and a transformative experience for our members.

The Department of Fraternal Leadership and Learning provides services that culminate in comprehensive support for our members, alumni, advisers, organizations, and councils. In addition to administration and planning, community member and council development, and leadership education, Fraternal Leadership and Learning provides advising to all three governing councils and three auxiliary organizations, house director support and training, chapter adviser support, intentional educational programming, and recruitment and intake management.

Office of International Programs (OIP)

international.olemiss.edu • 331 Martindale • 915-7404

The OIP offers a wide variety of services to international students, faculty, researchers, and staff. This office provides specific information about admissions, financial aid, international document processing, and health insurance. The OIP presents a wide variety of events that introduce Ole Miss students to the richness and diversity of our international community.

Office of Leadership and Advocacy

dos.olemiss.edu • Minor Hall • 915-7247

The Office of Leadership and Advocacy is a multifaceted operation serving students, faculty and staff, parents, alumni, and the general public. The Office advises student organizations; provides extra-curricular and co-curricular educational opportunities for students; and serves as a liaison between students, University faculty and staff, and the public.

Office of the Registrar

olemiss.edu/depts/registrar • 104 Martindale • 915-7792

The Office of the Registrar is the academic record-keeper for the University. The Registrar can provide students copies of their transcripts, proof of enrollment, and letters of good standing.

Office of Student Disability Services

olemiss.edu/depts/sds • 234 Martindale • 915-7128

Various services and materials are provided to eligible students for the purpose of allowing equal access to education. Eligible students must complete an intake process for verification at least two weeks prior to the first day of classes.

Office of the Vice Chancellor for Student Affairs

olemiss.edu/studentaffairs/ • 233 Lyceum • 915-7705

The Division of Student Affairs works to create and maintain a living-learning environment that promotes leadership development, academic achievement, and responsible and engaged citizenry. The Division complements and enhances the academic mission of the University by providing facilities, services, and programs to support students in their intellectual, personal, and vocational growth.

Office of Violence Intervention and Prevention

violenceprevention.olemiss.edu/ • University Counseling Center • Lester Hall • 915-1059

The Office of Violence Intervention and Prevention promotes awareness of the realities of dating violence, sexual assault, and stalking. The Office also provides education and training for students, faculty, and staff concerning these topics. Additionally, the program serves as a resource for victims and as a liaison between University departments and local resource groups.

Ole Miss Dining and Meal Plans

campusdish.com/en-US/CSS/OleMiss/MealPlans/ • 915-1467

This site provides a wealth of information and a map showing the various locations on campus for student dining. There is additional information describing meal plans offered to students.

Ole Miss Student Union

915-1044

The Ole Miss Student Union Office oversees the general operations of the Union while also serving as the event programming resource for the University. Along with the Student Activities Association (SAA), the Office often partners with campus organizations and departments to sponsor a variety of events and activities. The SAA provides campus entertainment and opportunities for student involvement in event planning. Special events, a movie series, musical entertainment, and pageants are among the more than 125 events sponsored each year.

Psychological Services Center

olemiss.edu/depts/psc • Kinard Hall, Wing G, 382 • 915-7385

This center provides diagnostic services such as evaluation of learning difficulties, attention problems, emotional problems, developmental delay, and impairment following brain surgery. Client fees are based on a sliding scale.

Student Disability Services (SDS) Testing Center

sds.olemiss.edu/sds-testing-center/ • Kinard Hall • 915-2524

The SDS Testing Center provides a centralized location for testing for those with verified test taking accommodations.

Student Housing

olemiss.edu/depts/stu_housing • Minor Hall • 915-7328

Student Housing serves the on campus housing needs of students. They also offer academic tutoring (olemiss.edu/depts/stu_housing/ed_support.html) in Martin/Stockard Halls.

Student Media Center

smc.olemiss.edu • 201 Bishop Hall • 915-5503

All students, regardless of major or classification, are invited to participate in multiple platform journalism at the S. Gale Denley Student Media Center. Many paid positions are offered in managing websites, social media, producting a daily newspaper, television newscast, staffing a 5,000-watt radio station, and producing the Ole Miss yearbook.

UM Box Office

olemiss.edu/depts/tickets/ • Ford Center for Performing Arts • 915-7411

The University of Mississippi Box Office is located in the Ford Center and provides ticketing services for non-athletic productions and events held on campus.

University Counseling Center

olemiss.edu/counseling • Lester Hall • 915-3784

The University Counseling Center assists students, faculty, and staff with many types of life stressors that interrupt day-to-day functioning. Professional services include crisis intervention, individual psychological counseling, support groups, meditation groups, substance abuse counseling, and wellness programs. Student services are free and confidential.

University Health Services

olemiss.edu/depts/stu_health • V.B Harrison Health Center • Rebel Drive • 915-7274

The Student Health Center is staffed by Family Practice and Internal Medicine physicians and Family Nurse Practitioners. The Center provides acute care for students.

University Museum

museum.olemiss.edu • University Museum • 915-7073

The University of Mississippi Museum and Historic Houses complex serves as a cultural center for the University community and beyond. Among its holdings are Southern folk art, Greek and Roman antiquities, 19th century scientific instruments, and American fine art. Part of the museum complex is Rowan Oak, a historic literary legacy that was once the home of William Faulkner, Nobel and Pulitzer Prize-winning author. Rowan Oak was renovated and reopened to the public in 2001 and continues to draw international visitors each year. The Museum also owns the Walton-Young Historic House – once home to critic and satirist Stark Young.

University Police Department (UPD)

olemiss.edu/depts/upd • Kinard Hall, Wing C, 322 • 915-7234

The five divisions that compose the University Police Department—patrol, investigation, crime prevention, security staff, and traffic support—are an integrated team striving to achieve excellence in police protection and to ensure a high quality of student-faculty life by promoting a tranquil, safe atmosphere conducive to the objectives of the University.

Writing Center

rhetoric.olemiss.edu • Lamar Hall • 915-7689

The Writing Center is part of the Department of Writing and Rhetoric and employs more than 30 student consultants to read and critique students' written assignments. The consultants also offer workshops and provide assistance with word processing and other software programs.